The Importance of SMEs as Innovators of Sustainable Inclusive Employment

New Evidence from Regional and Local Labour Markets

Christa Larsen, Jenny Kipper, Alfons Schmid, Marco Ricceri (Eds.)

The Importance of SMEs as Innovators of Sustainable Inclusive Employment

New Evidence from
Regional and Local Labour Markets

Rainer Hampp Verlag   Augsburg, München 2020

Bibliographic information published by the Deutsche Nationalbibliothek

Deutsche Nationalbibliothek lists this publication in the Deutsche Nationalbibliografie; detailed bibliographic data are available in the Internet at http://dnb.d-nb.de.

ISBN 978-3-95710-280-5 (print)
ISBN 978-3-95710-380-2 (e-book)
ISBN-A/DOI 10.978.395710/3802
First published in 2019

© 2020   Rainer Hampp Verlag   Augsburg, München
          Vorderer Lech 35   86150 Augsburg, Germany
          www.Hampp-Verlag.de

All rights preserved. No part of this publication may be reprinted or reproduced or utilized in any form or by any electronic, mechanical, or other means, now known or hereafter invented, including photocopying and recording, or in any information storage or retrieval system, without permission in writing from the publisher.

In case of complaints please contact Rainer Hampp Verlag.

Foreword

Analytical work of both researchers and international organisations has stressed evidence of increasing regional disparities within and between Member States as well as perceptions of a widening rural-urban divide. This concerns labour market outcomes and indicators of productivity and innovation, as well as social outcomes and subjective measures of life satisfaction and well-being.

At the same time, regional and local actors today are facing unprecedented challenges and responsibilities. Depending on the economic structures and skills profiles at regional and local level, firms and workers may find themselves disproportionately exposed not only to the direct effects on public health, but also to the massive demand shock that followed the outbreak of the pandemic. This holds in particular for regions with high employment shares in the tourism, hospitality and cultural sectors.

Moreover, regions are at the centre of the twin – green and digital – transition on which Europe has embarked and which is a cornerstone of our efforts to promote a fast and inclusive recovery. Support to regional strategies for a just transition will be a main focus of the EU policy agenda over the coming years, moving towards a more circular, climate-neutral and sustainable economy and society. Policy action at regional level further is central to the effective implementation of the European Pillar of Social Rights, including through enhanced access to essential services such as education, health, housing, energy and mobility. Last but not least, digitalisation, new forms of work and new modes of transport have a clear regional impact and can offer new opportunities in rural areas and peripheral regions.

Against this background, there is an increasing demand for timely and robust information on regional labour market developments. The European Network on Regional Labour Market Monitoring continues to play a significant role in this context, by bringing together and sharing widely the available analysis and intelligence at regional and local level, by promoting concrete activities and initiatives of regional and local labour market observatories at the European level and by furthering exchange and mutual learning between all relevant stakeholders.

Loukas Stemitsiotis

Head of Unit A4 - Thematic Analysis
European Commission, Directorate-General Employment, Social Affairs and Inclusion
Brussels (Belgium)

4

Changes in the Italian Labour Market

The labour market is essential to an economy, so much so that it determines its vital state. The Italian economic fabric, in terms of history and tradition, is mainly made up of small and medium-sized enterprises (SMEs). The model established in the 1970s, that of industrial districts, had its most widespread and successful period in the 1990s. Globalisation subsequently modified some of its characteristic aspects, especially in terms of work and territoriality. On the one hand, companies, with the opening of the global market, have experienced mostly positive effects. On the other hand, there has been a tendency to reduce labour costs, resorting to territorial areas where labour is underpaid. This has sometimes degenerated to the point of exploitation (even of minors). The risk posed by such behaviour would be to fall into the logic of an exasperated capitalism with the sole objective of profit maximization, debasing the noble and ideal part of SMEs. The definition of an industrial district, identified for the first time by the economist Alfred Marshall in the second half of the 19th century, was taken up by the Italian law according to which: industrial districts are defined as "local territorial areas characterized by a high concentration of small enterprises, with particular reference to the relationship between the presence of the enterprises and the resident population as well as to the productive specialization of all the enterprises". This definition emphasizes the link between industrial and social reality. SMEs, highly specialised and appreciated at national and international level, present in the same geographical area, benefit from the advantages of closer relationships between themselves to reduce the costs of production of a single supply chain and to better engage with local authorities, institutions and policies. This structure creates not only economic but also socio-cultural development. A valuable aspect of a system conceived in this way is the interaction of labour with its reference market.

The presence of large companies in Italy remains small and is, for the most part, the result of the privatisation of public companies.

Another dimension of the economy and of the labour market in Italy is linked to the spread of cooperativism, enshrined in Article 45 of the Constitution. The sectors most affected by this legal form are those of agriculture and transport as well as those linked to the needs of the territories. Cooperative credit banks also have a very substantial presence in the Italian financial system.

Still on the subject of analysis of the labour market, a great process of social transformation is underway in Italy. In this context, the public debate, first economic and then legislative, has highlighted how the third sector has taken charge of welfare between the State and the private sector. Through the recourse to regulations derived from other legislations, an autonomous legal system has been emanated. This reform, transversal to the entire economy, is generating profound changes also in terms of taxation and labour law. The Third Sector has been identified as the protagonist of a new economic model: the third pillar of development as part of the objectives set out in the UN 2030 Agenda. In Italy, the expression of this network is also represented by the National Forum of the Third Sector. The Forum, which followed the genesis of the reform, is a privileged observatory and contributes to the decisions of the Government by being part of the control room established at the Presidency of the Council of Ministers. The reform has introduced themes of the highest ethical content, especially in the world of work. Inclusion, reduction of the social gap, reduction in the range of salaries between different levels, personal care, are the vocation of all the realities that work to meet the needs of people and communities. The system of the Third Sector and volunteering represents a key factor in the evolution and identification of new paradigms of sociality. In this context, the theme of social enterprises and businesses dedicated to communities and territories intertwine with the future of SMEs and more generally with the concept of the Green Economy that will be at the heart of European policies.

The Italian experience, in the context of the meeting between demand and supply of labour, has been built both with the help of public instruments and private assets. An acceleration on labour policies was introduced with the Legislative Decree n.150 of 14 September 2015 "Jobs Act". which provides for a series of general regulatory interventions in the field of labour. Within this process of renewed attention to the world of labour, a predominant role is now played by ANPAL (National Agency for Active Labour Policies). ANPAL, whose statute was approved by the Council of Ministers in April 2016, acts to prepare new active labour policies both for the placement of workers seeking their first job and for the relocation of the unemployed. ANPAL, structured on a regional basis, coordinates with INPS, INAIL, the Employment Agencies and all accredited training bodies, including Italia Lavoro and INAPP (formerly ISFOL), Chambers of Commerce, Industry, Crafts and Agriculture, universities, and other secondary school institutes. It has among its tasks: -Manage and define the type of services for employment, placement of disabled people and activation policies for unemployed workers; -coordinate the activities of the EURES network; -produce new ways of profiling workers; -promote and support the use of European Social Fund programmes and national funds; -coordinate the information system of employment policies; managing the national register of subjects accredited to carry out functions in the field of active labour policies; -governing the national operational programmes and projects co-financed by the Community Funds; -creating new incentives for mobility; -favouring the management of the critical aspects of company crises in relations between workers and companies so as to limit the possible negative effects on employment data.

The coordination with INPS allows the Ministry of Labour to have feedback on the training and retraining of unemployed workers and on the methods of repositioning in the labour market. Another important element is the file that traces the path of each worker, which can be consulted by all stakeholders including Regions, Provinces and by the worker himself. A network has been set up to prepare an annual report on the labour market. It is the result of the collaboration developed within the context of the Framework Agreement between the Ministry of Labour and Social Policies, ISTAT, INPS, INAIL, and ANPAL, aimed at collecting harmonised, complementary and consistent information on the structure and dynamics of the labour market in Italy.

The element that creates added value to the labour market is given by active policies that take charge of the worker avoiding that, while waiting for placement or relocation, he remains unemployed. The new needs related to innovation, internationalisation and digitalisation are at the centre of training projects for workers to meet the needs of SMEs. The speed required to change economic system for it to become sustainable and not produce waste and inequality is too fast for SMEs to adapt alone. Enterprises are calling for continuous training and higher specialisation. The State favours and accompanies these pathways but, at the same time, it requires respect for each worker so that it can have a satisfactory and adequately remunerated work without undermining the fundamental rights of individuals.

Among employment policies, the debate on citizenship income (reddito di cittadinanza) has taken on an important role. With this measure, which is intended to be an instrument for increasing employment, the Government wanted to fill a gap. It is intended to guide, for a limited period of time, the unemployed towards finding a job. For them, the choice must not be weighed down by reasons related to the need for economic subsistence but there must be consistency between the employer's offer and their specific skills, training and acquired skills. There is no doubt that the citizenship income measure is in an experimental phase, especially regarding the job offer and the professionals who take care of its implementation. The value to be recognized to this legislative measure is that of having saved a group of citizens from a state of pre-poverty, which would have put thousands of people in a situation of "invisibility" with the risk of a very serious social and cultural crisis. Time and corrections will offer possibilities for the improvement of the measure in the sole interest of the economy, the well-being and happiness.

The Italian economic framework and its most recent evolution from the welfare state, towards the welfare society, are the mirror of a thought that focuses on the person, relational goods and the common good. Thus, also the labour market is part of this process. The meeting between labour supply and demand is enriched by new actors, new visions, and new tools. It is no longer a limiting space, delimited between the boundaries of an exasperated idea of profit for the company and the needs of mere survival of the worker, but rather a path of growth of entire communities towards an ethical and sustainable economy. In this way, tools are born that connect the evolutionary phases of each person in their work training. This must be consistent not only with the demands of businesses but with European and global challenges. All this to generate good globalisation, good economics, and good practices; focused on a reciprocal relationship between work and business that has as its objective the sustainable development of the planet.

The reflections made so far keep Italy on a path of profound change that puts the individual at the centre of its transformation. Unfortunately, however, 2020, which despite a temporary stagnation of the economy and uncertain forecasts on GDP, confirmed levels of employment growth in comparison to the trend of the last decade, has shocked the entire world population with the COVID-19 pandemic. Man, in his most fragile aspect, that of the disease, suddenly found himself defenceless and vulnerable. Health systems have revealed peaks of inadequacy due to short-sighted policies that had undermined their tools. Skills, on the other hand, have shown that, embodied in men and women of value, are able to deal with catastrophic events resolutely and promptly. Italy found itself having to move at the same time from observing the epidemic to taking measures to combat it and activating them. With an intuition that left little time for second thoughts, it immediately implemented a lockdown, at first in some regions and a few days later the whole national territory. The labour market suffered a painful impact already in the first month of lockdown. A series of decrees were immediately implemented to activate passive labour policies to face the liquidity crisis of the companies. A dialogue with the countries of the European Union was set up which, today more than in the past, shows the need for shared community policies. The pandemic has caused a shock to the global economy with effects that, it is assumed, will also have repercussions in the coming years. It will be necessary to develop further instruments to support the labour market and to overcome the crisis caused by the pandemic. These include co-planning between the State, social partners and employers who work mainly alongside SMEs and very small businesses.

Some productions have slowed their pace, others have stopped their cycles for over a month, others have not restarted. Labour seems to have changed its face during this period. To deal with the emergency, there has been both a use of passive policies and a massive increase in the use of smart working. But, despite the immediate response of the Italian Government, the indicators give us very worrying signals. The most at risk are the precarious workers, young people, and women. There has been a significant increase in the demand for unemployment benefits (Naspi). Once again, the workers with the lowest wages and those with fixed-term contracts are affected the most.

What future should we envision? The idea of a time that projects itself into the months and years to come cannot ignore concepts such as resilience and generativity. A healthy economy, like any organism, is characterized by the ability to draw new energy for its own recovery from a crisis. If the health disaster has not spared our best heritage, that of the older generations, it is our task and duty to support the new generations on the difficult path to recovery. It will be essential to identify the weaknesses of the economic systems that in the labour market identified the person with the hours worked. Respect for adequate and favourable conditions for the performance of one's tasks must play a priority role, given the fact that in Italy 49 per cent of workers must carry out their work in relation to and in the places of production. Agencies and Services of public and private nature will have to equip themselves with organizations that are even more efficient and appropriate to the challenge of digitalization, to offer expertise and effective actions. Training, both online and offline, must be the key element, not only for the unemployed but also for workers placed in redundancy funds. Better pathways will be created where people will be remunerated, valued and rewarded in relation to the projects carried out and the objectives achieved. Employment levels will increase if the needs of the person are taken into account, not only in relation to their working life, but also in relation to their personal life in a community that they welcome and share. Businesses, and especially SMEs, because of their social concern, will thus be able to implement production logics that meet the real needs of consumers. No more resources used to produce goods and services that do not correspond to real needs and requirements. No more a slave market of profit maximisation rules that creates boxes of debt. No more exploitation and destruction of the environment. No more levels of pollution beyond the permitted thresholds. History has confirmed how fragile these systems are and how cyclically they collapse causing incontrovertible crises.

Therefore, the future can only be declined in the sense of sustainability and ethics that respect the environment and man.

Senator Stanislao Di Piazza

State Secretary
Ministry of Labour and Social Policies
Italy

Homage: What Patrizio Di Nicola Has Left Behind

Renato Fontana

Since its very inception, Patrizio Di Nicola was one of the key figures of the European Network on Regional Labour Market Monitoring (EN RLMM). He passed away too early. He has left a void that cannot be filled. In these brief notes, I will try to outline the research paths on which he ventured and, at the same time, to understand how to gather and continue the very considerable contributions he left behind.

Patrizio delivered many studies, contributions, and suggestions that are difficult to put in order (because he was not a "tidy" researcher). The leaps he made were numerous and important. His contributions can be summed up in three key topics:

- The first concerns flexibility and precariousness in the labour market;
- The second has to do with his interests in the business world and in particular with the organisational dimensions in which the factors of production are combined;
- The third is the one that absorbed Patrizio's energies more than any other, namely, his studies on teleworking and smart working.

The topics are contained within a larger framework that recognises the sensitivity that the scholar Patrizio had for the social, political, and historical inequalities that have been growing dramatically in recent years. Before examining these three topics one at a time, it should be noted that it was very important to him to constantly compare his scientific work to everyday reality; a reality marked by social complexity that makes it complicated to define a clear boundary between the exploited and the exploiting subjects and hard to grasp the responsibilities. In times of "surveillance capitalism" (Zuboff 2018), it is quite easy to identify the exploited, weak, and poor subjects who pay the heaviest consequences according to this specific development model; but it is far less easy to discern the subjects responsible for the very serious injustices that split Europe and, for example, Italy in rich and poor. In fact, they do not have a face: they are corporations, companies, network enterprises; they are virtual places where responsibilities always belong "to others", or, at least, "to the system". I get the feeling that Patrizio fought against this elusive nebula of social and economic responsibilities.

The militant researcher. It is almost impossible not to grasp the militant nature of his studies, especially when he first faced the issue of flexibility and precariousness in the labour market. Patrizio's latest editorial was a jointly authored book entitled "Storie precarie: Parole, vissuti e diritti negati della generazione senza" ("Precarious Stories: Words, Experiences, and Denied rights of the 'Without' Generation") (Di Nicola et al. 2014).

As everyone knows, flexibility is a disaster that has hit the labour market since the second half of the Seventies and that continues to disrupt acquired rights, working conditions, and the lives of younger and older women and men. On the back cover can be read: "Being part of the 'without' generation means not being able to afford life plans, having no elementary rights, being worse off than one's parents despite having studied more: in a few words, workers live on the edge of the labour market, seeing themselves denied an important part of their own identity". The book collects the stories of 470 respondents and their message of complaint is very strong. In fact, this is not a book for academics but a book for everyone, even for those who have no academic experience or knowledge. For the purpose of putting this on public record, here is what a young woman with a postgraduate degree living in a region of central Italy complains about to the interviewer: "To be precarious means working six years without a contract, but having to do it to pay the rent. To be precarious is to obscure your life, but having to do it in order to study [...]. Precariousness is a way of life. Because if you know that today you work, but maybe not tomorrow, you have to design your choices, your needs, your desires not on the basis of what you have today, but on the basis of what tomorrow you may need to have. Precariousness is exhausting, it wears out your self-esteem. Building precariously means digging by the sea" (Di Nicola et al. 2014: 140). This is the life of many female and male workers who suffer the sad experience of precarious work. Everyone seems to be against precariousness, but there are also those who promote it, namely, hundreds of thousands of firms in Europe.

The academic researcher. Patrizio taught for years at Sapienza University in Rome and held courses and conferences around the world, particularly in the United States of America (USA). His contributions, above all, have underlined the consequences of the organisational and technological transformations that have gradually taken place in the business world. In the book "Visioni sul futuro delle organizzazioni: Persone e imprese nell'era della complessità" ("Visions on the Future of Organisations: People and Businesses in the Era of Complexity") (Di Nicola 2009), together with a team of young collaborators, he focused on the organisation and reorganisation of businesses, outlining the signs of a process that he calls "the great mutation", and which clearly draws its inspiration from Karl Polanyi's wonderful contribution, "The Great Transformation" (1974).

In his book, Patrizio wonders about the consequences of the crisis that started in 2008 and he is convinced that the same economic crisis and financial instability accelerate the change of modern businesses by bringing up new economic, psychological, anthropological, and philosophical skills. Looking at what he wrote, we can observe that the following lines can also be applied to the very serious current crisis caused by the COVID-19 pandemic: "Companies will have to rethink their organisational paradigms quickly. In fact, to deal with the difficulties, some basic rules should be applied. First of all, when production is reduced, companies must try to lay off as little staff as possible. Mass layoffs have the defect of striking indifferently, alienating even the most critical and indispensable professionals from the production cycles. In this way, in an attempt to survive in times of crisis, companies risk collapsing in the recovery phase, when they will no longer be able to resume production. Needless to say, those nations that avoid these mass layoffs within their workforce and those who maintain the social contract with the labour force and its unions, will have more chance of survival" (Di Nicola 2009: 17-18). His reasoning continues with the belief that time freed from work should be reserved for training as a driver towards more suitable forms of professionalism to face the risk of unemployment and towards the possibility of creating innovative products. Who can blame him? In my opinion, the suggested path is also very topical for the crisis that we are experiencing or that we are close to experiencing. I also observe how these prospects have not been pursued by businesses at all, but this opens a front that goes beyond these brief notes.

The committed researcher. In my opinion, the most important contribution of studies and reflections that Patrizio bequeaths to our scientific community concerns the thematic area of remote work, a research journey that could be summarised with "from teleworking to smart working". In 1997, Patrizio published one of the first books on the subject in question in Italy. Its title is "Il manuale del telelavoro: Nuovi modi di lavorare nella Società dell'Informazione" ("The Handbook of Telework: New ways of Working in the Information Society") (Di Nicola 1997). It is an important text that explains the spread of these forms of work and, at the same time, points out their advantages and disadvantages. This book is a sort of panegyric of the topic addressed. However, it does not hold-back from denouncing the main limits concerning "the isolation and reduction of external relational life" (Di Nicola

1997: 21), together with the workaholic syndrome, namely that syndrome suffered by "those who tend to get drunk on work by losing the distinction between productive activity and free time" (Di Nicola 1997: 23).

As a further evidence of the obstinacy with which Patrizio studied telework, the following year, he edited a new book entitled "Telelavoro tra legge e contratto" ("Telework Between Law and Bargaining") (Di Nicola 1998), which took the form of a guide to legislation, national and corporate bargaining, the design of workstations, the use of technology, and the areas of labour union relations. Clearly, it has been very useful both for workers and unionists.

In his paper "Dal telelavoro allo smart work: Una innovazione che fa bene a tutti?" (Di Nicola 2016), Patrizio focused on the transition from telework to smart work, carefully identifying and defining the similarities and differences between telework, smart work, and agile work. Then he had to stop his work, for reasons of *force majeure*. In this paper, Patrizio explains very well that the three terms teleworking, smart working, and agile work do not refer to the same activities and are not synonyms, even if, in common language, they are often confused. The curiosity remains as to what he would have written about remote work, now that millions of Italian and European workers practice it. What everyone calls smart working today is only a way to work from home, since it is not possible to go to the office; that is all. It does not open new horizons. It does not outline epochal organisational changes. It is not the sign of an enlightened management. It is a response to the pandemic. More precisely, it constitutes an improvised reaction that, once again, can be interpreted in terms of social and political stratification; I think that certainly would not have escaped Patrizio. The internal layering of the workforce becomes evident in the fact that, on the one hand, there are those who are able to stay at home to work, while on the other hand, many workers are pushed to go to the factory or to the office because they are an integral part of the "essential" production services.

I am convinced that Patrizio would have had something good to say, being motivated, as he was, by the propensity to fight social inequalities and claim a more participatory role for those classes dominated by profit and rampant capitalism. Now, all we can do is enhance his cultural heritage, with the certainty that new generations will want to gain from his teachings, both in studies and life.

References

Di Nicola, Patrizio (Ed.) (1997): Il manuale del telelavoro: Nuovi modi di lavorare nella società dell'informazione (The Handbook of Telework: New ways of Working in the Information Society). Roma: Edizioni SEAM.

Di Nicola, Patrizio (Ed.) (1998): Telelavoro tra legge e contratto ("Telework Between Law and Bargaining"). Roma: Ediesse.

Di Nicola, Patrizio (2016): Dal telelavoro allo smart work: Una innovazione che fa bene a tutti? URL: http://www.telelavoro-italia.com/wp-content/uploads/2016/01/Di-Nicola-LW-1-2016.pdf [25 June 2020].

Di Nicola, Patrizio/Rosati, Simona (Eds.) (2009): Visioni sul futuro delle organizzazioni: Persone ed imprese nell'era della complessità ("Visions on the Future of Organisations: People and Businesses in the Era of Complexity"). Milano: Guerini Scientifica.

Di Nicola, Patrizio/della Ratta-Rinaldi, Francesca/Ioppolo, Ludovica/Rosati, Simona (2014): Storie precarie: Parole, vissuti e diritti negati della generazione senza (Precarious Stories: Words, Experiences, and Denied rights of the 'Without' Generation). Roma: Ediesse.

Polanyi, Karl (1974): The Great Transformation. New York: Holt, Rinehart & Winston.

Zuboff, Shoshana (2019): The Age of Surveillance Capitalism: The Fight for a Human Future at the New Frontier of Power. New York: Public Affairs.

TABLE OF CONTENTS

Foreword
Loukas Stemitsiotis   3

Changes in the Italian Labour Market
Stanislao Di Piazza   5

Homage: What Patrizio Di Nicola Has Left Behind
Renato Fontana   11

TABLE OF CONTENTS   17

The Importance of SMEs as Innovators of Sustainable Inclusive Employment: New Evidence from Regional and Local Labour Markets
Christa Larsen and Jenny Kipper   21

1. SMES: CONCEPTS AND RELEVANCE FOR REGIONAL AND LOCAL LABOUR MARKET MONITORING IN THE PHASE OF PANDEMIC AND BEYOND

The Importance of SMEs as Innovators of Sustainable Inclusive Employment: Some Issues Resulting from Shocks to the Economy Imposed by the COVID-19 Pandemic
Ronald McQuaid and Aleksandra Webb   33

What Is New in SMEs? Innovation and Employment Sustainability in the Context of Italian Start-Ups
Renato Fontana, Ernesto Dario Calò and Milena Cassella   47

2. POLICY FRAMEWORKS FOR SUSTAINABLE AND INCLUSIVE EMPLOYMENT AND GROWTH OF SMES

2.1. Multiple Policy Fields and Collaboration

SMEs in Hungary and in Poland: A Comparative Analysis of Legal and Labour Relations
Gábor Mélypataki, Michał Barański, Zoltán Muszinszki and Katalin Lipták   79

Regional Public Policy on the Use of ICT to Support Innovation and Growth: How Can Micro-Businesses and SMEs Be Supported Through Collaborative Initiatives in Clusters?
Martine Gadille, Karine Guiderdoni-Jourdain and Robert Tchobanian   103

Employment in SMEs in the Context of Digitalisation: Opportunities and Threats. On the Examples of Russia and China
Irina V. Novikova, Olesya V. Dmitrieva and Roman I. Antonenko   129

Decent Work in the Basque Country
Borja Pulido Orbegozo   141

2.2. Challenges for Policy Makers

SMEs in the Economy of Russia: Regional and Industry Aspects
Nina Oding   159

Contributions of SMEs to Employment in Romania
Ciprian Panzaru and Cosmin Enache   179

SMEs in Brandenburg – Job Creation Motor, Adaptation Machine, Low Wages?
Daniel Porep   191

3. HUMAN RESOURCE MANAGEMENT IN SMES

3.1. Relevance of Training and Its Practice

Continuing Vocational Training and SMEs: Specificities, Practices, and Potentials
Aline Valette-Wursthen — 215

Skills for Smart Specialisation: Fostering SME Innovation Through New Training and Learning Pathways, Technological Transfer, and Skills Upgrading
Pirita Vuorinen and Cristina Mereuta — 231

SMEs and the Retrospective Acquirement of Vocational Qualification by Semi-Skilled and Unskilled Workers in the Federal State of Hesse
Oliver Lauxen and Christian Müller — 247

3.2. Human Resource Development and Retention Management

How Do SMEs Contribute to Sustainable Employability in Times of Crisis? An Explorative Study in Northern Italy
Mattia Martini and Dario Cavenago — 263

Innovation and Sustainable Inclusive Employment: Evidence from the „Regio Insubria" During the COVID-19 Outbreak
Moreno Baruffini — 281

Recruiting and Retention in SMEs in Hesse – Qualitative Insights
Jenny Kipper — 295

4. OUTLOOK – SMES ACROSS EUROPE

SMEs – Labour and the Challenge of Competitive Sustainability
Marco Ricceri 311

Afterword
Oliver Roepke 337

INFORMATION ON THE AUTHORS 341

The Importance of SMEs as Innovators of Sustainable Inclusive Employment: New Evidence from Regional and Local Labour Markets

Christa Larsen and Jenny Kipper

Introduction

Reflections on SMEs and Their Function for Securing Skilled Labour

In October 2019, the Scientific Committee of the European Network on Regional Labour Market Monitoring decided that in the following 12 months, its thematic focus would be on small and medium-sized enterprises (SMEs) and, more specifically, on their function as innovators of sustainable inclusive employment. This was based on the belief that SMEs are more than just a small version of larger companies. Approaches in recent years have shown many indications that SMEs – in the context of skilled labour shortages due to demographic changes – are particularly successful in the recruitment and retention of skilled labour. This stems from the following factors: (i) their particular, often family-oriented culture; (ii) an orientation towards their local and regional labour markets; (iii) their distinctive expertise of niche products and niche target groups, and (iv) an awareness of having to offer more customized working conditions to offset the lure of financial incentives found in larger companies. They succeed by offering individually tailored and flexible working conditions and career paths for their employees. They are also able to adapt to an employee's specific needs, which will change over time. It is about people and their interaction with their environment, their families, and their locality. Accordingly, creative and diverse solutions for the reconciliation of work and family, flexible working time models and much more are implemented. Employees for whom work-life balance is very important, especially many young workers, appreciate these framework conditions of SMEs and show high loyalty to their employers in the form of retention.

However, SMEs are not only highly adaptable and responsive to their employees, but also to their product or service markets in which they operate. Fast adaptation to emerging product or service requirements is a major advantage for SMEs. Short internal decision-making processes and often very close contacts with customers allow for high transparency and quick readjustment. In comparison, large companies with standardised processes and structures prove to be much more cumbersome when confronted with the need for fast and customised personnel and product/service solutions.

These observations by members of the Scientific Committee led to the question of whether SMEs offer good and contemporary solutions for securing skilled workers but also for the inclusion of target groups remote from the labour market. If so, they can be regarded as "modern" companies, as hidden champions. To grapple with this question, Network members were asked to contribute to this anthology.

SMEs in the COVID-19 Pandemic

During the preparation of the articles for this anthology, the COVID-19 pandemic broke out and sharpened our focus on the flexibility and possibilities of SMEs, especially with respect to the changed framework conditions. The current work context has been particularly affected by health-related measures across their respective labour markets. We wonder whether the characteristics of SMEs, such as flexibility (adaptivity and responsiveness), their orientation towards local conditions and the loyalty of their employees will prove to be factors that help these companies survive the crisis well, or even come out stronger.

The authors of the articles in this anthology show that there are no simple and, above all, no conclusive answers at this moment. Rather, they raise awareness that SMEs represent a heterogeneous group of companies. There are fundamental differences between a medium-sized company with up to 250 employees and a corresponding capital stock or a self-employed person. The latter in particular is affected far more severely and existentially by the pandemic in most regions of Europe. It is also clear that the company's industrial affiliation plays an important role. For example, while tourism, hospitality, culture industry and vocational training are extremely affected by the pandemic, this is hardly the case for most craft businesses. In many cases, SMEs may succeed by converting their production to protective equipment or disinfectants, or by offering their services online. In many cases, particularly SMEs that focus primarily on local and regional raw materials and sales markets are more stable through the crisis than those that depend on global supply and service chains. And, of course, it is a fundamental factor how politics acts in the individual states and regions. Here specifically, to what extent are support programmes available (wage replacement benefits, loans, and bridging funds) to assist endangered SMEs.

The articles of our Network members show that it is currently hardly possible to draw a precise picture of the SMEs' situation in Europe. This is not only due to the fact that the developments are still ongoing and that changes are occurring very quickly. Because SMEs are strongly embedded in heterogeneous local socio-cultural and economic structures and processes, they find both positive and negative framework conditions for their future development. Thus, their developments cannot yet be described with generalised statements. A systematic monitoring of the factors listed is not yet available in any country. In order to obtain the information necessary for political decision-makers to, for example, act more precisely in a crisis such as the current one, it requires a bottom-up perspective from the localities and regions. This can create a transparency that enables precise assessments of how SMEs are impacted by a crisis, the types of support that they need, and how the aid already provided is working. This requires continuous monitoring of local events and systematic feedback to the policy process. This can be done through the almost 700 regional and local labour market observatories in Europe. To this end, the authors of this year's anthology provide initial approaches and insights.

Importance of Regional and Local Labour Market Observatories in Supporting Evidence-Based Policy Making During the Pandemic

Since the start of the pandemic, transparency and orientation have been more important than ever for the political decision-making process. Evidence-based policymaking, long advocated, has been quickly implemented. For a long time, virologists, successively followed by economists and sociologists, have set the topics and politicians have made decisions and installed programmes based on their information. This top-down process has dominated in almost all countries. It is gradually becoming clear that local and regional decision-makers need more appropriate evidence for their political decisions, especially in the important area of the labour market and employment. The regional and local labour market observatories across Europe are already established within networks of stakeholders and policy makers and can take on the important task of continuously creating transparency.

Most regional and local labour market observatories have little specific information on SMEs. To a large degree, information from SMEs concern only the number employees or their affiliation with certain industries. The internal heterogeneity of

SMEs is not yet sufficiently mapped, due also to the limits of official statistics. In view of the current requirements, these also have the disadvantage that there is often a time lag of one year or more between the data generation and its accessibility, rendering such data hardly useful. Much of the Public Employment Services (PES) routine data is rather useful, due to their topicality and their small-scale mapping. Further qualitative information is required from the expert discussions already established in many observatories. Surveys of companies and their managements certainly contribute to exploring the ways in which public support programmes are effective and where further action is needed. Data from the internet (BIG DATA) may also be another source. The contributions in this anthology provide a variety of references to this data. They also provide various concepts and definitions for thematic focus ideas by region and need, with which the respective status quo can be provided to local decision-makers.

However, this approach is probably insufficient. The pandemic and the onset of a recession are causing massive short-term political interference through immense economic stimulus packages intended to minimize or even avoid the economic downturn. The immense financial support offers opportunities to "re-engineer" the economy and the labour market. The political target horizons for this can include the sustainable and inclusive growth approach of the Organisation for Economic Co-Operation and Development (OECD) and the International Labour Organization (ILO). In connection with this, the green economy concept, including digitisation, from the European Commission can serve as inspiration. For monitoring of the labour market, employment, and the economy in regions and localities, this means that the observed developments can also be assessed and classified by the extent they lead to sustainable and inclusive development. Labour market and local economy stakeholders, as well as the local policy makers, can leverage their decisions and actions to significantly enable SMEs, often local and regional, to pursue sustainable and inclusive strategies for their employees. Unlike large companies, SMEs are significantly more dependent on a local and regional support structure and corresponding networks. This close interdependency promotes the stability of companies and thus the regional economy, and it improves the quality of life within regions and localities.

How can regional and local labour market observatories adapt to the new challenges? And, what can they do to act as central players in a transformation process? This initially addresses the information content observatories make available and their roles and involvement in local networks. A strong focus on SMEs is essential.

It is highly likely that in most regions and localities, well over 90% of companies are SMEs. These are the promoters of the transformation process. For this reason, it is necessary to have differentiated information about these companies, their business and their personnel policies. Unmet needs and support structure gaps should be clearly identified. To generate such information, additional paths can be forged by involving new actors. For example, a standing group of experts could be established from representatives of local businesses, local training providers, local business development agencies, public employment services, and business advisors of the Chambers of Commerce and Crafts to assess the current situation. Estimates of the degree of transformation would also be relevant. The observatory could support this group by moderating discussions and contributing new knowledge, when necessary. The information stand can be prepared by the observatory for stakeholders and policy makers. The now widespread use of digital communication in SMEs, especially video conferences, can be intensified by the observatories. This enables more scheduling flexibility. It would also be important for observatories to provide tightly packed current information (real time) at short intervals, and to be thematically flexible, in accordance with the needs of the decision-makers. The increased use of information technologies can help to better reach decision-makers individually and in real time. As observatories succeed in becoming a reliable and central provider of information in the regions and localities, the more central and significant the role of the observatories in transformation processes will become.

In many European countries, the regional and local observatories are interconnected. This structure enables them to communicate findings between regions easily and efficiently and across regions to national decision-makers. The European Network on Regional and Local Labour Market Monitoring will also continue to monitor the transformation process in the future and bundle relevant findings. Appropriate measures to achieve this will be defined at this year's annual meeting.

Strategic Decisions Planned for the 15th Annual Meeting of the European Network on Regional and Local Labour Market Monitoring (EN RLMM)

For the first time in the Network's 15-year history, the Annual Meeting will not be held as a face-to-face event. The circumstances of the COVID-19 pandemic lead to the choice of a virtual format. This will enable Network members to gain experience with digitally supported exchanges and possibly receive new impulses for their work in the observatories. Two thematic focuses are planned to empower Network members for the challenges of the transformation.

The foundations of this empowerment are provided by the contributions in this anthology.

Focus 1: Assessing the Complex World of SMEs in the Pandemic and Beyond

It will be discussed how, according to Network members, SMEs are currently positioned in their regions to survive the pandemic. In particular, five thematic dimensions are under consideration:

- Differentiated according to various types of SMEs (different sizes, industry affiliations, locations, degrees of innovation and digitisation, qualification levels of employees), it can be determined which of these types are particularly well suited to the challenges of the crisis and what are the decisive factors.
- A focus is also on the extent to which specific concepts such as corporate social responsibility, employability, life-long learning, and green production can help to promote sustainable and inclusive employment and how these concepts can best be implemented by SMEs.
- It should be discussed how the digitisation implemented out of necessity by many SMEs in work, production, and marketing processes in recent months can be stabilized and sustainably anchored or expanded. Further, what can the companies achieve on their own and where would they need help from third parties.
- It will be discussed how local and regional policy frameworks should be designed to promote the existence and transformation of SMEs and their employees.
- Finally, the integration and networking of SMEs in their regions is of central importance, since they are often dependent on support from third parties for the recruitment, retention, and training of their employees due to limited resources. An exchange should take place about which actors are indispensable for such networks and how these networks should be designed as part of the regional governance structure.

For each of these thematic stands, it is also important to explore how relevant information on the respective topics can be mapped into a continuous regional and local labour market monitoring.

Focus 2: Preconditions and Functions of Regional and Local Labour Market Observatories During the Pandemic and Beyond

During the pandemic and its consequent transformations, the best possible transparency is continuously required so that companies (the majority of which are

SMEs), actors in their support structures (Public Employment Services, VET provision, innovation, and technical support, and so on), and policy makers are well-oriented and are able to make suitable decisions. The situation in most regions and localities is currently still characterised by non-transparency. Accordingly, there is a high need for action. If this need is met, evidence-based labour market and economic policies can be implemented. As mentioned above, regional and local labour market observatories form a solid basis for creating optimal local transparency. However, most observatories are not currently set up to do this job adequately. Against this background, it should be discussed where there is a need for action and which solutions and support can be used to improve it. Discourses must be conducted along four thematic dimensions:

- It is important to clarify the topics on which information needs exist in the regions and localities. In addition, it has to be discussed how this information can be made available at short intervals – if possible, in real time – and which actors not yet addressed should be involved in the generation and use of this information.
- It will also be discussed how observatories can become visible as competent and central actors locally and how they can systematically use the interface with the policy makers in particular. However, access to other information user groups, such as companies, should also be discussed.
- For observatories which have so far been operating in (regional) isolation, it is important to determine whether a support structure can be established or activated with the help of the European Network on Regional Labour Market Monitoring and how this structure should be designed.
- Finally, it can be discussed whether, and if so, how observatories in their regions and localities can influence the initiation and implementation of sustainable, inclusive, and innovation-oriented development.

At the Annual Meeting, the results of the virtual exchange will be documented and serve as a knowledge base for the network members, which can and should be updated by further exchanges.

Contributions in this Anthology

The 31 Network members, who have written 17 articles this year, show that dealing with SMEs can have many different facets. Basically, there are two main perspectives to be differentiated. On the one hand, some of the articles in Chapter 2 focus on the relevance of SMEs with the help of structural data and thus demonstrate their importance for regional and local economic areas. These descriptions are mostly linked to necessary policy frameworks. This shows how important the targeted support of SMEs is, so that they can secure sustainable and inclusive employment and at the same time maintain their economic stability. On the other hand, this anthology contains a number of articles in Chapter 3 that approach SMEs from an organisational perspective. The main focus is on human resource management and its specific conditions. These two groups of articles are framed by contributions in Chapters 1 and 4, which present definitions and concepts and localise the position of SMEs in the major development lines of international organisations such as the OECD and the European Commission and thus create an important basis to specify perspectives beyond the pandemic.

The chapters and the articles are described in more detail below.

In the introductory Chapter 1, Ronald McQuaid and Aleksandra Webb introduce the general topic of SMEs. They show different definitions and concepts in order to be able to grasp the diversity of SMEs. They also argue that SMEs are of central importance for the transformation of economy and labour, especially in times of pandemic. They speak of a necessary re-engineering that can be pursued with the aim of sustainable and inclusive employment. Finally, they summarise the thematic lines under which SMEs can be taken into account in regional and local labour market monitoring. In the second contribution of this chapter, Renato Fontana, Ernesto Dario Calò, and Milena Cassella open up a rather qualitative perspective on the subject of SMEs by historically deriving that the socio-cultural substance of SMEs (they particularly consider start-ups), are anchored deep in Italian society. This impressively shows that this is a special quality criterion of SMEs and that this anchoring at a local and regional level can bring about particular sustainability in employment and at the same time innovations.

Chapter 2 focuses on the policy framework that SMEs need for sustainable and inclusive employment and economic growth. First, various policy fields and their relevance for the support of SMEs are discussed in Chapter 2.1. It starts with Gábor Mélypataki, Michał Baránski, Zoltám Muszinki, and Katalin Lipták, a consortium of scientists from Hungary and Poland, who interdisciplinarily examine from an economic and legal perspective to what extent the legal framework can meet the special conditions of SMEs so that they can implement sustainable employment. Their finding is clearly negative. They point out, however, that the concept of corporate social responsibility can be provided. Martine Gadille, Karine Guiderdoni-Jourdain, and Robert Tchobanian take a different perspective by focusing on the field of economic policy. They show that cluster policy in particular cannot adequately do justice to SMEs. Rather, according to their findings, so-called meta organisations are needed, which have independent resources and can support SMEs very efficiently as a local service provider. Irina V. Novikova, Olesya V. Dmitrieva, and Roman I. Antonenko argue similarly with regard to support for digitisation. Using various examples from China and Russia, they show that a targeted digitisation policy, which in addition to technology also focuses on training people in SMEs, can lead to growth of SMEs. However, their results further show that systematic and sustainable support is needed to anchor digitisation well in SMEs. An appropriate policy framework is particular important in times of digitisation, which is often implemented ad hoc. While in the first three articles the focus is on a policy field, Borja Pulido Orbegozo demonstrates for the Basque Country how different policy fields can be interrelated under a regionally defined and future-oriented strategy. This promotes SMEs specifically but also simultaneously promotes inclusive employment. Thereby, the policy areas economy, labour market, and education are directly connected with each other. Pulido Orbegozo makes it clear that integrated or collaborative approaches can only be successfully aligned if they are supported by a common vision or objective.

In Chapter 2.2, the authors show that when designing policy frameworks for the promotion of SMEs, challenges can arise in the implementation, which have a clearly limiting effect on the efficiency of the support. In her article, Nina Oding shows that, unlike in many European Union (EU) countries, there is no historical and socio-cultural line in Russia that would support the establishment of SMEs. She argues that in the Post-Soviet states, SMEs play only a marginal role given the large corporate and production conglomerates. This also means that transitions into grey and black economies are smooth. Incentives from the policy framework to promote SMEs are difficult to grasp here since the grey market has established itself as a social practise. Ciprian Panzaru and Cosmin Enache outline another challenge in their article to the situation in Romania. They deal with employment growth in SMEs, which is promoted by a corresponding policy framework. However, their research shows that there is a kind of marshalling yard between individual industries. Employment growth in the services and construction sectors is to the detriment of employment in production. In his article, Daniel Porep from the Brandenburg region in Germany proves with elaborated and much differentiated data analyses that SMEs' funding does not automatically function as a job engine. This means that incentives for employment growth in SMEs embedded in policy frameworks cannot always achieve the intended effect. Therefore, research and evaluation, as in the articles presented here, is required to measure the effectiveness of policy measures.

Chapter 3 focuses on the perspective of SMEs as organisations and discusses how human resource management should be aligned in order to create sustainable and inclusive employment. Qualification and training seem to be of great importance. This is illustrated by the articles in Chapter 3.1. They show that, unlike in large companies, learning and training in SMEs is often carried out informally. This means that other than formal formats are applied. To grasp these precisely is an important task in regional and local labour market monitoring. Aline Valette-Wursthen conceptually introduces different types of SMEs. She particularly refers to the very small enterprises (VSEs), those are microenterprises with up to ten employees. She combines her descriptions of the different types of companies with the specification of the roles of the managers. According to her results, this has a significant influence on how training and learning are implemented in the company. In conclusion, she points out that the educational sector could still target some previously untapped educational potential in SMEs. Pirita Vuorinen and Cristina Mereuta from the European Training Fund (ETF) argue in a similar way. They argue that new training formats and learning pathways are required in order to significantly promote the ability to innovate as well as the relevant technology transfer in SMEs. It is also important to the authors that there is a systematic approach on how a skills upgrade is implemented for employees. Thus, significantly strengthening the employability of workers and securing sustainable employment. The topic of skills upgrade is also in the focus of the article written by Oliver Lauxen and Christian Müller. It deals with unskilled and semi-skilled workers in SMEs. Their upskilling is promoted in the state of Hesse in Germany so that practical work experience can be used as the basis for an external exam in order to obtain a formal vocational qualification degree. The results of the presented evaluation show that only certain types of SMEs are interested in such formal qualifications for their employees. Rather, it seems to be important for SMEs that the necessary knowledge and skills are available even without formal qualifications. To achieve this, companies use different strategies and approaches. In the following Chapter 3.2, Mattia Martini and Dario Cavenago show in a case study that maintaining employability is essential for SMEs. This also ensures the sustainability of employment. Employability is achieved or secured respectively by offering trainings. The authors show that employability is a key prerequisite for sustainable employee loyalty to the company. Moreno Baruffini also demonstrates in three case studies from the border region between Switzerland and Italy that the strategic orientation of SMEs in relation to the development of products and services can be closely interrelated with human resource management. His findings make clear that innovations in recruitment and employment can represent a good potential for product and service innovation and vice versa. This means that innovative SMEs also have good prerequisites for innovative personnel management and, thus, for a sustainable and inclusive employment. The conclusion of this chapter is the contribution of Jenny Kipper, who uses the analysis of six SMEs in Hesse to clarify that the founders and managers of the SMEs are decisive for employee retention, recruitment, and dealing with crisis situations. Jenny Kipper works out which indicators should be included in a quality-oriented monitoring that can capture insights into the logic of action of small businesses.

In the last Chapter 4, Marco Ricceri outlines a perspective, based on central key documents of the OECD, the ILO, and the European Commission, in order to be able to identify objectives for the transformation of economy and employment. He analyses that, however, there is still a need for readjustment, in particular with regard to better intersectional integration, new tools for intensifying the relationships between the regions and their businesses and sound governance for new environmental and social policies.

As editors of this anthology, we would like to thank the authors who have often written their contributions this year under the difficult conditions of the pandemic. Their contributions enable a unique panoramic view of the topic of SMEs in a situation in which there are very good reasons to rely on SMEs when it comes to securing and sustainably strengthening regional and local economy and employment. Thank you very much.

Without the active and professional support of Amelie Schultze and Daniela Holler at the Goethe University in Frankfurt am Main in Germany, this anthology would not have been possible in such a short time. Thank you very much for this.

And last but not least, Marco Ricceri and Ludovico Semerari from EURISPES in Rome have given us great support over the past few weeks. They were flexible enough to postpone their Network member's invitation to Sardinia from 2020 to 2022 and are now helping significantly to make it possible for the first time to host the network's annual meeting as a virtual meeting. We are very grateful to Marco Ricceri and Ludovico Semerari.

We would also like to thank Renato Fontana, with whom we would like to further anchor the memory of the work of Patrizio di Nicola in the Network. He supports this greatly.

At the end of this introduction, we would like to speak again as editors of the Network's anthology. After 15 years of dealing with regional and local labour market monitoring and the many activities that were developed within the network to convince policymakers in regions and localities in particular that evidence-based policies can generate the best possible development impetus, we look at the current situation. In many countries, politics in recent weeks have been more evidence-oriented than ever before. This is an opportunity for the actors in the network to create transparency through their observatories, that is to help them advance the transformation of employment and the economy in the crisis and afterwards. The exchange in the Network can help us all.

Frankfurt am Main, June 2020

1. SMES: CONCEPTS AND RELEVANCE FOR REGIONAL AND LOCAL LABOUR MARKET MONITORING IN THE PHASE OF PANDEMIC AND BEYOND

The Importance of SMEs as Innovators of Sustainable Inclusive Employment: Some Issues Resulting from Shocks to the Economy Imposed by the COVID-19 Pandemic

Ronald McQuaid and Aleksandra Webb

Introduction

This chapter briefly introduces some of the issues related to small and medium-sized enterprises (SMEs) in their roles as innovators of sustainable inclusive employment. There are multiple forms of SMEs that differ by size, reach and character, varying by industry and country. However, these enterprises are crucial to local and regional economies throughout the world, especially in terms of offering employment opportunities and contributing to economic growth (Acs and Audretsch 2010).

Adaptability and responsiveness are two commonly noted features of SMEs that provide business advantages in non-turbulent times as well as in times of crises (Drucker 1985). A flexibility in management policies and rules allows SMEs, firstly, to respond quickly to market opportunities by finding innovative solutions to existing or emerging problems, and secondly, to develop competitive advantages through niche organisational and strategic capabilities, which leads to increasing innovation and productivity (Audretsch and Thurik 2004). Utilising their know-how enables SMEs to respond to consumer needs, gain cost/strategic leadership and increase market-share. Such strategic leadership does not have to be limited to the market and financial success, as SMEs can also lead the work and employment innovation championing better work and creating more balanced, fairer and healthier workplaces (Schumacher and Gullingham 1979, Burchell et al. 2014).

Such roles seem to be of great value in the context of the health crisis caused by the COVID-19 pandemic. The pandemic has already altered some societal norms, caused consumer behaviour to change and negatively impacted national and regional economies. This chapter, firstly, briefly introduces key definitions and statistics related to SMEs and their socio-economic importance. Secondly, it draws attention to some of the immediately observed impacts of the health pandemic on local economies and the SMEs landscape, also suggesting the leadership opportunities and challenges such a crisis brings about.

Definitions and Importance of SMEs

There is no single definition of SMEs. One seminal UK report argued that:

> "[a small firm is] one that has a relatively small share of the market [...] is managed by its owners or part-owners in a personalised way, and not through the medium of a formalised management structure (...) is also independent in the sense that it does not form part of a larger enterprise and its owner-managers should be free from outside control in taking their principal decisions." (Bolton Report 1971: 1).

More broadly, quantitatively-based definitions, which vary between sectors, countries and time, are often based upon criteria such as employment, turnover, asset size, and ownership characteristics, although there are difficulties due to measuring, for instance, part-time versus full-time or temporary versus permanent employees and definitions may vary by industry and country (Glancey and McQuaid 2000). Qualitative approaches focus more on issues such as market share, the ownership or the control of the business, and attempt to capture the meanings, logics, beliefs and identities of actors in SMEs (Ekinci 2020) as well as behavioural aspects (such as identifying issues facing managers) that differ between small businesses and large firms (Curran and Blackburn 1994). Policy definitions of SMEs set out by the European Commission (2003) focus on staff headcount and either turnover or balance sheet totals. SMEs are those employing fewer than 250 persons, together with an annual turnover of no more than EUR 50 million or a balance sheet total of no more than EUR 43 million (Table 1).

Table 1: Definition of SMEs by the European Commission (2003)

Company category	Staff headcount	Turnover	Balance sheet total
Medium-sized	< 250	≤ € 50 m	≤ € 43 m
Small	< 50	≤ € 10 m	≤ € 10 m
Micro	< 10	≤ € 2 m	≤ € 2 m

Source: European Commission (2003).

Using financial measures such as turnover can be problematic if used across countries with greatly differing economic circumstances, for instance in high- and low-income countries, so Gibson and Van der Vaart (2008) suggest an SME definition that incorporates a formula that reflects volume of its turnover relative to the local economy.

Although it is clear that SMEs offer employment opportunities and contribute to economic growth, their importance varies by industry and country. For example, service and construction industries have the highest proportions of employment in small enterprises, while manufacturing has the lowest. In virtually all the European Union (EU) countries, more than 50 per cent of private service employment was in small firms in 2015. SMEs are crucial to local and regional economies and account for the vast majority of firms across the world (Acs and Audretsch 2010); however, their share of employment, investment, and value added is relatively lower than for larger firms. In the EU, 99 per cent of all business are SMEs (with under 250 employees), but they make up only 66.3 per cent of business employment and 56.5 per cent of value added (or lower percentages if financial businesses and the public sector are taken into account). The smallest employers, micro-businesses with less than ten employees, make up most firms (92.8 per cent,) but their shares of firms, employment and value added are relatively smaller at 29.1 per cent and 20.3 per cent respectively (Eurostat 2020).

Canada uses the term SME to refer to businesses with fewer than 500 employees (OECD 2017). In the USA, the definition of 'small' varies by industry (US SBA 2019), but around 99 per cent of all firms had under 200 employees in 2017, and they employed 39 per cent of all private employees; while for firms employing under 20 employees, the figures were 89 per cent and 16 per cent respectively (US SUSB 2018). While most employment remains in large firms, the job creation rate of small firms is higher (US SBA 2018). There is also considerable "churn" in SMEs, with only about half of all new establishments in the USA surviving for five years or more and about one-third surviving ten years or more (US SBA 2014). However, in times of recession the closure rate usually rises considerably, and the number of new starts drops, so there is likely to be a major short-term cyclical reduction in SMEs in the aftermath of the COVID-19 pandemic. This might be especially true for businesses that are focused on service provision rather than the sale of goods, and which tend to operate in face-to-face rather than online environment (education, arts, leisure, and sports among others).

Similar to the differences between SMEs and larger firms, there are many variations between types of SMEs that need to be taken into account when monitoring and analysing them. The following may often be significant. First, micro-businesses are those with under ten employees and whose characteristics and behaviours are likely to be quite different from larger SMEs. Second, family owned businesses are particularly important across the EU, but may have distinctive perspectives, knowledge and rationales compared to other SMEs, with greater emphasis placed on family and friendship rationales rather than solely business rationales for their decisions (Klein and Kellerman 2008; Seaman et al. 2014). Small family businesses often differ from other SMEs in the structure and operation of their social networks, including complex relationships through which they engage with the external socio-economic environment in which they operate (involving direct and indirect family, friendships, and business links); such relationships can act as bridges to outside sources of knowledge and expertise and hence to better exploitation of opportunities and innovation and the development or creation of new businesses (Seaman et al. 2017). Third, self-employed sole-traders (those with no employees) play a crucial role in many economies, but often have fewer financial reserves and have difficulty bearing the costs of major economic downturns, such as the pandemic. Sole traders, who vary from traditional skilled tradesmen to tutors and lifestyle coaches, are particularly prevalent in some service sectors and local economies.

Fourth, many people work informally within SMEs or the SMEs themselves operate in the informal economy (Webb et al. 2019). It is estimated that two billion workers worldwide are now employed informally, representing a majority of the global workforce (61 per cent) (ILO 2018a). This is particularly the case in rural areas (80 per cent) more than in cities (44 per cent), and in developing (90 per cent) and emerging countries (67 per cent) more than in developed countries (18 per cent).

The role of the "shadow" or "grey" economy also needs to be considered, otherwise the activities of SMEs and their links to local labour markets may be underestimated. SMEs might have different reasons for engaging with the informal economy, but commonly they arise from global and local competition rules and financial constraints (ILO 2015). However, the economic activities in the informal economy can be hidden from the authorities and institutions not just for financial gain, but also to avoid regulatory responsibilities (Medina and Schneider 2018; Williams 2011), including entrepreneurial activities in the early stages of product development or trading when higher risk of failure and financial loss is involved (Williams and Martinez 2014). For example, the evidence from the United Kingdom (UK) suggests that owners of small businesses resort to informal trading when starting their business to test the viability of their product or service. As the nature of the entrepreneurial process is focused on the recognition and exploitation of business opportunities (Webb et al. 2009), consequently, decisions concerning growth often lead to activities on the periphery or directly in the informal economy.

Fifth, many have argued that innovation is fundamental to entrepreneurship and to economic and social development (Drucker 1985; Schumpeter 1942 among others), and SMEs are important in developing and using knowledge as a significant source of competitive advantage (Audretsch and Thurik 2004) and innovation often underpinning sustainable growth in SMEs (Coad et al. 2016; Ismail et al. 2011). However, most SMEs are not particularly innovative (Bhide 2000) and carry out what Leibenstein (1968: 72) calls "routine entrepreneurship", involving routine management and coordination in an existing business with well-established and defined markets. Such entrepreneurship evolves around activities that are familiar and are conducted in familiar "tried and tested" ways with often limited time, knowledge and Research and Development (R&D). It is important to distinguish innovative SMEs who grasp opportunities, innovatively utilise resources or provide new products and services (even if they did not necessarily invent the new product or process themselves) from those who just carry out routine entrepreneurship (for example, OECD/Eurostat 2019).

Hence, it is important to take account of variations over time, location, industrial sector and various sub-groups of forms of SMEs. How SMEs recruit, train and develop their workers, how they finance themselves and how they develop their products and production processes are often quite different from the approaches of large firms; and it is crucial for labour market observatories and policy makers to take account of these differences. SMEs are important for local and regional labour markets, as they are more likely to recruit, train and develop vocational skills on a local basis and to rely more on local infrastructure and providers for related support and services than large firms.

SMEs and the Response to the Pandemic

The COVID-19 pandemic, a health pandemic that has affected the world deeply and which remains a threat of unprecedented magnitude, has put even the strongest world economies in a state of emergency. At the time of writing (May 2020), the economic crisis caused by the pandemic with the consequent downturn is particularly affecting certain sectors which employ large numbers of SMEs and self-employed (including restaurant, arts, entertainment and other leisure providers, transport such as taxis, accommodation, and real estate, and tourist operators among others). Countries and nations world-wide have currently implemented a range of approaches to manage this health crisis, but with limited certainty over how long this containment will take, or indeed whether consequent waves of the virus will reappear in months and years to come. For some businesses, the impact of pandemic will lead to the organisation ceasing to exist; or to their operation and development being heavily affected for many years, due to factors such as increased debt burden and reduction or loss of markets (to large firms or lower demand), with "knock-on" effects to others including their staff, suppliers, business collaborators, and owners. For others, it will need to spark a period of reinvention and adaptation. Of course, many businesses will thrive, taking advantage of opportunities generated by the current crises and of changes in consumer activities and habits. For example, in the UK, small shops selling bikes and garden supplies have recorded the highest sales in record, as the lockdown rules forced the public to stay at home but allowed for exercising outdoors.

However, for many SMEs this crisis may offer opportunities for a more *socially and environmentally sustainable (or "greener") recovery*, if investment in infrastructure, research and innovation and in social and employment support is targeted suitably. For example, governments' encouragement for using greener transport methods on return to work after the lockdowns accompanied with the public buy-in to support such transformation might contribute to the favourable conditions for SMEs with a green agenda (although some may move from public to private transport). SMEs are often considered to have the flexibility and speed to respond quickly to many of the opportunities, especially in the short term. As always, SMEs might also fulfil their expected role as leading technological and organisational innovators in response to pressing needs, for example, produce protecting personal equipment or developing medical technology. Although many innovations are likely to be mainly controlled by larger, better resourced organisations, SMEs might contribute in niches of economy or production.

The associated needs for developing the new and refreshing the existing, skills and various forms of training to ensure adequate recruitment are likely to be considerable. However, while there may be some positive scenarios, there is also a risk that existing vested interests will try to return the economy to "business as before" the pandemic and seek to replicate past socio-economic-environmental and employment structures. Nevertheless, some of these structures have changed during the pandemic. For instance, in the UK, social welfare support has been provided to those previously ineligible, including many self-employed, as well as wage support across large parts of the economy and different types of firms[1]. How these change in the future is still uncertain. However, this is yet another potential positive outcome which presents itself as an opportunity to carefully reengineer the economic system in line with the social principles of care and fairness. Still, the long-term consequences of support given to workers who lost income (including those in SMEs) and changes in the levels of trust towards the government and its policies remain to be seen; possible effect could include a greater compliance and a shrinkage of the activities in the informal economy.

In addition to reforms in *welfare systems*, and in the light of the lessons learned from the epidemic, new opportunities might emerge related to satisfying care needs (for example, for the sick or elderly). The epidemic has shown the importance of jobs that for a long time have been overlooked, undervalued and underpaid. Those jobs carry a high degree of medical risk of catching a disease and cannot be substituted by a digital/online service. For SMEs, this is a chance to take a lead in two areas; first, through filling the gap in the market and providing much needed services that will enhance the lives of people (for example, through provision of valuable and socially desired service). Second, it may involve re-structuring the business utilising sustainable models (such as social enterprise) and embedding

---

[1] In the UK, welfare rules were changed to support businesses and individuals through tax reliefs and furlough scheme, which they would have not normally been eligible for.

the principles of fairness and respect in their business cultures and human resources (HR) practices. In such ways, SMEs could provide high quality services and jobs that value both customers/clients and workers.

The reengineering of the economy should also include serious reflection on the widely utilised employment practices that tend to reduce *workers' conditions and health and safety protection*, in order to gain a competitive advantage. The lack of balance in the modern economy has been often criticised. On the one hand, the rise over recent decades of a modern version of the *gig-economy* (people working on the basis of short-terms jobs, often being self-employed) may increase with a greater desire for flexibility among employers (and aversion to taking on staff when there may be future health and economic disruptions). On the other hand, there may be countering effects as workers seek more job and health security and a more effective unemployment safety net. This type of "gig" or short-term work has a long history and in less "glamorous" situations such as "day labourers" in many developing countries or "lump labour" in the last century (where dock workers stood in a queue to be hired for a day at a time if they were needed). The historic struggles for job security from such jobs may be repeated by "gig" workers who found themselves without security during the pandemic. In addition, there may well be further shocks (such as demographic changes, climate change, economic dislocation, or another health pandemic) to the economy due to short or long-term financial, demographic and environmental pressures, and a more resilient and sustainable economy and society is needed to identify and respond to these future risks. It is likely that SMEs will have a major role in future socio-economic changes, especially those with flexibility, ability to scale up, and innovation histories. Hence, depending on how different tendencies towards better working conditions play out in different economies, SMEs may have a larger role in the creation of greater "decent work" as set out in the United Nations (UN) sustainable development goals (ILO 2018a) than has been acknowledged so far.

In terms of training, *local vocational training* has suffered major disruption during the COVID-19 pandemic, although SMEs tend to rely more on informal training (Kotey and Folker 2007). However, the pandemic is likely to make SMEs more aware of, and willing to use, national or even global online services (for example, for training or online subcontracting) and to invest more in home working and remote based operations with flexible work policies and adequate support for staff. Networks based on common interests (possibly sector, product, supply-chain or opportunity based) at national or wider levels, rather than local spatial proximity interests, may become more important to many SMEs. Although geographical, interpersonal and social links will remain important, regional observatories will continue to play a key role in regional economic development; their focus may shift somewhat towards wider online and other networks interconnecting SMEs and the markets, services and support used by SMEs. Interestingly, for those SMEs not totally reliant on face-to-face contact with customers (unlike many restaurants or local service providers), the move towards online sales and payments during the pandemic may have opened up markets beyond the local and regional, putting new demands on their development (such as new forms of marketing and supplying customers) and making them recruit staff from non-traditional groups or employ non-local staff who can work remotely. Hence, the COVID-19 pandemic might lead to a greater outward orientation for many SMEs, in contrast to historic pandemics which often resulted (at least in the short-term) in more local and social inward-looking orientations across society. Overall, the effects of the COVID-19 pandemic will require a rethinking of skills development programmes. It may also lead to different forms of interaction between observatories and regional policy makers and many SMEs; and potentially to the deepening of links between the countries of the EU, provided counteracting pressures towards national production and supply do not arise after the pandemic.

Conclusions

Major global economic challenges due to the COVID-19 pandemic put many SMEs in a state of insecurity, forcing them to find new ways to achieve inclusive employment for staff and also the owner-managers and using new structures to achieve this. They have to face situations where new ways of work and inclusion have to be built up in a very short time. Societies and economies will need to seek ways to provide greater employment and economic security for those particularly vulnerable to economic shocks, such as that caused by COVID-19, which may lead to a changed balance between flexibility and health and economic security among SMEs and the self-employed. As an effect of the crisis, the role of SMEs in the labour market may become more important.

The papers in this volume cover a range of important issues and provide new evidence for the importance of SMEs as innovators of sustainable inclusive employment in regional labour markets. They respond to a number of questions on how regional labour market observatories can address SMEs issues in two key areas: Data and Labour Market Intelligence and Employment/HR practice and Production Systems Innovations. Such questions include, but are not limited to:

Data and Labour Market Intelligence

- Which types of data do regional labour market observatories use in order to produce SMEs figures in different territories/cities and sectors (such as agriculture, industry, and services)? What data and methods do they use in order to measure and assess the contribution of SMEs to local development, the set-up of industrial districts, and the spread of new social models in the territories in relation to the organisation of different times of life and work and the related preferences of the people?
- What monitoring actions do they organize in order to assess the effects of national and regional public policies, university programmes, specialized centres and business plans in relation to the spread of corporate culture, the promotion of SMEs with the creation of start-ups, the involvement of young people in such initiatives, in particular the inclusion of NEETs in the production processes? Which types of action do they set up in order to support the development of SMEs? In which ways do they support or equip decision-makers concerning SMEs' issues?
- How are SMEs embedded within local actors' networks in order to proceed with training and labour market supply policies?

Employment, HR Practice, and Production Systems Innovations

- How are SMEs innovators of sustainable inclusive employment and what actions are required to support fair and inclusive practices in SMEs?
- What type of innovative HR practices and work organisations, if any, do SME develop when participating in sustainable development strategies?
- To what extent are SMEs or start-ups involved in the spread of new employment and new forms of work, for example, linked to the transformation of production systems induced by digitalisation and robotization (such as smart working, platform working among others) as well as by regional, national and global competition? Will these processes generate more jobs in some regions and less in others and therefore reinforce regional inequalities? Or will these processes create better jobs in SMEs?

- To what extent do SMEs contribute to changing value chains in current transformations of productive systems and manpower management? Examples in local or regional territories could be especially interesting.

The following papers in this anthology help set us in the right direction towards answering these important questions.

References

Acs, Z. J./Audretsch, D. B. (2010): Handbook of Entrepreneurship Research. In: Acs, Z. J./Audretsch, D. B. (Eds.): International Handbook Series on Entrepreneurship, 2nd edition. London: Springer, pp. 1-22.

Audretsch, D. B./Thurik, R. (2004): A Model of the Entrepreneurial Economy. In: International Journal of Entrepreneurship Education 2 (2), pp. 143–166.

Armstrong, M./Baron, A. (2002) Strategic HRM: The Key to Improved Business Performance. London: CIPD Publishing.

Bhide, A. (2000): The Origin and Evolution of New Businesses. Oxford: Oxford University Press.

Bolton Report (1971): Report of the Committee of Inquiry on Small Firms, Cmnd 4811. London: HMSO.

Burchell, B./Sehnbruch, K./Piasna, A./ Agloni, N. (2014): The Quality of Employment and Decent Work: Definitions, Methodologies, and Ongoing Debates. In: Cambridge Journal of Economics 38 (2), pp. 459–477.

Curran, J./Blackburn, R. (1994): Small Firms and Local Economic Networks: The Death of the Local Economy. London: Paul Chapman.

Drucker, P. F. (1985): Innovation and Entrepreneurship. London: Heinemann.

Ekinci, Y./Gordon-Wilson, S./Slade, A. (2020): An Exploration of Entrepreneurs' Identities and Business Growth. In: Business Horizons 63 (3), pp. 391-401.

European Commission (2003): Commission Recommendation of 6 May 2003 Concerning the Definition of Micro, Small and Medium-Sized Enterprise. URL: https://eur-lex.europa.eu/legal-content/EN/TXT/?uri=CELEX:32003H0361 [10 May 2020].

Gibson, T./Van der Vaart, H. (2008): Defining SMEs: A less imperfect way of defining small and medium enterprises in developing countries. Brookings Global Economy and Development. URL: https://pdfs.semanticscholar.org/7daf/d951bc399ecbbe4a15823c6b9e802614f63c.pdf [04 June 2020].

Glancey, K. S./McQuaid, R. W. (2000): Entrepreneurial Economics. Basingstoke: Macmillan.

International Labour Organization (ILO) (2015): World Employment and Social Outlook: The Changing Nature of Jobs. URL: https://www.ilo.org/wcmsp5/groups/public/---dgreports/---dcomm/---publ/documents/publication/wcms_368626.pdf [22 August 2019].

International Labour Organization (ILO) (2018a): Women and Men in the Informal Economy: A Statistical Picture. URL: https://www.ilo.org/global/publications/books/WCMS_626831/lang--en/index.htm [10 May 2020].

International Labour Organization (ILO) (2018b): Decent Work and the Sustainable Development Goals: A Guidebook on SDG Labour Market Indicators. URL: https://www.ilo.org/global/statistics-and-databases/publications/WCMS_647109/lang--en/index.htm [10 May 2020].

Ismail, H.S./Poolton, J./Sharifi, H. (2011): The role of agile strategic capabilities in achieving resilience in manufacturing-based small companies. In: International Journal of Production Research 49 (18), pp. 5469-5487.

Kotey, B./Folker, C. (2007): Employee Training in SMEs: Effect of Size and Firm Type - Family and Nonfamily. In: Journal of Small Business Management 45 (2), pp. 214-238.

Medina, L./Schneider, F. (2018): Shadow Economies Around the World: What Did We Learn Over the Last 20 Years? IMF Working Paper WP/18/17. URL: https://www.imf.org/~/media/Files/Publications/WP/2018/wp1817.ashx [22 August 2019].

Leibenstein, H. (1968): Entrepreneurship and Development. In: American Economic Review 58 (2), pp.72–83.

Organisation for Economic Cooperation and Development (OECD) (2017): SME and Entrepreneurship Policy in Canada. Paris: OECD.

OECD/Eurostat (2019): Oslo Manual 2018: Guidelines for Collecting, Reporting and Using Data on Innovation. 4th ed. Paris/Eurostat, Luxembourg: OECD Publishing. URL: https://doi.org/10.1787/9789264304604-en [04 June 2020].

Schumacher, E. F./Gillingham, P. N. (1979): Good Work. New York: Harper and Row.

Schumpeter, J. A. (1942): Capitalism, Socialism and Democracy. New York: Harper and Row.

Seaman, C./ McQuaid, R. W./Pearson, M. (2017): Social Networking in Family Businesses in a Local Economy. In: Local Economy 32 (5), pp. 451-466.

Seaman, C., McQuaid, R. W. and Pearson, M. (2014) 'Networks in Family Business: A Multi-Rational Approach'. In International Entrepreneurship and Management Journal 10 (3), pp. 523-537.

United States Census Bureau (SUSB) (2018): 2017 SUSB Annual Data Tables by Establishment Industry. URL: https://www.census.gov/data/tables/2017/econ/susb/2017-susb-annual.html [08 May 2020].

United States Small Business Administration (SBA) (2019): Table of small business size standards matched to North American Industry Classification System codes. Washington DC: U.S. Small

Business Administration. URL: https://www.sba.gov/document/support--table-size-standards [04 June 2020].

United States Small Business Administration (SBA) (2018): Small Business Profile 2018. URL: https://www.sba.gov/sites/default/files/advocacy/2018-Small-Business-Profiles-US.pdf [08 May 2020].

United States Small Business Administration (SBA) (2014): Frequently asked questions. URL: https://www.sba.gov/sites/default/files/FAQ_March_2014_0.pdf [04 June 2020].

Webb, A./McQuaid, R. W./Rand, S. (2019): "What, Who, Why and Ways out of the Informal Economy: A Brief Review of Key Definitions and Approaches". In: Larsen, C./Rand, S./Schmid, A./Bobkov, V./Lokosov, V. (Eds.): Assessing Informal Employment and Skills Needs: Approaches and Insights from Regional and Local Labour Market Monitoring. München: Rainer Hampp Verlag, pp. 23-40.

Webb, J. W./Tihanyi, L./Ireland, R. D./Sirmon, D. G. (2009): You Say Illegal, I Say Legitimate: Entrepreneurship in the Informal Economy. In: Academy of Management Review 34 (3), pp. 492-510.

Williams, C. (2011): Reconceptualizing Women's and Men's Undeclared Work: Some Results from a European Union Survey. In: Gender, Work and Organization 18 (4), pp. 415-437.

What Is New in SMEs? Innovation and Employment Sustainability in the Context of Italian Start-Ups

Renato Fontana, Ernesto Dario Calò and Milena Cassella

Introduction

The goal of the following observations is to reason on the relevance and the meaning of small and middle-sized enterprises (SMEs) in Italy, with particular attention to their regional distribution. In our country, more than in others in Europe, the diffusion of SMEs has been extensive not only for economic reasons, but also for social and anthropological ones. The management of an enterprise of this size suits the collective profile of a small entrepreneur better, whose margins of freedom and movement are far greater than those of the entrepreneurs belonging to the world of big enterprises, which are placed inside an organic logic, much more conditioned than any other. In other words, the need of freedom and creativity, typical of the Italian people, is better expressed in small and elastic contexts rather than in larger sized ones, where the system of rules does not allow any deviation from economic standards. The observation of the size of enterprises does not only mean understanding that one is bigger and another is smaller; it means rather that these organisations are born from different economic histories and that they can be tightly related to the territory (think of the so-called industrial districts), or in other cases, completely dissociated (consider the so-called cathedrals in the desert of Southern Italy).

A further reason is related to the fact that Italy has traditionally been a land dominated by "borghi" (villages), small municipalities, and the culture of localism. Starting from the past centuries, this has determined a propensity to craft work, favouring the opening of a myriad of handicraft shops in the surrounding territory.

During the Middle Ages, in most of Italy, but especially in the centre-north of the country, many of the small cities became "free communes", independent entities with their own specific traditions; then, during the Renaissance (1300-1600), the transformation of the free communes into small and big Lordships, governed by princes, dukes, marquises, and counts, stressed even more their independent nature. The development of craft work labs first and of small enterprises later, which found fertile soil for their development until the 1950s, when in Italy an industrial revolution took place and big industries were born, is founded on these premises. The so-called "economic miracle" was certainly a happy period for Italy's economy, but a bit less for the hundreds of thousands of male and female workers, who found themselves making "pieces" of products of which they knew neither the destination nor the final configuration in inhuman, and often menial conditions.

An impressive socio-economic development began in our country in the 1950s to decline twenty years later, when entrepreneurs, conditioned in their decisional power, started thinking that industrial giantism was no longer practicable in certain conditions, and in any case, it no longer kept its promises as it had done up to that moment: great profits, social peace, and continuously growing markets.

The entrepreneurs' reaction was violent. They followed the road of productive decentralisation. In *The Second Industrial Divide*, Michael Piore and Charles Sabel provide an explanation:

> "From the 1970s onwards, they decentralized production and entire units were transferred to small enterprises physically separated. This decentralization created work for various types of enterprises: traditional craftwork labs; the workshops opened at the end of the 1950s by specialized workers who had been expulsed from the big factories for political reasons; and new enterprises, many of which founded by mid-level managers coming from large enterprises that at the beginning had helped them. This decentralization was facilitated by the exodus from the big industries of specialized craft workers. When it became obvious that the workers' control of work organization would have meant neither political power, nor control of the industrial investments and strategies, the specialized workers started to resent the levelling of salaries and the abolition of traditional specialization levels, and were attracted by the perspective of higher earnings in small decentralized workshops." (Piore and Sabel 1984: 234f.)

The result of a process of these proportions was the rebirth of SMEs, together with the awareness that scale economies had lived their day: at least in the Western world, enterprises moved from a mass production model to a lean production one, where enterprises have to be slenderer, more reactive, and flatter in their hierarchical lines. What makes its way is the orientation that flexibility can be a suitable answer to emerging market uncertainties, to workers' and their representatives' requests, to the competition coming from the new Asian markets, apparently distant, but capable of cutting out a place for themselves in the Old Continent, Italy included.

Entrepreneurs no longer have convenience in investing in big size enterprises and for this reason they look for new solutions in productive units, where they can regain the power they need to make the professional performance more elastic, eluding the victories obtained up to that moment by the workers' movement. These initiatives are based on the assumption that decentralising production and spreading workforce in more production units, it is possible to regain the ground lost so far.

Production dispersion is the consequence of a situation in which it is no longer convenient to concentrate activities in large industrial plants. Savings on production costs, economic and political relationships with local bodies, hierarchical structure, administrative and trade simplifications disappear when it becomes difficult to control the workforce. According to this perspective, production decentralisation is the way of guaranteeing workforce flexibility, assigning to small entrepreneurs and factory managers the control of the widest number as possible of employees without damaging productivity (Calza Bini 1976).

Before the end of the last century, the entrepreneurial strategy, on one hand reactive, and on the other approximate, acquired other characteristics and made a further step in the direction of becoming a system. The decline of the great industrial districts gives way to the so-called enterprise-net, which expands and is dispersed in peripherical areas of the country with almost no industrial traditions. Following the introduction of a new mantra called "flexibility", enterprises undergo two important processes of remodulation: downsizing and outsourcing. This inverts the historical trend in favour of the growth of an enterprise's dimensions with a horizontal integration among enterprises instead of a vertical industrial integration inside the enterprise itself. Downsizing and outsourcing as much as possible are the two ingredients capable of providing new energy to small enterprises that were apparently undergoing an irreversible decline.

At the beginning of the new century, the production model moves from a sort of concentration without concentration, that is, a kind of paradox that allows to concentrate power without concentrating it. In other words, enterprises can now follow market fluctuations thanks to a sort of flexible specialisation. The latter goes along well with the impulses coming from technological innovation:

> "[T]hanks to computers it is today easy to re-programme and set-up industrial machinery. Also the speed of modern communication has favoured flexible specialization, making it instantly possible for an enterprise to have global market data. Furthermore, this way of producing requires taking quick decisions, and this suits better small work groups; in a large bureaucratic

pyramid, on the contrary, taking decisions is a task which can require a lot of time." (Sennett 1998: 51)

Flexible specialisation is opposite to Taylor-Fordism: while the latter is based on mass production, the former looks at a lean production in order to be able to renovate every time historical and economic circumstances make it necessary.

Piore and Sabel (1984) make explicit reference to the Italian model. They explain better than others that flexible specialisation is typical of the small enterprises of centre-north Italy, and in particular of the hinterland characterised by small and middle-sized cities. It is where the culture of industrial giantism has never been able to take root. Here, enterprises collaborate and compete at the same time to find new market segments and innovative products capable of adapting to the short production life of one good or another, trying to anticipate consumers' tastes rather than follow them with difficulty and often with poor results. In these areas industrial districts are very common.

In Italy, industrial districts are structures organised according to size and culture. The influence of size determines rather clear consequences: a SME valorises its employees for intrinsic work reasons, while a large enterprise valorises them especially thanks to its reputation. In the first case, the contents and work conditions are more gratifying, while in the second one, the enterprise's history and brand weighs more (besides the tasks effectively performed). Social relationships determine different configurations according to whether the enterprise is small, medium-sized or large. In the Italian context, relationships count a lot, at least as much as one's presence at the workplace.

These are the premises that make it possible for the continuous solicitations coming from the external market to determine the internal organisational set-up. The features described above require the acceptance of deep and decisive transformations in the world of enterprises. The transformations we are going to talk about in the following pages have their roots in the handicraft vocation of small Italian entrepreneurs, but at the same time, these professional figures (from certain points of view absolutely without precedent) are connected to the experimental nature of small high-tech enterprises mainly known as start-ups. We will try to understand their socio-economic significance in terms of employment innovation and sustainability in the labour market today.

Enterprises and Labour in Italy: A National and Regional Overview

Epochal changes which give shape and substance to innovation as we progressively move into the "fourth industrial revolution", inevitably have an impact on the way of thinking – even before the way of making – an enterprise. In the continuities, irregularities, and intermittencies which mark the course of time in a global historical perspective, the Italian research context confirms its relevance thanks to the traditional "liveliness" of small enterprises, that more than others face (and clash with) the particular needs of innovation dictated by digital transformation and by an ever growing need of flexibility and resilience. This widely shared entrepreneurial vision reflects directly on the current configuration of the national economic framework.

From the analysis of the first Permanent Census of Italian enterprises carried out by Istituto italiano di statistica nazionale (ISTAT) (2020a)[2] emerge 1,033,737 units. A number slightly lower than the one of the previous survey in 2011 (-1.3 per cent), counterbalanced by a modest increase of the total number of employees (12,680,488; +1.3 per cent) (ISTAT 2020b). In line with the distinctive traits of the wider European trend[3], 79.5 per cent (equal to 821,000) are micro-enterprises (with a work-force of three to nine employees) and 18.2 per cent (equal to 187,000) are small-sized enterprises (ten to 49 employees), while the medium-sized (50 to 249 employees) and the big ones (250 employees and over) are only 2.3 per cent of the total (respectively, 21,000 and 3,000) (table 1).

---

[2] The survey was carried out in a phase of radical transformation of census statistics inside ISTAT (Istituto italiano di statistica nazionale). These new measurements are characterized by a drastic reduction of the statistical summary intervals, moving from one every ten years to one every year (for the population), every two years (for public bodies) and every three years (for enterprises and no-profit organizations). Hence, they "allow to collect and release updated, timely and complete statistical information from the point of view of the phenomena observed" (see ISTAT 2020a: 1). The census was carried out between May and October 2019, in the respect of the provisions of the European Regulations n.177/2008 and n.696/1993 and following a harmonized methodology promoted by Eurostat. The year of reference of the acquired data is 2018.

[3] https://www.statista.com/statistics/878412/number-of-smes-in-europe-by-size/; https://ec.europa.eu/eurostat/statistics-explained/index.php/Statistics_on_small_and_mediumsized_enterprises#General_overview.

Table 1: Italian enterprises and employees per size class (absolute values and percentages)

Size class	2018		2011		2001	
	Enterprises	Employees	Enterprises	Employees	Enterprises	Employees
3-9	821,341	3,740,110	837,209	3,820,052	762,536	3,445,396
	79.5%	29.5%	79.9%	30.5%	78.8%	29.1%
10-19	136,908	1,796,404	133,955	1,757,584	128,644	1,705,238
	13.2%	14.2%	12.8%	14.0%	13.3%	14.4%
20-49	50,826	1,513,579	52,196	1,552,199	52,574	1,547,560
	4.9%	11.9%	5.0%	12.4%	5.4%	13.1%
50-99	13,801	942,005	13,586	928,425	13,562	927,758
	1.3%	7.4%	1.3%	7.4%	1.4%	7.8%
100-249	7,300	1,099,134	7,180	1,079,739	6,865	1,030,234
	0.7%	8.7%	0.7%	8.6%	0.7%	8.7%
250-499	2,050	700,947	2,002	686,149	1,923	659,331
	0.2%	5.5%	0.2%	5.5%	0.2%	5.6%
500 or more	1,511	2,888,310	1,465	2,698,566	1,338	2,509,163
	0.1%	22.8%	0.1%	21.5%	0.1%	21.2%
Total	*1,033,737*	*12,680,488*	*1,047,593*	*12,522,714*	*967,442*	*11,824,680*
	100.0%	*100.0%*	*100.0%*	*100.0%*	*100.0%*	*100.0%*

Source: ISTAT (2020a: 2).

In general, the sectorial development of Italian enterprises and employees confirms the trend in favour of a growing tertiary sector: over nearly twenty years, from 2001 to 2018, there is a growth of the service sectors equal to 158,000 enterprises and over two million employees (with particular intensity in accommodation and restoration services, in artistic and sport activities, in entertainment and services for companies). Overall, in this unit of time the employment weight of service companies increased by 20 percentage points. Over the same period of time, the industrial sector in strict sense lost 63,000 enterprises (-7.8 per cent) and over one million employees (-10.6 per cent), while the building sector lost 30,000 enterprises (-3.8 per cent) and 220,000 employees (-2.4 per cent) (Table 2).

A first important element of disparity concerns the territorial distribution of the enterprises. In fact, more than half of them operate in the North (29.2 per cent in the North-West and 23.4 per cent in the North-East), 21.4 per cent are located in the Centre and 26 per cent in the South of the country. This data confirms the idea of a "two speed Italy", which probably depends on the different contribution historically given by citizens and institutions to the economic development of the entire country, stressing as a consequence, the impossibility to overcome the differences between the northern regions, traditionally more industrial, and the southern ones.

Table 2: Italian enterprises and employees per economic macro-sectors (absolute values and percentages)

Macrosectors	2018		2011		2001	
	Enterprises	Employees	Enterprises	Employees	Enterprises	Employees
Industry	195,653	3,702,244	216,564	3,913,398	258,673	4,705,785
	18.9%	29.2%	20.7%	31.3%	26.7%	39.8%
Construction	110,911	861,375	144,023	1,109,369	140,331	1,084,695
	10.7%	6.8%	13.7%	8.9%	14.5%	9.2%
Services	727,173	8,116,869	687,006	7,499,947	568,438	6,034,200
	70.3%	64.0%	65.6%	59.9%	58.8%	51.0%
Total	*1,033,737*	*12,680,488*	*1,047,593*	*12,522,714*	*967,442*	*11,824,680*
	100.0%	*100.0%*	*100.0%*	*100.0%*	*100.0%*	*100.0%*

Source: ISTAT (2020a: 2).

Currently, a stimulus for growth in our popular "Knowledge Society" concerns the relationship with other enterprises and institutions. In 2018, over half of the Italian enterprises with less than three employees (52.6 per cent, over 540,000 units) declare to have stable production relationships, based on contracts and/or informal, with other enterprises or organisations. Such propensity increases with the growth in size of the enterprise (it concerns about 50 per cent of the micro-enterprises, 64.2 per cent of the small-sized enterprises, 76.3 per cent of the middle-sized enterprises, and 82.3 per cent of the large ones). In addition, the first fifteen provinces with a stable relationship capital belong to regions of the North, and this despite the fact that there is a sufficient level of inter-regional homogeneity.

For what concerns the level of internationalisation and the reference markets of Italian enterprises, 42.2 per cent operate in a local market that does not go beyond a regional ambit; 26.5 per cent widen their activity to the national market and about 31 per cent compete at an international level. Also, in this case, the extension of the context of competitiveness presents territorial features: the enterprises with at least ten employees in Sicily and Sardinia operate, respectively for about 60 per cent and 70 per cent, at municipality or regional levels; the same thing occurs for about half of the enterprises with headquarters in Calabria, Apulia, and Campania.

On the contrary, the industries of many northern regions (in particular, those of Friuli-Venezia Giulia, Lombardy, Veneto, Trentino-Alto Adige, and Piedmont) widen their horizon to markets abroad (Figure 1).

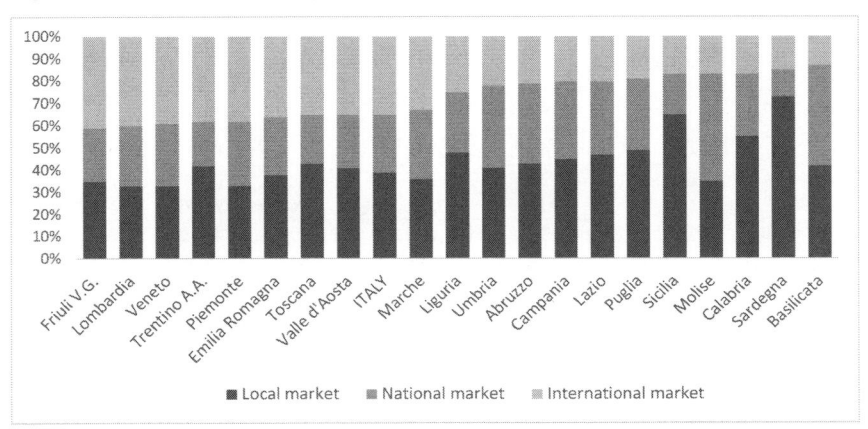

Figure 1: Reference market per region (%)

[Bar chart showing Local market, National market, and International market percentages for regions: Friuli V.G., Lombardia, Veneto, Trentino A.A., Piemonte, Emilia Romagna, Toscana, Valle d'Aosta, ITALY, Marche, Liguria, Umbria, Abruzzo, Campania, Lazio, Puglia, Sicilia, Molise, Calabria, Sardegna, Basilicata]

Source: the authors, based on ISTAT (2020a: 16).

The complexity of the development processes of Italian enterprises is reflected in the different propensity to invest. According to the same report, in the three years 2016 to 2018 only 64.8 per cent of the enterprises (a percentage that reaches 77.5 per cent in the case we consider only the enterprises with at least ten employees) make an investment in one of the "drive towards innovation" areas (research and development, technology and digitalisation, human resources and training, internationalisation, social and environmental responsibility). In general, investments are destined more to human resources and training[4] (54.3 per cent) and technologies and digitalisation (46.7 per cent), and less to research and development (27.4 per cent). The enterprises with at least ten employees investing in digitalisation declare a positive impact mainly in the greater facility of sharing information and

---

[4] In reality, as to staff training activities, one needs to distinguish between those performed as a consequence of precise legal obligations (compulsory training) and those connected to single company strategies. To this regard, in 2018 non-compulsory company training regarded little more than 230 thousand enterprises (equal to 22.4 per cent). The larger the company the larger is the propensity to favour training, involving only 18.4 per cent of micro and over 80 per cent of large enterprises.

knowledge inside the companies (52 per cent). Only 32.4 per cent observe a better efficiency of the production processes, and 13.7 per cent a greater facility in acquiring knowledge from outside. 14.6 per cent of the respondents do not notice any direct consequence, while an irrelevant percentage of enterprises perceive a negative effect of digitalisation, at least in its initial phase, on efficiency and productivity. As regards the personnel, there was the need of training to acquire the basics of digital technologies. At the request to indicate how they planned to manage criticalities of this kind, the Italian enterprises indicate the following practices: acceleration of turnovers (72.5 per cent), staff self-training (57 per cent), personnel training opportunities (56.9 per cent), increase of investments in automation (56.3 per cent), use of consultants (48.3 per cent), amelioration of the selection processes of the newly hired (44.3 per cent).

Meanwhile, the first results of the widening of users or customers by means of e-commerce emerge among the "smartest" enterprises. The digital channel involved in 2018 only one enterprise out of ten (about 100,000 companies with three or more employees – of which 75,000 with less than ten employees – are active on online platforms), recording a turnover of over 44 billion euro.

For what concerns the enterprises' environmental and social sustainability, 66.6 per cent of Italian companies with at least three employees take action to reduce environmental impact. 69 per cent seek to improve work wellbeing, equal opportunities, parenthood, and work-family balance. Little less than 65 per cent try to increase security levels inside the enterprise or in the surrounding territory; almost one third support or carry out initiatives of collective interest outside the enterprise or to the benefit of the economic fabric of the territory where the enterprise operates. Both environmental and social sustainability are looked at more in the manufacturing and building sectors, while the service sector shows less attention in both cases. Furthermore, the phenomenon reveals a clear dimensional connotation: large enterprises are more active in all "sustainable" actions, even though the presence of stricter legal obligations seems to be the main reason of the engagement in this direction. Indeed, the presence of taxes and/or specific subsidies address company strategies in 67.6 per cent of the cases; the second relevant reason is the consolidation of the links with the local community (58.1 per cent), followed by a better reputation of the enterprise (56.2 per cent) (Figure 2).

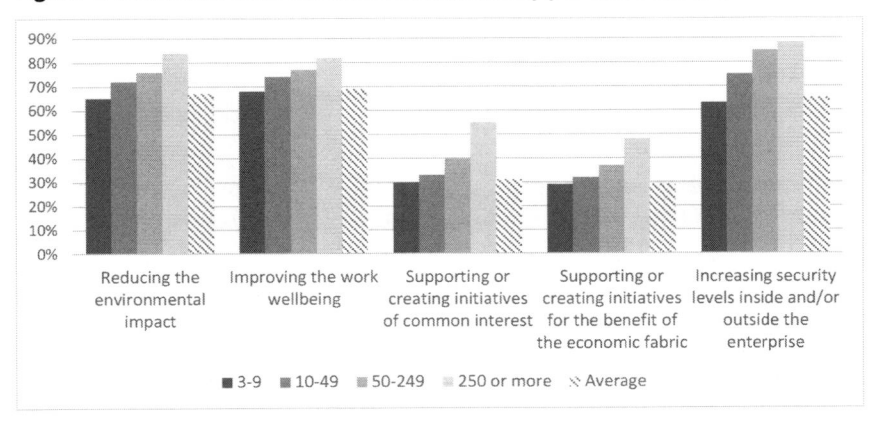

Figure 2: Social and environmental sustainability per size class (%)

[Bar chart showing percentages across five categories: Reducing the environmental impact, Improving the work wellbeing, Supporting or creating initiatives of common interest, Supporting or creating initiatives for the benefit of the economic fabric, Increasing security levels inside and/or outside the enterprise. Legend: 3-9, 10-49, 50-249, 250 or more, Average.]

Source: the authors, based on ISTAT (2020a: 27)

With reference to the national dynamics about the relationship between enterprise and labour, even if employment has reached its highest levels (59.1 per cent), Italy remains the country with the lowest employment rate in the EU (69.3 per cent) after Greece (ISTAT 2020b). The main factors that contribute to explaining the increase in labour market participation are a higher presence of women and middle-aged people, although we should not forget that the Italian rate of non-participation is double that of the EU average (19.7 per cent against 9.7 per cent). The differences with the EU are more marked for women and young people: in 2019, the employment rate gap varies from a minimum of 1.3 per cent for men between 50 and 64 years of age, and a maximum of 19 per cent for women between 15 and 34 (Figure 3).

Equally relevant is the high percentage in Italy of young people with no work experience: in 2019, we can insert in this category 26.6 per cent of the 25 to 29-year-olds and 13.3 per cent of the 30 to 34-year-olds; and the fact of having never worked could cause them difficulties entering the labour market, once they have concluded their studies. In concrete terms, there is a widening of the generational gap in favour of older people with a further aging of the workforce employed.

In spite of a little improvement in 2019 also of education levels, the already wide gap between the educated and the non-educated has worsened: the employment rate of the 15 to 64-year-olds varies from the 78.9 per cent of university graduates to the 64.9 per cent of secondary school graduates, dropping to the 44.1 per cent of the workers with a middle school diploma. Notwithstanding this, the poor demand of qualified labour in Italy provokes in some cases a sort of "downward competition", where university graduates take the job positions of people with secondary school diplomas, who in turn take the jobs of people with lower levels of education. The last mentioned find themselves cut out of the market.

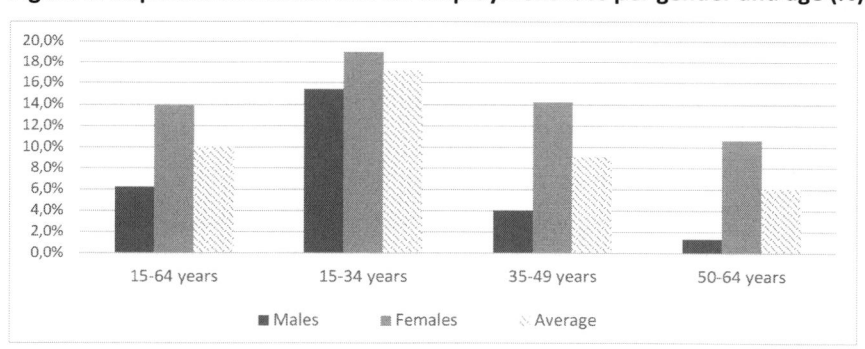

Figure 3: Gap between Italian and UE employment rate per gender and age (%)

Source: the authors, based on data by ISTAT.

Another critical aspect is the deepening of territorial disparities (Figure 4). In fact, in 2019, the gap between the employment rate in Southern Italy and that of the Centre-North is of over 20 per cent (44.7 per cent against 66.6 per cent) and the labour market non-participation rate in the southern regions is more than three times higher than in the rest of Italy (respectively 34.9 per cent and 11.8 per cent), probably because of the wider employment difficulties of the former geographic area traditionally more strongly characterised by undeclared work (Fontana *et al.* 2019).

There are signs of structural change that have brought to a reduction of the amount of work with the same number of employed. This emerged during the 2008 crisis, but it has never been corrected. The persistence of this trend also in the recovery phase depended on the spreading of part-time and discontinuous work relationships, in particular fixed-term and of short length. In fact, the full-time employed in 2019 are still 876,000 less than in 2008, the number of part-time workers has strongly increased, in particular *involuntary*[5] ones. Overall, the number of enterprises employing part-time employees for at least one month in the year 2018 is equal to 1.19 million (73.1 per cent of the total). If the increase of enterprises is equal to 3 per cent compared to 2014, the companies with only part-time employees (almost exclusively small enterprises) have increased by 12 per cent and the ones with both full-time and part-time employees by 9 per cent. Altogether, the enterprises using part-time have grown by 115,000, whereas the enterprises with only full-time employees have lost 74,000 employees. What we obtain is an overall picture where the growth of part-time employment is caused both by the diffusion of such working hour arrangements among enterprises and by an intensification of its usage among enterprises that already made use of it, contributing therefore, to the worsening of the quality of work and life of the employees (Table 3).

---

[5] In contrast with voluntary part-time employment, involuntary part-time work is a forced choice, in concrete perceived as a form of half-employment, but also of half-unemployment. The percentage of part-time employment is almost identical in Italy and in the EU, but there is a different percentage of involuntary part-time work (respectively 64.1 per cent and 23.4 per cent), confirming how the use of part-time employment in Italy is due more to enterprise flexibility strategies than to the needs of working people. This percentage is obviously higher among employees with fixed-term contracts (85.3 per cent towards the 59.7 per cent of employees with open-ended contracts), and part-time is more widespread among employees who provide services to families, in non-qualified professions and among atypical workers. Even if the percentage of part-time workers has grown also among men, the phenomenon is still much more common among women (respectively 8.5 per cent and 32.4 per cent).

Figure 4: Italian employment rate per geographical macro-area and their composition (%)

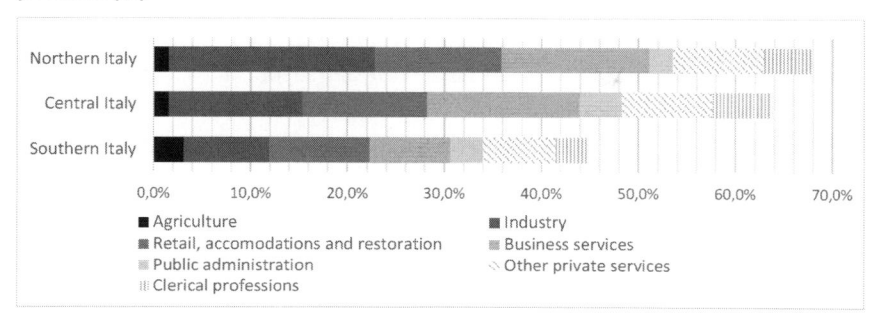

```
Northern Italy  [stacked bar chart extending to ~67%]
Central Italy   [stacked bar chart extending to ~62%]
Southern Italy  [stacked bar chart extending to ~45%]
                0,0%   10,0%   20,0%   30,0%   40,0%   50,0%   60,0%   70,0%
```

- Agriculture
- Retail, accomodations and restoration
- Public administration
- Clerical professions
- Industry
- Business services
- Other private services

Source: the authors, based on data by ISTAT.

Table 3: Italian employed workers per hourly regime and gender (2008-2018)

	2018	2018 (%)	2008 (%)	Δ 2008-2018	
				Abs. values	Percentages
Total	23,215,000	100.0	100.0	125,000	0.5
Full time	18,908,000	81.4	85.7	-876,000	-4.4
Part-time	4,307,000	18.6	14.3	1,000,000	30.3
involuntary	*2,760,000*	*11.9*	*5.8*	*1,432,000*	*107.8*
voluntary	*1,548,000*	*6.7*	*8.6*	*-432,000*	*-21.8*
MALES					
Total	13,447,000	100.0	100.0	-374,000	-2.7
Full time	12,304,000	91.5	94.7	-787,000	-6.0
Part-time	1,143,000	8.5	5.3	413,000	56.6
involuntary	*855,000*	*6.4*	*2.6*	*493,000*	*136.3*
voluntary	*288,000*	*2.1*	*2.7*	*-80,000*	*-21.8*
FEMALES					
Total	9,768,000	100.0	100.0	498,000	5.4
Full time	6,604,000	67.6	72.2	-89,000	-1.3
Part-time	3,164,000	32.4	27.8	587,000	22.8
involuntary	*1,905,000*	*19.5*	*10.4*	*939,000*	*97.2*
voluntary	*1,260,000*	*12.9*	*17.4*	*-352,000*	*-21.8*

Source: the authors, based on data by ISTAT.

The Innovative Start-Ups in Italy

The introduction of innovative start-ups in the Italian legal framework can be found in article 25, paragraph 2, of the Decree-Law No. 179/2012 (*"Misure per la nascita e lo sviluppo di imprese startup innovative"* – "Measures for the birth and development of innovative start-ups")[6]. Given the presence of an innovative component with a strong added value, the creation of start-ups in Italy as elsewhere, is promoted by national government authorities through a series of incentives (MISE 2017), among which there are the following:

- *The possibility to set them up online* (also in the case of statutory changes) *without a notary*, sending documents to the Chamber of Commerce;
- *Incentives to favour hirings*. The possibility to hire with fixed-term contracts is extended in the case of innovative start-ups. The contracts can last from six to 36 months. Once the 36 months are reached, it is possible to renew the contract for further 12 months, at the end of which it is necessary to hire with an open-ended contract;
- *Fiscal benefits for those who invest in innovative start-ups:* a natural person is recognised a deduction equal to 30 per cent of the amount invested up to an investment value of 1 million euro, while a legal person (entity) receives the same deduction for an investment of maximum 1.8 million euro;
- *Crowdfunding incentives*, that is the possibility to offer participation shares, facilitating access to the capital;
- *Direct access to a "Guarantee Fund"*, which facilitates access to credit by guaranteeing up to 80 per cent of bank loans.

According to the latest report of the Italian Ministry of Economic Development (MISE 2020), the 31st of December 2019, the number of innovative start-ups registered in the "special section" of the Business Register is equal to 10,882; 272 (+2.6

---

[6] According to the present article, a start-up is a limited company – not listed and set up also as a cooperative – with the following requirements: i) it is newly set up or less than five years old; ii) has its main headquarters in Italy, in another member state of the EU or part of the European Economic Area, as long as it has a production plant or a branch in Italy; iii) it has an annual production value less than five million euro; iv) it does not and has not distributed profits; v) its exclusive or prevalent corporate purpose is the development, production, and commercialisation of products or innovative services of high level of technology; vi) it has not been set up thanks to a merger, demerger or following a transfer of a company or of a business unit; vii) it possesses at least one of the following three indicators of innovativeness: 1) A share equal to 15 per cent of the highest value between revenue and annual costs can be attributable to research and development (R&D) activities; 2) The overall work-force is made up of PhD students, PhDs or researchers for at least one third, or of partners or collaborators with a Master's degree for at least two-thirds; 3) The enterprise is proprietor, depositary or licensee of a patent or registered software.

per cent) more than the previous quarter. Observing their distribution per economic areas, it is no surprise that 73.7 per cent of Italian start-ups provide services to businesses. In particular, the start-ups deal with software production and IT consultancy (35.6 per cent), R&D activities (13.9 per cent), and information service activities (9.2 per cent). In addition to B2B services, 17.6 per cent of these particular enterprises work in the manufacturing sector, especially in the production of industrial machinery (3.1 per cent) and of computers and electronic products (2.8 per cent), while 3.4 per cent of them deal with trade (Table 4).

Table 4: Italian innovative start-ups per economic areas (31 December 2019)

Economic areas	Distribution per economic areas	Absolute values	Weight on each area
Business services	73.66%	8,016	8.33%
Software production and IT consultancy	35.58%	3,872	37.93%
Research & Development	13.90%	1,513	68.55%
Information service activities	9.15%	996	13.91%
Manufacturing, energy, mining	17.58%	1,913	5.11%
Computer, electronic and optical products	2.81%	306	35.83%
Electrical equipment	1.56%	170	18.30%
Other machinery and equipment	3.13%	341	14.36%
Trade and distribution industry	3.36%	366	0.45%
Other areas	2.44%	266	1.00%
Construction	0.89%	97	0.18%
Agriculture and related activities	0.74%	80	1.12%
Tourism	0.58%	63	0.15%
Transportation and shipping	0.28%	30	0.23%
Unclassified areas	0.27%	29	6.56%
Insurance and credit	0.20%	22	0.26%
Total	100.00%	10,882	2.98%

Source: the authors, based on MISE (2020: 10).

Analysing the geographic distribution of the phenomenon, some criticalities already mentioned referring to the difficulties Italian entrepreneurs and policy makers have when trying to stimulate a united economic development in the regions of the North, Centre, and South re-emerge. In fact, confirming the presence of long term national peculiarities, the region with the largest number of innovative start-ups is Lombardy, that with its 2,928 units (2,075 only in the province of Milan), represents 26.9 per cent of the national total. It is followed by Lazio, the only other region to exceed the thousand (11.3 per cent of the total number, 1,227, of which 1,110 in the province of Rome), and Emilia-Romagna (931; 8.6 per cent). Little distant is Campania, by far the first region in the South, with 896 start-ups (8.2 per cent), followed by Veneto, with 889 start-ups. In the back we find Sardinia with 130, Basilicata with 104, Molise with 80, and Valle d'Aosta with 22 innovative start-ups (Figure 5).

Figure 5: Italian innovative startups per regions (abs. values and %)

Region	Value	%
LOMBARDIA	2,928	26.91%
LAZIO	1,227	11.28%
EMILIA-ROMAGNA	931	8.56%
CAMPANIA	896	8.23%
VENETO	889	8.17%
PIEMONTE	610	5.61%
SICILIA	514	4.72%
PUGLIA	429	3.94%
TOSCANA	423	3.89%
MARCHE	343	3.15%
TRENTINO-ALTO ADIGE	266	2.44%
CALABRIA	265	2.44%
FRIULI-VENEZIA GIULIA	231	2.12%
ABRUZZO	215	1.98%
LIGURIA	190	1.75%
UMBRIA	189	1.74%
SARDEGNA	130	1.19%
BASILICATA	104	0.96%
MOLISE	80	0.74%
VALLE D'AOSTA	22	0.20%

Source: the authors, based on MISE (2020: 12).

For what concerns the target markets of the Italian start-ups, 71.8 per cent answer to the demand of goods and services of other national enterprises (41.5 per cent to agreements with foreign enterprises, mainly signed by start-ups of the North-East), fully in line with business-to-business (B2B), while 49.5 per cent directly address consumers (31.2 per cent in the case of foreign consumers). Finally, the Italian and Foreign Public Administrations are a market only for a minority of enterprises:

little over 28 per cent do business with the Italian PA, while 11.1 per cent sign agreements with foreign PAs.

In terms of employment, the innovative start-ups employ 13,803 people. The average number of employees per start-up is equal to 3.2, but if we consider the partners of all the innovative start-ups registered till 2019, we should add 50,816 people (on average, each start-up has 4.7 partners). Hence, the overall number of partners and employees involved in the start-ups is 64,619. Since the second quarter of 2019 the workforce has gone up by 671, while the annual increase is of 8,116 (+15.1 per cent).

Briefly analysing the social characteristics of innovative start-ups, the preponderantly female ones, - that is, the ones in which shares and administrative roles are mainly in the hands of women – are 1,468, equal to 13.5 per cent of the total. The innovative start-ups, in which there is at least one woman in the corporate structure, are 4,704, equal to 43.2 per cent. Women are only 18 per cent of the partners and they differ from men for being younger (29 per cent of them are less than 34 years old compared to 25.9 per cent of their male counterparts). The preponderantly young innovative start-ups (under 35) are 2,153, 19.8 per cent of the total. Finally, the innovative start-ups with a preponderantly foreign corporate structure are 380, equal to 3.5 per cent of the total, while the ones with at least one non-Italian citizen are 13.9 per cent (1,515).

Table 5: Italian innovative start-ups per social characteristics (gender, age, nationality; abs. values and %)

Characteristic composition	Absolute values	Percentages
Preponderantly female	1,468	13.49
Preponderantly youth	2,153	19.78
Preponderantly foreigner	380	3.49
At least one female employed/partner	4,704	43.23
At least one youth employed/partner	4,830	44.39
At least one foreigner employed/partner	1,515	13.92

Source: the authors, based on MISE (2020: 11).

Focusing only on the founders and co-founders of innovative start-ups, the Italian start-uppers, 72.8 per cent have achieved a degree and about 16 per cent have a PhD (ISTAT-MISE 2018). However, a fact to reflect upon is that women, who possess on average higher qualifications (78.9 per cent have at least a degree and 21 per cent a PhD) are less present also in start-ups. The majority of operational partners[7] is qualified in technological-engineering subjects (42.1 per cent), followed by economic-managerial (20.7 per cent) and scientific (20 per cent) ones. Over 88 per cent of the partners with a degree believe to carry out an activity in line with their qualifications, even if this percentage drastically falls among the partners with lower levels of education (37 per cent for those with a middle school diploma and 67 per cent for those with a secondary school one).

The majority of start-uppers show strong territorial attachment; in fact, over 83 per cent have set up the enterprise with headquarters in the same region where training and work experiences take place. The personal reasons that push start-up founders to operate in their own region are often connected to the extremely lean structure of innovative start-ups and to the normative, administrative, and financial facilitations offered by government bodies. Around 55 per cent of them have had at least a training or work experience abroad: in 13.5 per cent of the cases it is a subordinate work activity, in 21 per cent a study programme, and in 10.3 per cent an entrepreneurial experience. In many cases the academic and professional experiences abroad have positively influenced in terms of foreign language knowledge. Around 96 per cent of the partners speak another language in addition to Italian,

---

[7] "Operational partner" is the co-founder of an innovative start-up that does not only provide economic resources, but also has an active role in the daily activity of the enterprise.

and it is no surprise that English is the most spoken (91 per cent), followed by French (21 per cent) and Spanish (11 per cent).

When asked what the main motivations are that pushed them to create a start-up, the "creation of innovative services or products" and the choice "to create a successful business with high profitability" seem to be the most common reasons (respectively, in 77.6 per cent and 62.9 per cent of the cases). Yet, despite the wish to see one's professional competences recognised, half of the partners declare that the set-up of a start-up has still not had significant effects on their income: almost half of them have seen their income unchanged since the beginning of the new entrepreneurial activity, little less than one third declare a worsening of their personal financial situation, and only two out of ten have noticed an increase in their income (Figure 7).

Considering the most relevant characteristics when referring to employees, a first significant fact is that 25 per cent of the Italian employees hired by these enterprises are women (18 per cent are partners). This gender distribution does not seem to vary according to the type of contract. More than half of the start-ups have hired employees (59.4 per cent), mainly workers and clerks with open-ended contracts (62 per cent), while the managers are 15.5 per cent (mostly men). Around one quarter of the start-ups use employees with atypical contracts instead to carry out their activities; in particular, the most common contract is for project work (46 per cent), while limited is the diffusion of fixed-term or temporary employment (only 2.7 per cent). Most start-ups hire staff between 25 and 34 years old (48 per cent), mainly coming from technological-engineering (45.9 per cent) and economic-managerial professions (15.5 per cent) (Figure 8). On the contrary of what is noticed among partners, the most widespread educational qualification among employees is a secondary school diploma (28 per cent).

Figure 7: Main motivations behind the startup creation and personal financial situation after its activation (%)

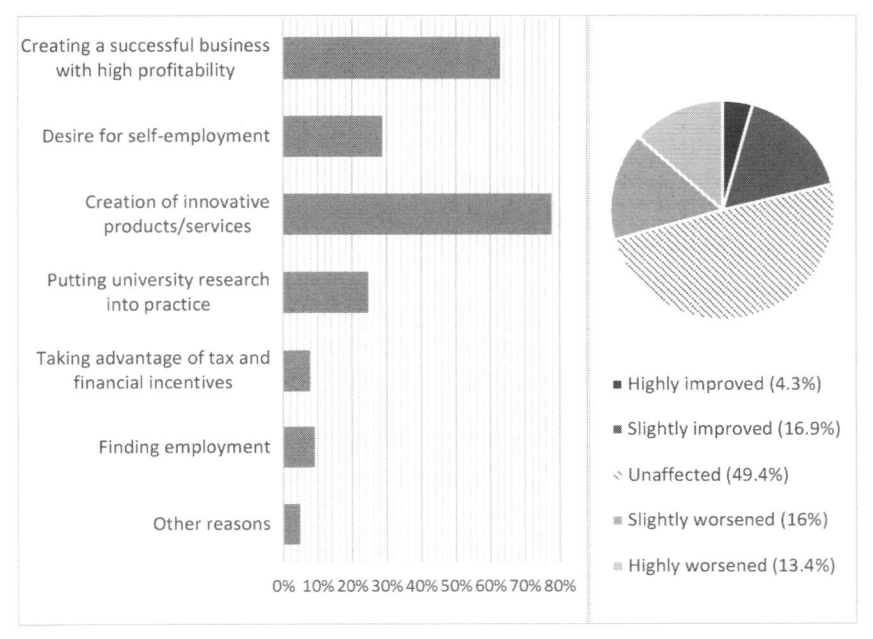

[Bar chart showing motivations:
- Creating a successful business with high profitability: ~60%
- Desire for self-employment: ~22%
- Creation of innovative products/services: ~75%
- Putting university research into practice: ~15%
- Taking advantage of tax and financial incentives: ~5%
- Finding employment: ~8%
- Other reasons: ~3%]

[Pie chart:]
- Highly improved (4.3%)
- Slightly improved (16.9%)
- Unaffected (49.4%)
- Slightly worsened (16%)
- Highly worsened (13.4%)

Source: the authors, based on ISTAT-MISE (2018: 27f.).

Finally, as observed among partners, territorial roots are strong also among employees: 80 per cent of them work for enterprises in the area where they had their previous training or work experiences, and they believe that their work activity is in line with their studies (in 79 per cent of the cases on average, which falls to a minimum of 51 per cent for those with a middle school diploma and rises to 94 per cent for those with a PhD).

Italian Innovative Start-Ups: Features and Trends

Among the data just presented, which try to give a picture of Italian enterprises, and in particular, of the so-called innovative start-ups, there are three great trends to be highlighted:

- The belonging of the activities to the *tertiary* sector: more than two thirds of the innovative start-ups are part of the sector "services to enterprises", and among these, the majority recall the Knowledge-Intensive Business Services (the so-called KIBS);
- The *geographic location* of the new enterprises: the territorial distribution of the start-ups concerns mainly precise regions of the country. However, this distribution does not seem to mirror the habitual division North/Centre-South, with the North better predisposed to adopting innovative activities compared to the South, which is lagging behind as usual. For instance, Lazio and Campania, both regions of the Centre-South, are respectively second and third for number of start-ups. The Italian innovative start-ups seem rather to be located in areas with specific features, around large urban centres (Milan and province, Rome and province);
- A *territorial vocation* of both founders and employees: the great majority of start-up founders have built-up their activity in the same region where they had their previous training and work experiences, despite the fact that over half of them have had a training or work experience abroad. The same trend emerges from the data about the employees, who equally work in the same area in which they had their previous training and/or work experiences, and who declare that their work is in line with their studies.

The three above-mentioned features find wide acknowledgement in literature (think about the entrepreneurial theories, the considerations about the impact of technology on markets and enterprises, or the role of innovation). However, a number of recent researches, some of which sociological, carried out moving from the Italian case, have stressed some particular specificities in the panorama of start-ups in Italy. If confirmed by further empirical evidence, that these specificities could provide new points of view on the theoretical knowledge of the theme. In what follows we will try to highlight these peculiarities and at the same time define the data provided in the previous paragraph.

For what concerns the first trend, the tertiary sector, it is not surprising that innovative start-ups operate in the market of services to enterprises, and that many of them are classifiable as KIBS. We are talking about B2B services with considerable knowledge content, since they require for their design and supply the use of an intellectual capital that is much higher than what is needed in other tertiary sectors or in manufacturing[8]. Also for this reason, these services are characterised by the

---

[8] In specific, with reference to the Ateco classification of economic activities, the KIBS include all the services connected to computer science, research and development activities, and part of

presence of an intense level of interaction between the enterprise providing the service and the client enterprise: for the very nature of good "knowledge" (Rullani 2004), the relational dimension of the relationship between the two organisations is extremely marked, to the point that scholars talk about a real "co-production" of knowledge between supplier and client (Bettencourt et al. 2002, Den Hertog 2000).

A concrete example of KIBS service provision between two Italian enterprises is the case of the car model *F12 Berlinetta*, built by the well-known car-manufacturer Ferrari in collaboration with Centro Stile di Pininfarina Spa (an enterprise specialised in the design of industrial products):

> "[T]he *design*, in the case here considered, is an essential ingredient to express the quality of the Ferrari brand, that has transformed into a strength the ability to combine extreme technical performance with the beauty of the bodywork and the interior trim. In substance, it is a multiplier of value that permits to transform a series of mechanical elements, however extraordinary they may be from a technical point of view, into an absolutely unique product. [...] A supplier such as Pininfarina sells its competences in the *design* of bodyworks and its ability to imagine new aesthetic shapes to Ferrari. It is evident that the value produced by Pininfarina does not depend on the *quantity* of the personnel used (as could happen for a service of a traditional kind) but on their *quality* in terms of preparation and creativity. It is equally obvious that the projects in which Ferrari works with Pininfarina require a lot of dialogue between the parties and *problem solving* joint activities." (Bettiol, Di Maria and Grandinetti 2012: 12-13)

Recent researches have focused on the observation of Italian enterprises offering services based on high levels of knowledge[9]. Among these, Bettiol, Di Maria, and Grandinetti (2012), on the basis of a quantitative study carried out using a database of more than 500 KIBS located in Veneto and 20 national and international history cases, have identified three evolutionary dynamics typical of the Italian case, but which could open up to new analysis perspectives also in other geographic areas.

First of all, the research in Veneto has highlighted how the great majority of enterprises have been able to find clients outside the regional borders (67.1 per cent) or even in foreign markets (10.8 per cent), when in literature physical proximity is generally considered a functional element necessary for an optimal management of the relationship between KIBS and the client enterprise (Andersson and Hellerstedt 2009). In the cases indicated in the research, we are talking about enterprises with a greater propensity to use Information and Communication Technologies

---

the activities regarding the so-called "services to enterprises", such as the design of systems or management consultancy (Bettiol, Di Maria, and Grandinetti 2012: 15f.).

[9] Cf. Di Maria, Grandinetti and Di Bernardo (2012).

(ICT), both in knowledge codification and organisation and in the dynamics of collaboration, for example using Customer Relationship Management (CRM) techniques. Secondly, KIBS have been found in sectors where traditionally you do not find them; for instance, in the manufacturing sector: in many *made in Italy* manufacturing enterprises that work in B2B sectors (for example, pre-sale services, machine tool installation, and after-sale services) the service component (strongly customised and with significant knowledge content) is so high that it overtakes the real product in value. Finally, the third feature concerns the KIBS that have widened their activity to include the management of entire supply chains, as in the case of design enterprises that integrate their typical services with the commercialisation of new products (Bettiol, Di Maria, and Grandinetti 2012).

In brief, the three features mentioned above seem to move towards a partial dissolution, or at least weakening, of the traditional and rigid barrier separating the manufacturing and the tertiary sectors. According to some scholars (Rullani et al. 2012), the contamination of the two different markets is welcome and could be beneficial on large scale with an increase of productivity.

In Rullani's opinion (2012), the path that has just started to be followed sees the convergence of three different subjects: neo-industries, neo-services, and neo-networks. The first subject is the traditional industry that virtuously uses its "generative knowledge"[10] to enrich its products (material) of certain valences (immaterial) given by the meanings of consumption and use value, decided downstream in the production process. The second subject is the service sector that, thanks to ICTs, is able to reduce the disadvantaged condition it had towards the industries producers of "material goods": by using digital technologies, service enterprises are no longer bound by physical proximity and are able to export their activity also in geographically distant areas, thanks to the codification of the procedures. At the same time, they can use the same technology to maximise the possibility of interaction and co-creation at a distance, succeeding in supplying the clients with complex and personalised performances. The third element at stake consists in the neo-networks,

---

[10] Rullani (2012) distinguishes between *"generative* knowledge" and *"replicative* knowledge". In the first case, it is a "knowledge capable of generating other knowledge, to adapt it or re-create it according to the circumstances". In the typical Italian model, which spread in the 1970s, it appeared "in the form of *widespread business intelligence and of close territorial relationships*". In the second case, it is instead a type of knowledge "that can be *codified and reproduced for free* once it is has been incorporated in a machine, in a standard product, in a *software*, in an advertisement, in an organisational procedure or in a juridical rule universally valid" (Rullani 2012: 28-31).

by which we refer to the immaterial aspects of relationships and communication, and which bring together all the supply chain, including the final consumers.

Knowledge is essential also to tackle the second point about the location of innovative start-ups in Italy. Other researches have examined the factors that have mostly influenced the birth and the location of start-ups, stressing the particular nature of an "innovative" start-up, and how, as a result, not all local economies possess the necessary features for its territorial development.

In fact, the high potential of innovation makes this kind of start-up different from the others, including the high-tech ones. Innovative start-ups are smaller in size, with greater liquidity and a strong investment propensity, and a more intensive usage of intangible resources (Finaldi Russo, Magri, and Rampazzi 2016). However, their most interesting feature is the presence of *knowledge spillover*, whether we refer to direct externalities of the knowledge coming from R&D departments of companies located in a specific area, or to the wider and still not fully investigated transmission mechanisms of knowledge and idea contamination (Breschi and Lissoni 2001). Regards to this, Antonietti and Gambarotto (2018a) underline how

> "On the contrary of the Fordist development model, based on scale economy efficiency, and of the post-Fordist model, based on the reduction of transaction costs and on district efficiency, the young innovative enterprises are founded on the usage and/or production of knowledge and efficiency associated with *knowledge spillover*. This means that not all local economies possess the actors and factors required for the birth and growth of innovative start-ups." (Antonietti and Gambarotto 2018a: 53)

By re-elaborating the data on Italian innovative start-ups updated until 2015[11], the above-mentioned authors reach some interesting results. First of all, it results that innovative start-ups are more frequent in areas with more heterogenous repositories of knowledge[12], exactly because the contamination of much diversified forms

---

[11] The research was carried out by comparing two different databases: on the one hand, the list of innovative start-ups present in the Register of Innovative Start-ups and SMEs of Unioncamere; on the other hand, the territorial distribution of enterprises and services analysed by ISTAT in 2015 on the basis of the 9th Industry and Services Census 2011.

[12] The authors refer to evolutionary economic geography literature (Frenken, van Oort, and Verburg 2007), that distinguishes between "a related (within-industry) variety and an unrelated (between-industry) variety. The former favors new ventures in nearby knowledge areas, and it exploits network externalities to reduce investment risks and expand new business opportunities. The latter stimulates new firm formation through the exploration and recombination of a very

of knowledge can create new ideas with greater facility (Antonietti and Gambarotto 2018b). Secondly, with reference to the division of the Italian territory in "Sistemi Locali del Lavoro (SlI)"[13], "Local Labour Systems" elaborated by Istat, the major concentration of innovative start-ups is in two particular environments: the SlI of the Centre-North cities, in particular Milan and its hinterland, and the SlI based on the "urban sprawl" model, that is the "urban areas characterised by a non-compact settlement model, typical of the North-East, of the plains of Lombardy and Emilia, of the coastline of the Marche, the Abruzzi, and the Pontine" (Antonietti and Gambarotto 2018a: 56)[14].

In harmony with previous researches about the diffusion of innovative start-ups in Italy[15], the authors declare that

> "[...] the big and medium-sized urban centres are the most fertile places to support the creation of innovative start-ups. Thanks to the presence of university centres, of a diversified economy and of a strong economic *performance*, innovative start-ups are more easily able in cities to overcome the critical phases linked to the transformation of an idea into a successful product/service. [...] The infrastructures in an economy based on knowledge are different from those which characterised the Fordist and Post-Fordist development phases. The connections

---

diverse array of knowledge sources. A greater local knowledge diversity suggests more entrepreneurial opportunities, though they may be more risky and uncertain" (Antonietti and Gambarotto 2018b: 562).

[13] The "Sistemi Locali del Lavoro" (SlI) have been divided into various categories: urban systems, industrial districts, systems with/without productive specialisation (Antonietti and Gambarotto 2018a: 53).

[14] With reference to the SlI specialisation typology, the innovative start-ups are concentrated more in non-manufacturing urban systems than in the *made in Italy* industrial districts or in the heavy manufacturing ones. Furthermore, they are located in the most productive SlIs, the ones with the highest added value per employee and where the cost of work per employee is also the highest; in other words, in the areas with the greatest amount of human capital (Antonietti and Gambarotto 2018a: 57f.).

[15] In particular, Colombelli (2016) observes how it is not only the quantity of *knowledge spillover* present in the area that guarantees the presence of innovative start-ups, but also its composition, especially for what concerns the technologies used. Ghio, Guerini, and Rossi-Lamastra (2016) stress the impact of academic knowledge on the creation of innovative start-ups: this certainly takes place close to university centres (it is, therefore, localised), but it can have effects also at a distance in the areas with "regional openness, as measured by the local presence in a geographical area of individuals with open-minded attitudes" (Ghio, Guerini and Rossi-Lamastra 2016: 296).

between universities and industries[16], the local interactions between inventors, entrepreneurs and *skilled people*, the accompaniment to local and non-local *networking* stand out."
(Antonietti and Gambarotto 2018a: 60)

The role held by human capital, and more in general, by the features of the people involved in the enterprises, can be useful when facing the last point in the list about the role of founders and employees in the particular enterprises we are here considering. The study by Colombo, Delmastro, and Grilli (2003) uses a micro-perspective to analyse the influence of firm-specific characteristics in determining some of the strategic choices made by New Technology-Based Firms (NTBF) when they enter the market. The data show how these choices concerning in particular the dimensional class of the enterprise, are influenced not so much by determiners of the sector of reference (industry-specific characteristics), as by the evaluations made by the founders according to their human capital and their ability to draw from external sources of finance. In particular,

> "[…] the founders' human capital, measured both in terms of educational level and of previous work experience, is a crucial factor in the initial dimension of the enterprise. The human capital has a double effect. On one hand, the founders with more business talent, with strong confidence in their means, and thus, with positive expectations about the future of the enterprise, start off with a relatively larger scale of operations. On the other hand, it is also true that better educated and more qualified entrepreneurs are generally richer and are less likely to be conditioned by financial constraints. In other words, *highly-skilled* people are more likely, *ceteris paribus*, to reach an initial enterprise dimension that they consider 'optimal'."
> (Colombo, Delmastro and Grilli 2003: 69)

The founders' human capital is equally essential to introduce organisational innovations in the following phases of an enterprise, for example, in the choice of whether or how to extend the NTBF's team. In the analysis by Colombo *et al.* (2011) emerge, for instance, two possible paths for a young enterprise: if the founders possess a high level of education but a work experience in sectors different from the one in which the enterprise operates ("generic work experience"), they will choose to widen the business team by inserting a new partner; in the case in which the founders have instead a great work experience in the sector ("industry-specific

---

[16] Buffardi and Savonardo (2017) refer to national initiatives with the aim of intensifying the contacts between the academic and the business worlds. Among these, we can indicate the Contamination Labs, university didactic laboratories of an interdisciplinary nature, tested since 2013 in some Italian universities with the goal of promoting knowledge contamination; or "innovative industrial PhDs", created in 2016 to qualify the study and research experience of PhD students in an industrial perspective, and addressed to the most disadvantaged regions in terms of development (Buffardi and Savonardo 2017: 209).

experience"[17]), the most convenient solution might be to insert the figure of a wage-earning manager inside the organisation. In the first case, the arrival of a new owner-manager touches the size and the competences of the business team, the division of tasks, and the balance of power among the partners, but not the organisational structure of an enterprise. In the second case, with the hiring of a wage-earning manager, there is the passage from a two level organisation (owners-managers and employees) to a three level pyramidal structure (owners-managers, wage-earning managers, employees), determining a real organisational innovation (Colombo *et al.* 2011: 517).

Finally, for what concerns the effects on employment, Santandrea and Lobello (2016) analyse the results of the regional actions performed by the region Apulia since 2009[18]. The authors underline how enterprise start-ups can be a useful tool to support dynamic labour policies, in particular for the weakest sections, such as young people, women, unemployed, or over 50-year-olds without work. With reference to this, relevant is not only the number of start-ups created, but also the number of start-ups capable of getting past their first five years of life:

> "[…] if start-ups, on the one hand, have the capability of immediately creating new net additional employment, on the other hand, they have a higher probability, compared to the consolidated ones, of closing up (with loss of employment); the winning ones reveal high employment rates in the post start-up phase, with a significant impact on overall employment growth. […] At national level, the attention given to enterprise start-ups as a tool of dynamic labour policies is still very poor, while a lot of emphasis is placed on 'innovative' start-ups to pursue the goal of productivity growth and technological innovation." (Santandrea and Lobello 2016: 500)

The present short excursus proposed in these pages, although not exhaustive, shows how to define the world of innovative start-ups - identify the environment in which they operate, establish the determinants of success, clarify the role played by human capital compared to structural aspects, and so on - is much more complex than expected. In particular, it suggests that the characteristics of asset-knowledge and the dimension of relationships between organisations and people

---

[17] Besides, that the founders's industry-specific experience is positively linked to the growth of young high-technology enterprises has been pointed out in various studies, as explained by Colombo and Grilli (2005).

[18] Among these, the support given to micro-enterprise start-ups newly created by disadvantaged entrepreneurs and the "Fondo Nuove Iniziative di Impresa della Puglia – NIDI" (Puglia's New Enterprise Initiatives Fund).

are the two most interesting aspects on which it would be important to reflect in further and more in-depth studies.

Conclusions: Can Italian Innovative Start-Ups Guide the Socio-Economic Revival?

In an attempt to conclude through some undeniably partial observations, in the following lines we propose some brief considerations about the possible consequences triggered by the catastrophe of the COVID-19 on the general socio-economic fabric, and in particular, on the SMEs.

Actually, nobody can know how things will change; we are in the midst of the storm. Therefore, there is no form of empirical evidence. The fact is that some European Countries such as Italy and Spain have been affected the hardest, while others have been less affected, such as those of northern Europe, Denmark, and Norway.

There are two certainties from which we think it is reasonable to start arranging a discussion on the theme, whereas scientifically supported observations require time, patience, and in-depth reflections on a wide spectrum. First, nothing will be as before. Second, the organisational transformations will be consequently very profound.

At this stage, we can only ask ourselves questions because we have no answers, but we can also assume hypothetical scenarios to be better examined later, in other times and places.

Given the general circumstances that impose a relational distancing (otherwise, there is a risk of Coronavirus infection), it seems that innovative start-ups set up on the web may represent an important point of the economic system on which the state, businesses, and individual entrepreneurs should concentrate resources and attention. Everything suggests that smart working will be further encouraged, especially for small working groups, spreading the emergence of virtual businesses (those without physical structures or, at most, with few essential physical relations).

The main consequences we imagine, declining them in a first, embryonic, form particularly for our country, are the following:

- *The downsizing of corporate structures*: recovering the historical inclination that has always characterised the Italian economic system made up of micro and small businesses, in the name of structural slenderness (and, paradoxically, aimed at the enhancement of human relationships). From this point of view, Italy seems favoured more than other countries, as we consider its entrepreneurial history and the average size of its businesses (Table 1);

- *The rebirth of the craftman vocation in the Italian connective tissue and the development of local businesses*: as we have seen, these traits represent a significant part of the new start-ups. Recovering this vocation would be a necessary act to get out of the shallows in which the current crisis has rejected us. Furthermore, it would also be a way to enhance the propensity for the collective spirit of the average Italian, that was silenced during the industrialisation boom but has never been completely dormant;
- *The expansion of mixed forms (in presence and remotely) of work performance*, including the probable surge in some professional profiles related to the world of Information and Communication Technologies (ICT) and, at the same time, the decline of other job figures strictly associated to the world of manufacturing industries, which can be replaced by robots, Machine Learning (ML) and Artificial Intelligence (AI);
- *The acceleration in the use of digital platforms and a more widespread use of the knowledge economy for increasing the share of co-workers in smart working* (Crowley 2016, Martone 2018). This is a typical trait of the variable geometry of network companies, where the social distancing can be taken intrinsically as an essential quality of this new way of conceiving professional activities, especially in complex organisational systems;
- *The spread of the "anthropological resilience" of the Italian people, and its ancestral ability to give its best in the most difficult conditions*. That is where the long history of *Made in Italy*, the industrial districts and the paradigm of flexible specialisation already mentioned in the first pages of these notes were born;

The fact is that the organisational and technological aspects we have observed require a change of course in the way we consume things and face *this* production model, which is highly criticised (Piketty 2013, Zuboff 2019) but always ready to rise from its ashes, like a phoenix that continually renews herself, a symbol of power and resistance.

Technology can be of great help in reversing the trend and giving breathing space to the aforementioned consequences. Neoliberal capitalism has so far used technology for the sole purpose of increasing profits, putting everything else (such as environmental sustainability, employment issues and the organisational well-being of employees) in the background; and the impact of this "cynical" approach is plain to see, all over the world.

Therefore, we need to question the bottlenecks in which we have wedged together. We have produced a form of senseless globalisation and, even more, we have been rooting for economic neoliberalism by trampling on the ethical principles of environmental sustainability and increasingly widening the gap between rich and poor. Again, we observe the presence of another gap, the one between employed and unemployed cultivated through the cult of regulatory flexibility (Sennett 1998) and applied with a certain ideological relentlessness both in Europe and in Italy. All these have led to exacerbate social and economic inequalities, causing for many women and men a series of dramatic consequences that can no longer be ignored in the business world, small and large.

References

Andersson, Martin/Hellerstedt, Karin (2009): Location attributes and start-ups in knowledge-intensive business services. In: Industry and Innovation 16(1), pp. 103-121.

Antonietti, Roberto/Gambarotto, Francesca (2018a): I luoghi fertili per l'innovazione: Uno studio sulla localizzazione delle start-up innovative in italia. In: Economia e Società Regionale 36(3), pp. 52-61.

Bettencourt Lance A./Ostrom, Amy L./Brown, Stephen L./Roundtree, Robert I. (2002): Client coproduction in knowledge-intensive business services. In: California Management Review 44(4), pp. 100-128.

Bettiol, Marco/Di Maria, Eleonora/Grandinetti, Roberto (2012): I servizi ad alta intensità di conoscenza si industriano. In: Economia e Società Regionale 11(3), pp. 12-23.

Breschi, Stefano/Lissoni, Francesco (2001): Knowledge Spillovers and Local Innovation Systems: A Critical Survey. In: Industrial and Corporate Change 10(4), pp. 975-1005.

Buffardi, Annalisa/Savonardo, Lello (2017): Contamination Lab, cultura digitale e imprenditorialità. In: Sociologia del Lavoro 147, pp. 201-219.

Calza Bini, Paolo (1976): Economia periferica e classi sociali. Napoli: Liguori.

Colombelli, Alessandra (2016): The impact of local knowledge bases on the creation of innovative start-ups in Italy. In: Small Business Economics, 47, pp. 383-396.

Colombo, Massimo G./Delmastro, Marco/Grilli, Luca (2003): La dimensione iniziale delle nuove imprese ad alta tecnologia: Il ruolo del capitale umano e delle fonti di finanziamento. In: Economia e politica industriale 119, pp. 43-75.

Colombo, Massimo G./Grilli, Luca (2005): Founders' Human Capital and the Growth of New Technology-based Firms: A Competence-based View. In: Research Policy 34(6), pp. 795-816.

Colombo, Massimo G./Grilli, Luca/Guerini, Massimiliano/Piva, Evila/Rossi-Lamastra, Cristina (2011): L'allargamento dei ranghi manageriali nelle giovani imprese: Il caso delle start-up ad alta tecnologia. In: L'industria 32(3), pp. 513-538.

Crowley, Dermot (2016): Smart Work: Centralise, Organise, Realise. New York: Wiley.

Den Hertog, Pim (2000): Knowledge-intensive business services as co-producers of innovation. In: International Journal of Innovation Management 4(4), pp. 491-528.

Di Maria, Eleonora/Grandinetti, Roberto/Di Bernardo, Barbara (Eds) (2012): Exploring Knowledge-intensive Business Services: Knowledge Management Strategies. Basingstoke: Palgrave Macmillan.

Finaldi Russo, Paolo/Magri, Silvia/Rampazzi, Cristiana (2016): Innovative Start-Ups in Italy: Their Special Features and the Effects of the 2012 Law. In: Politica Economica/Journal of Economic Policy 32(2), pp. 297-330.

Fontana, Renato (1981): Ristrutturazione del lavoro e iniziativa sindacale. Processo produttivo, qualifiche, salari nell'industria italiana. Milano: FrancoAngeli.

Fontana, Renato/Calò, Ernesto Dario/Cassella, Milena (2019): On the Reasons for an Informal Economy in Italy: The Motivations of Entrepreneurs and Workers. In: Larsen, Christa/Rand, Sigrid/Schmid, Alfons/Bobkov, Vyacheslav/Lokosov, Vyacheslav (Eds.): Assessing Informal Employment and Skills Needs. Approaches and Insights from Regional and Local Labour Market Monitoring. Augsburg, Munchen: Rainer Hampp Verlag, pp. 103-130.

Frenken, Koen/van Oort, Frank/Verburg, Thijs N. (2007): Related variety, unrelated variety and regional economic growth. In: Regional Studies 418(5), pp. 685-697.

Ghio, Niccolò/Guerini, Massimiliano/Rossi-Lamastra, Cristina (2016): University knowledge and the creation of innovative start-ups: an analysis of the Italian case. In: Small Business Economics 47: pp. 293-311.

Ingham, Geoffrey K. (1970): Size of Industrial Organization and Worker Behaviour. London: Cambridge University Press.

Istituto Nazionale di Statistica (ISTAT) (2020a): Censimento permanente delle imprese 2019: i primi risultati (retrievable through *https://www.istat.it/it/censimenti-permanenti/imprese*).

Istituto Nazionale di Statistica (ISTAT) (2020b): Il mercato del lavoro 2019 una lettura integrata, ISBN: 978-88-458-2009-0.

Istituto Nazionale di Statistica (ISTAT) – Ministry of Eceonomi Development (MISE) (2018): Startup survey 2016. La prima indagine sulle neoimprese innovative in italia, ISBN 978-88-458-1948-3.

Martone, Andrea (2018): Smart Working, Job Crafting, Empowerment. Milano: Wolters e Kluwer.

Ministry of Economic Development (MISE) (2017): Relazione Annuale al Parlamento sullo stato d'attuazione e l'impatto delle policy a sostegno di startup e PMI innovative (retrievable through *https://www.mise.gov.it/images/stories/documenti/startup_relazione_annuale_al_2017*).

Ministry of Economic Development (MISE) (2020): Startup innovative. Cruscotto di Indicatori Statistici. 4° trimestre 2019 (retrievable through *http://startup.registroimprese.it/isin/report_trim?fileId=4_trimestre_2019*).

Organisation for Economic Co-Operation and Development (OECD) (2014): Studies on SMEs and Entrepreneurship Italy: Key Issues and Policies. Paris.

Piketty, Thomas (2013): Le capital au XXIe siècle. Paris: Editions du Seuil.

Piore, Michael J./Sabel, Charles (1984): The Second Industrial Divide: Possibilities for Prosperity. New York: Basic Books.

Rullani, Enzo (2004): Economia della conoscenza: Creatività e valore nel capitalismo delle reti. Roma: Carocci.

Rullani, Enzo (2012): Produttività cercasi, disperatamente: Per un nuovo rapporto tra manifattura e servizi. In: Economia e Società Regionale 117(3), pp. 24-54.

Rullani, Enzo/Cantù, Chiara L./Paiola, Marco/Prandstraller, Francesca/Sebastiani, Roberta (2012): Innovazione e produttività: Alla ricerca di nuovi modelli di business per le imprese di servizi. Milano: FrancoAngeli.

Santandrea, Vincenzo R./Lobello, Alfredo (2016): Start up di impresa e politiche attive del lavoro. Il caso Puglia. In: Rivista economica del Mezzogiorno 30(2-3), pp. 467-502.

Sapelli, Giulio (2013): Elogio della piccola impresa. Bologna: il Mulino.

Schumacher, Ernst F. (1973): Small Is Beautiful: A Study of Economics as If People Mattered. London: Blond & Briggs.

Sennett, Richard (1998): The Corrosion of Character, The Personal Consequences of Work in the New Capitalism. New York-London: Norton.

Zuboff, Shoshana (2019): The Age of Surveillance Capitalism. The Fight for Human Future at the New Frontier of Power. New York: PublicAffairs.

Websites

European Union: https://ec.europa.eu

Istituto Nazionale di Statistica (ISTAT) business permanent census: https://dati-censimenti-permanenti.istat.it

Istituto Nazionale di Statistica (ISTAT) data: http://dati.istat.it

Istituto Nazionale di Statistica (ISTAT): https://www.istat.it

Ministry of Economic Development (Ministero dello Sviluppo Economico, MISE): https://www.mise.gov.it

Statista: https://www.statista.com

2. POLICY FRAMEWORKS FOR SUSTAINABLE AND INCLUSIVE EMPLOYMENT AND GROWTH OF SMES

2.1. Multiple Policy Fields and Collaboration

SMEs in Hungary and in Poland: A Comparative Analysis of Legal and Labour Relations[19]

Gábor Mélypataki, Michał Barański, Zoltán Muszinszki and Katalin Lipták

Introduction

Automation, digitalisation, and globalisation influence today's global labour market. The process of change has become increasingly apparent also in Hungary and in Poland. Both the employer and the employee must adapt themselves to the rapidly changing circumstances. The aim of this paper is to examine the requirements the novel processes and their labour market effects impose upon the potential labour force and labour law. We examine how the effects of globalisation affect the global labour market, and how high-level automation and digitalisation affect the expectations of labour market actors and the world of labour law. Since the 1990s, as an effect of globalisation, technology has replaced labour in production to an increasing extent. Labour force is gradually disappearing in the society of wage labour, which is a major problem. A redefinition of the concept of work is needed, as much of society has already been excluded from classical wage labour. We analyse some SMEs who carry out accounting tasks for other SMEs. The choice of this type of activity for analysis is particularly important due to the recently adopted provisions on the digitalisation of employee files in some national laws.

Our research question is: Is there a relationship between the competences related to a highly qualified job like an accountant and the size of a company? According

---

[19] This research was supported by the Project No. EFOP-3.6.2-16-2017-00007, titled "Aspects on the Development of Intelligent, Sustainable, and Inclusive Society: Social, Technological, Innovation Networks in Employment and Digital Economy". The project has been supported by the European Union (EU) and co-financed by the European Social Fund (ESF) and the state budget of Hungary.

to our hypothesis, accounting firms (which tend to be SMEs) do not have enough financial and human resources to handle the new situation and these activities can be easily mechanised.

Changing the Concept of Work in a Globalised and Digitalised World

According to Offe (1984), the central role of work has changed. Individuals see work only as a way to earn money, its social organising feature has ceased, and there has been a cultural shift that has resulted in a change in individual attitudes and relationships to work (Offe 1984). In Robertson's (1985) theory, volunteering, freely carried out for one's own needs, is a new element in contrast to paid work.

It is worth noting that not only the concept of work has been re-evaluated, but also working conditions and circumstances. According to Dahrendorf (1994), a critical point in the history of work is the impact of recent changes in modern social conflict. There have been many changes in the nature of work that have had an impact on the lives of individuals and the social structure. In his view, work is no longer the solution to social problems, but a part of the problem itself. He also sees modern societies as labour societies. He writes that "employment is the entry ticket to the world of supplies" and intensifies this when describing the group of workaholics. He says that most of its members constantly complain that they cannot distinguish between weekdays and Sundays and that they have not been on vacation for years, but in fact, this type of complaint is another form of wasteful consumption: "a showcase for the wealthy at work" (Dahrendorf 1994: 230). He questions whether it is still possible to call the modern society a labour society and concludes that, despite the numbers, we still live in a labour society because of the presence and situation of the unemployed: in a developed country, 20 per cent of the total population is not of working age, 20 per cent are retired, 10 per cent go to school, 15 per cent are looking for work, 10 per cent are unemployed and only the remaining 25 per cent have work. Dahrendorf (1994) analyses the relationship between economic growth and employment and uses the natural rate of unemployment (NAIRU rate), ideally taking 6 to 8 per cent. With less human effort, more can be produced, meaning that there can be fewer job opportunities, so some may be excluded from the labour market. He does not believe in achieving full employment; he writes that full employment requires the creation of peripheral or needless jobs, which obviously is problematic (Dahrendorf 1994).

As an effect of globalisation, technological developments are increasingly displacing human workforce from production, while capital needs the flexibility of the labour market. Unemployment is a natural consequence of capitalist production and its growth is a necessary consequence of globalisation, but the side effects intensified growth of unemployment hit lower qualified workers the hardest. At a time of economic boost, employment increases to a smaller extent than production, but at a time of economic downturn, it decreases faster than production. According to Rifkin (1995), one of the main reasons for the decrease in labour demand is the increase in mechanisation and automation.

The shift to mass production and the high degree of mechanisation also led to a change in the nature of work. Because of mechanisation, work has become less dangerous, but also, in some cases, tedious. From as humanist point of view, the change in work in market economies has destroyed the human personality, reduced curiosity and talent, and has made work boring and monotonous. According to Rimler (1999), due to changing conditions, a new concept of work is needed. In the past, the emphasis was on the social integration of work, while now it is on personal development. Technological development has also changed the demand for labour by significantly reducing direct human input. As a result of this, for many people, paid work no longer is a means of social integration, recognition, and acceptance. Furthermore, it is possible to link personal development to work more closely because of its richness in content. The view of the 20th century - production is for consumption - may be reversed: We need to consume to produce. Any activity intended to create or maintain a personal or interpersonal civilizational, cultural, legal, political, or economic value is regarded as work. The obvious purpose of economic work is to produce goods and services of economic value.

Török (2006) predicts that we are going to move beyond the wage-labour society; he believes that high unemployment may mean the end of the labour society. In his view, the restoration of full employment has moved to the world of illusions and is no longer feasible, due to the effects of globalisation such as the relocation of industrial mass production to cheaper countries. According to Artner (2006), in capitalism, most people can survive only by marketing their labour force. The term "human capital" thus serves to obviate the difference between the nature and capitalist application of labour and privately-owned means of production (capital), that is, to deprive both sides of the productive forces of their social determination. Thus, for most people, work is not only theoretically but literally life itself. While this work is a mere cost to the capital employed by them. Ruling economics do not talk about people or workers, it speaks about human capital. Csoba (2006) concludes in her book that although the historical "hour of wage labour society" has expired, the pursuit of an alternative has so far been only an attempt. In her later work, Csoba (2010) approached the concept of paid work from a completely new perspective: Decent work is a socially acknowledged, voluntary activity that ensures the costs of living of the person concerned and their family, as well as strengthening the fact of belonging to the community.

It can be stated that the society of wage labour is gradually losing work, which is a significant problem. A redefinition of the concept of work is needed, as a significant part of society has already been pushed away from classical wage labour. A lower proportion of people of working age are employed in traditional forms of employment, whereas in the more developed European countries, atypical forms of work can already be considered as typical, as they are predominant. When reinterpreting the concept of work, the first question is whether we only consider paid work as work. The answer is no, because work also includes self-sufficiency farming, community work, and volunteering among others. Thus, the following vision emerges from the academic literature on sustainable employment policies: Breaking with the illusion of full employment and boundless globalisation, employment in a global network of local communities is given a whole new framework of interpretation. By extending the material nature of economic definition of needs with its relational and self-realisation elements, the concept of work is also transformed. Employment does not stop at the boundaries of paid work, and work for non-financial rewards, such as the individual's self-fulfilment or the community well-being, also increasingly becomes accepted as work (Király et al. 2012).

In addition to the spatial reorganisation of global labour demand, there is an equalisation that reduces the gap between centres and peripheral areas (Lipták 2009). Very low wages are still evident in some countries of the Asian continent, but the results of the catching-up process are also evident. Indeed, technological advances and the increased use of machinery in manufacturing companies are pushing some workers out of the labour market, especially those with low levels of education. In the case of highly skilled workers (for example, accountants), adapting to changing conditions is much quicker; also, the mechanisation of non-manual workflows is more difficult than the mechanisation of the work of a regular worker, putting people with lower qualifications typically working in such traditional jobs at a higher risk of unemployment than others.

In the literature, the concept of the "20/80 society" is frequently listed as an effect of globalisation on the labour market (Rifkin 1995, Martin and Schumann 1998). According to this concept, 20 per cent of the total population being employed will be enough in the future to keep the global economy going. The future of the labour market raises several questions: What will happen to the workers excluded from the labour market? How can human workforce compete with machines and should this situation be conceptualised as competition at all? What new types of jobs and what kind of educational training will be needed in the future?

Globalisation and Digitalisation

Globalised markets have increasingly opened opportunities for digitalisation. The questions of digitalisation will require rethinking issues such as legal responsibility (Pusztahelyi 2019). Liability issues may require the reestablishment of a complex of legal institutions, perhaps along the lines of the theory of the liability of dangerous activities.[20] The transformation of the relationship between the decision-making competences of the employer and their legal responsibilities will be crucial. Due to the complexity of the issue, we cannot investigate the phenomenon in detail.

What is certain is that cooperative robots that support decision-making can change legal responsibilities (Bobkov et al. 2018). Easy access to smart robots, their lower cost of maintenance, and increased efficiency in their work are pushing lower-skilled workers out of the labour market. In this context, the question arises of how to create new jobs that also provide job opportunities for lower-qualified workers. Although these jobs will come into being, they will require a completely different interpretation of lower-skilled jobs. These jobs will also require workers to learn new competences. However, it should also be considered that the number of jobs created will not necessarily be as high as those that are lost. In addition, it must be considered that not all employees are able to learn these new competences. Issues related to the functioning of the social welfare system will be linked to labour law problems. The basic question will be, what kind of care should be given to those

---

[20] The use of digital technology is a high-risk activity. The law has an own category for this liability form: For example, a car is considered a high-risk technology; the driving or self-driving of a car therefore is considered a high-risk (or dangerous) activity. If digital technology is used in the labour market, the same strict liability forms for high-risk activities must be applied to both labour law and industrial relations.

who lose their jobs due to digitalisation and how long should they be supported financially?

The transformation of employment relations through digitalisation will affect all segments of economy. According to data from 2018, 68.8 per cent of the workforce was employed by small and medium-sized enterprises (SMEs).[21] Accordingly, these businesses also need to be prepared for change. However, it also becomes evident in a strategic document prepared by the Hungarian Government that the participation of SME employees in adult education is low. OECD countries show that employees in SMEs are 50 per cent less involved in training activities than employees of large companies. In 2015, the share of employees in continuous vocational training in Hungary was only about half of the European average and one third of the value measured in the Czech Republic.[22] The importance of this issue for the labour market is best illustrated by one of Martin Ford's ideas:

> "And, as a small business owner, I've watched as technology has transformed the way I run my business - in particular, how it has dramatically reduced the need to hire employees to perform many of the routine tasks that have always been essential to the operation of any business." (Ford 2015: 33)

This also means that those fewer workers must be better qualified. It should be emphasised from the data of the above-mentioned strategy that this requirement puts SMEs in a difficult employment situation not only in Hungary, but also in other Central European countries. When asked, 39.8 per cent of Hungarian SMEs reported that the biggest challenge for them was the recruitment of a qualified labour force, compared to 31.2 per cent in the Czech Republic and 26.6 per cent in Poland.

---

[21] https://www.kormany.hu/download/5/f7/b1000/KKV_Strategia.pdf.

[22] https://www.kormany.hu/download/5/f7/b1000/KKV_Strategia.pdf.

General and Labour Laws and Regulations of SMEs in Hungary and Poland

SMEs in Hungary

In order to clarify the general legal framework and the specific legal framework, it is necessary to look at what the abbreviation "SME" means. In Hungary, the definition of SMEs is determined in Act XXXIV of 2004[23], and the support provided to such enterprises is based on Article 2 of the Annex to Commission Recommendation 2003/361/EC[24]. According to this, there are three categories within the definition of SMEs: micro-, small, and medium-sized enterprises, which are commonly referred to as small and medium-sized enterprises, or SMEs (Szira 2014). In the EU, SMEs are companies with fewer than 250 employees, provided that they are independent of other companies and that their income does not exceed EUR 50 million. There are other categories within SMEs, which are mainly related to the employment rate. Based on these, enterprises with ten or less persons are considered micro-enterprises, enterprises with ten to 49 persons are small enterprises, and enterprises with 50 to 249 persons are considered medium-sized enterprises. The accounting firms we investigate are typically micro-enterprises and small businesses, but there are businesses with more than 50 employees, too.[25]

Due to their size, some of the labour laws and regulations legislated for typically large employers may not be applicable to these types of businesses or may be applicable only with significant changes. We understand that most of the collective labour laws and regulations are not applicable to micro-enterprises and small businesses in the categories listed above. A fundamental question is how the size of the company is related to the application of general legal and labour law frameworks. Contradictory effects should be investigated in parallel between the size of the firms and general labour law. Indeed, some studies confirm that the SME sector has the lowest quality of labour force (Homicskó and Kun 2015). It should also be noted that in small businesses, labour relations tend to be much more informal

---

[23] Hungary, Government Act of XXXIV of 2004 on Small and Medium-Sized Enterprises and Supporting Their Development.

[24] Commission Recommendation of 6 May 2003 Concerning the Definition of Micro, Small and Medium-Sized Enterprises (2003/361/EC).

[25] Commission Recommendation of 6 May 2003 Concerning the Definition of Micro, Small and Medium-Sized Enterprises (2003/361/EC).

than in larger companies. Basically, a stronger level of trust between employer and employee, usually stemming from family relationships between the parties (Biagi 1995), does not prevent labour law violations. The figures by the International Labour Organization (ILO) show lower wages and longer working hours in the SME sector, which is dependent on the above (ILO 2018). The human resources management (HRM) of an SME oftentimes is less professional than that of larger companies. This becomes well-illustrated when looking at the impact of digitalisation on recruitment and the quality of services provided.

The basic question is whether there is a legal need for a facilitated path for SMEs. There are several international examples that recognise the need for this. Many ILO conventions[26] permit differentiations based on the size of the employing company. There were also special provisions in Hungarian law for micro-companies, which limited the employer's liability for damages. Under Hungarian law, the employer's liability for damages is objective; only in a small number of cases may the objective responsibility be escaped. One such quasi-option was to limit the liability of an individual employing up to ten full-time employees. In the case of these micro-companies, the liability of the employer was subjective. This rule created the opportunity for a somewhat differentiated set of rules than would otherwise have been created for large companies (Marencsák 2010). The explanatory memorandum to the Hungarian Labour Code[27] and the minister's note also emphasises that the legislator does not want to impose stricter consequences on these "low-income" employers (mainly individuals employing employees on an ad hoc basis and the self-employed), as their resources are very limited. According to the minister's opinion, in the case of the objective liability of these "low-income" employers, the employer's obligation to compensate would deprive them of the resources necessary for their operation and eliminate the economic basis of their operation. In Decision 41/2009, the Hungarian Constitutional Court considered this solution to be contrary to the Hungarian Constitution regarding the right to work and the practice of international law.[28]

---

[26] For example, the following ILO conventions: International Labour Organization (ILO) C001 - Hours of Work (Industry) Convention, 1919 (No. 1); C030 - Hours of Work (Commerce and Offices) Convention, 1930 (No. 30); C081 - Labour Inspection Convention, 1947 (No. 81); and C158 - Termination of Employment Convention, 1982 (No. 158).

[27] Hungary, Government Act I. 2012 on the Labour Code.

[28] Hungary, Constitutional Court, Decision 41/2009.

As a result, Hungarian labour law and labour market rules do not directly regulate SMEs. However, this does not mean that there are no special labour market instruments that promote employment. During our research, we concluded that there are similarities between the Hungarian and Polish solutions. The Polish solutions are explained in more detail in the following sections, but we will highlight the similarities here already. A major common feature of the labour regulations in the two countries is the use of the employment agency activity as an employment policy instrument.

In Hungarian law, Article 6 of Act IV of 1991 on the Promotion of Employment and the Provision of Benefits to the Unemployed[29] deals with employment agency activity as an employment policy instrument. The significance of this act lies in the fact that it provides SMEs with the opportunity to "acquire" labour force through employment agency activity. Employment agency activity means a service designed to facilitate the meeting of jobseekers and employers, which includes the obligation to provide information. For Hungary, detailed rules are contained in the Government Decree 118/2001 (VI. 30.)[30]: According to Paragraph 11 of the Decree, the private employment agency has to inform jobseekers about the main characteristics of the positions, in particular about the qualifications needed, the experience required, the place and time of employment, the relevant work schedule, the working time schedule, and the expected earning potential. Beside the state employment body, employment agency activity can be carried out by a person who meets the requirements as stated in the decree.

Employment agency activity is usually accompanied by support programmes. These programmes are mainly funded by the European Union (EU), which seeks to improve the labour market situation. However, it is important to add that employment agency activity is different from temporary agency work. Labour market tenders for SMEs usually involve the compensation or temporary assumption of wage costs related to the employment of new labour. In many cases, these programmes can improve the chances for businesses to find and hire high-qualified workers.

---

[29] Hungary, Government Act IV of 1991 on the Promotion of Employment and the Provision of Benefits to the Unemployed.

[30] Hungary, Government Decree 118/2001 on Private Employment Offices and Hiring out of Labour.

Effects of the COVID-19 pandemic

In the light of the above-mentioned, we can note that ILO Recommendation No. 189 6.(1)(b) (ILO 1998) says the following: "Members should consider policies that create conditions which (...) ensure the non-discriminatory application of labour legislation to raise the quality of employment in SMEs". It is worth it to analyse if and how the recommendation of the ILO is implemented in SMEs of different economic sectors, including SMEs in accounting that we scrutinise.

Furthermore, the importance of digitalisation and the urgent need to implement it become quite clear against the background of the latest labour market difficulties caused by the COVID-19 pandemic. In this context, it might be also become visible that perhaps SMEs actually are able to adapt faster than large companies; at least so are accounting offices, since some of the accounting tasks are already done in teleworking/home offices. Thus, one could state that the dissolution of SME operations had already begun earlier. Crowdsourcing may be a solution not only for traditional accounting firms, but also in other segments. It refers to the activity when an enterprise or an organisation outsources a function previously performed by its own employees to a (typically large) outsourced to a group, not set out in advance in the form of an open call. The goal is to complete tasks quickly and efficiently. In addition, the parties are leaving their own local area in the virtual space, thus widening the labour market, and going beyond the local level. Typically, crowd work is an alternative in connection with jobs that are intellectual (non-manual) and creative, such as translation, selling iStockphotos, or accounting tasks analysed by us.

These new forms of employment fundamentally change the position of SMEs in the labour market and pose new challenges to classical SMEs, in particular because of the lack of specific legal regulation for this segment of the labour market. SMEs operating under existing labour law are trapped within the rules of large companies and therefore they are at a disadvantage in tackling this new challenge. The questions of how general the disadvantage is and how it is reflected in the accounting field are analysed below in connection with both Hungary and Poland.

The impact of COVID-19 in general should also be examined for the SME sector. When discussing the importance of the digital presence, we need to highlight the increased responsibility that comes with it. By this we do not mean general labour law responsibility, but social responsibility, hereinafter referred to as corporate social responsibility (CSR). The labour market situation caused by the pandemic generates the need for employers to use CSR tools outside the framework of labour law. The legal framework for CSR is not entirely clear, as it is not a legal concept (Szegedi-Mélypataki 2016, Mikonowicz et al. 2019, Balaton-Horváth 2019), but brings together several employment policy principles and labour law provisions that can help vulnerable employees. However, it should be added that the application of CSR is not quite common in the Hungarian SME sector, at least not its conscious application. In our view, sustainability requires an extended interpretation of social interest and responsibility that is achieved simultaneously with real economic goals. A good example of this is the UK Social Value Act[31], which aims to support SMEs and the Voluntary Community and Social Enterprise (VCSE) sector in gaining greater access to advertised projects and increasing their chance to compete for drawing up contracts with public institutions and authorities (Jakab and Ráczi 2019). Translating this into the domestic model would better support the conscious CSR activities of SMEs.

Such conscious activity can be experienced primarily in those small Hungarian companies that consciously deal with brand and branding. An essential element of the branding is human resources management (HRM) (Papp-Váry et al. 2020). The application of special labour law rules due to epidemiological measures has also aimed to reduce the burden on SMEs. This is because the turmoil in global systems will have a significant impact on the activities and services they can provide, so employment structure and recruitment practices will also adapt to this. Part of the relevant labour law rules related to the epidemic, which also affect SMEs, is laid down in Section 6 of Government Decree 47/2020 of 18 March 2020[32]. According to Section 6(4) of the Decree, the employee and the employer may deviate from the provisions of the Labour Code[33] in a separate agreement. Under this provision, within certain extended limits, the parties may conclude a contract concerning almost any legal provision. Gábor Kártyás emphasises that this one sentence moves the cornerstone of the entire labour law regulation. The main purpose of labour law, as a branch of law of protection, is to lay down minimum protection rules precisely for employees, from which the parties may not derogate by agreement or

---

[31] United Kingdom (UK), Government Act of 8 March 2012 on Public Services (Social Value Act).

[32] Hungary, Government Decree 47/2020 (18 March) on Immediate Measures Necessary for Alleviating the Effects of the Coronavirus Pandemic on National Economy.

[33] Hungary, Government Act I. 2012 on the Labour Code.

only for the benefit of the employee (Kártyás 2020). In our opinion, these legal provisions must be implemented in the context of social innovation, as innovative solutions that do not increase the vulnerability of employees will be the key for both businesses and workers.

SMEs in Poland

In Polish economic sciences, when defining SMEs, two groups of criteria are most often taken into consideration: quantitative (number of employees, turnover, and size of the market) and qualitative criteria (ownership and management unity, decision-making and financial independence, degree of flattening of the organisational structure, innovation, management system, and the market share) (Piasecki 2001, Barański 2019a).

In Polish law, there are definitely "strong correlations between the legal notions of an entrepreneur and an employer, though they rarely occur jointly in specific normative solutions" (Barański 2019a: 11). In the provisions of the Act of 6 March 2018 – Entrepreneurs Law[34], the legislator defined a micro, small and medium-sized entrepreneur. The average annual employment for a given entrepreneur, for the purposes of its possible qualification into one of the indicated categories of entrepreneurs, is determined in full-time equivalents, excluding employees on maternity leave, leave on maternity leave terms, paternity leave, parental leave and upbringing leave, and also being employed for the purpose of vocational training[35]. For this reason, it is emphasised in the literature that "under the Polish labour law, the main, if not the only, criteria for differentiating the legal status of employers are quantitative criteria - diversification due to the size of employment" (Barański 2019a: 17; see also Mikołajewska-Böning 2006: 40, Łaga 2016: 174). At the same time, the literature also formulates attempts to develop concepts of micro, small and medium-sized enterprises as employers, because the numerical criterion characteristic of labour law does not correspond to the provisions of the Entrepreneurs Law (Gładoch 2013, Szmit 2013, Barański 2019a).

---

[34] Poland, Government Act of 6 March 2018 - Entrepreneurs Law (Journal of Laws of 2018, item 646 with amendments).

[35] Poland, Government Act of 6 March 2018 - Entrepreneurs Law (Journal of Laws of 2018, item 646 with amendments), Article 7(3): "In the case of an undertaking operating for less than a year, its expected net turnover from the sale of goods, goods and services and financial operations as well as average annual employment is determined based on data for the last period documented by the entrepreneur".

More and more SMEs in Poland are finding innovative ways to recruit and retain skilled labour. What should be highlighted among modern employee recruitment techniques, from the perspective of Polish legal regulations, are first the solutions adopted based on the Act of 20 April 2004 on Employment Promotion and Labour Market Institutions[36]. Pursuant to Article 18(1) point 1 of that Act, conducting business activity in the field of job brokerage services (private job brokerage), along with personnel consultancy, occupational guidance, and temporary work, shall be a regulated activity and shall require an entry into the register of subjects operating employment agencies.

In turn, Article 18c(2) point 4 of the aforementioned Act[37] provides, among other things, that "collecting in the form of an electronic document and providing information on vacancies and sought-after job via IT systems does not require an entry into the register of subjects operating employment agencies". Unfortunately, provisions of Article 18(1) point 1 and Article 18c(2) point 4 of the Act, due to their far-reaching imprecision, raise the question about the mutual relationship between those provisions. In particular, it is not clear whether the services listed in Article 18c(2) point 4 of the Act fall within the conceptual scope of private job brokerage, or, on the contrary, whether they constitute services that cannot be classified as private job brokerage (Barański 2019b). In the case of services regulated in Article 18c(2) point 4 of the Act, their purpose was indirectly indicated by specifying the type of information collected and made available by the client. Since the information refers to vacancies and sought-after jobs, it should be assumed that those services "will usually be provided as an opportunity to conclude a contract" (passive job brokerage) (Barański 2019b: 139). At the same time, "the regulation in question should also cover contracts, the subject of which will be the collection and sharing of information about vacancies and sought-after jobs, for example for statistical purposes or as a part of the so-called business intelligence" (Barański 2019b: 139).

In the case of passive job brokerage, existing databases, or social networking sites, especially business-oriented websites are being used more and more. As part of

---

[36] Poland, Government Act of 20 April 2004 on Promotion of Employment and on Labour Market Institutions (Journal of Laws of 2004, No. 99, item 1001 with amendments).

[37] Poland, Government Act of 20 April 2004 on Promotion of Employment and on Labour Market Institutions (Journal of Laws of 2004, No. 99, item 1001 with amendments).

such modern recruitment techniques, applicants usually fill out an online application form or participate in talent acquisition programmes (also called talent management).[38] In economic sciences, those techniques are usually referred to as networking and e-recruitment (Olszak 2014). However, it should be remembered that the EU[39] and national provisions (for example, the Polish Labour Code[40]) on the protection of personal data always must be applied, also during any activities undertaken in connection with passive job brokerage.

Among other modern recruitment techniques used by SMEs, one should distinguish in particular a) the method of group psychological examination (also referred to as the "assessment centre" or "integrated assessment") and b) neurolinguistic programming (NLP)[41], which raises considerable doubts (including in the fields of human rights, labour law, and personal data protection law) (Borowska and Figiel).

One of the key issues in retaining skilled labour is age management. Age management understood in a traditional way corresponds to the cycle from the employee's entry into the organisation to their departure, including the following areas: recruitment, training, development and promotion, organisation of work, health care, termination of employment, and retirement (Wiktorowicz and Warwas 2017). The extended and more current approach to age management emphasises "competence management (knowledge, skills, motivations, attitudes, self-image) of mature employees, including training, knowledge development and management; WLB (Work-Life Balance), such as issues related to achieving a balance between

---

[38] Of course, such actions may also be undertaken by the employer (recruiters employed by the employer), provided that these actions are in accordance with the provisions of generally applicable law.

[39] European Union (EU), Regulation 2016/679 of the European Parliament and of the Council of 27 April 2016 on the Protection of Natural Persons with Regard to the Processing of Personal Data and on the Free Movement of Such Data, and Repealing Directive 95/46/EC (General Data Protection Regulation).

[40] According to Article 22(1), Paragraph 1 of the Polish Labour Code, "an employer demands a person applying for emplyment to provide the following personal data, including: 1) name(s) and surname; 2) date of birth; 3) contact data indicated by such a person; 4) education; 5) professional experience; 6) employment history". Poland, Government Act of 26 June 1974 - Labour Code (Journal of Laws of 1974, No. 24, item 344 with amendments).

[41] Neurolinguistic programming (NLP) is "a collection of knowledge about the way we operate, use and develop our mind (brain) in complicity with our body, which is the receptor (seeing, hearing, tasting, smelling, feeling) reality for that mind. NLP is both a system of theoretical models that understand the structure of human experience and activities, as well as a set of practical methods that support constructive change and development" (Olszak 2014: 290-291).

work and private and family life, including prevention and health protection; motivating, commitment and well-being of mature employees" (Wiktorowicz and Warwas 2017: 73).

In the case of younger employees, factors that determine if they stay in employment with a given employer often revolve around completely different issues. Those include the use of innovative tools and solutions or the provision of flexible working time and a sense of independence (Deloitte 2014).

However, the basic technique of retaining valuable employees is still represented by the introduction of appropriate pay regulations in workplaces (for example, bonus regulations including the so-called retention bonus, the amount of which increases with the course of employment). In that regard, measures that are becoming more and more popular are the package remuneration systems, in which employees have the option of choosing specific types of benefits within the amount provided for individual positions (taking into account the principle of equal treatment in employment).

Undoubtedly, various systems for improving one's professional qualifications are also of significant importance in employee retention (including the mentoring programs at the workplace, which connect employees of different generations and ensures effective transfer of knowledge).

The current global economic crisis caused by the COVID-19 pandemic may be a good reason to introduce changes in employers, including SMEs, by permanently integrating CSR with business operations. Certainly, "internal relations within the enterprise, especially regarding employees, are the sphere where corporate social responsibility should be particularly important during the crisis" (Bernatt 2010). Such actions will not only affect the retention of qualified employees, but also the search for valuable employees, even still after the economic crisis triggered by the pandemic has ended.

SMEs for SMEs

Digitalisation, which sweeps through all areas of life, also affects accounting. The 6D model of Peter Diamandis and Steven Kotler aims to show how digital technology is evolving and what change this evolution will bring to the world around us (Diamandis and Kotler 2015). The first stage (1D) is digitalisation itself, when the information is put into digital form, that is, it will be suitable for computer processing. In the field of the accounting profession, this means recording invoices into an accounting programme. In the next stage (2D), the nature of the digital process is described, which is characterised initially by growing slowly, unnoticeably, and then, after a point, its growth soars rapidly, and they are eliminated. After the destruction comes the stage (3D) when the positive effects of change due to digitalisation dominate, for example, when digital technologies become accesible for everyone and everywhere. As a result of digitalisation, a structural change is taking place in the focal points of the accounting service. Currently, data recording dominates, be it accounting data or tax data. This data recording-based service model is evolving today, with an increasing emphasis on consulting-focused service.

This section of our study presents this process through the example of a Hungarian accounting firm (Orosz 2018). We look at how the accounting firm makes use of the opportunities provided by digitalisation and how it looks from the standpoint of clients. The accounting firm was established in 2011 with the goal of providing accounting services to SMEs as well as sole proprietors, foundations, and associations. The firm is currently associated with a total of 86 companies, performs accounting and payroll tasks, and furthermore provides general legal advice to its clients. The managing director manages the day-to-day operations of the company, with the participation of four employees, and in a family atmosphere. Employees maintain close contact with their customers and are constantly available to them to resolve all possible issues and problems affecting their business.[42]

The firm opted for a cloud-based service, otherwise known as "cloud computing", to process its invoices. The benefits are clear: They are not tied to a fixed place and can have access to the materials they need to work with almost anywhere, anytime. This solution allows for flexible scheduling for both office staff and clients. By using a cloud-based service, the office is not only free from the cost of hardware and software purchases, but also from immense costs of maintaining the building of the office. After all, this solution supports not only flexible working hours, but also home offices. This flexibility has helped maintain and increase the competitiveness of the accounting firm in previous years. However, in the situation that emerged in March 2020 due to COVID-19, this is no longer just a means of competitiveness but also of survival.

---

[42] This form of relationship, as we shall see, does not require a personal presence. The solutions used by the firm allow for smooth working even during the COVID-19 crisis.

Accountants spend most of their time processing data, that is, processing incoming invoices. Suppliers' invoices are processed by the Billcity accounting software. The Billcity programme recognises the number of invoices, partner data, and amount on the invoices with 85 per cent accuracy. The Institute of Management Accountants (IMA) accounting programme makes cloud-based operations possible, which allows one to post and perform various queries from the posted data anywhere and anytime. The programme requires an active Internet connection and a Microsoft Windows operating system. The firm also uses a programme called Viki (a software assistant accountant), which helps accountants in a way that they do not have to manually send all kinds of tax and contribution notifications to their clients. The primary goal of the solutions presented so far has been to minimise the work involved in data management in the past. By now, the objective function has been expanded with flexibility, both in terms of working hours, place of work, and customer relations. But what about the company's advisory function? To get to know the expectations of the customers on that issue, we conducted a questionnaire survey.

The purpose of the questionnaire survey was to identify whether there was a need for clients to utilise a management reporting system to be developed by the accounting firm. The query was created by using Google Forms. The questionnaire consisted of the following sections: data on ownership and management, questions related to the operation of the business, and questions related to management information needs.

The questionnaire (in Hungarian) was sent by the head of the office to the clients. Out of 86, 57 customers (companies) completed the questionnaire. Of these, 64.92 per cent of the respondents are micro-, 33.33 per cent small, and 1.75 per cent medium-sized enterprises. The type of company is distributed as follows: 47.36 per cent are limited liability companies, 21.07 per cent sole proprietorships, 19.29 per cent non-profit organisations, and 12.28 per cent limited partnerships. In terms of sectoral classification, 22.8 per cent of the sample include companies operating in the field of education, 19.29 per cent in trade, 12.28 per cent in real estate, 7 per cent in financial and insurance activities, 7 per cent in construction, 19.29 per cent in other services, and 5.26 per cent in accommodation, food and beverages, and transportation and warehousing.

Of the respondents, 91.22 per cent have heard of a controlling approach or system before, although 78.94 per cent do not use controlling methods to increase competitiveness. When hearing the term "controlling", most of the customers think of controlling the operation of the company, but many are also aware that it also means planning, auditing, and providing information. Nevertheless, 17.54 per cent of all respondents consier controlling to be an expensive and meaningless system.

In the third part of the questionnaire, we examined how important the reports in the questionnaire were considered by the clients of the office. A five-point Likert scale was used for the measurement of importance (1: not at all, 2: less important, 3: moderately important, 4: important, 5: extremely important). Concerning reports on turnover, both limited liability companies and limited partnerships each give a 5 (extremely important); 83 per cent of sole proprietors rate the importance of the report on turnover with 5 (extremely important), too. However, the non-profit sector is divided on this question, with most organisations (60 per cent) considering the report on turnover to be moderately important (rated with 3). The evolution of costs is considered very important (rated with 4) to all respondents. In most cases, monthly reports would be preferred. Only 25 per cent of sole proprietors and 28 per cent of non-profit organisations think that a quarterly report on cost trends was sufficient (instead of a monthly report). All in all, clients would be happy to receive regular reports on the income statement (average of 4.6): Except for one response, only the scores of 4 (very important) and 5 (extremely important) are included in the responses. One respondent rate it with a 3 (moderately important), 22 respondents vote for the score of 4 (very important) and 34 for the score of 5 (extremely important).

Based on previous surveys (Fenyves and Tarnóczi 2019, Fenyves et al. 2018, Bozsik et al. 2019), reports on the cash flow are more informative for the managers of small companies than the reports on the development of the result. This survey could confirm this: For all forms of company, respondents considered cash flow reporting to be more important than income statement. Next, we will take a closer look at the average values and the proportion of the highest value in both cases:

- sole proprietor: average 4.5 to 4.7, proportion of highest value 58 to 67 per cent;
- limited partnership: average 4.4 to 4.9, proportion of highest value 43 to 86 per cent;
- limited liability company: average 4.7 to 4.8, proportion of highest value 74 to 85 per cent;

- non-profit organisation: average 4.4 to 4.7, proportion of highest value 36 to 72 per cent.

The need to receive reports on the most successful product or service varies widely. Customers consider this type of report to be moderately important (rated with 3). At the same time, we can see great differences for each form of company: The average for limited liability companies is 4.0, for limited partnerships 3.1, for sole proprietorships 2.3, and for non-profit organisations 1.4. In the case of the detection of the customers with the highest turnover, the same pattern can be observed. Most of the points were given by limited liability companies; of the limited liability companies, 77 per cent would like to see a summary made on their top customers, while sole proprietors and non-profit organisations typically gave 1 point (not at all important) to the reports that can be prepared about customers. Examining the claims, limited liability companies demand this type of report the most, with 5 points (extremely important) given by a total of 18 clients. This type of report is not important for sole proprietors, as 66.66 per cent of all micro-enterprises gave it only 1 point (not at all important).

In the survey, respondents were also asked about the services of the accounting firm. All respondents would welcome a report by the office on pre-calculated, expected annual results, and sales revenue. This would help them judge whether they are on the right track (through a comparison of plan-fact data). Businesses are open to self-control (87.71 per cent of respondents would like to expand their knowledge of controlling as well), as all the clients felt that it was necessary to expand the role of accountants towards consulting.

Conclusion

Concerning SMEs, the changed situation due to the crisis caused by the COVID-19 pandemic is speeding up several processes that would otherwise have been due only in the near future. SMEs are in an easy and a difficult situation at the same time. On the one hand, their situation is difficult because services provided by them demand personal relations with clients. On the other hand, it has also become easier for them than for multinational companies, because SMEs are able to adapt to the new circumstances faster, as their quantity of human resources that must be shifted to a different type of working method is lower. The crisis in the labour market will also affect human resources (HR) processes and the management of the existing workforce.

The crisis can also bring about interesting new phenomena. On the one hand, in both Hungary and Poland, the outflow of labour to the Western part of the EU has been a major problem. In the situation caused by the COVID-19 pandemic, this process is somewhat reversed: Some workers have returned from Western countries because of the virus and have no plans to go abroad again. Another trend is the challenges posed by digitalisation.

In our study, we have concluded that the current circumstances reinforce the examination of two proposed solutions. The accounting firm presented in our case study is a good example for the fact that digitalisation tools are not necessarily and always aimed at taking away jobs from employee but can also help them keep their jobs. Another important phenomenon is the relationship between CSR and SMEs. The importance of this stems, on the one hand, from the fact that neither Polish nor Hungarian labour law deals specifically with SMEs; thus, these businesses must invent alternatives within the legal framework. On the other hand, the globalised world has become narrow in the current situation; therefore, it is necessary to focus on local communities, in which CSR strategies can help to reconcile both careful removal and recruitment as well as foster a healthy work-life balance.

In our view, an important element of crisis management should be the development and review of the business strategies of SMEs, with a focus on supporting CSR activities that contribute to the development of fair requirements of employment, the whitening of the economy, and the transformation of HR processes.

References

Hungary, Ministry of Innovation and Technology (2020): A magyar mikro-, kis- és középvállalkozások megerősítésének stratégiája 2019-2030 (Strategy for Strengthening Hungarian Micro, Small and Medium-Sized Enterprises 2019-2030). URL: https://www.kormany.hu/download/5/f7/b1000/KKV_Strategia.pdf (25 June 2020).

Artner, Annamária (2006): A globalizáció alulnézetben: Elnyomott csoportok – lázadó mozgalmak. Budapest: Napvilág Publisher.

Balaton, Károly/Horváth, Dóra Diána (2019): Responsible Employment as a Strategic Issue, In: Nemec, Radek/Chytilova, Lucie (Eds.): Proceedings of the 13th International Conference on Strategic Management and its Support by Information Systems 2019 (SMSIS 2019). Ostrava: VSB-Technical University of Ostrava, pp. 16-24.

Barański, Michał (2019a): An entrepreneur as an employer in the Polish Legal System. In: Praca i Zabezpieczenie Społeczne 11, pp. 11-20.

Barański, Michał (2019b): Prywatne pośrednictwo pracy a świadczenie usług informacyjnych o miejscach pracy za pośrednictwem systemów teleinformatycznych. In: Acta Universitatis Lodziensis Folia Iuridica 88, pp. 131-141.

Bernatt, Maciej (2010): CSR – przedsiębiorca i jego pracownicy. Wartości konstytucyjne jako inspiracja dla budowania poprawnych relacji z pracownikami w czasie kryzysu: URL: http://odpowiedzialnybiznes.pl/artykuly/csr-przedsiebiorca-i-jego-pracownicy-wartosci-konstytucyjne-jako-inspiracja-dla-budowania-poprawnych-relacji-z-pracownikami-w-czasie-kryzysu/ [22 June 2020].

Biagi, Marco (1994-1995): Labour Law in Small and Medium-Sized Enterprises: Flexibility or Adjustment? In: Comparative Labor Law Journal 16, pp. 439- 454.

Bobkov, Vyacheslav/Kvachec, Vadim/Novikvoa, Irina (2018): International Systems of Labour Skills Monitoring in the Digital Economy. In: Larsen et al. (Eds): Developing Skills in a Changing World of Work. Augsburg, München: Rainer Hampp Verlag, pp. 385-394.

Borowska, Gabriela/Figiel, Agnieszka (n.a.): Nowoczesne metody selekcji pracowników stosowane w procesie rekrutacji. URL: www.sknprofit.ue.poznan.pl/publikacje/Nowoczesne%20metody%20selekcji.pdf [22 June 2020].

Bozsik, Sándor/ Musinszki, Zoltán/ Szemán, Judit (2019): A Central European Spproach to the Typology of Social Enterprises. In: Nemec, Radek/Chytilova, Lucie (Eds.): Proceedings of the 13th International Conference on Strategic Management and its Support by Information Systems 2019 (SMSIS 2019). Ostrava: VSB-Technical University of Ostrava, pp. 25-32.

Csoba, Judit (2006): Foglalkoztatáspolitika. Debrecen: University of Debrecen.

Csoba, Judit (2010): Segély helyett közmunka. A közfoglalkoztatás formái és sajátosságai. In: Szociológiai Szemle 20 (1), pp. 26-50.

Dahrendorf, Ralf (1994): A modern társadalmi konfliktus. Budapest: Gondolat Publisher.

Deloitte (2014): Big Demands and High Expectations: The Deloitte Millennial Survey. URL: http://www2.deloitte.com/content/dam/Deloitte/global/Documents/About-Deloitte/gx-dttl-2014-millennial-survey-report.pdf [22 June 2020].

Diamandis, Peter/Kotler, Dteven (2015): Bold: How to Go Big, Create Wealth and Impact the World. New York: Simon & Schuster Publisher.

Fenyves, Veronika/ Tarnóczi, Tibor (2019): Examination of the Expectations of Controllers on the Labour Market. In: Corporate Ownership and Control 17 (1), pp. 60-70.

Fenyves, Veronika/ Bács, Zoltán/ Zéman, Zoltán/ Böcskei, Elvira/ Tarnóczi, Tibor (2018): The Role of the Notes to the Financial Statements in Corporate Decision-Making. In: Corporate Ownership and Controls 4, pp. 138-148.

Ford, Martin (2015): Rise of the Robots: Technology and the Threat of a Jobless Future. New York: Basic Books.

Gładoch, Monika (2013): Oczekiwania zmian ustawodawstwa w zakresie statusu prawnego małych pracodawców — uwagi z perspektywy organizacji pracodawców. In: Goździewicz, Grzegorz (Ed.): Stosunki pracy u małych pracodawców. Warszawa: Wolters Kluwer, pp. 362-375.

Homicskó, Árpád/Kun, Attila (2012): A munkáltató „méretének" relevanciája a munkajogi szabályozásban a 41/2009 (III.27.) AB Határozat fényében. In: DIEIP 5 (2), pp. 1-22.

International Labour Organization (ILO) (1919): C001 - Hours of Work (Industry) Convention, 1919 (No. 1). URL: https://www.ilo.org/dyn/normlex/en/f?p=NORMLEXPUB:12100:0::NO::P12100_ILO_CODE:C001 [22 June 2020].

International Labour Organization (ILO) (1930): C030 - Hours of Work (Commerce and Offices) Convention, 1930 (No. 30). URL: https://www.ilo.org/dyn/normlex/en/f?p=NORMLEXPUB:12100:0::NO::P12100_ILO_CODE:C030 [22 June 2020].

International Labour Organization (ILO) (1947): C081 - Labour Inspection Convention, 1947 (No. 81). URL: https://www.ilo.org/dyn/normlex/en/f?p=NORMLEXPUB:12100:0::NO::P12100_ILO_CODE:C081 [22 June 2020].

International Labour Organization (ILO) (1982): C158 - Termination of Employment Convention, 1982 (No. 158). URL: https://www.ilo.org/dyn/normlex/en/f?p=NORMLEXPUB:12100:0::NO::P12100_ILO_CODE:C158 [22 June 2020].

International Labour Organization (ILO) (1998): R189 - Job Creation in Small and Medium-Sized Enterprises Recommendation, 1998 (No. 189). URL: https://www.ilo.org/dyn/normlex/en/f?p=NORMLEXPUB:12100:0::NO::P12100_ILO_CODE:R189 [22 June 2020].

International Labour Organization (ILO) (2018): The Impact of Social Dialogue and Collective Bargaining on Working Conditions in SMEs: A Literature Rewiev. URL: https://www.ilo.org/wcmsp5/groups/public/---ed_emp/---emp_ent/---ifp_seed/documents/publication/wcms_651378.pdf [25 June 2020].

Jakab, I. Nóra/Ráczi, P. Zsófia (2019): Issues of Public Social Responsibility in Great Britain and Hungary. In: Zbornik radova Pravnog fakulteta u Novom Sadu 54 (2), pp. 603-617.

Kártyás, Gábor (2020): Veszélyhelyzetre veszélyes munkajogi szabályok. URL: http://www.klaw.hu/2020/03/19/kartyas-gabor-munkajog/ [13. 04. 2020].

Király/Gábor, Köves/Alexandra, Pataki/György, Balázs/Bálint (2012): A fenntartható foglalkoztatáspolitika alapvonalai. Budapest: NFTT Műhelytanulmányok.

Lipták, Katalin (2009): Foglalkoztatáspolitika Magyarországon, különös tekintettel az időskorúak foglalkoztatására. In: Észak-magyarországi Stratégiai Füzetek 6 (1), pp .3-15.

Marencsák, Zsolt (2010): A KKV szektor differenciált munkajogi szabályozásának kérdései, különös tekintettel az Alkotmánybíróság 41/2009. (III. 27.) AB határozatára. In: Smuk, Péter (Ed.): Az állam és a jog alapvető értékei I. Győr: Széchenyi István Egyetem Állam- és Jogtudományi Doktori Iskola, pp. 358-367.

Martin, Hans-Peter/Schumann, Harald (1998): A globalizáció csapdája: Támodás a demokrácia és a jólét ellen. Budapest: Perfekt Publisher.

Mikołajewska-Böning, Marta (2006): Ochrona interesu pracodawcy w polskim prawie pracy, Toruń: Europejskie Centrum Edukacyjne.

Offe, Claus (1984): Arbeit als soziologische Schlüsselkategorie? In: Offe, Claus (Ed.): Arbeitsgesellschaft: Strukturprobleme und Zukunftsperspektiven. Frankfurt: Campus Verlag, pp. 100-120.

Olszak, Ewa (2014): Nowoczesny dobór personelu – kierunki rozwoju metod i narzędzi w rekrutacji i selekcji. Prace Naukowe Uniwersytetu Ekonomicznego We Wrocławiu 349, pp. 283-294.

Orosz, Éva (2018): Kontrolling tevékenység egy könyvelőirodában. Miskolc: University of Miskolc.

Papp-Váry, Árpád/Hajnal, Mónika/Czeglédi Csilla (2020): A személyes márkázás hatása a karrierépítésre - Egy egyetemi hallgatók körében végzett primer kutatás eredményei, In: Új Munkaügyi Szemle 1, pp. 38-45.

Piasecki, Bogdan (2001): Ekonomika i zarządzanie małą firmą. Warszawa, Łódź: Wydawnictwo Naukowe PWN.

Pusztahelyi, Réka (2019): Reflections on Civil Liability for Damages Caused by Unmanned Aircrafts. In: Zbornik Radova Pravni Fakultet (NOVI SAD) 53 (1), pp. 311-326.

Rifkin, Jeremy (1995): The End of Work – The Decline of the Global Labour Force and the Dawn of the Post-Market Era. New York: Tarcher/Putnam Publisher.

Rimler, Judit (1999): A munka jövője. In: Közgazdasági Szemle 46 (9), pp. 772-788.

Robertson, James (1985): Future Work: Jobs, Self-Employment, and Leisure after the Industrial Age. New York: Universe Books Publisher.

Szegedi, Krisztina/Mélypataki, Gábor (2016): A vállalati társadalmi felelősségvállalás (CSR) és a jog kapcsolata. In: Miskolci Jogi Szemle 11 (1), pp. 51-70.

Szira, Zoltán (2014): The Situation of the SME Sector in Hungary. In: Michelberger, Pál (Ed.): Management, Enterprise and Benchmarking in the 21st Century. Budapest: Óbudai Egyetem Keleti Károly Gazdasági Kar, pp. 107-118.

Szmit, Jakub (2013): Oczekiwania zmian ustawodawstwa w zakresie statusu prawnego pracowników zatrudnionych przez małych pracodawców z perspektywy związków zawodowych. In: Goździewicz, Grzegorz (Ed.): Stosunki pracy u małych pracodawców. Warszawa: Wolters Kluwer, pp. 376-389.

Török Emőke (2006): Túlléphetünk-e a bérmunka társadalmán? In: Szociológiai Szemle 16 (2), pp. 111-130.

Vobruba, Georg (1989): Arbeit und Essen. Frankfurt am Main: Suhrkamp Verlag.

Vobruba, Georg (2000): Alternativen zur Vollbeschäftigung: Die Transformation von Arbeit und Einkommen. Frankfurt am Main: Suhrkamp Verlag.

Wiktorowicz, Justyna/Warwas, Izabela (2017): Jak proaktywnie zarządzać wiekiem – MODEL STAY. In: Warwas, Izabela/Wiktorowicz, Justyna/Woszczyk, Patrycja (Eds.): Kompendium wiedzy dla pracodawców MŚP z zakresu utrzymania aktywności zawodowej osób w wieku 50+. Łódź: Wydawnictwo Uniwersytetu Łódzkiego, pp. 71-90.

Regional Public Policy on the Use of ICT to Support Innovation and Growth: How Can Micro-Businesses and SMEs Be Supported Through Collaborative Initiatives in Clusters?

Martine Gadille, Karine Guiderdoni-Jourdain and Robert Tchobanian

Introduction

In the early 2000s, at a time when the French national government was implementing a policy of developing selective competitiveness hubs to support regional communities of micro-businesses and small and medium-sized enterprises (SMEs), some Regional Councils embarked upon more regional development policies, inspired by the concept of "clusters" to support small businesses. The aim was for business associations to scale up their collaborative initiatives to the regional level as a means of driving economic development and innovation in the broadest sense. A regional cluster development policy was implemented in the Provence–Alpes–Côte d'Azur (PACA) region beginning in 2006, just as it had been in the Rhône Alpes region in the early 2000s. In the PACA region, the policy first involved issuing a request for proposals (RFP) to establish Community Economic Development Hubs (Pôles de développement économique solidaire, PRIDES) to be submitted by groups of businesses with similar economic circumstances and aims. In the case of PACA, "the size of the region's enterprises, which are smaller than the national average, can limit their development. One key aim is therefore to help them form networks (...) while improving their overall performance" (Région Provence–Alpes–Côte d'Azur 2007: 50). With financial support, these business groups would be tasked with activating five levers under the aegis of their strategic roadmaps: innovation, international activity, corporate social responsibility, staff training, and information and communication technologies (ICT). While the responsibility for the first four levers belongs to the region's economic leaders, this chapter focuses on the fifth component, ICT, which belongs to a cross-functional "Digital Innovation and Economy" department within the Regional Council. This department is specifically tasked with planning and leading the work of the other departments (economy, innovation, and research) through the allocation and distribution of ICT. It is also responsible for managing RFPs for the implementation of the ICT lever in the development of the clusters. However, it comes under a double strain: it has to overcome the digital divide that affects some SMEs and, at the same time, help implement networks and tools across shared business development strategies. While the issue of the digital divide between different types of enterprise often falls into the remit of the Chambers of Commerce and Industry (CCIs), with some regional support, in this case the region is trying to position itself as a leader through its financial support for digital innovation.

The purpose of this chapter is to study how these business associations respond to policies promoting the pooling of services, resources, and tools through the adoption of ICT.

From a theoretical point of view, we draw on the concept of the meta-organisation to analyse how public–private policies promoting economic development and innovation impact micro-businesses and SMEs. This concept, which is broader than that of the cluster (Martin and Sunley 2003, Porter 1998), enables us to consider the dynamic relationship between the practice of grouping businesses into local networks and policies that promote the construction of new geographical districts for network members. In light of both the rationale for networks's decisions to grant financial support and the way contracting processes work, there is a need to clarify and renegotiate the rules (Ganne 2000) governing the distribution of resources, and especially intellectual resources (Pecqueur 2007), with regard to market access. For our purposes, a meta-organisation is defined as a structure whose members are not individuals but organisations (Arhne and Brunsson 2004). In this respect, it has a transforming effect on a fragile environment because its own leadership, rather than that of the government, is what shapes its members's practices (Berkowitz and Dumez 2015, Dumez 2008, Gadille, Tremblay and Vion 2013). We focus on meta-organisations at the subnational level, with regional governance and implementation at the heart of our analysis. There are parallels between that regional governance and the role of intermediaries in the economic development of regions (Cooke and Morgan 1998, Scott 1998). More recently, the new economic landscape has called for a review of the regional clusters policy and the adoption of a multi-level governance model that regulates commercial and non-commercial relations between the different regional and external stakeholders. This region-specific approach to innovation would be based on sectoral diversification, international openness and a high level of diversity among stakeholders to reduce the risks associated with lock-in effects and self-referential behaviours (Cappellin 2010,

2017). However, organisations of organisations are not designed to be tools for improving our understanding of the relationship between new types of region-specific government policies and the construction of collective identities through business associations.

To answer our research question, we adopt a qualitative method that focuses on the analysis of three structurally different PRIDES: Culture Industries and Heritage, Business Tourism and Care Services.[43] Despite the differences in their activities, the distinguishing feature of these types of cluster is that they have regional groups and administrative bodies as clients, suppliers, and trustees.

After outlining our theoretical framework and methodology, we introduce the regional policy of the PRIDES as well as the geographical boundaries of each cluster. We then analyse how each meta-organisation has made use of the public incentives for innovation and development through the use of ICT. We conclude with a discussion on the relevance and limits of public policy with regard to the geographical boundaries of these very diverse business groupings, all of which include a significant number of SMEs.

Theoretical Framework

This section begins with a presentation of the theoretical and empirical approaches which, based on an understanding of organisational theory and industrial sociology, examine the relationship between the ways in which SMEs are involved in the social division of labour, and how resources and technologies are created and distributed within the environment through collaborative initiatives. This theoretical prism is complemented by research approaches that are more firmly rooted in economic geography and analyse the more territorial dynamics of businesses and how these dynamics lead enterprises to pool their assets to create new resources.

---

[43] The results presented are the fruit of a research project conducted by the authors, entitled "ICT-SME-CLUSTERS", and funded by the PACA region.

SMEs in Regional Economies: Between Domination and Emancipation as a Result of Collaborative Initiatives

The independence of SME owners in France has been a focus of research for many years. For example, on the subject of action by business owners during the institutionalisation of the cross-sector social conflicts (led at the start of the 1970s by the National Council of French Employers (Conseil national du patronat français/CNPF), Bunel and Saglio note that business owners with fewer than 100 employees[44] within the metropolitan areas of Saint-Etienne, Roanne, and Lyon wanted to steer clear of any collective action involving business owners and free to make decisions about their businesses unilaterally without the need to enter into any kind of bargaining (Bunel and Saglio 1979). According to Sellier (1984), the structural origin of this split within the world of business owners is the way in which larger businesses have developed in France, namely with excessive and economically detrimental technical engineering, bureaucratic organisational structures, and slow-moving consumer markets. By contrast, the work of SMEs is based upon the principles and practices of private reasoning (Sellier 1984). Indeed, in the second half of the twentieth century, any collective action led by SME owners tended to be characterised by urgent interventions in local production systems, that is in crisis situations, rather than by creative collaborative activity (Raveyre and Saglio 1984, Saglio 1991).

The creation of industrial districts has been an exception to the rule in French industry for a long time, despite policy around local production systems (systèmes productifs locaux/SPLs). The industrial districts used as a benchmark for the concept of clusters and related policies are given as a social and economic whole: their success is dependent on social and administrative aspects that go far beyond purely economic factors (Bagnasco, Sabel and Brusco 1994, Pyke and Sengenberger 1990) so they need to be considered in the context of global socioeconomic changes (Piore and Sabel 1984). In Italy, the traditional approach based on industrial districts suggests that they may have been the driving force behind the economic changes in the north of the country from the 1970s to the 1990s thanks to the specificities of the geopolitical and economic context, the social makeup of the entrepreneurs and the subculture prevailing in the spheres of politics, technology, and markets (Sabel 1994, Segreto 2006). In France, such structures are much rarer and have not always survived globalisation. In the case of France, however, Hancké (1998) pushes for an overarching strategy to improve the quality of French SMEs in

---

[44] Taken from a sample of over 50 employees.

the different regions based on vertical relationships with major contractors. Courault (2000) also argues that industrial districts should not be compared with French industrial systems that have a high proportion of SMEs. In the case of Choletais, a kind of industrial district for French textiles and apparel, Courault (2005) highlights its globalisation as an example of a successful strategic refocusing of SMEs. These enterprises now focus less on production and more on distribution, thereby requiring manufacturers to constantly update their offering. He concludes that this is a historically significant approach to economic development because, though rooted in tradition, it has survived in ways that largely ran counter to the dominant forms elsewhere in France (Courault 2006).

New Geographical Boundaries of Business Networks

The emergence of external economies of scale, with waves of international companies setting up operations and an increasingly educated working population, has transformed regional SME communities through swarming processes, often as a result of social plans (Garnier and Zimmermann 2006). At the same time, more spontaneous entrepreneurial activities have been undertaken by people with strong technical skills. These practices can be found within the newer types of SMEs that began to emerge during the crisis, whose leaders have been geographically mobile and are reasonably well educated (Ardenti and Vrain 2000). These leaders can rely not only upon horizontal networks between local SMEs but also on ones that transcend local boundaries (Raveyre 2005). Ganne thus refers to new geographical districts being established within the framework of globalisation: "for these SMEs, bringing all of their operations in house is less important than establishing themselves as members of dynamic specialised networks" (Ganne 2000: 70). These developments have made people reflect on these new types of public policy and question the logic of planning that is centred on redistribution and equity in order to ensure that each geographical district is designed to take advantage of and exploit its distinctive advantages (Ganne 2000: 72). The policy of clusters can be analysed from this point of view, whether it be a national policy (for example, competitiveness clusters and business clusters) or a regional one (for example, regional clusters, such as the PRIDES in the PACA region). According to the original definition, a cluster is a network that emerges in a specific geographical area, which may be on a number of different scales. The enterprises and institutions in these networks share close links, common concerns and an element of complementarity, leading to frequent and beneficial interaction between them (Porter 1998: 226).

For many authors, however, the concept remains too generic and unclear (Martin and Sunley 2003) and is not exhaustive enough to provide a suitable basis for decisions on government policy (Perry 1999). Bearing that in mind, we would argue that the concept of the meta-organisation is a valuable device. This type of organisation makes use of employer–employee relationships to plan and implement projects, using public and private funding, and not without tension or conflict, to influence the rules and working environments to which the stakeholders are subject (Arhne and Brunsson 2004, Berkowitz and Dumez 2015, Dumez 2008, Gadille, Tremblay and Vion 2013).

On the one hand, this concept makes it easier to identify the formal governance of a cluster, including both collaborative and subcontracted projects, along with the rationale for using public funds to try to promote the distinguishing features of the geographic zone. On the other hand, subnational meta-organisations belong to the wider industrial and professional structures through which stakeholders and other organisations interact, both locally and beyond.

The political representation of the meta-organisation as a stakeholder in the governance of a regional cluster, whether supported through public policy or on a more spontaneous basis, would therefore be reflected in the establishment of fora in which collaboration could be promoted and owners of micro-businesses and SMEs could work on their collective identities. This local but globally influenced confrontation between the rationales for reproducing or reconfiguring collaborative identities of micro-businesses and SMEs would lead to a part-restructuring of their division of labour. Whatever the scale of these changes, we would assume that, through the pooling of resources, these businesses's access to risk-sharing would still be closely related to their own involvement with different industrial organisations within their region or subregion (Gadille and Pélissier 2009). The results of our research on the use of ICT in SMEs reveal that, in order to be understood and applied, the adoption process needs to be integrated into targeted approaches that are both differentiated and specific to SMEs. These approaches form part of a continuum that ranges from subcontractor SMEs that do not even have a say in their internal processes to SMEs that have the freedom and autonomy to pick and choose which contracts they take on (Gadille and d'Iribarne 2000). Amabile and Gadille (2003) have shown that ICT adoption strategies within SMEs need to be seen in the context of the exploration and exploitation processes within their own organisations. These are partly determined by their strategic and even identity-based decisions on their degree of autonomy in vertical relationships. Finally, the use of ICT within SMEs is evolving not only alongside the emergence of more collaborative business models, but also through partnerships with trusted third parties when adopting more sophisticated e-business solutions (Brown and Lockett 2004).

The concept of the meta-organisation therefore provides a deeper understanding of how groups of SMEs choose whether or not to take advantage of opportunities to develop and use ICT to improve their operating environments, taking into account the governance and operational services with which they have been formally equipped. In our case, the PRIDES meta-organisation needs to try to balance the requirements of public policy with the different strategies and collective identities that existed beforehand, which led to their being approved as hubs (Gadille, Méhaut and Courault 2013). While the ICT innovation and adoption strategies in each of these hubs indicate the presence of existing collective identities, using public policy to harness the ICT lever could also provide an opportunity to enhance these collective identities. Collective identities are both the focus and potential outcome of a "transaction or negotiation" between social groups and institutions, or between social groups themselves (Wittorski 2008). At the same time, the sociology of entrepreneurs is focused on their companies's intensive use of local resources and on aligning their companies to local social regulations (Zalio 2004). The territoriality of these entrepreneurs can therefore be defined as the process through which they form a social and professional identity in relation to a specific geographical context (Zalio 2004). In our view, this context can be defined, on the one hand, by the characteristics of the productive systems to which the member enterprises belong (the value chains, sectors and any social and/or economic anchoring locally), and by the nature of the public policy (local, regional, and/or national) that is being implemented by the businesses themselves (Andreff 1996, Michun 2011). Moreover, the geographical identity of any social group implies the ownership and delimitation of a given space within the context of the increasingly complex organisation of social activities and relations (Crevoisier 2001, Savey 1994). Indeed, the meta-organisation is an indicator of this "territoriality" in that, together, the administrative and operational functions are supposed to promote improvements in the collaborative and autonomous capacities of the organised collective (Leys and Joffre 2014). It is therefore important to use qualitative, "bottom-up" approaches to obtain a better understanding of the operational behaviours at the interface between more flexible public requirements and private initiatives taken by businesses.

Research Methodology

Due to the investigative nature of our research on ICT among SMEs, we adopted a qualitative approach. Our research focused on five clusters, all of which were selected to be part of the PRIDES economic policy in the PACA region. Since two of the PRIDES studied are also competitiveness clusters, we focus here on the other three: the Care Services hub (Pôle service à la personne, PSP), the Cultural Industry and Heritage hub (Pôle industries culturelles et patrimoines, ICP), and the Business Tourism hub known as "Provence Côte d'Azur Events" (PCE). We conducted a series of semi-structured interviews (26 in total) and extensive analysis of documentary sources. Across the three clusters, 16 people were interviewed. These included civil servants from the administrative structures of the PRIDES, as well as individuals representing the member businesses and associations. As some of the latter are also members of boards of directors or other governance bodies, the data from those interviewed provided information on both the ICT policy and activities of their PRIDES clusters (in particular the services and provisions for member organisations) and on the expectations and uses of ICT by the member organisations themselves (micro-businesses and SMEs in particular). The interviews were conducted using two guides, one focusing on SMEs within the PRIDES and the other on hub administration.

The SMEs were asked about the perceived usefulness of ICT within their sector, the different tools used, ICT-related needs and the role played by the PRIDES in both analysing their ICT needs and the provisions being made to support their adoption of digital tools. Meanwhile, the leaders of the PRIDES (those running them, as well as the business leaders who were directly helping to set their objectives) were questioned about the role of ICT within the policy and strategies of the PRIDES, descriptions of the needs of member organisations, strategies for increasing ICT usage, specific activities proposed and evaluations of their implementation, and activities already being carried out, along with their results. The data collected were coded based on the categories in the interview guides and collectively analysed by the research team.

The Geographical Scope of the Hubs Before the PRIDES Policy

By analysing the geographical scope of these regional clusters, we can obtain a better understanding of the relationship between the administrations of the PRIDES, which are non-profit associations under French law, and the member micro-businesses and SMEs, that contribute to stakeholder activities to support the value chains targeted by the clusters's administrations. Our ultimate objective is to better understand how incentives for ICT adoption are implemented, and the roles of micro-businesses and SMEs as both stakeholders within, and beneficiaries of, the collaborative initiatives of the PRIDES.

The ICP PRIDES

The ICP hub was created and given PRIDES status in 2007. In 2010, it was also designated a "business cluster" as part of a new policy introduced by the Delegation for Regional Development and Policy (Délégation à l'aménagement du territoire et à l'action régionale, DATAR) to support SMEs within regional communities. However, the hub has also been strongly influenced by two earlier types of collective organisation. Firstly, as with all PRIDES, the ICP's sphere of activity could potentially cover the whole of the PACA region. However, it has a special relationship with the Arles area, and in particular with its CCIs. In 2012, over 40 per cent of the member organisations were established in this area (this rises to 60 per cent if we include the Bouches du Rhône area). It is this local aspect of being part of a geographical zone which strongly influences the relationship between the member organisations, the hub, and its administration. Secondly, because of relations previously established with universities and research laboratories, the hub's application for PRIDES status only materialised following the termination of an earlier plan to become a competitiveness hub focused on research and development (R&D) and innovation in the sectors covered by the hub. This background, along with the resources available for collaborative initiatives, led the ICP PRIDES to have a complex perimeter which is reflected in the identities of its stakeholders, the scope of its spheres of operation, and the structure and activities of its administration. This sectoral diversity strengthens the importance of the original geographical focus for the boundaries of the cluster.

Among the companies and associations in the hub, staff sizes are generally small (the ideal type of member for the hub, at least for businesses, is the micro-business). With regard to resources (ICT or otherwise), this naturally leads to a relationship between member organisations, with the hub functioning as a resource centre. The technology and expertise held by many of these micro-businesses also drives them towards collaborative arrangements between group members in tender bids, R&D projects, and shared technology- or information-based platforms.

The hub therefore plays an engineering role which supports these collaborative arrangements and solutions. At first glance, then, the ICP PRIDES lies somewhere between a structure like the CCI as a small business resource centre and a competitiveness hub, a hub for collaborative technological and/or innovative projects.

This complex identity is reflected in the spheres of activity of the member organisations. Within the heritage sector, three subsectors can be identified: natural heritage, manmade heritage, and cultural planning and outreach. Around these three areas, there are businesses, associations, and research and training organisations, as well as institutional stakeholders. It is therefore not so much a question of activating value chains within one or more sectors (as these would ideally go from R&D to distribution, via a marketing process), but rather the intervention of a set of stakeholders in the cultural or digital promotion of a given area, regardless of whether it involves technological, environmental, or cultural dimensions. One important objective of the hub is to create and maintain jobs directly or indirectly linked to these activities, and this has particularly been the case in the Arles region. More broadly, it is a question of developing collective engineering for this purpose, in which the PRIDES is responsible for both coordination and implementation.

The "Care Services" (PSP) PRIDES

The Care Services PRIDES (Pôle service à la personne, PSP) was created in January 2007 to bring together a significant number of third-sector organisations, and also private-sector companies operating within the social solidarity economy, in a network to increase and broaden their offerings, visibility and service quality, and improve their employees's training and prospects. In 2010, third-sector organisations (77 per cent) and private-sector companies (33 per cent) accounted for almost half of paid employment among the certified providers of the various social support services, from "comfort-related" services for households to children's services and assistance to vulnerable persons. At the beginning of 2011, the hub was also designated a "business cluster" in recognition of its support for regional networks of SMEs in the same sectors. More recently, in February 2017 when its PRIDES and "business cluster" initiatives were over, the hub signed a contract to be a national "care services" provider and extended the scope of its services to include health.

The PSP PRIDES in the PACA region was formed on the initiative of stakeholders and stakeholder associations from the care sector: those working in personal assistance and at-home care, departmental platforms, stakeholder associations, and groups of stakeholders from the social solidarity economy in the PACA region. The aim, according to the initial objectives, was to establish a supply chain model in the care sector (which is growing rapidly, for various reasons) that would be based on quality of service (either quality- or accreditation-based) as well as proactive human resources (HR) policies (skills, training, and social dialogue) in order to pursue objectives around social responsibility. This model, which relies on organised and licensed providers, differs from those based on direct employment of staff by individuals in need of care.

There is a geographical element to this hub, but the hub is made up of different types of stakeholders who are also part of other communities, locally and regionally, who share similar types of problems (as highlighted in the chapter by Julien Maisonnasse in this book). What is most important here, therefore, is the sector-specific aspect, even if public policy deals with it at the regional level.

The PCE PRIDES

The PCE PRIDES specialises in business tourism in the PACA region and was created in December 2007. It was formed on the initiative of four stakeholders: the Regional Chambers of Commerce and Industry (Chambres régionales de commerce et d'industrie) for the PACA region, the Regional Committee for Tourism (Comité régional de tourisme/CRT) for Riviera Côte d'Azur, the CRT for Provence–Alpes–Côte d'Azur, and Provence Méditerranée Congrès (PMC)[45], an association of 11 cities promoting their convention centres. The two CRTs bring together public stakeholders, such as the CCI, General Council and Regional Council, who subsidise and share the geographical area with them. Their objectives are to promote the region, generate tourism, and provide oversight and monitoring. For the PMC, which led the response to the PRIDES RFP, the strategic priority was essentially to develop the market for convention centre operators throughout the region, as well as the development of quality accommodation and seminar rooms for business tourism by extending capacity to host events for groups of up to 300 people, all of which would require an innovative and shared approach to marketing, based on the studies carried out. The leaders of the broadened PCE PRIDES therefore expanded its scope following a recommendation by the administration of the PMC, which was a founding member of the PRIDES. It led the integration of the two subregional convention

---

[45] Aix-en-Provence, Ajaccio, Arles, Aubagne, Avignon, Hyères-les-Palmiers, La Grande Motte, Mandelieu-La Napoule, Marseille, Saint-Raphael and Toulon.

centre associations (one in the east and the other in the west of the region) into a single association at the regional level. To broaden this network, the PRIDES system encouraged other stakeholders within the "business tourism" sector to join, including incoming tour operators and hotels, all of whom meet quality specifications.

The PRIDES also includes various subcontractors, partners, and corporate sponsors among its members, such as stand and furniture rental companies, sound and lighting companies, specialist and niche caterers, and specialist couriers. These are all niches that are occupied by SMEs and micro-businesses across both regions; membership would represent a significant cost that they may not necessarily be prepared to pay. The micro-businesses and SMEs in the value chain are represented in the strategic decision-making processes of the PRIDES in the form of a panel on the board of directors. However, the representatives of the convention centres and their institutional partners (CRTs, international development agencies and hotel industry federations) are still in the majority.

Hub-Based Collaborative Initiatives in Innovation and ICT

For over 20 years, public authorities at both the local and national levels have sought to encourage SMEs to adopt ICT and to use it innovatively and effectively, based on two implicit assumptions: the fear of a "digital divide" which would be detrimental to smaller businesses, and the hope that ICT, if adopted, would provide a strong boost to business development. A number of national and regional observatories and public support schemes for the adoption and use of ICT have been set up. The PRIDES have therefore emerged as logical places for such policies to be effectively deployed. They are a conduit for this policy, which they roll out to their member organisations and at the same time adapt to the characteristics and specific needs of the cluster. This locally relevant and, in principle, collaborative approach to deployment was one of the objectives of the PRIDES.

However, the resource centre teams realised fairly quickly that this policy was not always being properly implemented across all the PRIDES. This is why a specific RFP was launched with the aim of "supporting PRIDES and their SMEs with the adoption of ICT within their development strategies and activities" [46], in order to encourage their initiatives. The description in this RFP exemplifies the type of activity encouraged by the regional public authorities. This comprises two related elements. Firstly, the first objective for the administration of any PRIDES is defining its ICT

---

[46] Interview with a convention centre director, June 2011.

strategy, taking into account the current situation facing businesses in the cluster. Secondly, this strategy must then be deployed through collaborative initiatives among SMEs (through awareness raising and action plans).

However, the issue of ICT adoption by SMEs cannot be addressed from just one angle. Even if it is primarily dependent upon the capacities of a given organisation to make use of these tools, it also depends greatly on the economic context (in particular the lines of work or sectors) in which these SMEs operate, as well as on the shared support structures (clusters, professional associations, consultants and stakeholders, and policies).

An analysis of business practices among each of the three PRIDES under study revealed differences arising from the specific characteristics each case, but it also illustrated the sometimes-limited scope of institutional policies to support the adoption of ICT by SMEs and micro-businesses.

Innovation and ICT in the ICP PRIDES

This cluster appears to be made up mainly of micro-businesses, something which is characterised by its retention of a very local focus (the Arles region) with institutions and business networks that have existed for a long time. However, it is also characterised by its desire to promote collaborative innovation strategies, especially when it comes to joint tender bids or R&D projects. The role of ICT within the initiatives promoted by the administration of the PRIDES also reflects this diversity.

First, the shift towards a more CCI-style resource centre, targeted at micro-businesses, has led to a largely top-down offering aimed at a network that is itself made up of multiple micro-businesses.

The PRIDES introduced a regularly updated website to keep its member organisations updated on its activities. This website provides a range of business, social and technical news to the organisations within the hub. A collaborative platform was also announced with a General Education Diploma and collaborative tools for projects that involve several companies in the hub, something which had not been available before.

In terms of ICT, this can be seen most clearly in the initiatives of the Arles CCIs as reported on the website. The aim of these initiatives, which are not exclusive to member organisations within the hub, is to present customised digital tools at events that are open to members of the PRIDES. Once again, the CCI's ICT-related actions rarely come in response to requests. The offering is largely "top down" in nature. The plan was for this offering to be expanded through "Compétitic". This tool was set up regionally by the CCIs, the Regional Council and the government to give small businesses a better understanding of the wide range of ICT tools and applications available to them, which linked into their economic and management environment and the skills available in the region to help them set up their business.

Then, in parallel with this supply strategy, which focuses on the specific needs of different micro-businesses, the PRIDES seeks to promote innovation through collaborative initiatives between several members of the cluster.

The website keeps track of new RFPs and offers project engineering support. There is also a list of members called the "skills matrix". This list of businesses originally included a shared space for setting up projects, which enabled several enterprises with complementary skills to join forces. This matrix has since become just a list of the hub members. In reality, as we have seen, the types of collaborative engagement that the hub wants to promote often seem to require active intervention by the administration in order to help set them up.

Similarly, a project for a collaborative platform for heritage conservation and development has led to the creation of a business centre with coworking spaces for digital nomads, complete with access to shared equipment and a digital ecosystem. The region has dubbed this platform the "living PACA lab".

This strategy of collaborative initiatives and pooling of resources seems to be one of the hallmarks of PRIDES's help for SMEs.

However, it must also take into account the diversity within the different sectors that make it up. This leads to the question of how the PRIDES was able to help a cultural association organising a festival around Mediterranean cultures. This type of festival requires a lot of advance preparation in terms of organisation (selecting artists, negotiating with agents, scheduling, multiple channels of communication, managing bookings). This is followed by logistical organisation during the festival (welcoming artists and ticket management), and then finally there is the post-festival follow-up (managing and updating customer records). The use of ICT can transform the way in which such a festival is organised and managed, and streamlining the entire affair. Could the PRIDES help develop an app for all this, even though it would only be relevant to a small number of organisations within the cluster? The group ultimately decided to work with four other festival organisers outside the regional scope of the PRIDES to develop the app. In this situation, as has occurred with other clusters, there were more business needs in common with other SMEs throughout the country than with those in the local cluster. Collaborative initiatives, such as the development of apps, are therefore planned outside of the scope of the hub's administration.

The fact that the ICP PRIDES is largely established in a region like Arles means that the number of collaborative ICT-based initiatives that it can lead is limited, despite the fact that it covers various value chains. By contrast, in the area of awareness-raising initiatives and support for the adoption of generic "Compétitic"-type ICT tools, the hub's offering is more in line with the needs of the member micro-businesses. Collaborative platform initiatives therefore make it possible to align the geographical scope of PRIDES members and their specific skills with a view to generating greater synergies between them.

Innovation and ICT in the PSP PRIDES

In this PRIDES's member businesses, office-based staff managing at-home carers serving a range of end users make extensive use of digital tools in their work. For these staff, therefore, it is not the weakness of ICT tools that is an issue, but the way in which they are used.

Interviews with four business owners in this sector confirm the crucial role of ICT for both the assignment and monitoring of resources, as well as to inform performance indicators. They are therefore equipped with tools for this purpose. However, they encounter two limitations on use: one is financial constraints (linked in part to the "stop-and-start" of government policies), which restrict the level of provision, and the other is the multiplicity of the various regulatory bodies (and funders), which leads to a proliferation of tools and costs involved. This makes the management of these resources more complex, and makes their own oversight difficult.

The response of the PSP PRIDES to these business needs led to the creation of a website, including an intranet section for the administration and member organisations, and also e-mail newsletters.

The PRIDES also conducted a collective audit of its member organisations on their ICT uses and needs.

Finally, focusing on one service sector, the PRIDES expressed its interest in the emerging use cases of ICT at the very heart of this service, and in particular on the digital tools which facilitate care provision. It wanted to play a role in monitoring technologies and help with service innovation.

The ICT audit and management support from the PRIDES confirmed that ICT, which is needed to improve quality of service and the management of fixed costs, is often restricted by constraints imposed upon them by the funding providers. The costs of these uncoordinated external constraints limit their ability to invest in ICT tools that could directly support operational and management objectives within care organisations.

To respond to this at least in part, the PRIDES carried out a joint initiative with eight test enterprises to design and build a web-based management audit platform capable of meeting three sets of needs: those of managers striving to better understand their management environment, those of auditors or inspectors categorising the data to be taken into account, and those of developers when designing and building the tool. In addition, the project had to be able to integrate with business software already on the market to make it as user-friendly as possible. This web-based management spreadsheet had three objectives:

- To provide the subscriber businesses with a data repository that could rank their performance indicators, irrespective of the multitude of third-party payment systems. The aim was therefore to base the organisation of services on informed decisions (with actual costs), with each member having access to the strategic management data through the online service.
- To use this individualised (but anonymised) data for benchmarking purposes in order to find out the best (management) practices for a given service. Each organisation using the platform could therefore benchmark itself and discover solutions to help it improve its management environment.
- To offer an online service for managers with self-assisted learning in the form of practical online case studies on management challenges and suggested solutions. The idea was to grow the repository and develop a common narrative based on a shared pool of knowledge.

The design of this online tool was made possible because a major management issue arose among the organisations, and the hub's offer of support around these issues created an opportunity to standardise the audit approach that it was already conducting. However, this is still largely a "top-down" approach, and so its success depends on how well it is received by the SMEs that it is designed for. The tool was finally put online for member organisations of the PRIDES at the beginning of 2012, but it no longer seems to be part of the services offered by the hub today.

At the time of the survey, the expectations of the SMEs who were questioned regarding such a tool remained fairly low. Similarly, operational staff within the hub found that the website, and in particular the intranet part, was used less widely than they would have liked. In terms of initiatives to promote ICT-based knowledge and tools, it seemed that the hub took a very proactive approach that was in line with the ICT policy proposed by the region, but the organisations were more passive in their response, due to the importance of the issues that they had to deal with in their daily work.

Innovation and ICT in the PCE PRIDES

Takeup of ICT in the PCE PRIDES was essentially achieved through the design and implementation of a website platform with apps hosted by the key business stakeholders within the region. These shared apps could be divided into two categories: client services management and the production/sharing of marketing and business knowledge:

First, the front office function within the PRIDES is centralised. This approach is understandable, as 99 per cent of quotations are tailored to individual clients and require both adherence to agreed fees and a response within 48 hours. A contact function makes it possible for prospective clients to leave their contact details and specifications, along with their "type of venue", so that the provider could get in touch. After this initial communication via the website, e-mail, and telephone would then be the main means of communication with the service provider, allowing prospective clients to clarify their specifications, along with the negotiable and non-negotiable elements of the brief. The PRIDES does not directly position itself as a provider with a complete range of products and services, as these providers already exist. It is more concerned with generating initial proposals and quotes.

Second, access to formal and informal knowledge is pooled to support the strategic repositioning of the region's business tourism offering: market observations initially fielded by one of the two CRTs are made available to all members of the PRIDES. This includes providing statistical data based on both an exhaustive survey of the region's conference centres and on a survey carried out by ATOUT France and France Congrès of their members within the PACA region (Aix-en-Provence,

Antibes, Cannes, Marseille, Nice, and Saint-Raphaël), as well as research on the hotel and seminar industry. The aim is to evaluate the social and economic impacts of conference / event activities, to carry out an annual review of the offering of conference centres and seminar hotels, to measure footfall at their premises, and to follow up with clients and ensure their satisfaction. The results of the CRTs's studies (for example on conference delegates's spending) are also made available. The PRIDES therefore acts as an intermediary in disseminating information to its members and, more generally, to stakeholders visiting the site. In addition, the home page announcements of business tourism events (trade fairs, fairs, roundtables et cetera) in the region or further afield for members. The PRIDES manages the administrative side of registration centrally.

Beyond this platform, the offer of designing and equipping SMEs with digital tools does not appear to be one of the strategic areas to be developed for the cluster within the PRIDES administration. The education and training initiative implemented by the CCI for micro-businesses and SMEs, which is available on the website, is considered sufficient. There are two reasons for this:

- Given the membership requirements to join the PRIDES, there is a relatively high and sophisticated level of ICT adoption by most board members and the members of high-end hotels and international incoming tour operators. Some hotels are even developing smartphone apps, and the same applies to convention centres, with variations of websites that are accessible via Facebook and social networks. In addition, the creation of digital innovation groups by some major hotels is seen more as a search for differentiating commercial advantages, in which the PRIDES does not need to intervene. There is a fear of colliding with the rationales of companies to compete within the PRIDES itself.
- The interviews revealed that not many smaller subcontractors were involved in this; these companies used Doodle to coordinate their activities. At the same time, the administration of the PRIDES was aware that the 2015 hotel regulations might cause many small hotels (which do not form part of the current target) to close, with only the large or smaller character properties remaining.

The only other potentially relevant development in terms of digital services was the provision of a comprehensive overview of regional suppliers in database form. Initial quotes are prepared manually by staff who spend anywhere between a half day and a full day a month updating their service offering: they update their destination-specific rates as well as the names of the service providers that are associated with each conference centre. The various service providers are not all organised to generate and feed this supply of information into an internally shared database (for example price and product changes, et cetera). In the PMC, updating the database for each destination "would keep a full-time employee busy all year, more or less, for just eleven conference centre venues"[47], but it seems difficult to imagine that this resource could be maintained without further financial support, given that the cluster has now been extended across the region by the PRIDES system.

Ultimately, the PCE PRIDES, including its member organisations, does not think of itself as an integrative body. It can give out initial quotes and to put people in touch with the right person, depending on the prospective project's specifications. ICT does not have a significant role to play in these activities, and the adoption of ICT by micro-businesses and SMEs in the events industry is not considered a priority. Thus, differences still remain between the operating processes of large hotels and event agencies and the more bespoke methods of a broad range of SMEs, as well as the processes employed by small groups of around three providers working in collaboration within a local area (for social and sports events).

Discussion

The cluster policy, as defined in the PACA Regional Economic Development Plan (Schéma Régional de Développement Économique) under the National–Regional and European Community Plan (Plan Etat-Région et Communauté Européenne), was designed to support the growth of SMEs, even though they were not the focus of the policy on competitiveness hubs. By consolidating collaborative initiatives that were already being carried out by associations elsewhere, the region attempted to bring about structural change to foster innovation in the broadest sense (HR, ICT, marketing, organisational among others) within SMEs communities that were chosen strategically for the benefit of the regional economy.

By dint of the five levers that the PRIDES had to activate to improve the economic and social performance of their members, in particular micro-businesses and SMEs, the regional authorities identified an overall issue relating to the economic development of the region, of which ICT was only one component. In some ways, ICT can

---

[47] Interview with a convention centre director, June 2011.

even appear to be quite a technical resource compared to other more general levers such as innovation, skills, or opening up to external markets. However, by focusing on tools and making efficient use of them to tackle ongoing challenges, and on intellectually upskilling individual and collective stakeholders, this lever represented a key focus of public policy.

The administrations of the PRIDES, studied through the prism of their meta-organisations, generally sought to roll out strategies for how to achieve these objectives through internet/intranet sites, platforms adapted to their sectors, awareness-raising or training meetings, presentations of "off-the-shelf" tools, and incentives to engage in collaborative initiatives. But they also often found that supply outstripped demand, with SMEs seeking solutions to problems or needs which did not necessarily fit into the strategy of the meta-organisation or the overall strategy of the region. In 2011, the regional observatory of the information economy in the PACA region (ObTIC) drew up a comparative assessment of the use of ICT by all SMEs in the region (ObTIC 2011: 27). While technological equipment (computers) and software (office, management, internet, and messaging) were both widespread, other digital functionalities such as the existence of a website, customer relations, product management, collaborative tools, and digitised data management lagged behind. These observations are also undoubtedly true for all the micro-businesses and SMEs within the three clusters studied here. The aim of having PRIDES administrations activate an ICT lever was to reduce the extent to which micro-businesses in the field were lagging behind larger companies, and to trigger a wave of financially profitable innovation.

The findings of our research indicate that these meta-organisational strategies are strongly linked to the specialisations within these three clusters. Table 1 below outlines the identities and geographical boundaries of each meta-organisation analysed based on the following factors: the main objective of the meta-organisation and the area in which resources were pooled, the location of the member organisations, the regulatory bodies or public authorities, the location of the end users or clients, and the diversity of the business sectors and value chains involved. These factors determine the individuality of each meta-organisation with regard to the constraints on its activities, as well as the ways in which it can create and implement its own resources. The ICT strategies of these meta-organisations are rooted in these different factors, and are differentiated from one another even within the common context of public policy in support of ICT:

- The PSP PRIDES showed itself to be capable of using the skills of the people working within the meta-organisation to develop a truly innovative piece of software that surpasses the needs of its members, all of whom belong to the same industry and are subject to strict management constraints.
- The ICP PRIDES, which is firmly established in the Arles area and within the network of the CCI, offers support for the adoption of basic digital tools by micro-businesses and SMEs, and has attempted organisational innovations (coworking) which have been made possible by digital technologies, despite the fact that its member organisations come from a variety of different sectors.
- The PCE PRIDES provides an online platform which gives access to a front office service that pools information on services and products as well as shared market intelligence for organisations working in the same sector. It does this without identifying the issue of the digital divide among micro-businesses and SMEs within the sector as a priority.

Table 1: Analysis of the geographical boundaries of the regional clusters

	PSP PRIDES	ICP PRIDES	PCE PRIDES
Primary objective: shared resources	- To promote the provision of care services through organisations (rather than direct employment). - To offer organisational, intellectual and HR resources.	- To support three sub-branches: the improvement of natural, manmade, and cultural heritage. - To support clusters with resources and engineering expertise for micro-businesses and SMEs. - To incentivise collaborative innovation projects.	- To increase the visibility of quality business tourism services, including conference centres and event venues. - Support with client briefs and commercial database maintenance.
Locations of member organisations (local/ national/ international)	Throughout the region but sometimes grouped together at the departmental, regional, or national levels.	In principle at the regional level, but with a very high concentration in the Arles area.	- Local: convention centres, character hotels, incoming tour operators, small subcontractors (caterers, et cetera). - International: hotel chains, incoming tour operators.
Trustees/ public regulators	Largely regulated activities: dependency, care vouchers (third-party payers), but the	- Competitiveness: initiatives from the CCIs, region, national government.	Local networks to organise, streamline, and increase the supply capacity of the re-

	region does not provide funding.	- Cluster assistance with responses to RFPs and access to public funding.	gion's business tourism offering.
Location of end users/ clients	The whole region, as well as more local structures (department, communes, et cetera).	- Dependent on subsectors and the sizes of organisations and their ecosystems, but very concentrated in the Arles area.	National/European/International, local: Professional or academic associations, corporations, large organisations.
Uniformity/ diversity of industries represented and value chains	Common professional sector: care services through organisations. May cover all or (in most cases) part of the services involved.	Different sectors: natural/environmental heritage, architectural and manmade heritage, cultural outreach and promotion.	All aspects of the business tourism sector: conference centres, luxury hotels, incoming tour operators, service providers (caterers, leisure, culture).
ICT strategy	- Supporting tools strategy: shared platform for self-auditing of management. - Intranet for members. - Technology monitoring.	- Adoption of basic digital tools by micro-businesses/SMEs. - Corporate hotels, coworking spaces and support for collaborative projects. - Intranet for members.	- No strategy for micro-businesses and SMEs. - Web platform with centralised services for client brief support, promotion of services. - Use of digital technology for market intelligence.

Source: the authors.

The policy for leveraging ICT can be interpreted in two ways. On the one hand, there have been inconsistencies in deployment through "top-down" strategies, with micro-businesses and SMEs initially implementing the tools that meet their immediate needs, while meta-organisations establish strategies in accordance with the stakeholders who are heavily involved and represented in governance. On the other hand, incentives and support targeted at fostering innovation within SMEs could be made part of more bottom-up projects to promote the effectiveness of these government policies at the level of the meta-organisations of clusters that implement them.

In order to be better understood, these shortcomings must also be set in the context of national–regional relations. The regions first had to take over responsibility for administrative control and monitoring of compliance with legislation from central government (Law of 13 August 2004). Then, in 2005, new requirements were introduced for the development of regional economic development plans (schémas régionaux de développement économique). These proved extremely restrictive with regard to the conditions for negotiating agreements between the national government and the regions concerning the allocation of state aid to businesses. None of this was very conducive to taking into account the specific characteristics of individual meta-organisations's geographical area or to assisting neglected business communities.

Conclusion

The call for ICT-related projects to help develop businesses in the PRIDES led the strategies for micro-businesses and SMEs to adopt and use these technologies to be clarified. In this regard, our study shows that the hierarchy of issues affecting economic development is not the same as that observed at the regional level, as this sees the needs of SMEs and micro-businesses in a generic way, without the socioeconomic and geographical filter that legitimises the need for a meta-organisational layer. This analysis of the relevance and limitations of government policy with regard to the implementation of the ICT lever in SMEs within meta-organisations cannot be extrapolated to all the levers of the cluster policy. It also seems difficult to categorise clusters based solely on their strategic priorities in order to derive general rules as to the effects of government policy within these various clusters. These priorities tend to remain fluid and adaptable over time, depending on the prevalent or changing factors in play. Considering the aims of the policy with regard to SMEs and micro-businesses, the inclusion of meta-organisations within geographical and functional contexts that are specific only to them means that they are not necessarily a relevant layer, as Ganne (2000) observes in relation to dynamic business associations. At the same time, changes in the balance of power in national versus regional planning have not tended to grant the regions greater autonomy to offer incentives that are tailored to these new geographical configurations.

References

Amabile, Serge/Gadille, Martine (2003): Les NTIC dans les PME: Stratégies, capacités organisationnelles et avantages concurrentiels. In: Revue française de gestion 144 (3), pp. 43-63.

Andreff, Wladimir (1996): Les multinationales globales. Paris: La Découverte.

Ardenti, R./Vrain, P. (2000): De nouveaux profils de dirigeants dans les PME indépendantes. In: Courault, Bruno/Trouvé, Philippe (Eds.): Les dynamiques de PME: Approches internationales. Paris: Presses Universitaires de France, pp. 145-174.

Arhne, Goran/Brunsson, Nils (2004): Soft Regulation from an Organizational Perspective. In: Mörth, Ulrika (Ed.): Soft Law in Governance and Regulation: An Interdisciplinary Analysis. Cheltenham, UK: Edward Elgar, pp. 171-190.

Bagnasco, Arnaldo/Sabel, Charles F./Brusco, Sebastiano (1994): PME et développement économique en Europe. Paris: La Découverte.

Berkowitz, Héloïse/Dumez, Hervé (2015): La dynamique des dispositifs d'action collective entre firmes: Le cas des méta-organisations dans le secteur pétrolier. In: L'Année sociologique 65 (2), pp. 333-356.

Brown, David H./Lockett, Nigel (2004): Potential of Critical E-Applications for Engaging SMEs in E-Business: A Provider Perspective. In: European Journal of Information Systems 13 (1), pp. 21-34.

Bunel, Jean/Saglio, Jean (1979): L'action patronale. Paris: Presses Universitaires de France.

Cappellin, Riccardo (2010): The Governance of Regional Knowledge Networks. In: Scienze Regionali 9 (3), pp. 5-42.

Cappellin, Riccardo (2017): Ripresa degli investimenti, evoluzione della domanda e integrazione territoriale delle produzioni. In: Cappellin, Riccardo/Baravelli, Maurizio/Bellandi, Marco/Camagni, Roberto/Capasso, Salvatore/Ciciotti, Enrico/Marelli, Enrico (Eds.): Investimenti, innovazione e nuove strategie di impresa: Quale ruolo per la nuova politica industriale e regionale? Milano: Egea.

Cooke, Philip/Morgan, Kevin (1998): The Associational Economy. Oxford: Oxford University Press.

Courault, Bruno (2000): Districts italiens et PME-systèmes français: Comparaison n'est pas raison. In: La lettre du CEE 61, pp. 1-10.

Courault, Bruno (2005): Les PME de la filière textile habillement face à la mondialisation: Entre restructurations et délocalisations. In: La Revue de l'Ires 47 (1), pp. 59-78.

Courault, Bruno (2006): PME et industrialisation: Que sont devenues les PME du miracle choletais (1945-2004)? In: Lescure, Michel (Ed.): La mobilisation du territoire: Les districts industriels en Europe occidentale du XVIIe au XXe siècle. Paris: IGPDE, pp. 413-445.

Crevoisier, Olivier (2001): L'approche par les milieux innovateurs: État des lieux et perspectives. In: Revue d'économie régionale & urbaine février 1, pp. 153-165.

Dumez, Hervé (2008): Les méta-organisations. In: Le Libellio d'Aegis 4 (3), pp. 31-36.

Gadille, Martine/d'Iribarne, Alain (2000): La diffusion d'Internet dans les PME: Motifs d'adoption dans les réseaux et ressources mobilisées. In: Réseaux 104, pp. 59-92.

Gadille, Martine/Pélissier, Maud (2009): Les PME multimédia et logiciel éditeur dans le pôle de compétitivité «Solutions Communicantes Sécurisées»: Quel mode de gouvernance pour quelle intégration industrielle? In: Management & Avenir 25 (5), pp. 207-226.

Gadille, Martine/Méhaut, Philippe/Courault, Bruno (2013): Compétences et régulation des marchés du travail dans les pôles de compétitivité: Le cas du pôle Pégase. In: Revue d'économie régionale et urbaine avril 2, pp. 339-361.

Gadille, Martine/Tremblay, Diane-Gabrielle/Vion, Antoine (2013): La méta-organisation territorialisée: Moteurs d'apprentissages collectifs. In: Intervention économique: Association d'Économie Politique 48, pp. 1-12.

Ganne, B. (2000): PME, districts et nouvelles territorialités. In: Courault, Bruno/Trouvé, Philippe (Eds.): Les dynamiques de PME: Approches internationales. Paris: Presses Universitaires de France, pp. 51-74.

Garnier, Jacques/Zimmermann, Jean-Benoît (2006): L'aire métropolitaine marseillaise et les territoires de l'industrie. In: Géographie, économie, société 8 (2), pp. 215-238.

Hancké, Bob (1998): Trust or Hierarchy? Changing Relationships Between Large and Small Firms in France. In: Small Business Economics 11, pp. 237-252.

Leys, Valérie/Joffre, Patrick (2014): Méta-organisations et évolution des pratiques managériales: Une étude appliquée au champ de la santé. In: Revue française de gestion 338, pp. 45-51.

Martin, Ron/Sunley, Peter (2003): Deconstructing clusters: Chaotic concept or policy panacea? In: Journal of Economic Geography 3 (1), pp. 5-35.

Michun, Stéphane (2011): Les territoires au cœur du présent et de l'anticipation. In: Relief (Collection du Céreq) 35, pp. 47-67.

ObTIC (2011): Rapport de la démarche d'observation de la société de l'information en région Provence-Alpes-Côte d'Azur. Marseille.

Pecqueur, Bernard (2007): Des pôles de croissance aux pôles de compétitivité: Un nouveau partage des ressources cognitives. In: Réalités industrielles mai, pp. 38-43.

Perry, Martin (1999): Clusters Last Stand. In: Planning Practice and Research 14 (2), pp. 149-152.

Piore, Michael J./Sabel, Charles F. (1984): The Second Industrial Divide: Possibilities for Prosperity. New York: Basic Books.

Porter, Michael E. (1998): Clusters and Competition: New Agendas for Companies, Governments, and Institutions. In: Porter, Michael E. (Ed.): On Competition. Boston, MA: Harvard Business School Press, pp. 197-288.

Pyke, Frank/Sengenberger, Werner (1990): Industrial Districts and Inter-Firm Cooperation in Italy: Introduction. In: Pyke, Frank/Becattini, Giacomo/Sengenberger, Werner (Eds.): Industrial Districts and Inter-Firm Cooperation in Italy. Geneva: International Institute for Labour Studies, pp. 1-5.

Raveyre, Marie-Françoise (2005): De nouveaux dirigeants de PMI pour le milieu rural: Enseignements d'étude de cas. In: Norois: Environnement, aménagement, société 197, pp. 83-94.

Raveyre, Marie-Françoise/Saglio, Jean (1984): Les systèmes industriels localisés: Éléments pour une analyse sociologique des ensembles de PME industriels. In: Sociologie du Travail 26 (2), pp. 157-176.

Région Provence–Alpes–Côte d'Azur (2007): Contrat de projets état-région 2007-2013. Marseille.

Sabel, Charles F. (1994): Learning by Monitoring: The Institutions of Economic Development. In: Smelser, Neil. J./Swedberg, Richard (Eds.): The Handbook of Economic Sociology. Princeton, NJ: Princeton University Press, pp. 127-165.

Saglio, Jean (1991): Échange social et identité collective dans les systèmes industriels. In: Sociologie du Travail 33 (4), pp. 529-544.

Savey, S. (1994): Espace, territoire, développement local. In: G. Duche (Ed.): Territoires en mutation: À la mémoire de Jean Le Coz. Montpellier, France: CIHEAM-IAMM, pp. 39-41.

Scott, Allen J. (1998). Regions and the World Economy. Oxford: Oxford University Press.

Segreto, Luciano (2006): Le regroupement districal dans l'industrialisation italienne après 1945. In: Méditerranée: Revue géographique des pays méditerranéens 106, pp. 49-56.

Sellier, François (1984): La confrontation sociale en France. Paris: Presses Universitaires de France.

Wittorski, Richard (2008): La notion d'identité collective. In: Kaddouri, Mokhtar/Lespessailles, Corinne/Maillebouis, Madeleine/Vasconcellos, Maria (Eds.): La question identitaire dans le travail et la formation: Contributions de la recherche, état des pratiques et étude bibliographique. Paris: L'Harmattan, Logiques Sociales, pp. 195-213.

Zalio, Pierre-Paul (2004): Territoires et activités économiques: Une approche par la sociologie des entrepreneurs. In: Genèses 56 (3), pp. 4-27.

Employment in SMEs in the Context of Digitalisation: Opportunities and Threats. On the Examples of Russia and China

Irina V. Novikova, Olesya V. Dmitrieva and Roman I. Antonenko

Introduction

For SMEs, the use of digital technology is a strategically important solution for the handling of employment relations; still, it is often compared to revolutionary transformation. Information technology (IT) has opened up new opportunities for the development of SMEs, such as new markets and forms of employment among others (ILO 2019). A business that works using modern information and communication technologies in a competitive and efficient way is able to access and to integrate itself into international markets and function under global threats even when stationary employment is impossible.

Digitalisation is manifested primarily in the development of robotics, wireless technology, the Internet of things, and artificial intelligence (Schwab 2018). The introduction of such technologies can increase labour productivity in companies up to 40 per cent (WEF 2018) and minimise the consequences of different global threats of an epidemiological, terrorist, or endogenous (meaning natural disasters) kind. What is more, taking into consideration the latest epidemiological outbreak of COVID-19, the problem of distant work organisation might become an urgent issue. Digitalisation is a solution for this problem, as far as digital technologies modify existing working environment according to more "distant standards".

At the same time, information technologies come with certain risks of their own; for example, the possibility of digitising jobs can also mean the dismissal of large numbers of employees (van Est and Kool 2015). Therefore, it is necessary to keep a balance between the introduction of IT and the use of human labour (Novikova 2019). This balance can be reached only by means of working out an effective strategy for the development of employment in SMEs in the context of digitalisation.

China's Experience in Using IT for Increasing Employment in SMEs

The role of the state in supporting a sustainable development of employment in SMEs is primarily in the formation of infrastructure and financial mechanisms. China's experience of a state's active participation in the formation of infrastructure can serve as an example. One of the examples of the use of digital technologies for the development of employment in small businesses is Taobao Villages (Qi, Zheng and Guo 2019).

China experiences not only an industrial and economic boom and rapid urbanisation, but also has a multimillion population living in rural areas below the poverty line. It was among such Chinese villages that a new type of settlement arose; the economy of such settlements depends entirely on the production of goods by small enterprises, which are sold through the largest Chinese online stores. Figure 1 shows the dynamics in the growth of the quantity of Taobao Villages.

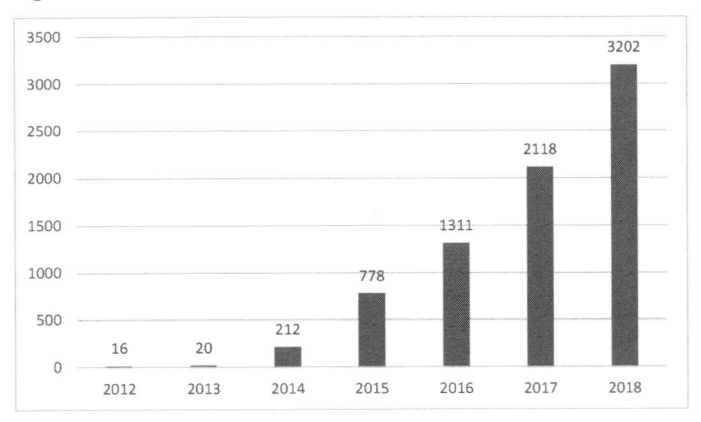

Figure 1: Total number of Taobao Villages (2012-2018)

Year	Number
2012	16
2013	20
2014	212
2015	778
2016	1311
2017	2118
2018	3202

Source: Sherry Tao Kong (2019).

There was a drastic increase in the absolute number of Taobao Villages reached between 2017 and 2018. This was because in November 2016, the Chinese State Committee on Poverty Alleviation, together with 16 ministries, issued recommendations for a massive development of e-commerce in rural areas. The state provided the most remote settlements with the necessary infrastructure, roads, and a broadband Internet network. It allowed slowing down the migration process of the population to big cities, as many people were able to start their own businesses and enter the nation-wide e-commerce sales market via the Taobao Internet platform. A digital platform (Figure 2) in a broad sense is a communication and transactional environment whose participants benefit from interacting with each other (Gribanov 2019).

An information and communication infrastructure that covers the entire territory of a country and provides access to international information resources makes it possible for SMEs to develop an innovative strategy aiming at sustainability. In fact, states that support the development of infrastructure and the creation of digital platforms provide the foundation for the development of SMEs. The development of information applications and digital platforms as well as the formation of an economic ecosystem are prerequisites for the transformation of the economy and its transition to digital reality (Berg Insight 2019).

Figure 2: Key elements of a digital platform

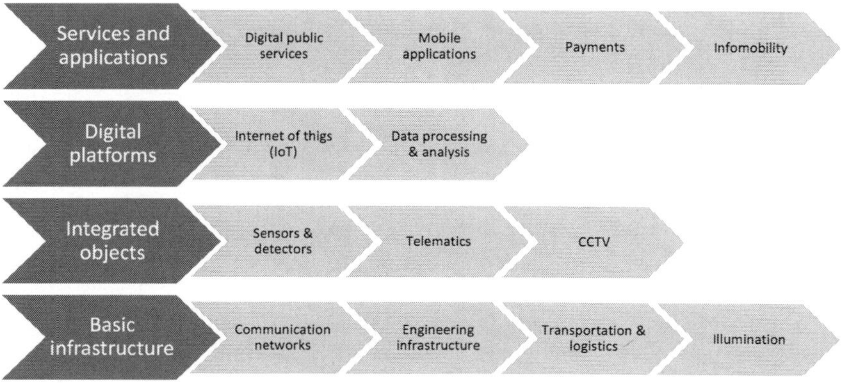

Services and applications	Digital public services	Mobile applications	Payments	Infomobility
Digital platforms	Internet of thigs (IoT)	Data processing & analysis		
Integrated objects	Sensors & detectors	Telematics	CCTV	
Basic infrastructure	Communication networks	Engineering infrastructure	Transportation & logistics	Illumination

Source: the authors, based on McKinsey & Company (2017).

The basic construction of the facility includes a whole set of parts, subsystems, interfaces, and technological processes as well as both fixed (basic) and variable (peripheral) components, varying from situation to situation. The successful operation of digital platforms requires a well-developed infrastructure and connected devices. The gradual construction of such an architecture creates new possibilities not only for communication, but also for the use of big data for commercial purposes, the introduction of artificial intelligence, the development of the Internet of things, and cloud technologies. It directly affects the development of SMEs.

Despite the regional economic differences in China, the measures taken by the Chinese government as part of the digitalisation project had a positive impact on the development of SMEs in various regions of China on a macroeconomic level. The total number of enterprises established under the Taobao Villages programme is shown in Table 1.

Another important factor for the development of the programme is private investment. The Alibaba Corporation has invested 10 billion Yuan into the construction of 100,000 Taobao service centres, the development of logistics infrastructure, and the teaching of local entrepreneurs on how to enter the Taobao market. The central government has signed an agreement with Alibaba and Jingdong (JD)[48] to set up another platform for the development of electronic commerce (e-commerce) in poor areas of the country. In 2010, Ant Financial (the financial division of Alibaba) launched a microfinance programme for small businesses. Since then, Ant Financial has issued loans whose total amount is four times bigger than the amount of loans that has been issued by the Grameen Bank[49] for 39 years.

Table 1: Total number of enterprises established in Taobao Villages in various regions of China (2012-2017)

Year	Region of China			
	East	Centre	West	North
2012	46,792	1,132	280	352
2013	73,650	1,434	716	448
2014	126,764	1,816	1,679	519
2015	170,850	2,433	1,844	590
2016	208,562	2,973	4,006	634
2017	235,221	3,277	4,086	702

Source: Liu et al. (2018).

---

[48] Alibaba and Jingdong (JD) are both e-commerce companies based in China.

[49] Grameen Bank is a Banglasdeshi community development bank which provides small loans to the impoverished.

Russia's Experience with the Development of Employment in SMEs in the Context of Digitalisation

Though the digitalisation process began in Russia about ten years ago, the official political decision to accelerate the introduction of digital technologies in the economy and social sphere was only made in the Decree of the President of the Russian Federation on 7 May 2018.[50]

The report by McKinsey & Company states that SMEs in Russia have a lot of potential to help speed up the digitalising of the Russian economy. They are ready to keep a continuous process of innovation and to cooperate with industrial companies, educational and research organisations, and high-tech companies (especially small innovative enterprises and start-ups) (McKinsey & Company 2017).

The current Information Infrastructure programme in Russia, which is supposed to run until 2024, could also have a positive impact on the development of employment in small businesses through the usage of information technologies. The main objectives of the programme are

- the provision of 100 per cent of households with an Internet connection;
- the provision of 100 per cent of medical organisations of the state and municipal healthcare system (hospitals and clinics) with an Internet connection;
- the provision of state (municipal) educational organisations of general and secondary vocational education with an Internet connection;
- the provision of Government bodies, local governments, and state extra-budgetary foundations with and Internet connection;
- the provision of the federal highways with mobile radiotelephone communication ("emergency call system");
- and increasing the number of industries which use 5G communication networks.

The state plays the key role in the implementation of digital technologies. The formation and development of infrastructure projects as well as the improvement of the transport and logistics systems within the country will allow trading operations in the segment of SMEs to increase drastically.

In the following, Table 2 shows changes in factors reflecting the level of digitalisation in Russia. The growth of all the indicators presented in the table indicates the

---

[50] Decree of the President of the Russian Federation No. 204 of 7 May 2018, On National Goals and Strategic Objectives for the Development of the Russian Federation for the Period up to 2024.

development of infrastructure for the formation of sustainable growth of SMEs in the context of digitalisation.

Table 2: Dynamics of changes in factors reflecting the level of digitalisation in Russia

	2014	2015	2016	2017	2018
Share of organisations that have Internet access with at least 2 Mbit/s in the total number of organisations	50.9 %	52.2 %	55.3 %	58.4 %	62.7 %
Number of Internet users per 100 citizens	67.0 %	70.0 %	73.0 %	76.0 %	81.0 %
Share of government bodies that have Internet access with at least 2 Mbit/s in the total number of federal, regional, and local government bodies	51.5 %	53.1 %	57.2 %	60.1 %	63.9 %

Source: the authors, based on data by the Rosstat.

The development of digital platforms and the creation of digital solutions and applications in Russia can be described with the following characteristics:

- a propriety of created device-dependent exemplary solutions combined with paucity of copies (which affect their quality and costs);
- an extremely limited functionality (consisting only of monitoring), plus a minimum level of automation of telemetry data processing;
- a large number of small players who are not able to develop their own products or solutions within the framework of the isolated systems concept;
- and the unavailability of commercial consumers who are ready to pay for the inefficiency of such solutions.

Despite the difficult conditions and a significant lag behind the leaders of digital transformation, digitalisation of SMEs in Russia could become a reliable mechanism for structuring the economy as a whole. The formation of fundamentally new approaches to managing business processes will allow Russia to build a system of sustainable socio-economic development.

Econometric Assessment of Opportunities and Threats of Employment: Development in SMEs in the Context of Digitalisation

To analyse the key factors of digitalisation in Russia that determine the level of employment in the segments of SMEs, the authors conducted a study using linear regression tools via the least square's method.

The timespan of the research stretches from 2014 to 2017. The study of this time interval involves the analysis of various aspects of digitalisation in the context of a low volatility of foreign currencies exchange rates and the absence of sharp market changes in the macroeconomic environment. The sample represents observations of the different regions (entities) in Russia, including federal cities, republics, autonomous regions, and capitals of federal subjects over a one-year observation interval. Observations for which there are no values of the dependent or independent variables were excluded from the final sample. The final sample is an array of 378 observations. Information for the study was downloaded using the toolkit of the statistical data showcase of the Russian Federal State Statistics Service.

In the course of this study, the absolute value of the number of employees in the segments of SMEs was used as a dependent variable; the natural logarithm for normalization was derived from the variable.

The following parameters were used as explanatory: the proportion of the population that receives public services through the Internet (EGOV); the share of medical institutions with an Internet access (EMED); the proportion of the population with access to the Internet (INT); the natural logarithm of the absolute amount of investment into Information and communication technology (IT); and internal research and development costs as a percentage of the gross regional product (RAD).

An equation of linear regression of the dependence of the level of employment in the segments of SMEs on the key factors of digitalisation in the regions was then formed as follows:

$$\text{SME} = 0{,}161 - 0{,}001 * \text{EGOV} - 0{,}003 * \text{EMED} + 0{,}009 * \text{INT}^{(*)} + 0{,}726 * \text{IT}^{(*)} - 0{,}013 * \text{RAD}^{(*)},$$

with (*) being significant in the 95 per cent confidence level.

At the next stage of the study, a linear regression equation was compiled using only explanatory variables that were significant in a 95 per cent interval:

$$\text{SME} = -0{,}158 - 0{,}013 * \text{RAD} + 0{,}008 * \text{INT} + 0{,}724 * \text{IT}.$$

The level of correlation between explanatory factors does not exceed 0.4, which may indicate the absence of multi-collinearity in the model.

The R-squared model is 0.723; the standard error is 0.760. A Darbin-Watson criterion of 2.006 rejects the hypothesis of autocorrelation in the model. The value of statistics on the Broes-Pagan-Godfrey test, equal to 0.0000, made it possible to reject the hypothesis of heteroskedasticity. In turn, the lack of autocorrelation, of heteroskedasticity, and of multi-collinearity as well as the high R-square value allows for the conclusion that the model has a high explanatory ability.

When interpreting the simulation results, further conclusions could be made:

1. The positive value of the coefficient under the variable INT (the share of the population with access to the Internet) indicates that the provision of Internet access for households is directly related to the level of employment in the segments of SMEs. This in turn allows for the hypothesis that the Information Infrastructure programme by the Russian government could become an effective tool for solving social and economic problems, since it is going to increase employment in SME segments.

2. The positive value of the coefficient under the IT variable (the natural logarithm of the absolute volume of investments into ICT) allows for the conclusion that employment in SME segments depends directly on investments into ICT. Practically speaking, the presence of a positive relationship between these variables may be a signal that, in the current macroeconomic and microeconomic realities, some Russian regional entities would be able to use the Taobao Village experience to increase employment in SME segments.

3. The negative value of the coefficient under the RAD variable (internal research and development costs as a percentage of the gross regional product) suggests that an increase in costs in the RAD segment has the opposite effect on employment in SME segments. In the context of the current study, the authors suppose that the negative correlation between variables might exist due to the redistribution of

funds in favour of scientific and innovative activities from the private economy to the state sector of economy, which, consequently might cause "brain drain" from SMEs to governmental corporations and state establishments. However, since the current study is limited to a short-term period, the authors do not reject the hypothesis that investment in research and development today can become a decisive factor in balancing employment in SMEs in the long term.

Conclusion and Comments on the COVID-19 Pandemic

Russia is only now facing a milestone in digitalisation revolution: Businesses and the society have already developed appropriate consumer habits and other patterns of consumer behaviour to accelerate and facilitate digitalisation processes. From the empirical perspective, we believe that overall, there exist some macroeconomic, geopolitical, and even geographical similarities between Russia and China. China faced exactly the same problems in 2010 that Russia has to face now, such as a modest level of digitalisation especially in distant regions and a level of digitalisation that can no longer satisfy existing business needs. We believe that the successful "digital" experience in China might become an appropriate stimulus for developing and implementing digital processes in Russia for both social and business needs. Taking into consideration this hypothesis, we have conducted research and concluded that various aspects of digitalisation do positively impact employment in Russian SMEs. Thus, we hope that our research could become a recommendation for further digitalisation of the Russian economy.

The COVID-19 pandemic revealed major difficulties in different countries to withstand threats of such a magnitude, also economically. The unstable situation at the stock markets is likely to result in a new global financial crisis. So far, no economist has been able to calculate losses and describe possible structural changes in the global economy at the level of transnational corporations, individual countries, or business entities.

The events of the crisis caused by the COVID-19 pandemic have changed the perception of security, external threats, responsibility, and cultural differences. Suddenly, the fragility and vulnerability of the socio-economic balance of all countries became apparent. At the same time, it has become obvious how useful digitalisation is in times of "social isolation". Food delivery, educational platforms, and digital medical solutions have become important or even vital for many people who are in isolation.

The International Labour Organization (ILO) predicts a reduction of workers in the world by 25 million people as a result of the crisis caused by the COVID-19 pandemic. However, digital technologies could significantly mitigate this crisis and provide new opportunities for building a digital economy.

References

Berg Insight (2019): IoT Platforms and Software. URL: http://www.berginsight.com/ReportPDF/Summary/bi-platforms-sum.pdf [18 May 2020].

van Est, R./ Kool, L. (2015): Working on the Robot Society: Visions and Insights from Science Concerning the Relationship Between Technology and Employment. The Hague: Rathenau Institute.

Gribanov, Y. (2019): Digital Transformation of Socio-Economic Systems Based on Development. URL: http//freedocs.xyz/docx-461882302 [18 May 2020].

International Labour Organization (ILO) (2019): World Employment and Social Outlook: Trends 2019. Geneva: ILO.

Kvint, V. L. (2015): Strategy for the Global Market: Theory and Practical Applications. New York: Routledge.

Liu, M./ Huang, J./Zhang, Q./Gao, S. (2018): What Drives the Development of E-Commerce in Rural China? Empirical Evidence from the Emergence of Taobao Villages, 30th International Conference of Agricultural Economists.

McKinsey & Company (2017): Digital Russia: A New Reality. URL: https://www.mckinsey.com/ru/~/ media/McKinsey/Locations/Europe%20and%20Middle%20East/Russia/Our%20Insights/Digital%2 0Russia/Digital-Russia-report.ashx [18 May 2020].

Novikova, I. V. (2019): Strategic Management of Labor Resources of the Enterprise in Industry 4.0. In: Economic Revival of Russia, 2019 61 (3), pp. 181-184.

Schwab, K. (2018): The Fourth Industrial Revolution. Moscow: Eksmo.

Sherry Tao Kong (2019): The Chinese Economic Transformation: E-Development in Rural China. URL: https://www.jstor.org/stable/j.ctvp7d4j8.14 [18 May 2020].

Wold Economic Forum (WEF) (2018): Digital Transformation Initiative: Unlocking $100 Trillion for Business and Society from Digital Transformation: Executive Summary. URL: http://reports.weforum.org/digital-transformation/wpcontent/blogs.dir/94/mp/files/pages/files/dti-executive-summary-20180510.pdf [18 May 2020].

Qi, J./Zheng X. /Guo, H. (2019): The Formation of Taobao Villages in China. In: China Economic Review 53 (C), pp. 106-127.

Websites

Alibaba (Chinese e-commerce company): https://www.alibaba.com/

Jingdong (JD) (Chinese e-commerce company): https://corporate.jd.com/

Grameen Bank (Banglasdeshi community development bank): https://www.grameen.com

Russian Federal State Statistics Service: https://showdata.gks.ru/finder

Decent Work in the Basque Country

Borja Pulido Orbegozo

Introduction

"Decent work" sums up the aspirations of people in their working life. It involves opportunities for work that is productive and delivers a fair income, security in the workplace and social protection for families, better prospects for personal development and social integration, freedom for people to express their concerns, organise and participate in the decisions that affect their lives, and equality of opportunity and treatment for all women and men.[51]

The concept of "decent work" has become a universal objective, as it is a key factor to achieve fair globalisation and reduce poverty. It was added as the central tenet of the International Labour Organisation's new 2030 Agenda for Sustainable Development. More specifically, it was defined as Goal #8 of the 2030 Agenda that "calls for the promotion of sustained, inclusive and sustainable economic growth, full and productive employment and "decent work". According to the ILO programme for the working community, decent work is based on "job creation, rights at work, social protection and social dialogue, with gender equality as a crosscutting objective".[52]

Concept of "Decent Work"

During the 1990s, European economies, pushed by technological change, underwent a profound restructuring. Globalisation on the one hand and the surge of the information society on the other hand led to the outsourcing of the economy. This triggered a reallocation of resources from the industrial and primary to the services sector, where the expertise of many people became obsolete and new skills were needed.

Workers have had to accept functional and geographical mobility, as they never had to do previously. The flexible organisation of production has forced them to

---

[51] https://www.ilo.org/global/topics/decent-work/lang--en/index.htm.

[52] https://www.ilo.org/global/topics/decent-work/lang--en/index.htm.

constantly change and to assume risks. We have moved from a "work society" to a "risk society", where the precarious, the individual and the imprecise are rooted. The difference between the "industrial" and the "risk society" is that we have shifted from a logic of wealth production/distribution to a logic of risk production/distribution, with risk being considered as the set of future threats, which depends on the decisions made at all times (Beck 2007).

The origin of the "decent work" concept was born in the globalisation process, which completely transformed the job market and labour relations with elements such as a flexibilization of the job market, changes to employment legislation, and a weakening of trade unionism and collective bargaining negotiation among others. In other words, it led to a loss of employment quality, which we could call a crisis. As a result of this deterioration of job quality, the term "decent work" needed to be coined and placed as one of the main cornerstones for the future evolution of the job market.

Basque Country

The Government of the Autonomous Community of the Basque Country considers the 2030 Agenda to be an opportunity for the Basque Country as it fully coincides with our priorities, namely, human development that guarantees essential services for everyone and sustainable growth that generates better quality employment opportunities. This is the Basque social wellbeing and growth model, which has now been furthered and bolstered with the unveiling of the "I Euskadi Basque Country 2030 Agenda"[53].

The I Euskadi Basque Country 2030 Agenda reflects the degree of alignment and contribution of the "Government Programme of the XI Parliamentary Term of the Autonomous Community of the Basque Country"[54] and of the enacting sectoral polices with the goals and targets linked to the 17 Sustainable Development Goals (SDGs) of the United Nations[55].

It thus links the Government Programme and the UN agenda in keeping with the latter and bearing in mind that the UN SDGs are not conceived to tell us what we

---

[53] https://www.euskadi.eus/.

[54] https://programa.irekia.euskadi.eus/.

[55] https://sustainabledevelopment.un.org/.

have to do, but rather to define a common universal context to help us fix priorities considering our territorial reality.

The I Euskadi Basque Country 2030 Agenda covers the period from 2017 to 2020, the same period as the lifetime of the Government Programme. The Agenda is focused on those objectives and commitments of the Government Programme that are most closely linked with the UN SDGs and which will be specifically monitored using the governance instruments and channels that the Agenda establishes. Thus, Goal #8 of the Agenda is to "promote inclusive and sustainable economic growth, employment and decent work for all", where eight commitments are defined and which lead to different initiatives and measures.[56] Those commitments, actions and initiatives can be consulted on the Basque Government's Irekia website, which is accessible to everyone.

The Partnership Agreement between the Basque Ministry of Work and Justice and the Basque Institute of Equality and Social and Labour Audits-IVAS-ASEE[57] in 2011 was signed to better comply with the Sustainable Development Goals of the 2030 Agenda and to contribute to a quicker and more effective achievement of those goals.

The Basque Government's Tools to Foster "Decent Work"

The Basque Government has tools both to directly support quality employment and to indirectly help empower workers.

Direct Tools

Enforcing the Law by Means of Sufficiently Frequent and Far-Reaching Inspections and Penalties and with Sufficient Coercive Power

Since the 2011 agreement, the Basque Country has performed the inspection function in its territory. Without prejudice to the necessary coordination and cooperation with the Spanish Central Government, the Autonomous Community of the Basque Country, in its territory and areas within its jurisdiction, carries out the tasks of the inspection function pursuant to current legislation. In any event, those tasks

---

[56] https://www.irekia.euskadi.eus/.

[57] https://www.euskadi.eus/.

include: (i) overseeing and enforcing compliance of the legislation, regulations and regulatory content of the collective bargaining agreements; (ii) technical assistance, that is, provide technical information to companies and to their workers, provide technical assistance to Social Security entities and bodies, issuing reports, helping and cooperating among others; (iii) arbitration, conciliation, and mediation.

In this last parliamentary term, for example, the Labour Inspectorate has intensified its work by reinforcing the aspect of combatting employment discrimination against women among other aspects of the Labour Inspectorate Campaign Plan since 2017[58].

Mechanisms to Receive Anonymous Complaints from Workers and Check Them by Means of Inspections

The Social Security and Labour Inspectorate has different contact channels for a person to make a complaint anonymously. This department of the Basque Ministry of Work has a Labour Fraud Box on its portal, a direct telephone number, and in-person assistance in its offices. Furthermore, this department has territorial delegations in the three provinces with contact telephone numbers and emails.

Employment Support Programmes

In most cases, employment support targets the most disadvantaged group, with the aim of helping them to enter the job market, if quality employment is guaranteed; in other words, provide jobs that guarantee "decent" working conditions. The different forms of support according to the groups which they are aimed at are described in Table 1.

Table 1: Employment support programmes (by target group)

Target Group	Employment support programme
People with disabilities	The Basque Employment Service-Lanbide has: (i) support aimed at maintaining the jobs of people with disabilities in special employment centres; (ii) support for fostering the employment of people with disabilities on the ordinary job market; (iii) support aimed at Supported Employment measures in order to foster the insertion of people with a severe disability on the ordinary job market.

---

[58] https://www.irekia.euskadi.eus/.

Target Group	Employment support programme
People with disabilities (continued)	Its purpose is to help companies not only to meet their legal obligation to contract workers with disabilities, but also to develop their Corporate Social Responsibility (CSR) strategy. Specifically, Supported Employment will offer support to a company when it wants to deploy CSR in the area of people management in order to guarantee equal job opportunities when contracting people with disabilities. Supported Employment means that experts will be made available for the company at no extra cost, and who will help it in the process to integrate people with disabilities in the company's workforce. Those professionals have a dual mentoring role, both for the company and for the person with a disability and in all the necessary job induction and retention processes. It means customised and individual mentoring whose aim is for the people with disabilities to perform their task independently and effectively, in similar conditions to other workers in similar posts and in accordance with the requirements of the company.
Women	**Domestic workers** Lanbide also supports the contracting of domestic workers to formalise their status and provide them with coverage by the Social Security system. **Women in vulnerable situations** Lanbide has championed the Emaktiva programme[59] for this group. The programme combines training and brokering actions with companies to improve access to employment for women in vulnerable situations. As a result of this programme, nearly half of the mentored women have found employment. **Women who are victims of gender-based violence** Lanbide includes equality criteria in its subsidy calls with clauses such as the following: (i) increasing the amounts of subsidies to contract women in sectors where they are underrepresented; (ii) obligations regarding equal opportunities and treatment in job tests, interviews, and selection; (iii) guaranteeing non-sexist use of documentation, advertising and images or materials used; (iv) women or women victims of violence as preferential groups in the access to some calls; (v) assessable training in equality of the workers of the entities that opt to the call; (vi) assessable track record in equality of the entity; (vii) balance representation of women and men in the workforce of the entity.

---

[59] http://emaktiva.org/es/pagina-de-inicio/.

Target Group	Employment support programme
Long-term unemployed people	Support for contracting the long-term unemployed aged 30 and older in work centres in the Autonomous Community of the Basque Country. Pursuant to this call, subsidies may be available for indefinite contracts, temporary contracts of 12 or more months and temporary contracts of six or more months, whose purpose is for jobs in work centres based in the Autonomous Community of the Basque Country.

The 2020 Budget has a heading for plans to retrain the long-term unemployed in green jobs, but this has not yet come to fruition. |
| People under 25 years of age | One of the initiatives from the Euskadi Basque Country 2030 Agenda is to drive a Youth Employment Plan. The plan pinpoints the following support:

The first is the programme Lehen Aukera [60]. This programme seeks to promote the recruitment of young people who are unemployed and without previous or hardly any work experience in jobs related to their qualifications. The programme tries to improve their employability through the acquisition of professional experience and to consolidate their entry into the job market.

Lanbide also has a programme called Youth Return[61]. This programme provides support to help contract young people under 35 years old who are returning to the Autonomous Community of the Basque Country, by Basque companies and to foster their entry into the Basque job market. Part of the support is aimed at funding the travel costs associated with returning to the Autonomous Community of the Basque Country.

Apart from those programmes, Lanbide has grants for training actions aimed at the social-occupational activation of low-skilled young unemployed (between 16 and 25 years old) of the Autonomous Community of the Basque Country.

It also regulates the non-work experience in companies that have signed agreements with Lanbide-Basque Employment Service, and is aimed at qualified young unemployed who, due to their lack of work experience, have employability problems. |

---

[60] https://www.lanbide.euskadi.eus/inicio-lanbide/.

[61] https://www.lanbide.euskadi.eus/inicio-lanbide/.

Target Group	Employment support programme
People under 25 years of age (continued)	Furthermore, there is the HEZIBI Programme[62]. This programme includes two types of support: • Hezibi companies: sign a training and learning contract of at least one year with (i) students for whom Education has authorised the conversion of the Training Cycle they are studying into a dual project, or (ii) students for whom Lanbide has approved a "sandwich course" (a training project alternating with employment) aimed at obtaining a Certificate of Professional Standards for which they are studying. • Hezibi training entities: allow the approval of a "sandwich course" aimed at obtaining a Certificate of Professional Standards.
Entrepreneuers	It is another key group of initiatives in the Euskadi Basque Country 2030 Agenda. The support includes the following: • In conjunction with the Basque Finances Institute and Elkargi, a new financing instrument has been designed for the new business initiatives. The aim of this new instrument consists of providing long-term financing for small and medium enterprises (SMEs). • The call for grants for entrepreneurs for 2020. The support to cover the selecting, mentoring, and/or tutoring of the entrepreneurs awarded by the grants is included.
Others	Lanbide has signed an agreement with the Institute for Basque Language and Literacy for Adults (HABE) to run Basque language skills courses, aimed at the unemployed and people in work who are taking part in training actions programmed or authorised by Lanbide. Lanbide has an Online Company Advisory Service, which deals with queries and answers enquiries regarding work contracts and allowances to support and monitor companies.

Source: the author.

Work-Life Balance

Every year, Lanbide offers a series of measures to foster the work-life balance of workers. The aim of this support is to encourage the contracting of the registered unemployed, for example, by substituting employees or cooperative members who

---

[62] https://www.lanbide.euskadi.eus/inicio-lanbide/.

have taken leave or a shorter working day to look after children or dependent or extremely ill relatives. It seeks to support workers' access to this type of leave (care for relatives) by facilitating businesses for the rapid and effective coverage of the workplace for the duration of the situation.

Progress in Safety at Work

Every year, Osalan[63], the Basque Occupational Health and Safety Institute, launches calls for private or public entities that run Basic Level training for Prevention Officers of the companies or of work centres of the Autonomous Community of the Basque Country. In 2018, Osalan launched calls for grants for research projects in the field of health and safety at work. In this parliamentary term, the emphasis has also been on implementing the Basque Health and Safety at Work Strategy from 2015 to 2020.

Indirect Tools

As has already been mentioned, there is also a series of indirect tools to support the goal of increasing the quality of employment throughout the Basque Country. We can classify them as follows:

Skills-Building of Workers and Jobseekers

One of Lanbide's fundamental purposes is to train jobseekers and workers. Every year, Lanbide runs courses aimed at improving employability and helping people enter the job market. The courses are programmed in two different lines, one prioritising the unemployed, many of whom with a hiring commitment, and the other mainly aimed at people in work.

These training actions, taught both in person and remotely, focus on the various levels of skillsets (from basic skills to those for the highly skilled aiming at a university education or other higher vocational training).

The training offer is divided into two specialities: the accreditable ones, which are the training specialities linked to a Certificate of Professional Standards, and the enrolled ones, with are the other training specialities not linked to Certificates of Professional Standards. Certificates of Professional Standards are an instrument to

---

[63] https://www.osalan.euskadi.eus/osalan/.

officially accredit professional qualifications in the field of the labour administration. Those certificates, which are official and valid throughout Spain, accredit the set of professional skills required to carry out certain work.

One of the new practices run by Lanbide is the so-called "Training Account", a service to increase individuals' employability by means of training itineraries adjusted to each professional profile. This tool is supplied with a person's academic information and the job market indicators. This means it can advise or re-focus jobseekers according to their professional skills, but also help them to adapt to the needs of the job market. However, it not only can be used to advise the unemployed, but it also guides companies to direct or redirect the skills of its professionals to meet market demands and helps them to increase the employees' skills and productivity.

In 2019, 7,409 training actions were conducted in Lanbide with 79,461 people taking part; 2,021 actions were aimed at the unemployed, involving 25,596 people (22 per cent of the average unemployed during that year); 5,388 were aimed at people in work with 53,865 people taking part. These figures do not include the company actions for their own workers, which do not enter in the concept of actions offered by Lanbide, but rather only involve mere financing of the companies' own actions.

Cooperation with Business Associations and Clusters

Related to the action described above, another way of supporting decent work is to cooperate with business associations and different clusters in order to give the best possible response to the challenges of the future job market. Thus, Lanbide has first-hand knowledge of the companies' needs and shortcomings to improve the training offered. The response will be more effective if the information that the Employment Service and the information that companies have as experts are shared than if each of the stakeholders tries to do so individually.

One of the examples that we could cite regarding this type of ventures would be the meetings held with different clusters. Lanbide takes part in the annual meeting organised by the Basque Government's Ministry for Economic Development and Infrastructures with all the clusters of the Basque Country. That meeting leads to meetings with the clusters that so request it and those meetings are opportunities to try to answer the clusters' questions regarding future employment challenges. For example, if a cluster tells Lanbide that it is going to find it hard in the future to find people trained in a specific occupation, they will be given information about the different training courses in Lanbide that could help them to train their workforce. If those courses do not help them to meet their needs, they are given the option of designing ones adapted to their specific needs.

Lanbide has entered into a Partnership Framework Agreement for Employment and Skills in the Basque Country from 2018 to 2020 with Confebask, the Basque Business Confederation. The aim is to work together to respond to the need of Basque companies to cover 100,000 jobs in the Basque Country during those three years.

Information for Citizens

Empowering workers is another way in which a government can obtain quality employment, and information is one of the keys to empower people.

For some time now, the Basque Government and all its ministries have published generated data on the Open Data Euskadi portal [64], where citizens will find a large catalogue of data to consult. One of the goals of this type of tool is for citizens to have access to the data that the different ministries produce. After all, the reason for preparing data and indicators lies in their use. Other objectives besides that are transparency and the fighting of corruption.

The use of the Futurelan tool[65] and Placement Surveys[66] could be one example of how information could help to empower citizens regarding the goal of "decent work".

Lanbide's Technical Office conducts an annual survey of all university and vocational training (VT) graduates to investigate the level of insertion into the labour market of each field of knowledge, university degree, or professional familiy. The published data includes employment, activity and unemployment rates, number of graduates, time interval between end of study and first job, and wage among others by sex, region, branch of activity, and occupation. The survey is conducted three years after graduating in the case of those who studied at university and after one year if they have a vocational training qualification. Once the survey is conducted and the data exploited, indicators are obtained on the job placement figures of each of degrees from different universities and VT modules. The information is then shared both with the students, who must decide on a professional career to follow,

---

[64] https://opendata.euskadi.eus/inicio/.

[65] https://www.lanbide.euskadi.eus/inicio-lanbide/.

[66] https://www.lanbide.euskadi.eus/inicio-lanbide/.

and with career advisors. Thus, objective information based on the data helps with the difficult decision to decide between one professional career or another.

Along with that information, the Lanbide Technical Office offers further support through the Futurelan portal, where information is available on the expected evolution of certain activities and occupations in the coming years, based on econometric models and the assessment of experts. That information is used to produce occupational datasheets on key jobs in the future that will have to be considered.

Thus, students can use the results of the Placement Studies and the Futurelan data to make their decisions objectively, using a scientific, data-based hypothesis on the evolution of the selected occupation on the job market.

Technological Upgrading

For many years now, the Basque Government has been working on supporting companies by helping them to access new technologies. It has two important entities for this task: SPRI (the entity of the Basque Ministry of Economic Development and Infrastructures tasked with promoting Basque industry)[67] and Innobasque (the Basque Innovation Agency)[68].

SPRI is working with companies to facilitate access to digitalisation and cybersecurity or even support them in founding the company in the first place. This entity is working different areas, one of the most important is Research and Development (R&D), which entails tasks such as investing in the development of new products and in the improvement of existing ones, experimenting with new materials, and managing day-to-day matters in a different way among others. It is what makes Basque companies cutting-edge, competitive, and relevant.

Another key area is Nanotechnology. SPRI is driving the "nano Basque" strategy, which aims to incorporate micro- and nanotechnologies in Basque companies to enhance competitiveness in the main business sectors and foster the diversification of the industrial fabric.

Robotics is also an area to mention. Robotics is undeniably one of the levers for ensuring that companies are competitive. That is particularly true in the case of small and medium-sized enterprises (SMEs), which need to automate their processes with flexible solutions that rapidly adapt to changes in their manufacturing

---

[67] https://www.spri.eus/es/.

[68] https://www.innobasque.eus/.

orders. SPRI offers training and economic, technological, and other advisory services.

In 2007, Innobasque was established with the mission of driving the development of innovation, the latter in conjunction with other stakeholders. The organisation now has around 1,000 member and has thus created a private-public partnership. Innobasque also provides the so-called Free Technological Advisory service to foster the digital transformation through customised and practical deployment of technologies that help make businesses more competitive. The service is aimed at Basque self-employed, entrepreneurs or micro-SMEs employing less than ten people.

Innobasque furthermore offers collaboration grants for university students who want to be involved on a compatible basis with their studies in Research Groups of the Basque University System, Basic and Excellence Research Centres (BERC), Health Research Institutes (IIS), or Cooperative Research Centres (CIC).

Innobasque also offers grants aimed at stimulating and incentivising research, development, and innovation in different sectors to enhance their efficiency, improve their competitiveness, contribute to sustainable growth, and foster cooperation between different sectors.

Supporting Entrepreneurship

The Euskadi Basque Country 2030 Agenda defined eight commitments, such as Goal #8 that includes "supporting entrepreneurship", meaning to "promote inclusive and sustainable economic growth, employment and decent work for all".

Among the various initiatives coming with this commitment, it should be highlighted that, in collaboration with the Provincial Councils, the Basque Entrepreneurship System is being enhanced to activate the cultural entrepreneurship in society and attract entrepreneurial talent from abroad, particularly among young people.

Another initiative prepares and implements the Support for Entrepreneurs Plan from 2017 to 2020[69]. It contains tax measures and economic incentives, along with the setting up of a "one-stop window" (*Ventanilla Única*) that oversees the streamlining of the formalities to set up companies, provides information on all entrepreneurial advisory services and actions, and focuses on helping and mentoring young

---

[69] https://www.euskadi.eus/.

entrepreneurs, women entrepreneurs, and self-employed. Within this commitment, for example financing formulas for start ups are developed and the recognition and social value of entrepreneurial activity and entrepreneurs is searched.

Fostering Participation

"Fostering social dialogue and participation" is also among the eight commitments. There are different initiatives within this commitment, including, for example, the reinforcement of the Basque Labour Relations System. Part of the Basque Government is the Labour Relations Board, a public institution set up as a standing meeting and dialogue body between business and trade union confederations, and as a socio-occupational advisory body.

One goal of the initiative is fostering social dialogue by means of creating and bolstering this standing social dialogue body made up of representatives of the Basque Government and of representatives of the most important businesses and social organisations.

The initiative also works on stimulating collective bargaining to improve employment quality, stability, and business competitiveness and to encourage the participation of the workers in companies. To give an example, the Basque Government awards grants for worker participation in companies. The subsidised activities are developing and implementing methods and tools that facilitate and improve the participation of workers in the management and in the bodies of Social Economy Enterprises, and the subscription of shares or stakes by employees among others.

And as a good practice, the design of the Employment Strategic Plan from 2017 to 2020 includes a participatory process for contributions to be submitted by business, trade unions, and social stakeholders as well as from other institutions.

Fostering Corporate Social Responsibility

"Fostering corporate social responsibility" is another commitment. The main initiative of this commitment is to "foster the corporate social responsibility (CSR) culture in our companies, with an emphasis on transparency as a tool to ensure the involvement of the different areas of the company in its development". In 2019, calls for grants were therefore launched to disseminate and deploy CSR in the companies of the Autonomous Community of the Basque Country. The grants financed activities such as preparing CSR training methodologies, the analysis of quantified benefits of applying CSR in companies, and the disseminating of CSR culture by means of identifying best practices.

Indicators of Quality of Employment in the Basque Country

Given the difficulty of building a synthetic indicator that measures the situation of the labour market in terms of quality, we selected indicators that allow for a vision of the concept. There are many indicators that, in one way or another, relate to the concept of quality (for example, in a project carried out in the Technical Office of Lanbide, more than 50 indicators were accumulated). These indicators are classified into two typologies: context indicators and impact indicators. Table 2 shows some of the indicators that were selected for the analysis titled "The Future of Work in the Basque Economy: Demography, Technology and Occupational Change"[70].

Table 2: Indicators of quality of employment

Dimension	Indicator	2010	2019	Variance %	Variance Absolute
Context indicators					
Employment - Unemployment	1- Activity rate (%)	58,2	56,2	-3,4	-2
	2- Employment rate (%)	52	51	-1,9	-1
	3- Indefinite hiring rate (%)	77,6	75,7	-2,4	-1,9
	4- Long-term unemployment rate (%)	3,5	4,7	34,3	1,2
Dialogue - Conflict	5- Working days lost by strikes	303.578	388.624	28,0	85.046
Economic Structure	6- GDP growth rate	0,8	2,2	175,0	1
I+D	7- Expenditure on I+D (% of GDP)	2,04	1,85	-9,3	-0,19
Impact indicators					
Work situation	8- Self-employment rate (%)	15,2	14,3	-5,9	-0,9
Wages	9- Average annual gross wage (€)	26.594	28.204	6,1	1610,79
Stability	10- Temporary employment rate (%)	22,38	24,30	8,6	1,925
	11- Part-time employment rate (%)	14,10	16,70	18,4	2,6
	12- Temping agency contracts (% of all contracts)	16,62	20,94	26,0	4,32

[70] Notes: Indicators 4, 7, 23 and 24 correspond to 2018 data and indicators 9 and 13 correspond to 2017 data. Indicator 24 ("Poverty risk rate") measures the percentage of the population below the poverty risk threshold. The poverty line is drawn at the value of income below which a person or family is considered to be at risk of poverty. It is a figure that varies depending on the income of the population of the country or region concerned; as the incomes rises, so does the poverty line, and as the incomes decreases, so does the poverty line, too. The poverty line is at 60 percent of the median income per unit of consumption for the people in a country or region.

No discrimination	13- Gender pay gap (%)	-23,60	-23,60	0,0	0,0
Health and security	14- No occupational accidents with sick leave/ People in work (%)	4,06	3,91	-3,7	-0,15
	15- Fatal accidents/ People in work (%)	0,0048	0,0032	-33,3	-0,0016
	16- Occupational diseases/ People in work (%)	0,29	0,33	13,8	0,04
Qualification	17- Employment with basic training level (%)	26,6	21,3	-19,9	-5,3
	18- Employment with medium training level (%)	23,0	21,5	-6,3	-1,45
	19- Employment with high training level (%)	50,5	57,20	13,4	6,75
Balance	20- Part-time workers with family responsibilities (%)	28,4	23,3	-18,0	-5,1
	21- People in work with general possibility of organising their working day (%)	4,2	4,2	0,0	0
	22- Inactive women where family responsibilities are given as the reason (%)	26,8	16,2	-39,6	-10,6
	23- Low degree of difficulty when combining aspects of work-life balance/ Working population (%)	47,2	38,4	-18,6	-8,8
Poverty	24- Poverty risk rate (%)	11,70	8,60	-26,5	-3,1

Sources: the author, based on data by EUSTAT, INE (Encuesta anual de estructura salarial, Encuesta de condiciones de vida, Microdata E.P.A.), Osalan, and Ministerio de Trabajo y Economía Social.

To summarise, with an overall balance of economic growth, labour indicators show more unemployment and lower employment. That employment is characterised by an increase of 11.3 per cent in part-time employment and a decrease of 16.6 per cent in job stability. The given period (from 2010 to 2019) furthermore was characterised by less labour conflict, an improvement in the conditions of conciliation, a decrease of the poverty rate, an increase in the levels of qualifications of the population, and an improvement in the parameters of occupational health and safety. At the time, the elements of discrimination between women and men and were not siginificantly decreased and there was a loss of purchasing power in wages.[71]

Conclusion

This assessment has sought to highlight the importance of generating and protecting "decent work" and quality employment, in contrast to the growing precariousness since the financial crisis in 2008. Both national and regional governments,

---

[71] Still, the above proposal of labour market quality indicators is only an approximation and requires a greater depth of indicators, analysis, and consensus.

along with business associations and trade unions, can develop and provide their societies with the tools to create a job market providing "decent work". Financial assistance is necessary, but not enough, as it oftentimes comes up only to ultimately one-off measures for specific moments in time.

New rules, business incentives, and policy measures targeting the economy can direct investments better towards areas of the economy that advance "decent" jobs, gender equality, and sustainable development, and at the same time provide a foundation for high value-added activities[72] (ILO 2019: 49).

Still, it is also necessary to change the current functional distribution of wealth, which is based on the allocation of income to the factors involved in the production processes (namely, work and capital). The functional distribution of wealth has changed over the past 20 years in many Western countries, where the weight of capital income has increased relatively to the work income. This has been happening in the last 20 years and is therefore not the result of a temporary situation, but a clear trend. "Decent work" is one of the fundamental elements to ensure equality and inclusive growth, and it is necessary to adequately reward the labour force, change the capital-work ratio, and make work gain more weight in the face of capital. In order to achieve this end, it is vital to have policies that protect all workers in the formal and informal economy and to follow the law on non-discrimination and the minimum wage.

*COVID-19 Annex

We have so far analysed the approach of the Basque Country to "decent work" and the emphasis it places on it. However, the foundations of the local and world job market have been shaken to the core by the world health crisis since March this year. Therefore, we cannot currently analyse the job market situation without considering the COVID-19 crisis and ensuing state of alarm decreed by the Spanish Government on 14 March 2020. In the Basque Country, both the employment figures and the number of people registered with the Social Security system in the first two months of the year gave reason to believe that they were going to be the best of the historical series (if they continued like this). However, the health crisis put a stop to that.

---

[72] High value-added activities are activities that generate high profits.

In the situation when millions of jobs are forecast to be destroyed worldwide, the Spanish Government's goal has been to safeguard jobs by applying temporary lay-offs, and both the Central Government and Provincial and Regional Governments have provided a series of aid for both companies and workers.

There are 41 distinct types of aid in the Autonomous Community of the Basque Country, including subsidies, financing, changes in procedures, new legislation, and labour measures among others. One of the groups most suffering from the economic effects of the health crisis are the self-employed; therefore, the Basque Government has placed special importance on protecting them.

The world is facing an unprecedented challenge. A disruptive element has joined climate change, demographic changes, and modern technologies. The world faces a pandemic produced by an unknown virus, decreed states of alarm aiming at softening the impact on people's health, and an ensuing paralysation of the social and economic life. The impact of the crisis on the job market is still unknown.

References

Beck, Ulrich (2007): Un nuevo mundo feliz, la precariedad del mercado de trabajo en la era de la globalización. Barcelona: Paidós.

International Labour Organization (ILO) (2019): Work for a Brighter Future. URL: https://www.ilo.org/wcmsp5/groups/public/---dgreports/---cabinet/documents/publication/wcms_662410.pdf [11 June 2020].

Ramos Salazar, Javier (2020): El futuro del trabajo en la economía vasca: demografía, tecnología y cambio ocupacional. In: Revista Ekonomiaz - XXXV. Aniversario, 2020.

Websites

Emaktiva: http://emaktiva.org/es/pagina-de-inicio/

Estatistika Erakundea (EUSTAT). Instituto Vasco de Estadística - Indicadores Estructurales - https://www.eustat.eus/movil/indicadores/indicadoresEstruc.html

Euskadi (Autonomous Community of the Basque Country): https://www.euskadi.eus/inicio/

Innobasque (Basque Innovation Agency): https://www.innobasque.eus/

International Labour Organization (ILO): https://www.ilo.org/global/lang--en/index.htm

International Labour Organization (ILO) - Decent Work: https://www.ilo.org/global/topics/decent-work/lang--en/index.htm

Irekia (tool of Open Government in the Basque Country): https://www.irekia.euskadi.eus/

Instituto Nacional de Estadística (INE) (Statistical Organisation in Spain) - Encuesta anual de estructura salarial, Encuesta de condiciones de vida, Microdata E.P.A.: https://www.ine.es/en/

Ministerio de Trabajo y Economía Social, Gobierno de España (Ministry of Work and Economy, National Government of Spain): http://www.mitramiss.gob.es/

Open Data Euskadi: https://opendata.euskadi.eus/inicio/

Osalan. Instituto Vasco de Seguridad y Salud Laborales (Basque Occupational Health and Safety Institute): https://www.osalan.euskadi.eus/osalan/

SPRI Group (Basque business development agency, Basque Ministry of Economic Development and Infrastructures): https://www.spri.eus/es/

United Nations (UN) - Sustainable Development Goals (SDGs): https://sustainabledevelopment.un.org/

2.2. Challenges for Policy Makers

SMEs in the Economy of Russia: Regional and Industry Aspects

Nina Oding

Introduction

Small and medium-sized enterprises (SMEs) are a relatively new phenomenon in the economic and social life of Russia. This form of organisation provides jobs for millions of workers. According to state statistics, the number of these enterprises is constantly increasing. However, the share of small enterprises in the economy is still small when compared with developed countries, which makes sense from a historical point of view. In Europe, medium-sized and large enterprises grew from small enterprises, while in the post-Soviet countries, where large enterprises predominated that had lost the tradition of the small business, private initiative developed only with difficulty.

In recent years, the organisation of SMEs in Russia has become easier. However, a successful participation of SMEs in the market is challenged by laws and the increasing regulation of various industries through several requirements and rules.

When SMEs first developed in Russia, they mainly did so in the area of trade. In recent years, their presence in other sectors of the economy has also become noticeable. This development was facilitated by the expansion of opportunities for organising production in new industries, the development of cooperative ties, and stimulation by the state. Also, the search and hiring of personnel of the appropriate qualifications in SMEs is highly flexible.

The main resource for SMEs is employees. Also, the structure of the enterprise and the management system are different from those inherent in large enterprises. Accordingly, the task of selecting and organising the work of personnel oriented towards the performance of multitasking functions is extremely important for ensuring efficient functioning. To reduce costs, the employer offers employees to combine various functions in a small enterprise, which requires the use of new methods of selection and motivation of staff.

Development of SMEs in Russia

Compared to European countries, the share of SMEs in Russia is significantly smaller; SMEs make up for 21 per cent of the gross domestic product (GDP) in Russia, whereas they make up for more than 60 per cent of the GDP in the economies of the European countries. Furthermore, the number of SMEs per 1,000 people in Russia is at 27.6, which is lower than the figures for Europe, China, and the world (OECD 2019).

Traditionally, SMEs operate in the areas of trade, service, repair, and construction. In other words, SMEs work in service sectors with low entry costs and resource requirements, notably wholesale, retail trade, and construction. As noted in the OECD survey (OECD 2019), relatively fewer SMEs operate in the manufacturing sector. SMEs in the manufacturing sector can be found in those areas that are capital or knowledge-intensive, requiring a larger scale of production. Nonetheless, SMEs even dominate some knowledge-intensive services such as advertising, market research, and other professional, scientific, and technical activities as well as legal, accounting, and management services (OECD 2019).

The OECD study points at the connection between sectors with lower productivity and lower wages. Although SMEs can outperform large enterprises in some services sectors, most new firm and job creation takes place in sectors with below average productivity levels. In addition, new firms are often born small, which causes productivity gaps between small and large firms at the aggregate business level. The lower productivity of SMEs has resulted in more low-paid jobs. SMEs, even the larger ones, typically pay employees around 20 per cent less than large firms. Between 2010 and 2016, close to 90 per cent of the new jobs in France, 75 per cent in the United States, and 66 per cent each in Germany and the United Kingdom were in lower-wage sectors. SMEs as drivers of job creation need higher investment in skills, innovation, and tech to boost wages and productivity (OECD 2019).

The main problem of SMEs in Russia is not their small share of the country's economy, but the lack of significant dynamics and of a growth in the number of and employment at them.

In Russia, statistically, the number of SMEs seems stable, with a slight upward trend. A certain increase in growth rates between 2016 and 2018 was an exception, and the real pace is more modest. Moreover, the tendency to a decrease in the number of employees at SMEs has stabilised, too (Figures 1, 2).

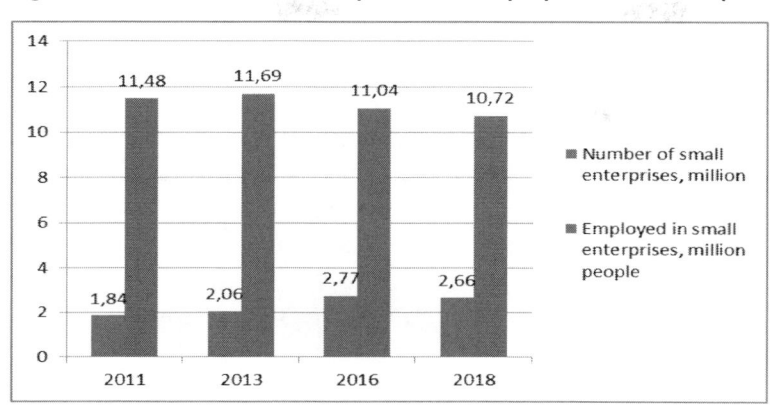

Figure 1: Number of small enterprises and employment in Russia (2011-2018)

[Bar chart showing:
- 2011: Number of small enterprises 1.84 million; Employed 11.48 million
- 2013: 2.06; 11.69
- 2016: 2.77; 11.04
- 2018: 2.66; 10.72]

Source: Rosstat (2013a: 632, 2019a: 634).

Figure 2: Employment in medium-sized enterprises in Russia (2012-2018) (in thousand people)

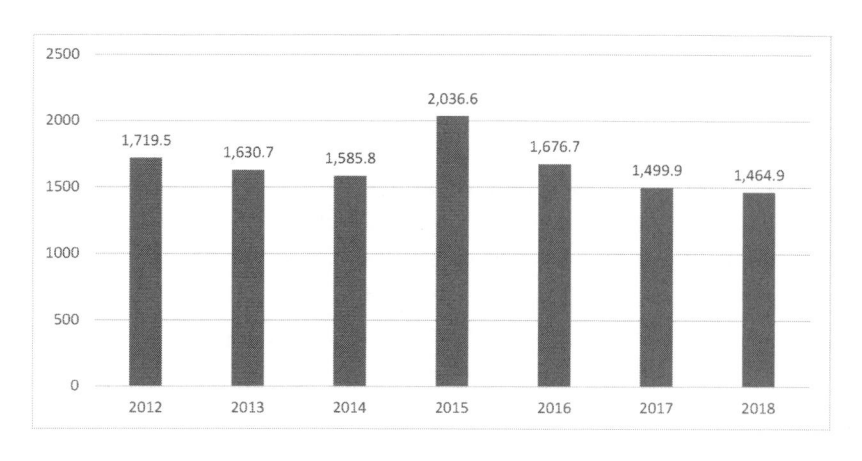

[Bar chart showing:
- 2012: 1,719.5
- 2013: 1,630.7
- 2014: 1,585.8
- 2015: 2,036.6
- 2016: 1,676.7
- 2017: 1,499.9
- 2018: 1,464.9]

Source: Rosstat (2013b: 9).

According to the Audit Chamber (2019), the number of workers employed in the SME sector (including microenterprises) did not change significantly, rising between 2015 and 2018 from 18.9 to 19.3 million people only. The number of SMEs (again, including microenterprises) remained at approximately the same level, namely, rising in the same period from 5.5 to 6 million only, while the number of medium-sized enterprises decreased from 20.4 to 16.7 thousand (Audit Chamber 2019).

Why does the number of new enterprises and jobs in the SME sector not increase? According to estimates of the SberData project by the Sberbank from August 2018 to March 2019[73], the number of active SMEs in Russia increased by 0.3 per cent; a year earlier, the growth rate was much higher with 11.8 per cent for the same period of time (calculations are based on data from the SME registry by the Federal Tax Service and bank transactions with Sberbank). Sberbank explains the figures by the stabilisation of the situation after the rapid recovery of company activity between 2017 and 2018 (Matovnikov et al. 2019) (Figure 3). An alternative explanation may be that in recent years, several regulatory legal acts have been adopted to legalise the informal sector of the economy, which has led to an increase in growth rates. It should be borne in mind that in about 50 regions (more than half of the regions of Russia), the number of SMEs decreased, but in most regions, the number of microenterprises (which are included in the concept of SMEs) nevertheless increased. The criteria for referring to small and medium-sized enterprises in Russia are the number of employees and the annual volume revenue. In the Russian statistics, microenterprises are considered separately, and they are not included in the number of SMEs.[74]

Such developments might be rooted in the new, widespread practice of adapting small businesses to new risks. For example, new enterprises are often re-registered old businesses that seek to fall under tax holidays and avoid inspections. In addition, small enterprises take advantage by transferring staff to individual contracts, thus transforming a small enterprise into the status of an individual entrepreneur.

---

[73] The SberData project is an initiative of Sberbank for processing and analysing big data. Based on information obtained from payment systems and publicly available sources, bank experts provide quantitative characteristics of the socio-economic processes taking place in the country at the macro and microeconomic levels.

[74] Per definition commonly used in Russia, medium-sized enterprises employ fewer than 250 people and their annual revenue does not exceed 2 billion roubles. Small enterprises employ not more than 100 people and their annual revenue does not exceed 800 million roubles. Microenterprises employ not more than 15 people and their annual revenue does not exceed 120 million roubles.

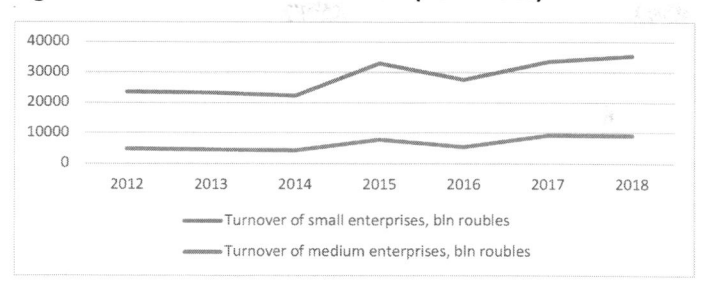

Figure 3: Turnover of SMEs in Russia (2012-2018)

```
40000
30000
20000
10000
    0
      2012   2013   2014   2015   2016   2017   2018
         ——— Turnover of small enterprises, bln roubles
         ——— Turnover of medium enterprises, bln roubles
```

Sources: Rosstat (2013a: 632, 2019a: 634, 2019c: 9).

There are still disputes in the Russian society over the poor development of SMEs in the country. In their study on the Development of Small and Medium-Sized Businesses in Russia, Sberbank claims that only 2.9 per cent of Russians conduct their own legal SMEs in March 2019, and the reason for this is that Russians are weak in entrepreneurship (Matovnikov et al. 2019). However, that does not exhaust all the possible explanations for this phenomenon. It should be borne in mind that between 25 to 40 per cent of the Russian economy consists of undeclared business. The low share of SMEs in Russia could also be explained by the tendency to stay undeclared business, as businesses do not trust the state and its capability to insure risks. The number of SMEs in Russia will only increase if business conditions change and if entrepreneurs start to officially register their businesses.

The COVID-19 crisis revealed once again the attitude of the Russian state towards SMEs. At first, there was no help at all, and then, in the light of negative comparisons with the actions of Western governments, the Russian government was finally forced to take action, but provided only partial and insignificant measures, such as delaying fines for non-payment of rents.

Small businesses are trying to strategically occupy niches that are predicted to be still in demand in the future, such as trade and catering, while other industry branches are avoided because they are fraught with high risks. Some small businesses with low profitability remain in the realm of undeclared business, thus avoiding the payment of taxes. Other small enterprises conduct business on the Internet for the purpose of saving on taxes as well as on rent. In other words, small businesses are adapting to the government regulation in the form a mere survival strategy, whereas large businesses (primarily the fuel and energy complex) profit from state support.

The nature of small business is transforming. The so-called one-day firms dominate the field and the majority of small enterprises remains in the realm of undeclared business because of an unfavourable business environment. Small businesses face excessive regulations and inspections and the demand of the population decreases due to the reduction of real incomes. This explains the lack of growth dynamics of the SME sector in Russia and a decrease in the number of employees in this sector.

Current Problems

Traditionally, the development of SMEs is considered as one of the main strands of diversification of the Russian economy. Nowadays, the development of SMEs has become one of the federal priorities; the goal is an increase in the number of employees in SMEs by six million people. According to the Strategy for the Development of Small and Medium-Sized Enterprises in Russia[75], the share of employees in SMEs of the total employed population should be 35 per cent by 2030. Considering the current state of SMEs in Russia, it is questionable if this goal can be achieved.

Although formal conditions have improved, as can be seen in the Doing Business 2020 ranking for Russia by the World Bank Group (2020), regional differences are great and the negative effects due to businesses remaining unregistered/informal prevail. The SMEs sector declined due to a decrease in demand, the introduction of online cash registers, and an increase in the value added tax (VAT). The official tax burden published by the Federal Tax Service for several types of activities ranges from 2 per cent to 10 per cent on average. However, the real costs for entrepreneurs are much higher, including Plato (a charge for heavy vehicles), overhaul fee for residents, environmental tax, excise taxes, trade tax, the recently introduced tourist tax, and increased port taxes. According to various estimates, the number of all kinds of mandatory non-tax payments amounted up to 50 or 70 in 2016. Revenues from so-called "quasi taxes" are close to 1 trillion roubles per year, according to estimates by the Audit Chamber (2019).

---

[75] http://static.government.ru/media/files/jFDd9wbAbApxgEiHNaXHveytq7hfPO96.pdf

The Russian state has created a multilateral system of support for SMEs, which includes direct and indirect support measures through infrastructure and development institutions. Direct measures include the provision of subsidies, soft loans, and special conditions for public procurement under federal procurement laws. Indirect measures include special tax regimes, simplified accounting, statistical reporting, free consultations, business training, and free admission to exhibitions and fairs.

In the literature, these measures of state support were estimated with mixed results. The calculations of many authors have shown that unexpected effects accompany massive support (such as subsidies and loans), effective entrepreneurs are ousted from the market (Shane 2009), and productivity and efficiency decrease.

The Russian authors Barinova and Zemtsov (2018) examined whether state support influences the development of SMEs in the different regions and why state support in Russia has little effect or affects an insignificant share of small enterprises only. Related problems are poorly developed institutions of social control (audit and antitrust control), little competition in the Russian market, little effects of direct support measures on the development of SMEs, and a weak SME sector in general. The volume of state aid is insufficient for the tasks of real growth of small businesses and diversification of the economy (Barinova and Zemtsov 2018).

The non-government Association "Support for the Development of Foreign Economic Activity" studied the conditions for SMEs in 2017 and found that small businesses enjoy almost no state support and/or know very little about the possibilities of such. Only about 2 per cent of small enterprises and 3.1 per cent of individual entrepreneurs use state support measures. Even though at the federal, regional, and local level, there are about 600 programmes in total, entrepreneurs oftentimes do not have any information about them, where to go, and whether they meet the criteria for these programmes.[76]

Paradoxically, participation in public procurement procedures often involves SMEs in corruption. According to the reports of the Audit Chamber, there are cases of splitting firms, financing various organisations belonging to the same person, and creating one-day firms to receive state support. Therefore, in the Kaluga region, all

---

[76] http://www.np-srv.ru/stati/5-prichin-pochemu-malyy-biznes-v-rossii-ne-rastet-kak-v-evrope/.

financial support went to four companies, the co-founder of which is the same individual; in the Bryansk region, out of 60 legal entities that received support, 22 organisations were registered only immediately before receiving assistance (Audit Chamber 2019).

According to the Strategy for the Development of Small and Medium-Sized Enterprises in Russia[77], the share of small businesses in public procurement every year should not be lower than the increasing quotas for purchases from SMEs.

In the period between 2016 and 2018, the share of direct participation of SMEs in the state procurement has increased from 15 to 25 per cent of the total. Still, there are many obstacles for small businesses in this area. The Center for Expertise and Analysis of Entrepreneurship Problems, Opora Russia[78], lists the need to undergo voluntary certification among the main problems with participating in government tenders, because the costs of such a service can go up to 1.5 million roubles. Furthermore, there are difficulties associated with price dumping in public procurement procedures. In several industries, the contract price is reduced by up to 60 per cent. As a low price oftentimes is the main reason for government institutions to select a company to be hired, arguments of quality come short many times and a company whose professional staff is not prepared for the implementation is given the job. Another requirement for all participants is to provide a bank guarantee with an amount of 5 to 30 per cent of the initial price of the contract, or to transfer their own or credit funds to the customer's account.[79]

SMEs in the Industries

For many years, SMEs have not only been present in trade, but also in industry and construction (Figure 4).

---

[77] http://static.government.ru/media/files/jFDd9wbAbApxgEiHNaXHveytq7hfPO96.pdf.

[78] https://opora.ru/en/.

[79] https://opora.ru/en/analytics/.

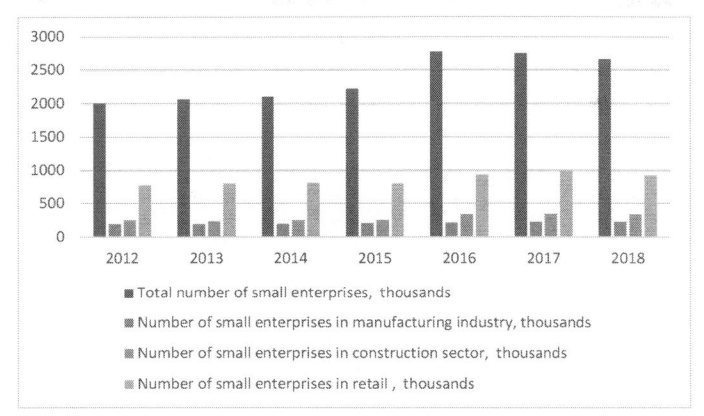

Figure 4: Number of small enterprises by main sectors (in thousands)

- Total number of small enterprises, thousands
- Number of small enterprises in manufacturing industry, thousands
- Number of small enterprises in construction sector, thousands
- Number of small enterprises in retail, thousands

Source: Rosstat (2013a: 633, 2019a: 636).

A more detailed examination of small enterprises in the industry shows that they operate in all sectors of that branch of economy and in some, such as real estate, even constitute the majority of companies (Figure 5).

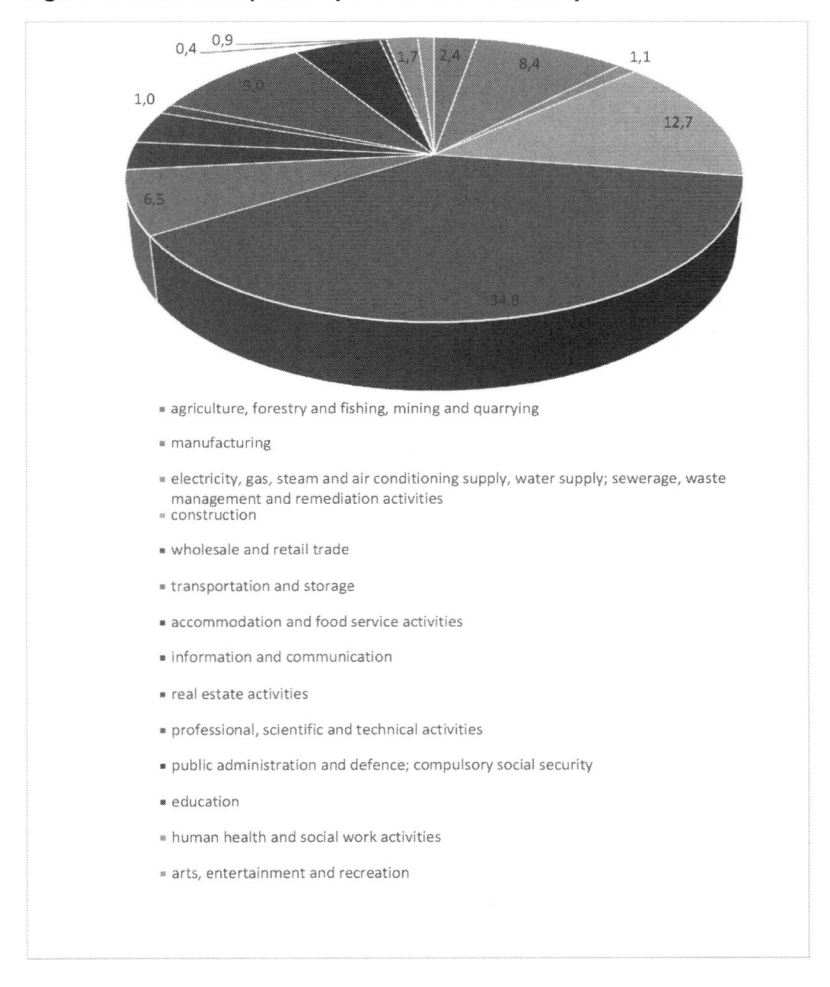

Figure 5: Small enterprises by branches of economy

- agriculture, forestry and fishing, mining and quarrying
- manufacturing
- electricity, gas, steam and air conditioning supply, water supply; sewerage, waste management and remediation activities
- construction
- wholesale and retail trade
- transportation and storage
- accommodation and food service activities
- information and communication
- real estate activities
- professional, scientific and technical activities
- public administration and defence; compulsory social security
- education
- human health and social work activities
- arts, entertainment and recreation

Source: Rosstat (2019b: 371).

About 8 per cent of small enterprises (adding medium-sized enterprises, more than 20 per cent) belong to the manufacturing sector. Such enterprises are characterized by problems with investments in fixed assets and the cost of loans. They were also negatively affected by devaluation and a decrease in demand. A constraining factor in attracting personnel for such enterprises is low salaries.

For the small businesses of transport and communications, the main challenge are the fees they must pay for the transportation of large goods through the Plato system. Some enterprises were forced to leave the market, unable to withstand the fierce price competition under such conditions. Increased excise rates on fuel in recent years also hit small businesses in the transport sector, affecting other industries dependent on transportation services.

The sector of SMEs varies significantly between different regions. In some regions, the development of small companies is a priority; in others, the economic potential is fully concentrated in large companies and the public sector. Therefore, measures of differentiated support are required, which are absent in most of the current legal acts.

In Russia, certain types of regions have developed in terms of development of SMEs. A comprehensive typology of the regions in terms of SMEs development was created by Zemtsov (2016), reflecting the state of art as well as the potential development of SMEs.

The author identified regions with a high level of development of SMEs as well as high growth potential of this sector. Regions that are dominated by active SMEs support policies are Belgorod Oblast, Republic of Tatarstan, Kaluga, Tyumen, Ulyanovsk, and Perm Territory. The last five regions represent innovative territorial clusters that are actively supported by the regional authorities and designed to intensify the interaction between SMEs and large enterprises (Zemtsov 2016).

Another group includes the regions with large cities, such as the regions of Omsk, Rostov, and Sverdlovsk, where the modern services sector is actively developing; here, the highest entrepreneurial activity, but also low rates and a weak growth potential can be found. A favourable business environment has developed in these regions, but competition is high and niches for SMEs are already occupied. SMEs are significant in Moscow and St. Petersburg as well as in the regions with active youth entrepreneurship, such as the regions of Novosibirsk and Tomsk, as well as in the regions with a high share of foreign trade relations, such as the Kaliningrad Region, Primorsky, and the Khabarovsk Territories (Zemtsov 2016).

Figure 6 shows the federal districts (blue) and by regions (green). The number of SMEs is high in the Central Federal District, North-West Federal District, Volga Federal District, and Siberian Federal Districts. However, in these districts the majority of SMEs are concentrated in one or two regions. For instance, in Volga Federal District with 14 regions in total, the majority of SMEs is located in the Republic of Tatarstan; in the Southern Federal District with eight regions in total, most of the SMEs are concentrated in the Krasnodar Territory. The highest numbers of SMEs are located in the Central Federal District with Moscow in first position and the North-western Federal District with St Petersburg second. In fact, it is in these few regions that SME activity is significant (Zemtsov 2016).

Figure 6: Number of small enterprises by federal districts and regions in Russia (in thousands)

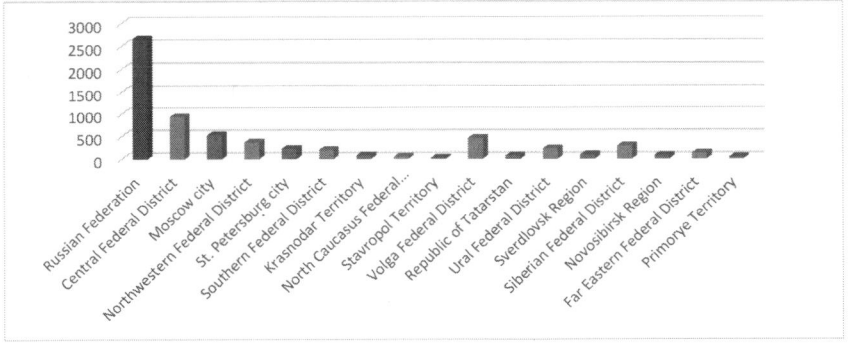

Source: Rosstat (2019b: 372).

More than half of the workers in SMEs are concentrated in ten regions of the country; more than 20 per cent are in Moscow and 8 per cent in St. Petersburg, where a steady demand for services, a diversified economy, and a well-educated population can be found (Zemtsov 2016).

Innovative SMEs and New Employment

Furthermore, another sector should be considered, conventionally called "innovative", which includes SMEs that develop or use high technology. Statistically, its share of innovative SMEs is insignificant. Here, the development potential is concentrated in the form of qualified specialists and business ideas. Traditionally, such enterprises are concentrated in the Information Technology (IT) sector. It is difficult to answer the question unequivocally whether a small business can be innovative, since the criteria for innovation themselves are very vague and subjective. However, a small business today may well become both a "conductor" of innovation, actively mastering new technologies, and a direct creator of innovative products. The last phenomenon can be shown in the experience of Western countries, where small businesses quite successfully make innovations part of their work.

Foreign experience in fact does show that SMEs contribute to innovative development, as the number of innovations per scientific researcher is significantly higher in SMEs than in large organisations. In several Russian regions, small enterprises (especially those working in high-tech) were brought together to create an effect of agglomeration, creating incubators, special economic zones, technopoles, and technology parks. Examples are the IT park Innopolis in Tatarstan and the pharma cluster in St. Petersburg as well as Skolkovo in Moscow.

Such solutions are popular in relatively rich regions; however, despite the intensification of the process of creating and organising the activities of small enterprises in one territory, there is no evidence of significant effects, especially regarding tax and rental benefits. Nevertheless, recent studies (such as by Madaleno et al. 2018) have also shown that the overall effect of such measures is positive. The authors suggest that co-working spaces, incubators and accelerators can be conceived of in four ways: as cities in miniature; as tools for bridging or structuring a range of relational distances or proximities; as ways to structure and de-risk entrepreneurial learning; or as economic communities or communities of practice.

However, existing measures to support innovative SMEs can become a barrier to development, since the development of their activities can lead to the abolition of subsidies. Particularly controversial is the situation in the pharmaceutical industry, where specific regulatory problems such as compulsory licensing, parallel import, lack of standardization of active ingredients, and impurities play a role.

In Russia, the localisation of SMEs in one pharmaceutical cluster has so far proven to be successful. Since 2010, the pharmaceutical market of St. Petersburg has experienced a five-fold increase, with a growth of the volume of production of medicines amounting to about 20 per cent of the nationwide production between 2015 and 2016 only. Since 2011, there has been a significant increase in the export volume; of pharmaceutical products, ranging from USD 500 to 600 million per year (though when looking at the absolute numbers, the effect does not seem so impressive). The top ten consumers include the Commonwealth of Independent States (CIS) and neighbouring countries as well as countries with a high demand for specialised drugs (such as vaccines). This is because preclinical studies of drugs in many cases are insufficient to bring development to the markets of developed countries with the relevant standards of clinical and laboratory practice.

Box 1: Priority projects of SMEs in pharmaceuticals and medical technology

Farm-Holding CJSC - conducting research in the field of peptide preparations, plus development and implementation of technologies to produce new drugs on their basis;
Vital Development Corporation OJSC - development and organisation of pilot production projects for clinical diagnostics;
JSC Orion Medic - a project for the development and production of medical products of a wide range (such as laser ophthalmic complexes and low-vision devices among others);
Inmed - a project to develop a technology of composite net materials based on biopolymers to produce applicative haemostatic materials;
"Nord Place" - a research and production complex for the development and industrial production of innovative protein substances for a wide range of applications.

Source: Russian Investment Forum (2017).

SMEs and Employment

Difficulties of Employment

As pointed out in the Deloitte Report (Deloitte 2018), today's tight labour market creates new challenges that can affect time to hire. Consider that candidates of the future will likely require a complex mixture of soft, interpersonal as well as detail oriented digital skills. Tackling recruitment in 2018 and beyond may require new thinking and business processes designed to attract candidates best able to create consumer moments that truly matter.

According to the annual Opora Russia surveys of SMEs, the main problems of SMEs are related to the availability of financial resources and tax arrears. Not every third small and medium-sized enterprise has difficulty in finding workers.

Some enterprises note difficulties with the selection of personnel of highly skilled workers, and especially technical specialists and workers.[80]

On the one hand, during recent years, the key problem for SMEs in the manufacturing sector was the lack of qualified personnel. The labour market is not capable of satisfying the needs of companies for qualified engineers and technicians or skilled workers. Even the selection of specialists for non-productive units (such as accountants or administrators) often proves difficult.[81]

On the other hand, the quality of jobs offered by SMEs is not always high. Low productivity does not allow paying decent salaries, and there are more professional risks for workers than at state enterprises. More than half of the managers state that finding engineers and technicians is either difficult or almost impossible. However, there are also possibilities for SMEs to organise special additional training and educational programmes for their employees. This could help them acquire the skills and expertise in such areas as the preparation of business plans, quality management, marketing and promotion, export, finance, the production process, and the development of new products. Nevertheless, almost 40 per cent of the study participants were not able to comment on issues related to the availability and quality of educational programmes, which shows a low awareness of companies about existing opportunities in the field of advanced training.[82]

(New) Forms of Employment

The increase in the scale of non-standard and flexible forms of employment at SMEs reflects the general trend towards a more flexible labour market. The literature notes that so far, the use of temporary employment is often identified with "poor", low-paid jobs that lower the level of well-being of the population. On the other hand, temporary employment can positively affect productivity and innovative activity, reduce labour costs, and increase the competitiveness of an enterprise (Gimpelson and Kapeluyshnikov 2006).

Many academic papers focusing on SMEs argue that there are many risks for employees related to lower pay, lack of guarantees, non-compliance with labour

---

[80] https://opora.ru/en/analytics/.

[81] https://opora.ru/en/analytics/.

[82] https://opora.ru/en/analytics/.

laws, delays in payment, and uncertain work patterns. It has been noted in several studies that in the last decade, there has been an expansion of precarious employment and growing of a new precariat (Krylova 2009). This is especially true for the small business sector (though the analysis is complicated by a lack of statistics) (Toksambaeva 2017). In a modern economy, a small enterprise is considered the most flexible regarding frequent economic changes.

Non-standard forms of employment (such as distance employment, flexible employment, and agent employment among others) are developed in connection with the intensive spreading of high-speed means of transmitting information. The limitations caused by the COVID-19 crisis added to increased use of such new forms of work. In the future, a virtual workstation with access to the network with all the information, the possibilities of virtual meetings, and cloud technologies could become a full replacement for a stationary workplace in the office. This would change not only the real estate market through a decreasing demand for office space, but also create a competitive advantage on the labour market for companies that will provide opportunities to work from home. According to a survey of companies in 15 cities across Russia, employers and employees have already realised the benefits of remote work using the appropriate IT services (IKSMEDIA 2018).

The scheme of search and selection of personnel for the large companies is not relevant for SMEs because of their resources' limitations. In many small enterprises, the process of employment is not structured. One of the strengths of small businesses is their freedom to adapt responsibilities and ability to fast changes of the economy and market. The lack of a multi-level organisational structure leads staff to understand their careers as a process of expanding and complicating functional responsibilities, increasing professionalism, increasing wages, and not promoting them.

SMEs with the lack of a full-fledged Human Resources (HR) service are focusing on aspects that can provide them with a competitive advantage in recruiting. This is especially the case in high-tech companies and makes SMEs to some extent innovators in the field of Human Resources Management (HRM). In general, SMEs practice the following approaches to staff recruitment:[83]

---

[83] Impressions of the St. Petersburg International Labour Forum 2020, 27-28 February. The forum is organised by the Government of St. Petersburg, St. Petersburg State University, and

- Determination of selection criteria, formulation of competencies that are necessary for an employee function in a particular position or workplace
- Consideration of the education system as a "supplier" of certain competencies
- Mandatory use of digital technology in the search for workers by social networks and forums
- Reduction and subsequent combination of administrative and functional duties at the enterprise
- Increasing the significance of the recommendations of the candidate compared with formal evidence of qualifications
- Attention to social capital and candidate soft skills ("universalism priority")
- Individual approaches and individualized contracts with various options for a flexible schedule
- Provision of indirect motivating conditions such as payment for work travel, assistance in rental housing, and subsidized meals at the enterprise
- Introduction of flexible forms of payment that stimulate initiative and effectiveness
- Informing about the current situation within the enterprise and relations with customers
- Formation of communications within the enterprise

The task of selecting and organising the work of personnel oriented towards the performance of such multitasking functions is extremely important for ensuring the effective functioning of SMEs. This requires the use of new methods of selection and motivation of staff.

Specific labour relations (the main elements of which are listed above) are fraught with many risks for both parties, employers as well as employees. The urgent task for SMEs is to develop a good balance between responsibility and risk and between independence and effectiveness, which will contribute to the sustainability and effectiveness of small businesses.

---

the ExpoForum-International Company, and supported by the Ministry of Labour and Social Protection of the Russian Federation.The Forum aims to become the largest platform in the country to discuss the issues related to the human capital development and to promote the integrated Strategy Creation to Develop the Human Capital of the Russian Federation that are based on advanced research and global best practices.

References

Audit Chamber (2019): Otzenka sostoyaniya garantiynoy podderdzki I mikrifinansirovaniya malogo I srednego predprinimateleljstva v Rossiyskoy Federatcii v 2015-2018 I pervom polugodii 2019 (Assessment of Guaranteed Support and Micro-Financing of Small and Medium Entrepreneurship in Russia between 2015 and 2018 and during the first half-year of 2019). URL: http://audit.gov.ru/upload/medialibrary/46a/46a9f2d742498488fca4d297cf187a11.pdf [13 June 2020].

Barinova, Vera/Zemtsov, Stepan (2018): Predprinimateljstvo I instituty: estj li svyazj na regionaljnom urovne v Rossii (Entrepreneurship and Institutions in Russia: Is there a Link at the Regional Level?). In: Voprosy ekonomiki 2018 (6), pp. 92-116.

Deloitte Centre for Industry Insights (2018): Retail, Wholesale and Distribution Outlook. An Industry in Transition. URL: https://www2.deloitte.com/content/dam/Deloitte/us/Documents/consumer-business/us-cb-retail-wholesale-distribution-outlook-2018.pdf [13 June 2020].

World Bank Group (2020): Doing Business 2020. Economy Profile Russian Federation. URL: https://www.doingbusiness.org/content/dam/doingBusiness/country/r/russia/RUS.pdf [08 July 2020].

Gimpelson, Vladimir/Kapeluyshnikov, Rostislav (2006): Nestandartnaya zanyatostj v rossijskoy ekonomike (Non-Standard Employment in the Russian Economy). Moscow: Izdateljstvo GU VSHE.

IKSMEDIA (2020): Kakova distantcionnaya zanyatostj v Rossii? (What is Distance Employment in Russia?). URL: http://www.iksmedia.ru/news/5254023-Kakova-distancionnaya-zanyatost-v.html [23 June 2020].

Krylova, Elena (2009): Maloe predprinimateljstvo I zanyyatostj naseleniya (Small Entrepreneurship and Employment of the Population). In: Problemy prognozirovaniya 2009 (1), pp. 125-132.

Madaleno, Margarida/Max, Nathan/Overman, Henry/Waight, Sevrin (2018): Incubators, Accelerators and Regional Economic Development. In: CEP Discussion Papers 2018 (1575), pp. 1-26.

Matovnikov, M./Korzhenevsky, N./Kamrotov, M. (2019): Zanyatostj v MSP: daleko li do tzeley Strategii-2030 (MCN Employment in SMEs: Is it far to the Goals of the Strategy 2030?).

Organisation for Economic Co-Operation and Development (OECD) (2019): SME and Entrepreneurship Outlook 2019. Paris: OECD Publishing.

Rosstat (Russian Federal State Statistics Service) (2013a): Regions of Russia.

Rosstat (Russian Federal State Statistics Service) (2013b): Small and Medium-Sized Entrepreneurship in Russia.

Rosstat (Russian Federal State Statistics Service) (2019a): Regions of Russia.

Rosstat (Russian Federal State Statistics Service) (2019b): Russian Statistical Yearbook.

Rosstat (Russian Federal State Statistics Service) (2019c): Small and Medium-Sized Entrepreneurship in Russia.

Source: Russian Investment Forum (2017): Quality of the international Level. Pharma Cluster. In: Russian Investment Forum 2017 (208), p. 15.

Shane, Scott (2009): Why Encouraging More People to Become Entrepreneurs is Bad Public Policy. In: Small Business Economics 33 (2), pp. 141-149.

Toksambaeva, Majrash (2017): Precarious Employment in Small Business with Diverse Status. In: Bobkov, V. (Ed.): Precarity of Employment: Global and Russian Context of the Future of Work. Moscow: Real Print, pp. 229-242.

Zemtsov, Stepan (2016): Tipologiya regionov dlya tceley razvitiya malogo I srednego predprinimateljstva (Typology of Regions for the Development of Small and Medium-Sized Entrepreneurship). In: Gosudarstvennoe I munitcipaljnoe upravlenie Uchenye zapiski SKAGS (4), pp. 99-102.

Websites

Association "Support for the Development of Foreign Economic Activity": www.np-srv.ru

Audit Chamber: http://audit.gov.ru

IKSMEDIA (business portal): www.iksmedia.ru

Opora Russia (Center for Expertise and Analysis of Entrepreneurship Problems): www.opora.ru

Opora Russia (Center for Expertise and Analysis of Entrepreneurship Problems) - Studies: https://opora.ru/en/analytics/

Rosstat (Russian Federal State Statistics Service): https://www.gks.ru

Sberbank: www.sberbank.ru

Sberbank - Development of Small and Medium-Sized Businesses in Russia (SberData project): www.sberbank.ru/common/img/uploaded/analytics/about-issledovaniya/smb_22_july_2019.pdf

Sberbank - Strategy for the Development of Small and Medium-Sized Enterprises in Russia: http://static.government.ru/media/files/jFDd9wbAbApxgEiHNaXHveytq7hfPO96.pdf

Contributions of SMEs to Employment in Romania

Ciprian Panzaru and Cosmin Enache

Introduction

Small and medium-sized enterprises (SMEs) are seen as the main driver for job creation and boosting economic growth and competitiveness.

Micro-enterprises and SMEs represent 99.8 per cent of all businesses in the EU. In 2018, there were almost 25 million SMEs in the European Union (EU). They generated EUR 3.9 billion in revenues, accounting for 56.4 per cent of total value added and providing jobs for 90 million people (66.6 per cent).

In Romania, SMEs represent about 99.7 per cent of all businesses. In 2018, they generated 52.7 per cent of total value added of the non-financial business sector and held approximately 65.8 per cent of the total employees in the non-financial business sector of the country. Romania has 29 micro companies and SMEs per 1,000 inhabitants, well below the European average (58 SMEs per 1,000 inhabitants). Also, the average productivity of Romanian SMEs, calculated as total value added for each employee, is about EUR 15,100, significantly lower than the EU average of about EUR 44,600. However, Romanian SMEs employ an average of 5.5 people, exceeding the EU average of 3.9 (European Commission 2019).

The importance of this sector was perhaps, more than ever, highlighted in the context of the COVID-19 pandemic. The first economic support measures were aimed primarily at SMEs. Most of the European Regional Development Agencies have implemented urgent measures to provide mainly help to SMEs, thus recognising their key role in the economy.

Immediately after the COVID-19 crisis erupted, Romania set up a programme called SME INVEST designated to provide help to SMEs strongly affected by the lockdown. The programme provides loans for SMEs, with a budget of over EUR 3 billion. Moreover, the programme allows SMEs to benefit from state guarantees for loans for investments and financing of working capital.

However, the importance of SMEs in the European economy was confirmed earlier, in 2008, when the European Parliament adopted the Small Business Act (EU

SBA). Among other support measures, it emphasises the role of SMEs in supporting employability. José Manuel Barroso, president of the European Commission in 2008, highlighted that the EU SBA is an essential support in implementing the Lisbon Strategy for Growth and Jobs.

Considering SMEs as an important source of job creation is not accidental. The contributions of SMEs to employment has been discussed also by a number of authors in literature.

For instance, a recent ILO report (Kok and Berrios 2019) examines the SME enterprises contribution to total employment. The main findings were that SMEs (including self-enterprises) account for the largest share of total employment. The study was based on data from a labour force survey from 99 countries in all the world regions (not including North America).

Some authors have also suggested that there is a strong relationship between the emergence of SMEs and employment. For example, Rotar, Pamić and Bojnec (2018) investigated whether SMEs employment affects employment in the EU-28 using panel data models during the period from 2005 to 2016. They found that SMEs play an important role in job creation and also in the reduction of unemployment.

The same issue has also been explored in a study by Mavlutova, Lesinskis and Olevskis (2017). The authors provide information on the role of the SME sector of high-tech manufacturing industries in employment. They suggest that the significance of SMEs in the economy is increasing and growingly contributes to the employment and labour market. However, the research shows that employment in the service sector in the developed countries is still widely focused on traditional sectors of activity (such as hotel services and public catering, wholesale and retail trade, and real estate activities among others).

A series of recent studies employed in Romania (Herman 2012, Aceleanet al. 2014) also indicated that SMEs are an important generator of jobs, even though the average value of labour productivity is lower compared to large enterprises.

Although studies have been conducted worldwide, the contribution of SME enterprises to employment is still insufficiently explored in some countries, including Romania. Our research intends to contribute to the understanding of the role of SMEs in the Romanian economy during the last 20 years. We use secondary data from Eurostat and the Romanian National Institute of Statistics to investigate whether employment through SMEs affects total employment in Romania.

Characteristics of the SME Sector in Romania

The business environment in Romania has been affected by major changes over the last 20 years. One of the most significant changes was the rapidly growing number of SMEs. According to the latest available data (Eurostat 2018), there are more than 500,000 SMEs active in Romania, which is a significant increase from 316,293 in 2000 (Figure 1; the year 2000 is set as index 100). The data cover the "non-financial business economy", which includes industry, construction, trade, and services (NACE Rev. 1 sections C, D, E, F, G, and H to K for the period from 2000 to 2007; NACE Rev. 2 sections B to J, L, M, and N for the period from 2007 to 2019).

Figure 1: Number of SMEs in Romania 2000-2018

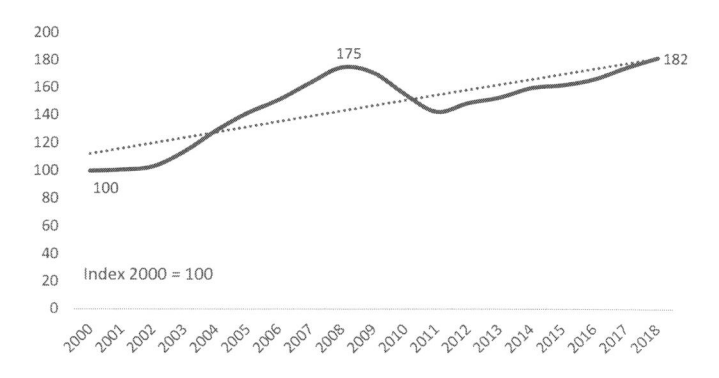

Source: the authors, based on data by the Romanian National Institute of Statistics.

The SME sector is an important employer. For instance, in 2018, the SME sector (industry, construction, trade, and services) attracted more than 65 per cent of the total labour force. It should be noticed that the number of persons employed in the SME sector increased at a faster rate than the number of persons employed in other sectors (Figure 2; the year 2000 is set as index 100).

Figure 2: Number of employees in SMEs and large enterprises in Romania 2000-2018

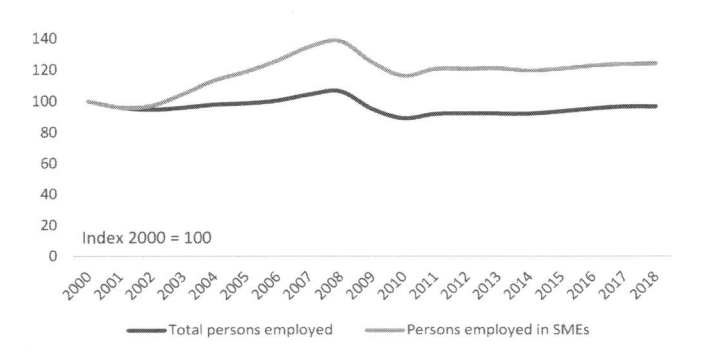

Source: the authors, based on data by the Romanian National Institute of Statistics.

When considering trends over time, one notices that both the number of SMEs (Figure 1) and the number of employees of SMEs (Figure 2) experienced an upward sloping trend for the period from 2000 to 2008. After 2008, the impact of the economic crisis was major, and some figures regressed to the same level as in 2004/2006. However, the evolution of the number of SMEs has stabilised after 2010.

The number of SMEs employees is well balanced between the domains of trade, services, and industry, but a lower percentage of employees is noticed in the construction domain. For instance, in 2018 (the last year for which there are statistical data available), the share of employees was 27 per cent for industry, 28 per cent for trade, 33 per cent for the services, and only 11 per cent for the construction. However, the number of employees has increased significantly for all those domains since 2000; the services and industry domain have increased almost threefold (Figure 3; the year 2000 is set as index 100).

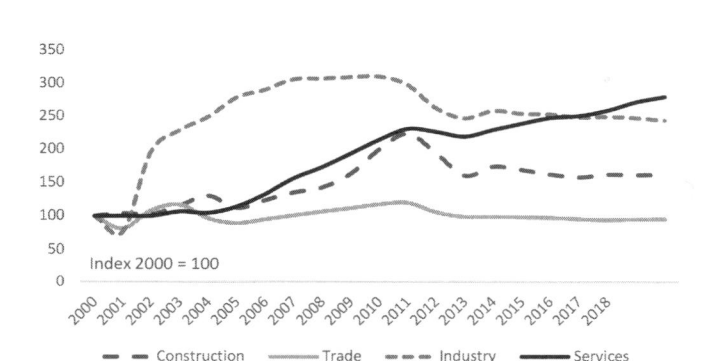

Figure 3: Employees in SMEs in Romania 2000-2018, by NACE - 1 digit (%)

Source: the authors, based on data by the Romanian National Institute of Statistics.

There is a relatively equal distribution of employees over the different size classes. Thus, 33.1 per cent of employees are employed in micro-enterprises, 33.6 per cent in small enterprises, and 33.3 per cent in medium-sized enterprises (Figure 4; the year 2000 is set as index 100).

Figure 4: Number of employees in SMEs in Romania 2000-2018, by size class

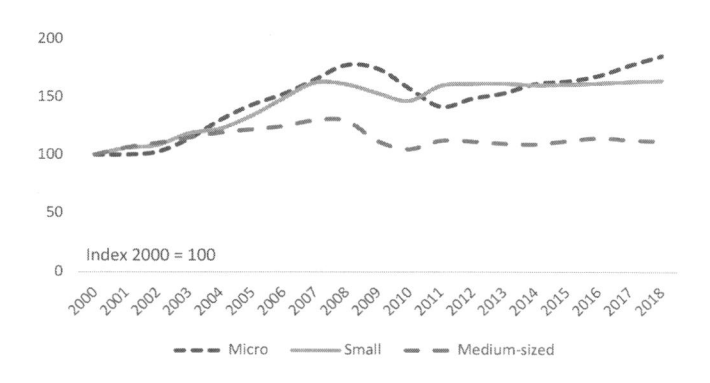

Source: the authors, based on data by the Romanian National Institute of Statistics.

The distribution of SMEs differs between regions and depends on the level of economic development (as indicated by the GDP; correlation of r = 0.97). On the other hand, there is no connection between the volume of population and the number of SMEs (Figure 5).

Figure 5: Share of SMEs, population, and GDP in Romania, by NUTS 2[84] (2018)

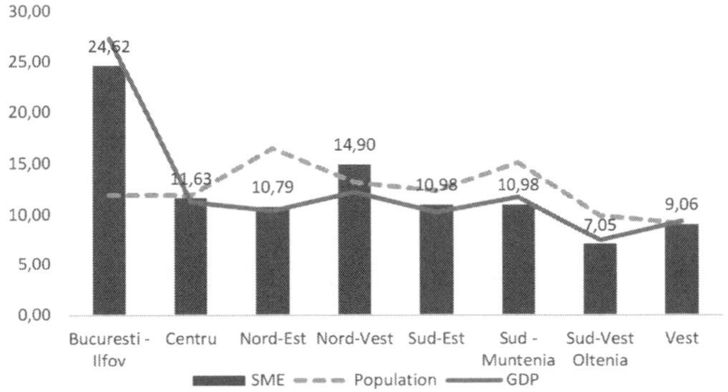

Source: the authors, based on data by the Romanian National Institute of Statistics.

When considering the performance of the SME sector (analysed in terms of total value added at factor costs), it can be noticed that after 2008 (data were available only for the period from 2008 to 2018), there was an increase year by year with only a few exceptions (Figure 6; the year 2000 is set as index 100).

---

[84] NUTS (Nomenclature of Territorial Units for Statistics) is a hierarchical system for dividing up the economic territory of the EU set up by Eurostat. NUTS 2 comprises basic regions for the application of regional policies.

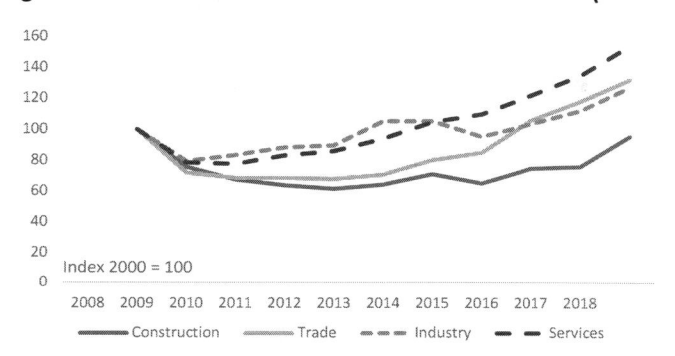

Figure 6: Total value added to factor costs in Romania (in EUR million) (2018)

Index 2000 = 100

Construction, Trade, Industry, Services — 2008 to 2018

Source: the authors, based on data by Eurostat.

The highest total value added is provided by services (34 per cent), followed by trade (30 per cent), industry (23 per cent), and construction (11 per cent).

Overall, Romania presents a dynamic picture regarding the SME sector, performing almost similar to the EU-28 (of 2018, including the United Kingdom/UK), both in terms of share of enterprises and persons employed, but with a notable difference in terms of total value added (Figure 7).

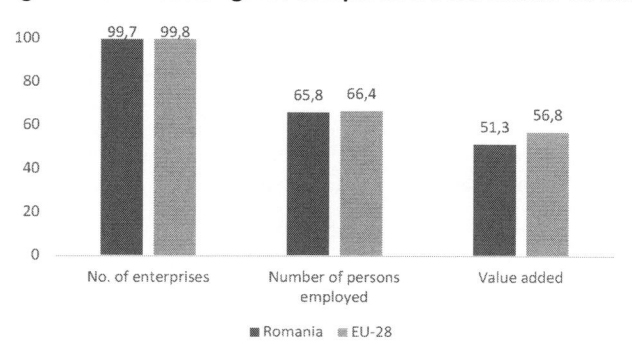

Figure 7: SME basic figures comparison between EU-28 and Romania (2018)

	Romania	EU-28
No. of enterprises	99,7	99,8
Number of persons employed	65,8	66,4
Value added	51,3	56,8

Source: the authors, based on data by Eurostat.

Over the years, the Romanian legislation regarding SMEs has changed significantly. However, now, there is a well-defined legal framework which is congruent with the one of the EU. For example, taking as a landmark the measures contained in the EU SBA, Romania has implemented nine out of ten of the proposed policy measures through various governmental programmes (Table 1).

Table 1: Policy measures under the EU SBA implemented (+) and not yet implemented (-) by Romania

1	Create an environment in which entrepreneurs and family businesses can thrive and entrepreneurship is rewarded	+
2	Ensure that honest entrepreneurs who have faced bankruptcy quickly get a second chance	+
3	Design rules according to the "think small first" principle	+
4	Make public administration responsive to SMEs	+
5	Adapt public policy tools to SME needs	+
6	Facilitate SME access to finances and develop a legal framework and business environment supportive of timely payments in commercial transactions	-
7	Help SMEs to benefit more from the opportunities offered by the EU single market	+
8	Promote the upgrading of skills and all forms of innovation	+
9	Enable SMEs to turn environmental challenges into opportunities	+
10	Encourage and support SMEs to benefit from growth markets	+

Source: European Commission (2019).

SMEs play a key role in the Romanian economy. They have become an important job provider and a pillar of welfare. Both the number of SMEs and the number of persons employed in the SME sector have constantly increased during the last years. An important increase was also noticed in terms of total value added. Moreover, Romania almost fully implemented the EU SBA measures and recently

(April 2020) set up a governmental programme to help the SME sector during the COVID-19 crisis.

Analysis of the Contributions of SMEs to Employment in Romania

In order to further investigate whether SME employment affects total employment in Romania, we used a simple econometric model. Due to data availability issues, our econometric analysis will be focused only on industry, services, construction, and trade sectors, according to NACE Rev. 2 classification.

We used total employment (TE) as the dependent variable in all the four selected economic sectors, which accounts for roughly two thirds of total employment in Romania. A small set of independent variables was selected, following relevant previous empirical studies on this matter (Mavlutova, Lesinskis and Olevskis 2017, Rotar, Pamić and Bojnec 2018). As the variable of interest, we used SME employment (SMEE) in the same four selected economic sectors. Alternatively, in a second estimation, we used SME employment in industry (SMEINDE), services (SMESERE), construction (SMECONE), and trade (SMECOME). In both estimations, as control variables we used labour cost (LABCOST) and gross domestic product per capita (GDPPC).

Data for all variables for the period from 2000 to 2017 were extracted from Eurostat (Annual Structural Business Statistics Database[85]). The relevant descriptive statistics for all variables (raw data) are given in Table 2.

---

[85] www.ec.europa.eu/eurostat/web/structural-business-statistics.

Table 2: Descriptive statistics

	TE	SMEE	SMESERE	SMEINDE	SMECONE	SMECOME	LABCOST	GDPPC
Mean	3,927,232	2,415,523	606,773.4	734,822.5	303,228.3	770,698.7	16.43	15,037.5
Median	3,902,656	2,475,437	666,369.5	699,821.5	309,815.0	745,419.0	14.45	16,708.7
Maximum	4,340,175	2,838,983	836,913.0	848,360.0	427,998.0	906,625.0	46.60	26,631.9
Minimum	3,638,764	1,971,850	313,380.0	624,837.0	214,866.0	675,757.0	4.00	5,848.8
Std. Dev.	181,934.8	240,323.0	172,575.3	74,443.1	55,740.1	68,797.3	12.68	6,406.4

Source: the authors, based on data by Eurostat.

As a method of estimation, a simple linear regression (OLS) was used. All variables were transformed into natural logarithms, so all estimated coefficients are elasticities.

Table 3: Estimation results

Variables/Method	Model (1) OLS AR (1)	Model (2) OLS
SMEE	0.454*** [0.104]	
SMESERE		-0.165 [0.142]
SMEINDE		0.280*** [0.069]
SMECONE		-0.095** [0.031]
SMECOME		0.387*** [0.102]
LABCOST	0.045*** [0.014]	0.039*** [0.011]
GDPPC	-0.048 [0.038]	0.182* [0.098]
Constant	8.849*** [1.199]	7.731*** [1.075]
Adj. R-squared	0.891	0.895
F-statistic	26.678***	25.125***
DW stat	1.97	1.61

Robust standard errors in parentheses; *** $p < 0.01$, ** $p < 0.05$, * $p < 0.1$.

Source: the authors, based on data by Eurostat.

Both SME total employment in industry, services, construction, and trade sectors (SMEE) and labour cost (LABCOST) have a significant and positive impact on total employment in these sectors (Model 1). This result could be useful for government decision makers, which could develop and implement public policies aimed at facilitating and stimulating SME employment. When SME sector variables are used in estimation, one notices that only SME employment in industry (SMEINDE) and trade (SMECOME) have a significant and positive impact on total employment. Consequently, these should be the target sector for SME public policy measures. Both SME employment in the services (SMESERE) and construction (SMECONE) sectors seem to have a negative effect on total employment (although the negative coefficient for SME employment in the services sector/SMESERE is statistically not significant). This shows that in these two sectors, new jobs are taken by people already employed in other economic sectors (and not by unemployed persons) and/or, moreover, SME business development and job creation in these sectors replaces business and leads to job destruction in other sectors suggesting a creative destruction phenomenon (Davis, Haltiwanger and Schuh 1996). Last but not least, given the short time span and the fact that gross domestic product per capital affects SME employment (SMEE) and labour cost (LABCOST) to a certain extent, the estimations results should be considered with caution.

Conclusions

This paper presents an overview of the development of the SME sector in Romania, examining the contribution of SMEs to the Romanian economy with a focus on employment. Descriptive data shows that SMEs play a significant role, as they represent a sector which attracts a considerable number of employees and brings over half of the total value added to the Romanian economy.

This paper has also investigated whether SME employment affects total employment in Romania, using an econometric model based on simple linear regression. The evidence is mixed, showing that on the one hand, SME total employment in the industry, services, construction, and trade sectors has a positive impact on total employment in these sectors, but that on the other hand, only SME employment in industry and trade has a significant and positive impact on total employment.

Given the limited time series, the results should be interpreted with caution. Nevertheless, our study provides a framework for further in-depth analysis. It could also help decision makers to develop and implement public policies focused on facilitating and stimulating SME employment.

References

Aceleanu, Mirela I./Traşcă, Daniela L./Şerban Andreea C. (2014): The Role of Small and Medium Enterprises in Improving Employment and in the Postcrisis Resumption of Economic Growth in Romania. In: Theoretical and Applied Economics 21 (1), pp. 87-102.

Davis, Steven J./Haltiwanger, John/Schuh, Scott (1996): Job Creation and Job Destruction. Cambridge: Massachusetts Institute of Technology (MIT) Press.

European Commission (2019): 2019 SBA Fact Sheet Romania. URL: https://ec.europa.eu/growth/smes/business-friendly-environment/performance-review_en#sba-fact-sheets [03 June 2020].

Herman, Emilia (2012): SMEs and Their Effect on the Romanian Employment. In: Procedia Economics and Finance 2012 (3), pp. 290-297.

Kok, Jan de/Berrios, Mario (2019): Small Matters: Global Evidence on the Contribution to Employment by the Self-Employed, Micro-Enterprises and SMEs. Geneva: International Labour Organization (ILO).

Mavlutova, Inese/Lesinskis, Kristaps/Olevskis, Grigorijs (2017): Contemporary Role of SMEs in Employment in Manufacturing and Service Industries. In: 5th International Scientific Conference on Contemporary Issues in Business, Management and Education. Vilnius: Vilnius Gediminas Technical University.

Rotar, Laura J./Pamić Kontošić, Roberta/Bojnec, Štefan (2019): Contributions of Small and Medium Enterprises to Employment in the European Union Countries. In: Economic Research (Ekonomska Istraživanja) 32 (1), pp. 3302-3314.

Websites

European Commission, SBA Fact Sheets: www.ec.europa.eu/growth/smes/business-friendly-environment/performance-review_en

Eurostat: https://ec.europa.eu/eurostat/data/database

Eurostat, Annual Structural Business Statistics Database: www.ec.europa.eu/eurostat/web/structural-business-statistics

Romanian National Institute of Statistics: http://statistici.insse.ro:8077/tempo-online/#/pages/tables/insse-table

SMEs in Brandenburg – Job Creation Motor, Adaptation Machine, Low Wages?

Daniel Porep

Introduction

The economy of the Federal State of Brandenburg (Germany) is characterised by a particularly large number of small and medium-sized enterprises (SMEs). Accordingly, most of Brandenburg's employees work for such businesses. This structure - marked by the strong presence of small enterprises with up to 49 employees - carries both positive and negative implications. On one hand, SMEs possess a high growth potential. In the past, these businesses have enjoyed a notably large proportion of Brandenburg's positive labour market development. In addition, SMEs can react to shifts in the market with considerable flexibility, which allows them to adapt well to economic change. On the other hand, SMEs lack the resources of large businesses and are less frequently bound by collective bargaining agreements. They pay lower wages and offer fewer opportunities for the organisational representation of employee interests. In this interpretation, the drawbacks of the flexibility of SMEs lie in their lower wages and somewhat uncertain employment circumstances.

The following report examines these tensions in the context of Brandenburg. It places special weight on employment structure, employment dynamic, and employee compensation, and analyses these factors based on company size. The report foregrounds the following three questions:

- What features characterise the employment structure of SMEs, with regard to qualification structure and working hours?
- What is the relationship between employment dynamics and company size in Brandenburg?
- What is the relationship between wages and company size in Brandenburg?

Preliminary Remarks

The following study places emphasis on the connections between company size and both employment dynamics and wages. For the examination of employment dynamics as they relate to company or enterprise size, data at the level of individual businesses can be used (Wagner 2007; Bauer et al. 2008a). Assessment at this micro-level offers the advantage of clearly depicting growth and contraction processes over time. This register of analysis for example reveals whether and to what degree SMEs develop into large companies or adjust their activities; however, the necessary data at the micro-level was unavailable. Alternately, aggregate information concerning size classes of companies can be used (Bauer et al. 2008a; Fuchs and Weyh 2007). Such aggregate data allows for analysis along various vectors such as the number of companies, number of employees, employment relationships, and wages. The following study, which uses statistics from the German Federal Employment Agency (*Bundesagentur für Arbeit*), draws on data aggregated based on the number of employees at a company.

A "company" (*Betrieb*) can be defined as the regional subsidiary of an "enterprise" (*Unternehmen*). An enterprise may consist of multiple companies but, in many cases, the company and the enterprise are one in the same entity.[86] As some enterprises have no employees, this study focuses only on companies with at least one employee subject to social security contributions.[87]

---

[86] "For the purpose of employment statistics, a 'company of employment (*Beschäftigungsbetrieb*)' is a regionally delimited and industry-specific entity with employees. The company of employment may consist of one or more subsidiaries (branches) of an enterprise (*Unternehmen*). The term 'company of employment' is always used to designate an entity for which a company number (*Betriebsnummer*) can be or has been issued. The municipality (*Gemeindebereich*) is the standard regional demarcation of the company of employment" (German Federal Employment Agency 2020).

[87] "The qualifier 'subject to social security contributions (sozialversicherungspflichtig)' (...) designates individuals who meet the following criteria: 1. The employee has issued a registration for social security. 2. The employment is subject to insurance in at least one of the sectors of social security (pension insurance, health insurance/long-term care insurance, unemployment insurance). 3. The individual is engaged in independent employment, namely work, which is generally compensated with a wage (periods of interruption, for example, parental leave, are an exception). 4. The individual works at least one hour per week" (German Federal Employment Agency 2020).

In analysing the development and significance of enterprises of varying sizes, SMEs - notable for their relevance to employment and considerable growth potential - often play a key role. Various economic assistance programmes frequently target these business categories directly (Bauer et al. 2008a: 5). Drawing on the definition of SMEs by the European Union (EU), the following analysis subsumes under this category the two size classes of SMEs and incorporates all companies with one to 249 employees.[88] The EU concept of SME, though imprecise, is used for the sake of simplification. Furthermore, rather than analysing enterprises as legal entities (as is common within this field of study), this assessment foregrounds companies as subsidiaries of enterprises.

SMEs – Between Job Creation Motor and Adaptation Machine

Most employees in Germany work for SMEs. In public perception, these companies are often ascribed the function of being motors of job creation. According to this "mid-sized company hypothesis", these businesses exhibit above average job growth.

Borrowing from what Austrian political economist Joseph Schumpeter described as the process of "creative destruction", SMEs can have a considerable impact on the adaptability of both society and the economy (Schumpeter 1934, 1942). The creation and liquidation of enterprises leads to an adjustment of societal resource allocation. These processes reflect an extreme form of this adaptation process (Bauer et al. 2008: 2). Such adaptation processes also appear, however, in the growth and contraction of enterprises. In this context, SMEs can be described as "adaptation machines".

In analysing employment growth and adaptation processes, the concept of internal and external labour markets becomes particularly relevant. The disposition of dynamic employment seen in SMEs suggests that they rely on external labour markets and that employment development in these businesses is characterised by the influence of market forces more than in others. External labour

---

[88] The European Commission has recommended designating, under the umbrella of SME, smallest, small, and medium-sized enterprises, based on number of employees or revenue. The smallest enterprises are those with up to nine employees. Small enterprises are those with ten to 49 employees. Medium-sized enterprises have 50 to 249 employees (European Commission 2003).

markets are characterised by limited periods of employment in each company, higher inter-company mobility among job holders, and the particular importance of market forces. Internal labour markets, by contrast, are distinguished by long periods of employment, higher intra-company mobility, and the importance of company-specific qualifications (Weingärtner 2019: 101). The process of employment-side adaptation within companies can take place through both external and internal labour markets.

Although the „mid-sized company hypothesis" has been criticised when measured against longitudinal empirical data, it nevertheless clearly suggests that SMEs are both positively and negatively impacted by a particularly dynamic employment disposition. This dynamic relates to changes not only in the total number of employees, but also in the number of initiated and terminated employment relationships (Bauer et al. 2008b; Fuchs and Weyh 2007; Haltiwanger et al. 2007). In comparison to large companies, SMEs appear to use external rather than internal markets for their adaptation processes. With these assumptions in mind, this report argues that SMEs, in comparison to large enterprises, display a more dynamic employment disposition when measured along three vectors, namely, the number of employees, the number of initiated and terminated employment relationships, and the length of time employees remain at the company. This employment dynamic is evident in above average rates of growth and contraction among employees, in above average labour turnover, and in shorter periods of employment. SMEs can thus be characterised as sites of adaptation, a process in which they utilise the labour market more readily than large enterprises.

These dynamic adaptation processes vis-à-vis numbers of employees have diverse causes. In differentiating between SMEs and large companies, legal regulations implemented by the state or collective advocacy groups such as business associations likely play a large role (Haltiwanger et al. 2007). They for example can be found in laws and ordinances regarding occupational safety and employment protection, or in the company's employee representation. Regulations pushed by trade unions and employer associations can impact many areas such as employment protection, wages, recruitment, and training practices. The scope of regulations concerning labour contracts is much greater in large companies than in SMEs. In Brandenburg, the proportion of SMEs bound by collective bargaining agreements lies between 14 and 57 per cent, depending on the size of the company. In large companies, this figure hovers around 75 per cent (MASGF 2019: 74). In other words, SMEs are much less regulated by collective bargaining agreements than large companies. This point explains why SMEs respond to fluctuations in demand more readily through expansions and cutbacks in numbers of employees. At the same time, this tendency can lead to less favourable working conditions for employees in SMEs as compared to large businesses, particularly in terms of wages. On account of both economies of scale as well as longer company histories, large businesses frequently produce with a higher capital intensity. This tendency leads to greater productivity and thus to greater latitude in paying higher wages. Building from these considerations, this report argues that SMEs pay lower wages than large companies.

Independent of these considerations about employment dynamics and wage differentials, such statistical analysis necessarily blurs distinctions between individual companies. This analysis employs only composite data. Thus, it is possible that the results of this study do not apply to some individual businesses. For example, wages in some SMEs may top those of some large businesses. The consolidation of SMEs under one umbrella brings together a very diverse collection of enterprises. This study nevertheless frequently employs the category "SME" in order to facilitate productive comparisons with large businesses. Any assessment of the results of this study must keep in mind that differences within the category "SME" can be significant.

This report does not aim to track labour conditions in order to judge the attractiveness of certain jobs as a whole. Wages certainly play an important role. Compensation, however, is hardly the only element that shapes working conditions. Substantive demands, forms of hierarchy, substantive and formal room for manoeuvre, and the compatibility of work and private life among other factors also carry considerable weight. The empirical data in the following sections should not be read as an overall assessment of the appeal of SMEs as employers.

Overview – Brandenburg in the National Context

Approximately 99.5 per cent of all companies in Brandenburg have fewer than 250 employees. Only about 0.5 per cent have 250 or more employees and can be defined as "large companies." Even when most of Brandenburg's employees subject to social security contributions (for definition, see above) are employed at SMEs, large companies are of greater significance for overall employment. The dominance of small businesses with up to 49 employees appears self-evident when one looks at the total number of companies. The picture changes, however, when one analyses numbers of employees. Although approximately 78 per cent of all companies have fewer than 10 employees, large companies employ the highest total proportion of workers. Approximately 23 per cent of all employees work at large companies. In addition, when one examines companies with 50 to 249 employees, one finds that approximately 54 per cent of workers are employed by such firms. These large and medium-seized companies, however, constitute only 4.4 per cent of all companies (Table 1).

Table 1: Companies and employees subject to social security contributions in Brandenburg, by company size (30 June 2019)

	TOTAL	1-9	10-19	20-49	50-99	100-249	≥ 250
Company	66,745	52,237	6,810	4,679	1,634	1,018	367
	100%	78.3%	10.2%	7.0%	2.4%	1.5%	0.5%
Employees Subject to Social Security Contributions	854,164	159,208	91,384	142,017	112,839	154,425	194,291
	100%	18.6%	10.7%	16.6%	13.2%	18.1%	22.7%

Source: the author, based on statistics by the German Federal Employment Agency.

In Table 1, the structural prominence of SMEs in Brandenburg's economy becomes evident. The considerable significance of SMEs represents a key feature of Brandenburg's economy. Compared nationally, one finds that, in 2019, approximately 66 per cent of workers in the federal states in western Germany were employed in SMEs, on average. In the federal states in eastern Germany, the total figure registered at approximately 72 per cent and at 77 per cent in Brandenburg. This national comparison reveals that, for Germany as a whole, most employees work at SMEs. Nevertheless, regional differences are sizeable. In comparison to both eastern and western Germany, SMEs in Brandenburg employ a notably large proportion of workers (Table 2).

Table 2: Proportion of employees subject to social security contributions, by company size (30 June 2019)

REGION	1-9	10-19	20-49	50-99	100-249	1-249	≥ 250
Brandenburg	18.6%	10.7%	16.6%	13.2%	18.1%	77.3%	22.7%
Eastern Germany	16.6%	9.9%	15.7%	12.9%	16.7%	71.7%	28.3%
Western Germany	14.7%	9.3%	14.1%	11.9%	15.6%	65.6%	34.4%

Source: the author, based on statistics by the German Federal Employment Agency.

SMEs are not evenly spread across industries. Rather, the presence of such businesses is strongly industry specific. Table 3 lists the proportion of companies categorized by company size and industry. The table underscores which industries consist predominantly of SMEs and which are more heavily populated by large companies. In the construction industry, for example, 81.7 per cent of all businesses have between one and nine employees. In the field of public administration, only 2.7 per cent of all businesses have 250 employees or more. A large proportion of the smallest companies can be found in agriculture, construction, financial services/real estate/scientific services and other service industries. The areas of mining/utilities, manufacturing, and public administration, however, are more clearly characterised by medium and large companies (Table 3). By comparison, these industries feature a higher concentration of employees in fewer companies. In manufacturing, for example, approximately 56 per cent of all employees work in companies with 100 or more employees. In public administration, that same figure is around 65 per cent. The industries of mining/utilities and manufacturing likely require notably higher capital investments and only become profitable beyond a certain company size. Public administration and education are strongly characterised by large administrative and educational institutions.

Table 3: Proportion of companies in Brandenburg, by industry and company size (30 June 2019) (*for the purpose of data protection, figures are anonymised)

INDUSTRY	1-9	10-19	20-49	50-99	100-249	≥ 250
Overall	78.3%	10.2%	7.0%	2.4%	1.5%	0.5%
Agriculture, Forestry, Fishing	80.8%	9.7%	7.6%	1.3%	*	*
Mining, Energy and Water Supply, Waste Disposal	58.7%	13.2%	14.4%	7.7%	4.4%	1.6%
Manufacturing	63.2%	14.3%	12.4%	5.0%	3.6%	1.4%
Construction	81.7%	11.0%	5.7%	1.2%	*	*
Retail, Transportation, Logistics, Hospitality	77.9%	11.8%	7.1%	1.9%	1.1%	0.2%
Financial Services, Real Estate, Scientific and Technological Services	87.2%	7.0%	3.9%	1.0%	0.7%	0.2%
Other Company-Oriented Services	76.5%	9.4%	7.3%	3.6%	2.2%	0.9%
Public Administration, Education and Schooling	53.5%	15.0%	15.5%	7.0%	6.3%	2.7%
Health and Social Services	75.7%	8.5%	8.1%	4.2%	2.3%	1.3%
Other Services, Private Households	89.4%	5.8%	2.7%	1.2%	0.8%	0.1%

Source: the author, based on statistics by the German Federal Employment Agency.

An analysis that distinguishes between industries clearly shows a strong link between industry affiliation and company size. On account of the specific economic and organisational demands of certain industries, large company structures have an advantage in some industries, whereas others allow for a greater proportion of SMEs.

Employment Structure

Following from this general overview of the importance of different company sizes to Brandenburg's economy and labour market, the following section describes and compares the employment structures of small and large companies.

Here, interesting patterns regarding qualifications and employment periods for small and large companies emerge.

Qualification Structures

It is quite difficult to establish well-grounded claims about qualification structures of employees that can be categorized in terms of company size. Working from the fact that SMEs rely more heavily on the labour market than on internal personnel development, two plausible conclusions can be drawn. One, employees at SMEs possess lower qualifications than those at large companies, given that the relevant labour force is easier to recruit from the labour market. Or two, SMEs expect employees to possess sufficient qualifications already, since long training processes, both initial and advanced, are difficult to implement in such businesses.

One possibility for assessing the qualification demands of companies is to differentiate between employees based on required levels of training. Training requirements depend on the complexity of the relevant position. They are closely connected to the qualification requirements of the job, but they also consider informal education and work experience (German Federal Employment Agency 2020). The required level of training for helpers is less complex, and no vocational training is necessary. For skilled workers, demands are greater, and vocational training is often required. Specialist must be able to carry out highly complex tasks and extensive vocational training or a bachelor's degree are prerequisites. Experts have the highest level of necessary training and often require a master's degree.

An assessment of employees subject to social security contributions based on required levels of training and company size shows that smaller companies with up to 49 emloyees have a lower proportion of helpers. Notably, these companies have a particularly high proportion of employees with mid-level training requirements and, in comparison to large companies, fewer helpers, specialists, or experts. Those points indicate that SMEs and especially smaller companies with up to 49 employees have lower levels of internal specialization. At the same time, a large proportion of employees needs to possess a moderate degree of qualifications and knowhow. On these grounds, SMEs enjoy greater flexibility without simultaneously needing to bear the high costs of employing high-qualified workers. That means that the effectiveness of the vocational education and training system is of elevated importance, particularly for smaller companies with up to 49 employees. Large companies, by contrast, are likely able to implement internal divisions of labour on a large scale and make greater use of both high-qualified workers as well as helpers.

Table 4: Employees subject to social security contributions, by required level of training and company size in Brandenburg (30 June 2019) (*for the purpose of data protection, figures are anonymised)

REQUIRED LEVEL OF TRAINING	TOTAL	1-9	10-19	20-49	50-99	100-249	≥ 250
Overall	100%	100%	100%	100%	100%	100%	100%
Helper	16.3%	13.8%	13.5%	15.7%	20.0%	16.7%	17.7%
Skilled Worker	61.0%	66.7%	66.7%	64.5%	59.4%	61.2%	51.7%
Specialist	11.2%	10.9%	9.9%	9.9%	10.7%	11.4%	13.0%
Expert	10.7%	8.6%	9.9%	9.8%	9.9%	10.2%	14.7%
No Assignment/ No Information/ Error	0.8%	*	*	0.2%	*	0.6%	2.8%

Source: the author, based on statistics by the German Federal Employment Agency.

Working Hours

In an interpretation of SMEs as particularly flexible sites of economic activity with less financial capacity to pay workers higher wages, one can conclude that SMEs have a large proportion of part-time employees. Given these reduced working hours, these employees receive lower wages and make it possible for businesses to directly adapt to fluctuations in demand. Particularly in those small companies with fewer than ten employees, it is conceivable that new recruitment would occur only very cautiously, in direct response to increased demand and initially only with reduced working hours. Observing the proportion of part-time employees by company size and industry confirms this assumption (Table 5). Across all industries, approximately 40 per cent of employees in the smallest companies work part-time. In large companies with 250 employees or more, that figure drops to just 27 per cent. In SMEs with ten to 249 employees, the importance of part-time work registers higher than in large companies but lower than in the smallest companies. In this segment, however, values vary only modestly between companies of different sizes.

The proportion of part-time employees varies dramatically between different industries. The figure of 6 to 11 per cent in manufacturing is relatively low. The significance of part-time employees is much greater in the service industries, though, with figures between 28 and 48 per cent. In nearly all industries, however, SMEs employ far greater numbers of part-time workers than large companies. The sole exception appears in the field of "other company-oriented services." Here, large companies employ a large proportion of part-time workers.

Overall, SMEs - particularly the smallest companies among them - employ much higher levels of part-time work than large companies. The data do not address, however, whether this tendency comes at the request of employees or employers. The difference between SMEs and large companies offers a strong indication that operational and organisational considerations of companies play a large role.

Table 5: Proportion of part-time employees of all employees subject to social security contributions, by company size and industry in Brandenburg (30 June 2019) (*for the purpose of data protection, figures are anonymised)

INDUSTRY	TOTAL	1-9	10-19	20-49	50-99	100-249	≥ 250
Total	31.3%	40.4%	31.0%	28.1%	31.0%	31.0%	26.7%
Agriculture, Forestry, and Fishing	13.6%	23.9%	11.2%	7.9%	*	*	*
Mining, Energy and Water Supply, Waste Disposal	6.6%	14.6%	*	7.7%	*	*	4.4%
Manufacturing	9.7%	24.6%	15.2%	10.0%	7.8%	7.6%	6.6%
Construction	11.0%	19.1%	9.9%	6.3%	4.9%	*	*
Retail, Transportation, Logistics, Hospitality	35.0%	46.8%	37.8%	31.1%	32.9%	27.3%	25.9%
Financial Services, Real Estate, Scientific and Technological Services	27.7%	40.0%	24.4%	20.5%	19.7%	23.8%	21.9%
Other Company-Oriented Services	37.5%	38.8%	33.8%	27.3%	32.9%	42.1%	42.8%
Public Administration, Education and Schooling	41.3%	47.2%	47.3%	42.9%	42.6%	44.9%	36.6%
Health and Social Services	48.3%	54.7%	53.5%	57.6%	59.3%	51.9%	35.2%
Other Services, Private Households	45.3%	57.8%	*	44.9%	29.1%	*	*

Source: the author, based on statistics by the German Federal Employment Agency.

Employment Dynamics

As described above, this report interprets SMEs as flexible sites of economic activity with a high potential for adaptation via heavier use of the labour market. As such, SMEs do not necessarily have a strong job growth but display higher numbers of initiated and terminated employment relationships as well as employment relationships of shorter duration.

The assessment of employment dynamics makes it possible to observe the development of the numbers of employees subject to social security contributions up to a cut-off date. This method reveals whether employment has expanded or contracted over time. The state of employment, however, offers no insight in the processes of initiating or terminating employment relationships taking place on the labour market. For that purpose, one must observe flow quantities during a defined period.

Employment Growth

Analysing employment development with reference to employees subject to social security contributions between the years 2003 and 2019 reveals a decrease in employees between 2003 and 2005, and continuous growth between 2005 and 2019. Though the impact on SMEs was slightly above average during the period of decreasing employment, they above average growth during the period of employment growth (Table 6).

Table 6: Quantity of employees subject to social security contributions in Brandenburg, annually (30 June 2019)

YEAR	TOTAL	1-9	10-19	20-49	50-99	100-249	≥ 250
2003	735,641	153,637	81,852	122,972	94,607	120,080	162,493
2005	704,143	148,128	76,541	114,000	91,593	115,360	158,521
2019	854,164	159,208	91,384	142,017	112,839	154,425	194,291
2003-2005	-4.3%	-3.6%	-6.5%	-7.3%	-3.2%	-3.9%	-2.4%
2005-2019	21.3%	7.5%	19.4%	24.6%	23.2%	33.9%	22.6%

Source: the author, based on statistics by the German Federal Employment Agency.

Changes in employment figures within individual company size classes, however, varied considerably. In recent years, the smallest companies with up to nine employees showed a growth rate of 7.5 per cent, which measures clearly below the total average. Notably higher than this figure, though also below average, was growth in companies with between ten and 19 employees. In comparison, the increase among medium-sized companies with more than 20 employees measured distinctly above average. Conspicuously large was the growth in total employment among companies with 100 to 249 employees. Growth among large companies with 250 or more employees was also above average, though only slightly so. Within Brandenburg's employee structure, one observes a trend toward large companies. Positive economic development has enabled companies to implement growth processes. The trend toward a higher significance of large companies to employment, however, also appears nationwide. In the total employment figures from eastern and western Germany between 2005 and 2019, the role of large companies increased. While, in Brandenburg, companies with 100 to 249 employees grew in significance, nationwide in both eastern and western Germany it was, on average, large companies with 250 or more employees that saw this increase.

Measuring the development of employees subject to social security contributions by company size offers an overall very heterogeneous portrait. This data, however, does not suggest that SMEs in comparison to large companies are characterised by a particularly pronounced employment dynamic. In medium-sized companies with 100 to 249 employees, though the number of workers increased dramatically during the growth phase, the prior decrease measured slightly below average. In both the growth and the contraction phases, employment development in the smallest companies was below average. It is possible, however, that many small companies expanded sufficiently during the growth phase that they entered a new size class.

Initiated and Terminated Employment Relationships

Analysing the quantity of employees at a specific reference date only offers a picture of the overall results of the processes taking place in the labour market. Concealed behind these figures are a multitude of recruitments, terminations, and job changes. In order to develop a full view of movement in the labour market, employment relationships initiated and terminated within a certain timeframe must be evaluated in addition to assessments of the number of employees subject to social security contributions during a certain period.[89]

---

[89] An initiated employment relationship exists when an individual is hired as an employee subject to social security contributions. A terminated employment relationship is recorded when employment subject to social security contributions is terminated. Initiated and terminated employment relationships are also recorded when a shift between different kinds of employment (training, employment, marginally compensated employment, short-term employment) takes place (German Federal Employment Agency 2020).

Data for initiated and terminated employment relationships includes cases in which employment began or ended as well as instances of change between different forms of employment. Changes in the registration of companies on account of fusions or divisions are also included in these figures. In these situations, there are no actual changes in employment relationships. As such, the number of initiated and terminated employment relationships exaggerates the real movement within the labour market. The statistics used in this report also occasionally include personnel changes within existing companies. These figures should thus be read only as clues about actual movement within the labour market. In order to compare the employment dynamics of various company size classes, numbers of initiated and terminated employment relationships must be analysed in relation to total employment. Figures for hirings and terminations likely increase automatically proportional to the total number of jobs. Other studies analyse dynamics in the labour market using labour force fluctuation rates or labour turnover rates (LTR). In this manner, they put the number of excess initiated or terminated employment relationships in relation to total employment. Shifts between different forms of employment and changes in company registration, however, remain uncounted (Rhein 2010: 4f.; Knuth et al. 1999: 27f.). Thus, these statistics can be compared only to a limited degree with the figures that appear below.

Table 7 depicts the number of initiated and terminated employment relationships for different company size classes. These figures show that the total number of changes in employment relationships vary with the total number of employees. Companies with higher numbers of employees also tend to have greater numbers of changes in employment relationships. An examination of the three largest company size classes reveals, however, that many more personnel changes were reported in companies with one to nine employees as well as in those with 100 to 249 employees than in large companies. In order to assess personnel movement, it is useful to measure the number of initiated and terminated employment relationships in relation to total employment. Table 7 displays these figures based on LTR. It is calculated based on the following formula, drawn from Knuth et al. (1999: 27):

$$\text{LTR} = \frac{\text{initiated employment relationships} + \text{terminated employment relationships}}{2 \times \text{the number of employees}}.$$

LTR represents the proportion of jobs impacted by personnel changes during a given year. For Brandenburg, the LTR indicates that SMEs experience personnel changes on a much larger scale than large companies. Personnel changes had the greatest significance in the smallest companies, where approximately 35 per cent of all jobs were impacted. Personnel movement is least significant in large companies, at about 22 per cent. SMEs - especially smaller companies with fewer than 20 employees - display very pronounced employment dynamics regarding personnel changes.

Table 7: Initiated and terminated employment relationships in Brandenburg in 2018, by company size

INDICATOR	TOTAL	1-9	10-19	20-49	50-99	100-249	≥ 250
Initiated Employment Relationships	262,269	55,783	32,336	44,254	33,829	51,607	44,091
Terminated Employment Relationships	254,199	55,328	28,418	39,155	31,265	44,207	40,020
Initiated and Terminated Employment Relationships	516,468	111,111	60,754	83,409	65,094	95,814	84,111
Employees Subject to Social Security Contribution	849,148	159,068	90,984	138,965	114,380	155,270	190,481
Labour Turnover Rate (LTR)	30.4%	34.9%	33.4%	30.0%	28.5%	30.9%	22.1%

Source: the author, based on statistics by the German Federal Employment Agency.

Duration of Employment Relationship

In addition to employment growth and the total number of changes in employment relationships, the length of employment relationships also points to conclusions about the nature of employment dynamics. The greater the volume of personnel changes within companies, the shorter the duration of employment relationships. One can infer from this that the length of employment relationships in SMEs is shorter than in large ones.

The median length of employment relationships[90] confirms this assessment (Table 8). The larger the company, the longer employment relationships last. The

---

[90] The median length represents the length of employment relationships that separates the total number of employment relationships into two groups of equal number. In other words,

data reveals that employees in large companies are employed for significantly longer periods. In addition to the considerable importance of personnel changes, founding events also play a significant role in smaller companies with up to nine employees. The duration of employment in newly founded companies is inevitably shorter than in older companies. In sum, the analysis of the length of employment relationships makes a case for more dynamic employment in SMEs, particularly in the smallest companies.

Table 8: Current median duration of employment relationships in Brandenburg, by company size and in months (31 December 2018)

TOTAL	1-9	10-19	20-49	50-99	100-249	≥ 250
51.2	39.7	42.7	46.2	50.2	53.6	78.3

Source: the author, based on statistics by the German Federal Employment Agency.

Wages

An examination of gross earnings[91] for all full-time employees subject to social security contributions reveals a clear link between company size and employee wages. Wages increase notably with company size. In large companies with 250 employees or more, the median wage is approximately 70 per cent higher than in the smallest companies with one to nine employees. The difference between large companies and all other company size classes is particularly salient. Within the category of SMEs, however, one also observes differences. Among SMEs,

---

50 per cent of employees have worked a shorter amount of time and 50 per cent have worked longer.

[91] "Monthly gross wages comprise wages declared in the notification procedure for social security. In accordance with §14 SGB IV, gross wages subject to social security contributions consist of all on-going and one-time income. To allow for comparable data, wage statements are standardized to a period of one month and are generally restricted to full-time employees from the core group subject to social security contributions. The median - that is, the "50 per cent quantile"- is accepted as the average value, given that the calculation of an arithmetic middle (weighted average value), on account of the peculiarities of the notification procedure (contribution assessment ceiling), is not practical. The median value can be interpreted [in] that half of employees receiv[e] a lower wage, half receive a higher wage" (German Federal Employment Agency 2020).

wages increased with increasing company size by approximately EUR 660 or 32 per cent (Figure 1).

Figure 1: Gross monthly wages for full-time employees subject to social security contributions in Brandenburg, by company size (31 December 2018)

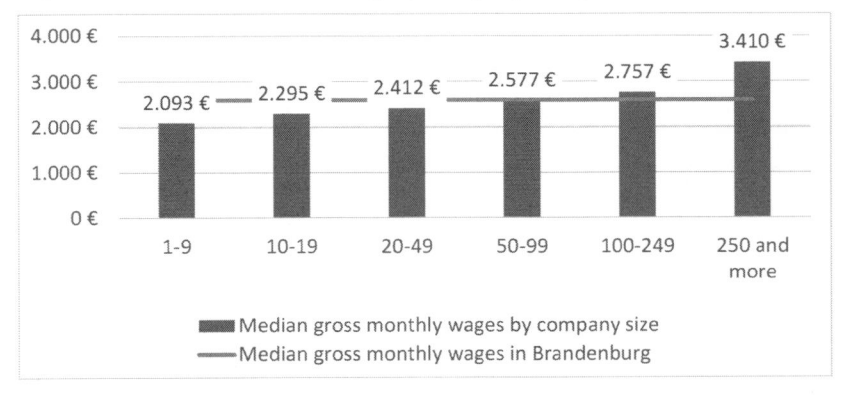

Company size	Median gross monthly wages
1-9	2.093 €
10-19	2.295 €
20-49	2.412 €
50-99	2.577 €
100-249	2.757 €
250 and more	3.410 €

Source: the author, based on statistics by the German Federal Employment Agency.

Income differences between company size classes also appear when employees are divided based on the level of training their work requires. Generally, the more complex their work, the higher their necessary qualification level and the required educational investments in those workers. In Brandenburg, the labour market faces a considerable labour shortage for skilled workers. This shortage increases with increasing qualification requirements.[92] In this context, it is expected that the higher the required training level, the higher the wages. This assumption bears out when one examines employees of all qualification levels. In December 2018, the median wage of experts measured double that of helpers (Table 9).

---

[92] The rate of unemployment for individuals without vocational training measured 26.5 per cent in 2019. By comparison, the rate of unemployment for individuals with an academic education was significantly lower at 2.2 per cent (Statistics by the German Federal Employment Agency, Qualification-Specific Unemployment Rates, Yearly Average, 2020).

Table 9: Median gross monthly wages for full-time employees subject to social security contributions in Brandenburg, by company size and required level of training (31 December 2018)

REQUIRED LEVEL OF TRAINING	TOTAL	1-9	10-19	20-49	50-99	100-249	≥ 250
Helper	1,922€	1,850€	1,937€	1,860€	1,880€	1,924€	2,200€
Skilled Worker	2,440€	2,034€	2,197€	2,316€	2,482€	2,628€	3,222€
Specialist	3,366€	2,377€	2,858€	3,137€	3,280€	3,606€	4,144€
Expert	4,431€	3,372€	3,759€	4,012€	4,233€	4,558€	5,351€

Source: the author, based on statistics by the German Federal Employment Agency.

At each individual level of required training, wages in large companies are higher than in smaller companies. The only exception are helpers in companies with ten to 19 employees. These workers earn more than in large companies with 20 to 249 employees. Differences in income in SMEs with up to 249 employees are not particularly large. In large companies, however, helpers earn notably more than in SMEs. Skilled workers, specialists, and experts earn more the larger their company is. Salary differences here, in comparison to those among helpers, are considerable. In large companies with 250 or more employees, wages for mid-level workers and experts measured approximately 58 per cent higher than in smaller businesses with up to nine employees. For specialists, the difference was nearly 74 per cent.

Differences in income between the companies of different sizes cannot be explained in terms of different employee structures regarding required levels of training. It is possible, however, that differences in income are contingent upon industry affiliation and that what appears an ostensible correlation with company size masks a correlation with industry affiliation. Table 10 lists monthly wage of employees by company size and industry affiliation. Alongside the strong differences based on company size, this data also shows considerable differences by industry. The median wage across all company size classes varies between individual industries, from EUR 1,940 in agriculture to approximately EUR 3,690 in mining and utilities.

An analysis of the income structure by industry confirms the influence of company size on income. In nearly all industries, employees earn more the larger their company is. Particularly extreme are the differences between the smallest companies and large companies. One also finds differences, however, within SMEs, between the smallest companies with one to nine employees and medium-sized companies with 100 to 249 employees.

The only exception to this pattern can be found in the field of "other company-oriented services." Employees in this field earn more in smaller companies with up to 49 employees than they do in those of medium size. Differences in income between company size classes in this industry are, overall, slight. Labour leasing also falls under this rubric. The corresponding enterprises likely have a higher number of employees. Payment, however, is oriented toward the enterprises leasing workers rather than to the companies ceding them. This point could clarify why a difference in income between large companies and SMEs in this industry is scarcely noticeable. Similarly, the income differences between institutions of different sizes in public administration as well as in education and schooling are scant.

Differences in income between large companies and SMEs vary by industry. Except for "other company-oriented services," these differences are evident in all industries. Income differences between small companies with up to nine employees and large business measure between 11 per cent in public administration and approximately 81 per cent in the field of mining/utilities. These statistics reveal that income differences between company sizes in private industries are notably higher than in public administration. Though obligations to collective bargaining agreements are more common in all companies in the fields of education and schooling as well as in public administration, similar obligations likely appear in private industries only for large companies, which are much less often bound by such agreements. Company size appears to stand in close connection both to the use of collective bargaining agreements and to wages (MASGF 2019: 70ff.).

Table 10: Median gross monthly wages for full-time employees subject to social security contributions in Brandenburg, by company size and industry (31 December 2018) (* for the purpose of data protection, figures are anonymised)

INDUSTRY	TOTAL	1-9	10-19	20-49	50-99	100-249	≥ 250
Total	2,593€	2,093€	2,295€	2,412€	2,577€	2.757€	3.410€
Agriculture, Forestry, and Fishing	1,940€	1,860€	1,929€	1,917€	2,024€	2.736€	*
Mining, Energy and Water Supply, Waste Disposal	3,687€	2,370€	2,614€	3,070€	3,118€	3.407€	4.300€
Manufacturing	2,684€	2,073€	2,223€	2,295€	2,449€	2.536€	3.681€
Construction	2,378€	2,204€	2,330€	2,456€	2,644€	2.931€	3.603€
Retail, Transportation, Logistics, Hospitality	2,206€	1,889€	2,111€	2,204€	2,380€	2.330€	2.684€
Financial Services, Real Estate, Scientific and Technological Services	3,352€	2,483€	2,980€	3,398€	3,595€	3.979€	4.430€
Other Company-Oriented Services	1,957€	1,982€	2,053€	1,961€	1,891€	1.887€	2.051€
Public Administration, Education and Schooling	3,489€	3,290€	3,392€	3,357€	3,309€	3.527€	3.650€
Health and Social Services	2,777€	2,016€	2,300€	2,507€	2,530€	2.891€	3.305€
Other Services, Private Households	2,426€	1,800€	2,420€	2,616€	2,538€	2.882€	*

Source: the author, based on statistics by the German Federal Employment Agency.

In sum, it can be concluded that company size has a positive effect on employee compensation, both directly and indirectly via obligations to collective bargaining agreements. In addition to commitments to collective bargaining agreements, economic performance on account of economies of scale can also be of particular importance.

Conclusion

In the assessment of employment dynamics and wage conditions, company size plays a decisive role. In the context of the analytical approach adopted in this report, smaller businesses with up to 19 employees do not appear as powerful motors of employment growth in the economy. In the growth phase from 2005 to 2019, employment growth in large companies measured even greater than that of SMEs. Disguised behind this tendency, however, is a much more substantial labour market dynamic among SMEs. The number of initiated and terminated employment relationships is vastly greater in SMEs than in large companies. This trend accompanied the shorter duration of employment relationships. In contrast to large businesses in recent years, SMEs do not function as growth motors for employment. On account of their highly dynamic rates of employment expansions and cutbacks, however, they nevertheless appear as sites of economic adaptation. Given that these processes unfold in the external labour market, they certainly imply the risk of unemployment for individual employees. Nevertheless, they also imply greater opportunities to secure jobs. Here, it is possible to view SMEs as fulfilling an important integrative function for the labour market.

In positioning themselves to carry out their economic functions, SMEs and especially smaller enterprises with up to 49 employees tend to draw on workers with mid-level training and employ them part-time. Because these workers can be deployed in a wide range of capacities and because their working hours can be extended as necessary, these SMEs maintain a high level of flexibility. This constellation can pose a problem for both workers and companies, if the part-time working hours are not voluntary and if incentives exist for workers to changes jobs. This emphasis on mid-level qualifications within SMEs also limits unskilled workers' ability to benefit from the potential integrative function of these companies. For SMEs in general, the effectiveness of the vocational training system is significant.

The causes of the more dynamic employment disposition among SMEs are most likely not only to be found on the side of the companies. The analysis of compensation revealed that large companies pay higher wages. Employees are thus more likely to end employment relationships in SMEs than in large businesses. Differences in compensation can be partially explained by differing obligations to collective bargaining agreements and differing levels of economic performance. Brandenburg's economic structure skews toward SMEs, which poses potential problems considering the corresponding lower incomes associated with such businesses.

Given such considerations about adaptive capacities and wage conditions, it appears that a "good" mix of businesses of varying sizes is crucial for both regional development and living conditions. The excessive predominance of large companies can lead, over time, to constraints on adaptability and, ultimately, to unemployment. An insufficient presence of large companies, however, can limit workers' earning potential and thus living conditions. What such a "good" mix of businesses might look like cannot be determined from the data analysed in this report. However, comparisons with eastern and western Germany suggest that a greater role for large companies in Brandenburg is desirable.

References

Bauer, Thomas K./ Schmucker, Alexandra/ Vorell, Mathias (2008a): KMU und Arbeitsplatzdynamik: Eine Analyse auf Basis der Beschäftigten-Historik-Datei. In: Journal for Labour Market Research (Zeitschrift für ArbeitsmarktForschung/ZAF) 02 and 03/2008, pp. 199-221.

Bauer, Thomas K./ Schmucker, Alexandra/ Vorell, Mathias (2008b): Viel Umschlag, wenig Gewinn: Beschäftigungsbeitrag von kleinen und mittleren Unternehmen. In: IAB-Kurzbericht 23/2008.

European Commission (2003): Commission Recommendation of 6 May 2003 concerning the Definition of Micro, Small and Medium-Sized Enterprises. URL: https://eur-lex.europa.eu/legal-content/EN/TXT/HTML/?uri=LEGISSUM:n26026&from=DE [12 June 2020].

Fuchs, Michaela/Weyh, Antje (2007): Die Determinanten des Job-Turnover im regionalen Vergleich. In: Institut für Wirtschaftsfotrschung (ifo) Dresden Bericht 2007 14 (2), pp. 25-36.

German Federal Employment Agency (Bundesagentur für Arbeit/BA) (2020): Glossar der Statistik der Bundesagentur für Arbeit (BA). URL: https://statistik.arbeitsagentur.de/Statischer-Content/Grundlagen/Definitionen/Glossare/Generische-Publikationen/Gesamtglossar.pdf [12 June 2020].

Haltiwanger, John/Scarpetta, Stefano/Schweiger, Helena (2006): Assessing Job Flows Across Countries: The Role of Industry, Firm Size and Regulations. In: Institute for the Study of Labor (IZA) Discussion Paper Series No. 2450.

Knuth, Matthias/Mühge, Gernot/Müller, Angelika (1999): Der Preis des Wandels: Wirtschaftliche Umstrukturierung, Arbeitskräftefreisetzung und Arbeitslosigkeit in Westdeutschland. In: Graue Reihe des Instituts Arbeit und Technik 1999/08.

Ministerium für Arbeit, Soziales, Gesundheit, Frauen und Familie des Landes Brandenburg (MASGF) (2019): Entwicklung von Betrieben und Beschäftigung in Brandenburg: Ergebnisse der dreiundzwanzigsten Welle des Betriebspanels Brandenburg. URL: https://msgiv.brandenburg.de/sixcms/media.php/9/Forschungsbericht%2043_Web.pdf [12 June 2020].

Rhein, Thomas (2010): Ist Europa auf dem Weg zum „Turbo-Arbeitsmarkt"? Beschäftigungsdynamik im internationalen Vergleich. In: IAB-Kurzbericht 19/2010.

Schumpeter, Joseph A. (1934): The Theory of Economic Development. Oxford: n/a.

Schumpeter, Joseph A. (1942): Capitalism, Socialism, and Democracy. New York: Harper & Row.

Wagner, Joachim (2007): Jobmotor Mittelstand? Arbeitsplatzdynamik und Betriebsgröße in der westdeutschen Industrie. In: Quarterly Journal of Economic Research (Vierteljahrshefte zur Wirtschaftsforschung) 2007 76 (3), pp. 76-87.

Weingärtner, Simon (2019): Soziologische Arbeitsmarkttheorien: Ein Überblick. Wiesbaden: Springer Verlag für Sozialwissenschaften (VS).

Websites

Statistics by the German Federal Employment Agency (Bundesagentur für Arbeit/BA), Qualification-Specific Unemployment Rates, Yearly Average, 2020:

https://statistik.arbeitsagentur.de/nn_31892/SiteGlobals/Forms/Rubrikensuche/Rubrikensuche_Form.html?view=processForm&resourceId=210368&input_=&pageLocale=de&topicId=1250828&year_month=aktuell&year_month.GROUP=1&search=Suchen

3. HUMAN RESOURCE MANAGEMENT IN SMES

3.1. Relevance of Training and Its Practice

Continuing Vocational Training and SMEs: Specificities, Practices, and Potentials

Aline Valette-Wursthen

Introduction

Nowadays we can assume, thanks to substantial literature (Salais and Storper 1993, Bentabet 2008, Régnault 2011), that small and medium-sized enterprises (SMEs) are specific and that they should not be regarded as large firm in the making. Several works also show that they are a very diverse and heterogeneous group. The main political discourse asserts that there is a need to break down the locks that are holding back the growth of SMEs linked to the hypothesis that "bigger is better". But do owners of SMEs really want their companies to grow? Is it perhaps time to stop considering being small naturally to be a handicap for an enterprise?

On one hand, in France, only few data, analysis, and research are available on the topic of SMEs. The New Enterprises Information System (Système d'information sur les nouvelles entreprises/SINE)[93] survey, regularly produced by the French National Institute of Statistics and Economic Studies (L'Institut National de la Statistique et des Études Économiques/INSEE)[94] is the main device studying the profile of firm creators and analysing the first years of activities of their enterprise. But the topic of SMEs is still not much exploited due to a lack of means (time and human resources/HR in particular), a lack of visibility, and the absence

---

[93] www.insee.fr/en/metadonnees/source/serie/s1271.

[94] www.insee.fr/en.

of a large availability for researchers. On the other hand, even though many actors support and advise SMEs and very small enterprises (VSEs)[95], there is a lack of stepping back, capitalizing on, and dissemination of this field knowledge in order to produce information for policy makers.

First, we will introduce the article with some contextual data on the SME landscape in France and explain why researchers in France talk about the "galaxy of VSEs" (Letowski 2019) and the features of such companies. In the second part, we will illustrate specific behaviours, characteristics, and the diversity of VSEs regarding training, based on data on the topic of continuing vocational training (CVT) by the French Centre for Research on Education, Training and Employment (Centre d'études et de recherches sur les qualifications/Céreq) (Dubois et al. 2016).

Contextual Data on French SMEs and VSEs

Eurostat figures of 2015 show that enterprises employing fewer than 250 persons (SMEs) represented 99 per cent of all enterprises in the European Union (EU) (Eurostat 2018). The vast majority of those are VSEs with less then ten employees. In 2017, they represented 93 per cent of the total of the 24.5 million SMEs in the EU (Statista 2019). In terms of number of employees, SMEs employed 66.3 per cent of total EU employees in 2015 (Eurostat 2018).

In France, "in 2017, 2.3 million companies" are active in the private sector (other than agriculture and expected self-entrepreneur status), but only 5,646 companies (0.25 per cent) have 250 or more employees. Companies with 10 to 249 employees represent 6 per cent, whereas firms with less than 10 employees representes 94 per cent of the total. Among the 2.1 million of VSE's, 57 per cent do not have any employee. Next to this VSE population, the total estimated number of self-entrepreneurs[96] is around 1,000,000. All in all, the landscape of French

---

[95] In this article, SMEs are defined as firms that employ less than 250 employees. VSEs constitute a subgroup of the SME population; per definition, they employ less than ten employees.

[96] The status of self-entrepreneur (micro-entrepreneur), created in 2009, simplifies business registration formalities and reduces and simplifies social contributions. An "micro-entrepreneur" is a sole proprietorship that falls under the tax regime for micro-enterprises and the micro-social regime for the payment of social security contributions. This simplified regime has been created to facilitate the procedures for setting up and managing businesses, while

SMEs is very similar to the one in the EU. French enterprises (companies and sole proprietorships) with one to nine employees account for 19 per cent of salaried employment in the private sector (excluding agriculture), which made it 3.3 million employees on 31 December 2018. Such enterprises employ an average of three employees, but 38 per cent of these have only one employee. Also, more than three quarters of employees in VSEs work in the tertiary sector; the remaining employees work in the construction and energy sectors, where craft enterprises are concentrated. So, when adding employees working in VSEs and self-entrepreneurs, it amounts to nearly four million workers (INSEE 2019).

The proportion of part-time employees in VSEs (27.5 per cent) is higher than that of companies with ten or more employees (17.6 per cent). It ranged from 10.8 per cent of employees in construction to 52 per cent of employees in the "private education, health and social action" activities of the tertiary sector. In 2018, nearly 450,000 employees in VSEs (13.2 per cent) are on fixed-term contracts. The use of fixed-term contracts is more widespread in VSEs than in larger firms. By way of comparison, in companies with ten to 19 employees, 9.9 per cent of employees were on fixed-term contracts on 31 December 2018 (INSEE 2019).

After setting the scene from a statistic perspective, we will now enter what Letowski (2019) calls the "galaxy of VSEs". The next part will focus on the smallest of SMEs (less than ten employees); still, a large part of our findings could also be extended to the next bigger group of companies (with less than 50 employees).

"The Galaxy of VSEs": Key Role of VSE Leaders

In line with the work on SMEs and VSEs by Céreq (Bentabet 2008), which highlights the diversity of socio-productive configurations in which small businesses evolve and the central role of the leader profile, Letowski (2019) speaks about the "galaxy of VSEs". The author points out that we need to understand the behaviours of SMEs in the context of goals defined by their leaders and their specific strategic orientation. In the field of VSEs, leaders differ immensely according

---

allowing people to benefit from dedicated social protection and other advantages (simplified administrative formalities; simplified method of calculating; paying social security contributions and income tax; social protection such as health coverage and retirement among others; and a right to vocational training).

to their preferred type of investment (human, social, cultural, and financial capital among others), which makes the landscape of VSEs so diverse. For Letowski (2019), there are three key characteristics of the small businesses leader profile that help understand the decisions they make for their enterprises: firstly, the leader's motivations and life plan, secondly, their training and previous working life, and thirdly, their environment.

The SINE survey mentioned by Letowski (2019) allows us to investigate what motivates business creators. The most common item mentioned by interviewees is the "search for independence" (60 per cent): "being their own boss", "decide on their own", "seek accomplishment in that position", and "create their own job" all seem to be important incentives for people to found their own company. An increasing income is not one of the main motivations; it is only cited by one out of five people. Furthermore, it should be noted that independence refers to the awareness of obstacles and constraints and to having a structured project for the business started from the outset. Entrepreneurship is only cited by 30 per cent of the people interviewed, mainly by those who have a substantial growth perspective. For the majority of creators, the most important issues are the successful installation and the sustainability of their business, not its growth. According to themselves, business creators make enormous personal investments (in particular, time) to reach those goals for their businesses; at the same time, they strongly express their satisfaction with their experience as a leader (Letowski 2019).

The second key characteristic in "the galaxy of VSEs" (Letowski 2019) concerns the training pathway and the previous working life of the creator. Cultural and relational capital are the fundament of business creation. SINE figures show a large diversity of the level of education among creators: roughly half of them (54 per cent) have the equivalent of the French baccalauréat (bac) or less (level 4 or less of the European Qualifications Framework/EQF), whereas the other half (46 per cent) got a higher education diploma, including 20 per cent who have a diploma equivalent to EQF level 7 or 8. As for the previous working life, around 30 per cent of creators are former business leaders, with 36 per cent coming directly from an employee's position and 26 per cent from unemployment. In the French context, there is a trend to valorise business creation as a successful career development, even though this type of entrepreneurship represents a minority share in firm creator profiles. Whatever the previous status - craftsman, skilled worker, or manager -, relational network is always present, used, and important (Letowski 2019).

The third and last characteristic concerns the economic environment. The ability to participate and compete in the market and the state of the economic climate are important factors in the development and sustaining of a business. VSEs faced more difficulties after the economic crisis in 2008 than larger firms, mainly due to difficulties in accessing bank funding and improving their visibility in the market (Letowski 2019).

As Letowski concludes in his article (2019), the VSEs landscape is complex and goes beyond the characteristic of company size. This heterogeneity can be imagined as two opposite conceptions of firms and entrepreneurs that could be placed at the extremities of an axis, centred on the behaviour of the entrepreneur. One end of the axis reflects a manager whose primary objective is to create their own job in the form of a self-employed activity and therefore a company adapted to this objective; the other end of the axis reflects an entrepreneurial manager of an SME whose objective is the growth they would like to see on a permanent basis. Managers of VSEs are mostly located close to the "creator of their own job", but with many variations: some will employ a small number of people; others will have positioned themselves "naturally" on market niches through their know-how. A common feature they all share is the entangling between their private person and their company (Letowski 2019).

The analytic approach that focuses on the business leader can also be found in the book by Bentabet and Gadille (2019). In this book, VSEs and SMEs are understood as diverse social worlds. As Bentabet, Gadille, and Trouvé (2019) define them, social worlds are a whole with an internal coherence. In the tradition of the approach by Céreq that is based on the term of "socio-productive configuration", researchers furthermore tend to make a strong link between strategic orientation and human resources management (HRM) practices in SMEs.

We still need to acquire more knowledge on VSEs and SMEs. Currently, we lack academic research on the subject in general and specifically qualitative analysis as well as regular, monitored, and coherent statistics. We need a real understanding of VSEs and SMEs; therefore, we need a reading grid to analyse collected data, to anticipate the role such companies play in the economy and society, to refine appropriate support policies, and finally to advise policymakers on policies targeting this kind of company.

Concerning training behaviours of French VSEs and SMEs, several studies conducted by Céreq (that we will refer to later) provide us with original knowledge and help us analyse the specificities of French VSEs and SMEs.

Training Behaviours of SMEs and VSEs

Thanks to several surveys conducted by Céreq, such as the French version of the fifth European Continuing Vocational Training Survey (CVTS-5) survey or the French Dispositif d'Enquêtes sur les Formations et Itinéraires des Salariés (DEFIS) survey,[97] we can update our knowledge about training access for SMEs employees. The latest exploitations of data on employees' access to training by Céreq highlight inequalities usually observed according to the size of the companies. While 48 per cent of all French employees followed a training scheme in 2015, the proportion ranged from 25 per cent of employees working in small companies to 63 per cent of employees working in large ones (Dubois et al. 2016). It is on basis of this observation that public authorities and social partners are calling for an increased training effort in VSEs and SMEs.

Investment of SMEs in Continuing Training: Irregular, Defined by Compulsory Training Schemes and Low due to a Lack of Time and Need

While companies with more than 50 employees make constant training efforts, the behaviours of smaller enterprises are rather irregular. Only 45 per cent of companies with ten to 20 employees train them every year. For the remaining 55 per cent, the need for training is not systematic and irregular (Dubois et al. 2016).

Indeed, training spending of VSEs and SMEs is irregular, too, and shows a stronger link to economic activity and market developments than those of larger firms. In other words, small enterprises have a more instrumental view of training than the big ones. They would train first and foremost when they feel they need it. Their training effort is stronger when they are involved in dynamics of improvement, development or general reorientation. The data provided by

---

[97] www.cereq.fr/en/data-access/lifelong-learning-and-vocational-training-surveys-defis-cvts-base-reflet, www.cereq.fr/en/training-employees-trajectory-surveys.

Céreq show that 84 per cent of SMEs become "training companies"[98] as soon as their leaders want to change the field of company activity or aim at a new market positioning. Only 56 per cent of SMEs become "training companies" because sustaining activity is their leaders' main objective. Many SMEs also declare that the impact of training on the economic performance of their company is important to them, which is why their evaluation is similar (22 per cent of training companies with ten to 49 employees compared to 19 per cent of those with 500 or more employees) (Béraud 2015).

One reason for the irregularity of the training effort of SMEs could also be the cycle of training renewal that is dictated by regulations companies have to comply with. Training obligations place a much greater burden on the budget of the smallest businesses compared to the larger one: Nearly 20 per cent of the companies with ten to 49 employees spend almost all or all of their training budget on compulsory training schemes[99] (Béraud 2016) (Table 1).

Table 1: Weight of regulatory training, by size of the company

	Share of companies which fund compulsory and regulatory training schemes (%)	Share of companies which spend almost all or all of their training budget on compulsory training schemes (%)
ten to 49 employees	61	18
50 to 249 employees	87	13
250 to 499 employees	95	9

---

[98] The concept "training companies" entails all firms that have completed at least one training scheme, regardless of its form, during the interrogation year (Béraud 2015).

[99] A training course is said to be compulsory when it is required by law to be carried out by the employer. These texts have two sources: on the one hand, the legal constraints stemming from the Labour Code, which govern health and safety obligations and all employers, and, on the other hand, all the legal conditions specific to the way in which activities are carried out (specific permits, mobilization of tools, dangerous environment, etc.). Compulsory training can be divided in two main areas: health and safety training and other regulatory authorisations and certifications (main ones are authorisations to drive machinery; compulsory training for drivers; different levels of electrical authorisations) (Béraud 2016).

500 employees and more	96	7
All companies (average)	63	16

Source: Béraud (2016: 3).

When SMEs and VSEs report on the obstacles to their training investment, the cost of training seems only secondary. When explaining why they do not train or why they limit their training effort, small companies primarily cite the following two reasons: the lack of need and the lack of time. The lack of need for continuing education is the most frequently quoted reason: 75 per cent of firms do not consider themselves in need for continuing education and 54 per cent expressed that they prefer to recruit new employees with the qualifications and skills required. Half of the companies indeed prefer to give priority to initial training. Time is a resource that is often in short supply: 62 per cent of companies assume that the workload of continuing training would be too heavy and that there is not enough time for staff to be trained. Far behind the absence of need, financial costs of training are mentioned as an obstacle by only two companies out of five (Marion 2017) (Table 2).

Table 2: Reasons for limited training efforts (firms with ten to 49 employees)

Staff qualifications and skills match the needs of the company	75%
Workload is too heavy, and staff are short of time	62%
The company's preferred strategy is to recruit people with the required qualifications and skills	54%
The company has given priority to initial training rather than continuing vocational training	50%
The costs of continuing vocational training courses or internships are too high	41%
It is difficult to assess the company's continuing vocational training needs	31%
Significant training efforts have been made previously	28%
There are no courses or internships on the market adapted to the needs of the company	18%

Other reasons	16%

Source: Marion (2017).

In SMEs with ten to 19 employees, other factors influence training access rates, such as the fact that the company belongs to a company group[100], the share of qualified jobs within the firm, or the level of the manager's degree (Figure 3) (Marion 2017). Indeed, within SMEs from ten to 19 employees belonging to a company group, training access of employees reaches 34 per cent when it is only 23 per cent in those of the same size which not (Marion 2017).

A Three Groups Typology Combining SMEs Training Practices and Business Strategy

Deepening researches concerning training strategy of French SMEs, recent work by Céreq highlights that there is a large heterogeneity among SMEs. DEFIS survey exploitation makes it possible to distinguish more precisely three business configurations among companies with three to 49 employees. In each of these three configurations, training practices are adjusted to particular development strategies (Béraud and Noack 2019). The first configuration includes the so-called "managerial and training companies", whose training practices are the closest to those of large companies. The second and third configurations include firms of the studied group (firms with three to 49 employees) with little training. The second pattern concerns so-called "traditional companies", where training is limited to legal and regulatory aspects. The third pattern, called "entrepreneurs", brings together those whose more specific skills needs are not well covered by the training offered; as a substitute, these companies develop more apprenticeships in the workplace (Béraud and Noack 2019).

"Managerial and training companies": This configuration includes 37 per cent of small businesses and is characterised by a very specific profile of managers. The vast majority of them have higher education qualifications and their main objective is to grow their company's business. In order to achieve this goal, they

---

[100] In this article, a group of companies or "group" means a group of companies with distinct legal personalities, but with direct and indirect links that are mainly financial (for example, shareholdings or control) but also frequently organisational (management and strategies), economic (pooling of resources), or commercial (sales and purchases of goods or services).

attach great importance to all strategic elements, such as price competitiveness, innovation, and originality of products or services. Consequently, these companies are characterised by a training policy that is just as developed and institutionalised as that of large companies, which is reflected, for example, by the existence of a person dedicated to training (Béraud and Noack 2019).

With an average of nine employees, they are slightly larger than companies of other configurations. More than one in three is part of a company group, a network of brands, or a franchise. Many of these "managerial and training companies" are part of specialized services, such as accounting, pharmacies, opticians, or legal activities. Some of them can be described as "small professional enterprises" attached to liberal professions (such as architectural firms, real estate agencies, and chartered accountants). The construction sector is under-represented in this business type, and the proportion of blue-collar workers is lower than in the others. The market for companies of this type is primarily local; still, a quarter of them expands their production nationally and more than one in ten even internationally. The favourable economic prospects that many of them report proves the success of their dynamism. More than eight in ten companies of this configuration are training companies and they largely continue to train, with important schemes, new employees after their recruitment. Their positioning on innovative strategies and specialized services contributes to making the development of their employees' skills a central issue. Moreover, like large companies, these companies often work with all types of employment training partners (such as training organisations, Chambers of Commerce, employers' organisations, consultants among others) in order to support and develop their training policy (Béraud and Noack 2019).

"Traditional small companies": Companies of this type declare limited training needs. These companies are the oldest, often resulting from a family transmission or takeover. Their managers have few qualifications and mainly aim at maintaining rather than further developing their business. Accordingly, such companies declare only few trainings needs and recruit little. For example, only one employee in four had access to training in 2014, mainly for regulatory reasons. Characterised by a mainly blue-collar workforce (45 per cent), these companies are present in all sectors where small structures are concentrated, particularly in traditional catering, construction, and car repair. They are distinguished by a strong territorial anchoring and few of them extend their production beyond the local market. A quarter of them report poor overall conditions and only 10 per cent have a workforce that has increased over the last three years. It is important to note that these companies, which do not have an asserted strategy other than a trivialized cost-competitiveness form, are the ones that most frequently declare that they have no specific skills needs. 41 per cent of these companies train mainly to meet regulatory requirements, for example updating an electrical or a machine operator's certificate. In these small, traditional companies, training adjusts to a production situation that seeks to maintain itself and changes only to meet regulatory requirements (Béraud and Noack 2019).

"Entrepreneurs": Companies of this type look for distinctive skills. Like those in traditional businesses, the managers of small entrepreneurial structures have few qualifications. However, 80 per cent of them have started their own business. Most of them (68 per cent) declare that they want to develop the company's activity on the basis of an original project or a customised production or service. Created by their current manager and based on strategic guidelines of differentiation or specialisation, these companies can thus be described as "entrepreneurial". However, they have some points in common with the "traditional" ones: They are present in the same sectors of activity, and their employees occupy relatively low-skilled positions. But they differ by the fact that they were established more recently and are positioned in a larger market (23 per cent operate on the national market and 10 per cent on the international market); they also have better economic dynamics, as proven by an increase in the workforce, good economic health, and prospects that are more frequently positive than for "traditional companies". While they place a strong emphasis on compulsory training, these companies also seem to seek to develop skills through and at the workplace rather than in an organised framework. Their managers, like those in "managerial and traditional companies", to a majority of 57 per cent believe that skills are mainly acquired on the job. Indeed, more than the others, these companies make use of apprenticeships (34 per cent), and oftentimes have appointed an employee as a trainer or tutor (41 per cent, whereas its only 23 per cent of the "traditional companies"). Furthermore, even when those companies are not identified as "training companies", they nevertheless report more frequently than others that they have trained employees on the job (38 per cent). "Entrepreneurs" recruit frequently (72 per cent have hired one or more people in the last three years) and most of them provide training after recruitment. For these recruitments, which must meet specific skills needs, managers rely mainly on personal networks (47 per cent). They also frequently request the help of outside organisations to advise them in implementing their training policy. Despite limited recourse to training, these companies often develop specific know-how through work activities. It is perhaps mostly in this configuration that, in addition to the frequent use of apprenticeship contracts, informal and unconventional training methods can be found (Béraud and Noack 2019).

In each of the above-described configurations of small businesses, the profile of the leader plays an important role. We will now elaborate on this aspect a little more.

The Entrepreneur: Driving Force Behind the Training in Small Businesses

When we cross lessons derived from studies based on DEFIS surveys (see above) and the analysis by Letowksi (2019), it shows that the entrepreneur's relationship to training explains to a significant extent the intensity of use of training in their company. A manager who has experienced initial education for themselves is more inclined to promote continuing training for their employees. The impact is tangible: While 42 per cent of companies with ten to 19 employees and executives without a degree are "training companies", the rate rises to 83 per cent for companies with executives holding a Bac+3 or higher degree (Marion 2017, Letowksi 2019) (Figure 3).

Figure 3: Share of training companies, by the manager's level of education

No degree (equivalent to EQF 1)	42%
CAP/BEP (equivalent to EQF 3)	52%
Baccalauréat (equivalent to EQF 4)	57%
Bac+2 (equivalent to EQF 5)	69%
Bac+3 and more (equivalent to EQF 6 and more)	83%

Source: Marion (2017).

There are two other factors that can have a positive impact on the use of training in a company: first, the company's director is a member in different networks;

and second, they are open to new forms of training. In order to raise the awareness of managers about training possibilities, "coaches" are necessary: Data show that the share of "training companies" and employee access to training depend largely on the support the manager receives to develop training courses. Excepted certified public accountants that are not training specialists, whatever type of organisation is requested to help with the training, the impact on the rate of employee access to training has proven to be significant. For example, the rate of employee access to training can be increased by 15 percentage points after a company with fewer than 20 employees has received support by a training course consultant for the implementation of a training policy (Marion 2017).

In France, the funding and provision of continuing training is organised by the OPCA[101], which is explicitly mandated by the social partners and public authorities to compensate for the lack of internal resources dedicated to training in the smallest companies. These support services are only used by 33 per cent of the companies with ten to 19 employees. When companies aim at obtaining a quality label or at encouraging employee mobility, companies prefer consultants to help them, sometimes in conjunction with OPCAs (as some OPCAs offer their member companies a list of consultants from the HR support register). The use of a consultant is also more frequent when the company director or HR manager participates in a network or association of entrepreneurs or human resources development (HRD). One third of small enterprises also turn to training organisations, more specifically with the aim of achieving a specific training action (Marion 2017).

Conclusion

This article explained how SMEs and VSEs are specific regarding their training behaviours. One of their distinguishing characteristics is the significant role of their leader (their profile; the strategy they chose for the company). Several works conducted by the team of Céreq, based on European and French surveys, allowed us to confirm the diversity that exists among SMEs and VSEs. Still, more

---

[101] The Organisme Paritaire Collecteur Agréé (OPCA) is responsible for collecting, pooling, and redistributing the financial obligations paid by companies for vocational training. The OPCA ensures the financing and the administrative management of the training actions implemented by companies.

data and analysis of as well as research on those special types of companies are necessary in order to understand them better.

Three configurations of companies with three to 49 employees, where training practices adjust to particular development strategies, emerged, namely, the "managerial and training companies", the "traditional small companies", and the "entrepreneurs".

However, the classification of a company within a particular configuration may evolve. A new positioning on the market, the development of a new product, a change in management are all factors that influence a company's training practices. The heterogeneity of small business development strategies and the related extend of training practices are a challenging issue for public policies aimed at improving employees' access to training. Such policies can be an important support for those companies that engage in the development of specific, sometimes original activities and seek to develop distinctive skills for their employees. All in all, support by skills operators remains an important issue. The recognition of on-the-job training, introduced by the recent French reform on vocational training[102], could also be addressed in this context by encouraging the formalisation and development of such training practices.

In order to conclude, we could take up some recommendations made by Céreq for the French case (Marion 2017), assuming that they certainly can be adapted to other national contexts. We need to

- promote the access to information on training and continuing training to business leaders,
- train and inform accountants
- and promote cooperation between the different types of support staff (Chambers of Commerce, consultants, and training organisations among others) in order to better integrate the development of vocational training in the strategy of companies.

---

[102] The French Government Act 2018/771 of 5 September 2018 for the freedom to choose one's professional future, indicates that the training action, defined as "a pedagogical pathway leading to the achievement of a professional objective", can be carried out in a work situation.

References

Bentabet, Elyes (2008): Très petites, petites et moyennes entreprises: Entre tradition et innovation: Une recension des travaux du Céreq (1985-2007). Marseille: Céreq.

Bentabet, Elyes/Gadille, Martine (2019): Les mondes sociaux des TPE-PME: Modèles et logiques d'actions. Toulouse: Octarès.

Bentabet, Elyes/Gadille, Martine/Trouvé, Philippe (2019): Les mondes sociaux: Un concept migrateur entre deux paradigmes. In: Bentabet, Elyes/Gadille, Martine (Eds.): Les mondes sociaux des TPE-PME: Modèles et logiques d'actions. Toulouse: Octarès, pp. 7-34.

Béraud, Delphine (2015): Les PME s'intéressent de plus en plus aux effets de la formation. In: Céreq, Bref no. 330.

Béraud, Delphine (2016): Les formations obligatoires en entreprise : Des formations comme les autres ? In: Céreq, Bref no. 350.

Béraud, Delphine/Noack, Edmond (2019): Training in Small companies: A reflection of Their Strategic Positioning. In: Céreq, Training and Employment no. 142.

Dubois, Jean-Marie/Marion-Vernoux, Isabelle/Noack, Edmond (2016): Le dispositif d'enquête Defis: Un nouveau regard sur la formation en entreprise. In: Céreq, Bref no. 344.

Eurostat (2018): Statistics on Small and Medium-Sized Enterprises. URL: https://ec.europa.eu/eurostat/statistics-explained/index.php/Statistics_on_small_and_medium-sized_enterprises#General_overview [26 May 2020].

French National Institute of Statistics and Economic Studies (L'Institut National de la Statistique et des Études Économiques/INSEE) (2019): Les entreprises en France: Édition 2019. Paris: INSEE.

Letowski, André (2019): L'approche de la galaxie des TPE. In: Bentabet, Elyes/Gadille, Martine (Eds.): Les mondes sociaux des TPE-PME: Modèles et logiques d'actions. Toulouse: Octarès, pp. 49-68.

Marion, Isabelle (2017): Point sur: La formation dans les petites entreprises. URL: https://www.cereq.fr/point-sur-la-formation-dans-les-petites-entreprises [08 July 2020].

Régnault, Gérard (2011): Les mondes sociaux des petites et très petites entreprises. Paris: L'Harmattan.

Salais, Robert /Storper, Michael (1993): Les mondes de production. Paris: Editions de l'École des Hautes Études en Sciences Sociales (EHESS).

Statista (2019): Number of Small and Medium-Sized Enterprises (SMEs) in the European Union in 2018, by Size. URL: https://www.statista.com/statistics/878412/number-of-smes-in-europe-by-size [26 May 2020].

Websites

French Centre for Research on Education, Training and Employment (Centre d'études et de recherches sur les qualifications/Céreq): www.cereq.fr/en

French Centre for Research on Education, Training and Employment (Centre d'études et de recherches sur les qualifications/Céreq) - Training and Employees Trajectory Surveys: https://www.cereq.fr/en/training-employees-trajectory-surveys

French Centre for Research on Education, Training and Employment (Centre d'études et de recherches sur les qualifications/Céreq) - Lifelong Learning and Vocational Training Surveys (Dispositif d'Enquêtes sur les Formations et Itinéraires des Salariés/DÉFIS, Continuing Vocational Training Survey /CVTS, base Reflet): https://www.cereq.fr/en/data-access/lifelong-learning-and-vocational-training-surveys-defis-cvts-base-reflet

French National Institute of Statistics and Economic Studies (L'Institut National de la Statistique et des Études Économiques/INSEE): www.insee.fr/en

French National Institute of Statistics and Economic Studies (L'Institut National de la Statistique et des Études Économiques/INSEE) - New Enterprises Information System (Système d'information sur les nouvelles entreprises/SINE): www.insee.fr/en/metadonnees/source/serie/s1271

Skills for Smart Specialisation: Fostering SME Innovation Through New Training and Learning Pathways, Technological Transfer, and Skills Upgrading

Pirita Vuorinen and Cristina Mereuta

Introduction

Smart specialisation is an important objective of the Cohesion Policy of the European Unions (EU). Since 2014, developing a Research and Innovation Strategy for Smart Specialisation (RIS3) that requires each country or region to identify and develop its own competitive advantages has been a prerequisite to receive funding under the European Structural Funds (ESF). The role of smart specialisation was further underscored in the 2017 Communication on Strengthening Innovation in Europe's Regions which linked it to regional innovation policy.

The smart specialisation approach has been recognised beyond the EU as a strategic approach to increase evidence-based public investment to foster growth and competitiveness and wellbeing of citizens. The European Commission has been sharing the benefits of the approach beyond EU borders, where, despite different framework conditions, the approach is seen as having potential to foster decentralised and innovation-led economic transformation as well as promote interregional and cross-border partnerships. The EU neighbourhood countries are connected to the EU agenda for smart specialisation, either in the context of the EU enlargement process (countries of South Eastern Europe) or overall economic and political cooperation process with the EU neighbourhood countries.

The contribution of vocational education and training (VET) to innovation, growth, and competitiveness is reflected in the EU VET policy cooperation framework set out in the Copenhagen Declaration in 2002 (Cedefop 2002) and consolidated through subsequent ministerial declarations, including the Riga Conclusions in 2015 (European Commission, Latvian Presidency of the Council of the European Union, and Ministry of Education and Science/Republic of Latvia 2015) which underscores the role of VET and skills in the European growth and jobs agenda. However, in the framework that guides the design of smart specialisation strategies, VET is not given the same importance as higher education. Therefore, investment in VET is disconnected from smart specialisation.

Growth and competitiveness of small and medium-sized enterprises (SMEs) depend on their ability to innovate, reap the benefits of digitalisation, and access skills in the smart specialisation priority domains. However, recently, the COVID-19 pandemic has brought the economy to a halt and SMEs in particular are receiving a blow. Many sectors have seen plummeting demand, while the supply side struggles with logistic constraints.

Against this backdrop and because of the limited resources and relative inability of SMEs to absorb the costs and risks associated with in-house technology development, they must often utilise the process of technology transfer to take advantage of the benefits gained by technology and innovation.[103] However, this, too, requires relevant human resources (HR), the lack of which is likely to inhibit the access of SMEs to external technology.

Various studies and assessments, including the regular Small Business Act assessment carried out by the OECD, EBRD, and ETF (OCED, ETF, EU and EBRD 2019) reveal that SMEs invest significantly less in skills development and upgrading than their larger counterparts and depend on the labour market to supply them with qualified labour. In order for SMEs to survive and prosper, new targeted training and learning pathways, technological transfer, and skills upgrading are needed.

The present paper builds on a project initiated by the European Training Foundation (EFT) to develop a toolkit to address the skills dimension, specifically VET, in developing and implementing smart specialisation strategies.[104] Initiated in 2019, the project includes a testing phase in which selected priority economic domains identified in the (draft) smart specialisation strategies are further analysed in terms of skills potential, demand, and supply imbalances as well as potential education and training actions fit to address the emerging skills needs. Three countries were selected for the testing phase, namely, Montenegro, the Republic of Moldova (at national level), and Ukraine (two pilot regions).

---

[103] https://www.indersciencelonline.com/doi/pdf/10.1504/IJTTC.2002.001781.

[104] ETF Country Reports on Skills for Smart Specialisation (forthcoming).

Following the testing, the project will be followed up by a methodological consolidation phase in which lessons, challenges, and adjustments are pooled together in a methodological toolkit and report to help future replication and adaptation in other countries or regions and their priority domains.

This paper summarises the methodological approach and preliminary findings of the first testing done in Montenegro and the Republic of Moldova (thereinafter "Moldova"), where research took place from mid-2019 to March 2020. Therefore, the results presented are indicative.

Moldova and Montenegro are among the first countries outside the EU having started working with the European Commission to develop their smart specialisation strategies. Montenegro initiated the development of its smart specialisation strategy in 2018 and established an inter-ministerial working group, which included business, academia, and non-government organisations. Moldova joined the Smart Specialisation Platform of the Joint Research Centre in 2016 and since then has worked on the identification of smart specialisation priority domains under the coordination of the Ministry of Education. Preliminary priority domains identified by Montenegro and Moldova represent the starting point for the research.

In 2020, the ETF is reviewing and adapting the methodology to the regional context in two pilot regions (Rivne and Kharkiv) in Ukraine. The complete toolkit on how to approach analysing skills implications of economic prioritisation, such as smart specialisation strategies, is planned to be published in 2021.

Research Approach

Efforts to pursue the smart specialisation approach are at the intersection of economic, industrial, innovation, labour market, and education and training policies. The Entrepreneurial Discovery Phase (EDP) of smart specialisation approach (when the "mapping" of economic potential leads to the identification of priority domains) secures the background for the identification of emerging needs for new or updated sets of skills. Labour market requirements, as expressed by employers or business sector representatives during the consultation process for smart specialisation, call for relevant VET programmes and targeted up-skilling or re-skilling services to SMEs. The use of new technologies or new production or trade patterns indicate a need for a forward-looking approach on skills provision in the context of smart specialisation and a stronger role for lifelong learning.

The basic assumption in the research was that newer and more focused economic priorities set out in smart specialisation agendas would shape short to long-term demand for skills. Given the complex nature of specialisation and various drivers such as technological and environmental factors or demographics, the research approach included multiple angles and investigation instruments.

This included skills data exploration at sub-sectoral and local/regional levels and skills relatedness including the potential of inter and intra sectoral labour shifts in a context of competitiveness and innovation.

The analysis focused on two priority areas identified as a result of the smart specialisation process in the country. In Montenegro, it focused on renewable production of energy and health tourism; while in Moldova, it focused on food-processing and (renewable) energy.

Below, the main research steps are summarized:

- Quantitative based assessment of skills dimension (supply and demand) in terms of qualifications, occupations, and skills by key characteristics (gender, age, education level, region/localisation);
- Qualitative assessment of skills (demand and supply aspects including utilisation at workplace, skills development, emerging shortages) through questionnaires and semi-structured interviews with employers, employees, and other key stakeholders such as incubators, industrial, chambers of commerce and industry, central and local public administration (relevant for chosen priority areas);
- Review of the content of existing training offer for initial vocational education and training (IVET), continued vocational education and training (CVT), training for SMEs, and other types of skills development initiatives;
- Identification of current and emerging skills trends and eventual gaps in terms of occupations, qualifications, and skills;
- Analysis of the capacity of training providers to match emerging requirements and develop recommendations for improving training content.

As presented in the figure below, the main goal was to analyse the implications for human capital development of innovation, growth, and competitiveness in two priority areas chosen from those selected for smart specialisation.

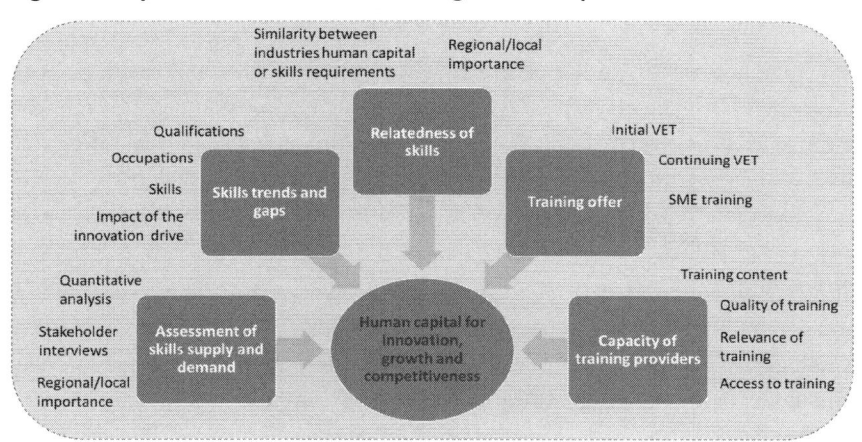

Figure 1: Key elements in the methodological development

Source: ETF Country Reports on Skills for Smart Specialisation (forthcoming).

The research work in the two countries took into account the relevant policy setting in the area of VET and continuous training and the institutional arrangements for engaging representatives of non-state actors in education and training (that is, sectoral committees or similar collaborative formats), and relied on existing ETF tools and methodologies such as the skills mismatch analyses and the small business act/SBA (OCED, ETF, EU and EBRD 2019), on holistic analyses of VET systems such as the Torino Process (ETF 2019a), and on the results of the smart specialisation process (that is, mapping of economic potential and entrepreneurial discovery process).

The practical implementation of the methodology revealed that capturing the skills profile and changes in sub-sectors clustered as priority domains requires both quantitative and qualitative investigation, with emphasis on the latter. Although clustered together, sub-sectors reveal very different skills profiles and need to be given the specificity of economic activities and associated technologies among others. Data and information vary greatly, as they are shaped by policy and institutional frameworks, existing statistical infrastructure (including relevant previous research) as well as raw data and broader economic and political context. Considering the specific context and limitations, each sub-sectoral analysis focused on gaining a sound understanding of the sub-sector/priority area, the key drivers of change, and interlinkages with other parts of the economy. Moreover, they focused on developing a detailed profile of occupations, jobs, and human capital, with a focus on skills.

A combination of quantitative and qualitative techniques was used, such as interviews with key players and stakeholders; a descriptive analysis of relevant data related to employment, skills, and educational level; and desk research using existing data, studies, and reports. Such combination was necessary to overcome limitations in data availability at sub-sectoral level, which is crucial for this type of study.

The main quantitative data used for the analysis were Labour Force Survey (data disaggregated by sectors, ISCO[105] groups, and regions among others), survey and administrative data on companies, wages/revenues, unemployment, vacancies, and education (including education offer and enrolment at secondary and tertiary level in the relevant qualifications or specialisation programmes as well as continuous training available).

Skills Dimension of Smart Specialisation Agenda (Preliminary Results)

The methodology, briefly described in the previous section, revealed several data and information limitations. The quantitative analysis, which relied greatly on Labour Force Survey data, demanded fine-grained data on sectorial, sub-sectorial, or cross-sectorial level (at three-digit or four-digit level of NACE[106] classification), or on specific occupation clusters, demographic characteristics, or territorial distribution of labour force.

Therefore, the qualitative analysis weighed more in the process of information gathering, interpretation, and assessment of the skills supply and demand aspects relevant for the priority areas linked to smart specialisation.

---

[105] ISCO: International Standard Classification of Occupation.

[106] NACE: Nomenclature statistique des activités économiques dans la Communauté européenne.

The main (preliminary) findings with regards to skills demand dimension of selected priority areas are presented below, clustered by country and economic (sub-)sector or priority.[107]

Renewable Energy Production in Montenegro

Energy is an important sector for Montenegrin economy, as it generated 8 per cent of the gross domestic product (GDP) in 2018. According to the Ministry of Science of Montenegro, the increase in production from renewable energy sources in relation to final production in 2018 was 33 per cent and is expected to reach 42 per cent by 2022 and it shows a great potential given the geographical and climate characteristics (for example, potential to produce both wind, solar, hydro or biomass based energy).[108] The energy sector also provides better employment opportunities in terms of jobs availability and earnings.

The competences needed to perform in the area of renewable energy encompass a wide spectrum, including technical, engineering, multilingual (English particularly), and digital skill as well as personal and social competences.

Most of the interviewed companies reported skills gaps when they initiated business operations or when hiring new employees (including recent graduates). Companies had to invest in staff education mainly through in-house trainings and mentorship. However, many companies used specialised trainings resources/specialists from abroad for the specific technologies not available in Montenegro.

In small companies, most employees are engineers, and low-skilled labour force is engaged for different operational tasks (for example, the installation of solar panels) on a part time basis. In larger companies, there is a constant need for new and good workers who are skilled, educated, and willing to work and learn.

The labour force mobility is not considered a problem in Montenegro (given the size of the country and distances between cities and regions) and there is a strong connection and relatedness between industries which are shrinking (for example, from manufacture to renewables and similar). Industry representatives expect that the adoption of new technologies, artificial intelligence, and digitalisation will soon become a change they cannot avoid if they want to stay

---

[107] ETF Country Reports on Skills for Smart Specialisation (forthcoming).

[108] http://www.mna.gov.me/en/ministry.

competitive and survive in the market. This will request employees with digital, information technology (IT), and multilingual skills.

It is interesting to note that no matter the company size, the education/skills of managers was stressed as crucial for managing processes efficiently and securing the sustainability of systems.

The educational system in the country is to some extent in line with the market needs in the renewable energy sector, although practical knowledge and more internships for students would be of great importance for having better skilled and knowledgeable labour force. In science, technology, engineering, and mathematics, specific knowledge and qualifications seem to be of crucial importance. Therefore, efforts should be made to encourage more students to follow such educational programmes. Also, setting up a training centre in the field of renewable energy might help attract more candidates from the whole country and, possibly, from the broader region.

Priority on (Renewable) Energy in Moldova

In Moldova, three key sub-domains have been identified as having the highest potential for smart specialisation: heating solutions, alternative energy sources, and efficient technologies.

Renewable energy technologies and an increase in the energy efficiency of residential and industrial sectors as well as of transport and agriculture would include innovation in the support of smart networks or the elimination of energy waste. This offers large opportunities for SMEs. While the supply of energy was until recently largely a public service, a deregulation of the industry and a growing interest in renewable energy production is an area where SMEs could play an important role.

The employment and salary levels in the energy sector have been growing in the past years, following also the overall positive developments on the labour market. In addition, the number of relevant vacancies at various levels has been increasing. Based on the existing data, research, and interviews with employers, it has become evident that the current demand for workers, both skilled and less skilled, exceeds the supply in the energy sector.

Small companies in the energy sector are employing experienced people, especially with the specialisation in engineering, while larger companies employ both fresh graduates and experienced specialists. The lack of specific technical knowledge and skills is usually tackled with additional training at the workplace. In general, employers consider the overall level of professional and generic skills among the existing workforce as inadequate. This is especially true for the middle-skilled workers in comparison to those with high skills.

Given the increasing use of new technologies, there is a higher need for specialised/technical skills. The employers stress, for example, that ICT skills are important for both high and middle-skilled workers, who are key for the operation and maintenance of modern technologies. Another gap identified is the knowledge of foreign languages among the high-skilled, a general lack of analytical and problem-solving skills, and a low motivation to learn among the middle-skilled.

The growing renewable energy sector accelerates the change in skills demand and raises new expectations of vocational and higher education providers. The technical staff with specific knowledge of renewable energy technologies is missing to a considerable extent.

Health Tourism in Montenegro

Montenegro promotes health tourism as a solution of diversification of tourism and of increased opportunities for employment. The main aim is to extend the touristic season throughout the whole year, focusing on therapeutic rehabilitation programmes, wellness, and spa (such as physiotherapy, preventive medicine, weight loss, aesthetic surgery, and wellness but also treatment and rehabilitation in case of respiratory diseases, back problems, and stomatology among others). Such prioritisation secures synergies with other sectors, for example, with agriculture in the production of healthy and organic food.

Based on the existing data and interviews with employers, it can be concluded that in Montenegro, skilled workforce currently mainly exists in the area of health. In the case of tourism, the country relies a lot on foreign workforce; also, the quality and quantity of the workforce is conditioned by its current seasonal characteristic and a high staff turnover.

In case of the health sector, the existing occupations are concentrated in the groups of professionals, technicians, associate professionals, and sales and service workers. Many hotels and related facilities also offer spa and wellness services, which are considered among those with the highest potential for the development of health tourism.

Within the Montenegrin health tourism area, the needs for technical skills are related, for example, to the ability to handle health service equipment, whereas technical/scientific knowledge is related to health services. Besides the technical/professional skills, there is a high need for the knowledge of foreign languages, especially English, and digital competences. Soft skills are also required, such as good communication skills, service-orientation, presentation skills, teamwork, resilience, or the ability to effectively manage time and planning.

To contribute to the development and innovation in the field of health tourism, there will be a need for therapy and fitness professionals, medical specialists, support staff, customer service workers, and supervisors.

In addition, to boost the competitiveness of SMEs in the sustainable and health tourism priority domain, their integration into global digital value chains is key. To drive such change requires new means of understanding training needs of SMEs. At present, training needs analyses in Montenegro are of limited scope and do not delve extensively into specific needs of SMEs.

Food Production in Moldova

Largely for natural reasons (soil resources, biological diversity, climate, and geographical conditions), the agriculture and food processing are well developed in Moldova, accounting for around 16 per cent of the GDP, 45 per cent of exports, and 27 per cent of employment. The greatest potential for growth would be in the production of organic food and in conventional crops.

The level of skills demanded by companies is increasing because of trade and technological change. Skill gaps identified in the Food Processing priority area encompass health and hygiene, quality, production, and marketing. Employers stress the lack of technical skills, poor work ethic, and motivation of the young employees (newly graduates).

Personal characteristics, such as the interest in personal development, responsibility, ability to cope with change, positive work ethics, and an interest in the job, are often identified as lacking.

There is a demand for specific skills, such as the understanding of food hygiene, understanding of quality standards, dexterity, machinery/technology operation and maintenance skills, health, and safety. Traditional manual skills are less and less required.

The rising level of mechanisation, automation and computerisation of the food processing operations requires specific professional skills to operate, regulate, and ensure the maintenance of modern techniques and to increase the levels of IT skills.

Some SMEs mentioned the need of "multi-skilling", that is, a mix of skills required to operate a machinery and carry out its maintenance or work in the processing/production section and to work in customer services at the same time, as processing, production, and sales are most of the time integrated. There is also a growing demand in skills and knowledge regarding organic food.

Foreseeable Impact on Education and Training Systems

Technological, environmental, and demographic changes as well as alongside globalisation are changing the nature of work, the content of jobs, and the demand for training.

Across the ETF partner countries, there is a need for continuous review and updating of the formal education and training provision; furthermore, the role of non-formal and informal learning is growing exponentially.

The competitiveness of countries and their regions depends on their flexibility and capacity to effectively adapt to global changes and related skills and competences. All countries need to ensure (i) that skill shortages and mismatch do not inhibit growth; (ii) a workforce with a skills mix needed for innovation (such as soft skills, digital skills, and entrepreneurship key competences); (iii) a flexible provision of Vocational Education and Training (VET); and (iv) lifelong learning to respond to future skills needs and to improve the adaptability and employment mobility of an ageing workforce.

The skills dimension of smart specialisation analysis done in Montenegro and Moldova revealed a mix of qualifications, skills, and competences required to fill in the needs of companies and secure the expansion of these priority areas. They entail technical and engineering qualifications in all selected priority areas and a stronger digital base as transversal skill. A common thread is the multilingualism, particularly English competences, reflecting the increase of technological transfer, compliance with international and European standards and cross-border trading, and cooperation relations. Key competences such as teamwork and the ability to learn scored high as well.

To achieve smart specialisation priorities, new modalities to sustain demanded training and learning are important, such as enhanced cooperation or partnerships to secure technological transfer and innovation between education and training systems, academia, and innovative companies among others.

The EU initiative of promoting Centres of Vocational Excellence[109] reflects the priority given to VET transformation and modernisation with the goal to cater for multiple groups of learners and support smart and inclusive economic growth. Linking the concept of Centres of Vocational Excellence with the smart specialisation approach is opening new opportunities to collaborate with other countries and regions based on matching priority domains. In doing so, smart specialisation lays the ground for establishing Centres of Excellence that advance vocational excellence, both by deepening and extending their relationship with employers and by cooperating and coordinating with other skills providers (such as schools, companies, universities, research organisations, and specialist development agencies among others) to boost VET quality and effectiveness. Targeting high value-added activities in areas such as the digital or green economies as well as innovative technology and manufacturing processes in traditional sectors unlocks new training and mentoring pathways for initial and continuing vocational education and training. Such Centres of Vocational Excellence could nullify the size of disadvantages of SMEs by facilitating SME specific training and skills, upgrading through interregional and cross-border partnerships for new technology development and transfer, and overcoming diseconomies of scale in innovations within priority domains for smart specialisation.

---

[109] https://ec.europa.eu/education/policies/eu-policy-in-the-field-of-vocational-education-and-training-vet_en.

Concluding Remarks

The ETF will continue to test the methodological approach in two regions of Ukraine, thus complementing the national approach already tested in Moldova and Montenegro. A full report on methodological lessons and country findings is planned for the end of 2020; in 2021, a practical toolkit will be developed to secure replication in other countries and priority areas.

So far, the experience with the practical implementation of the methodology has revealed that data at the sub-sectoral level is crucial for such a type of analysis. The experiences both in Moldova and Montenegro showed that as smart specialisation addresses new domains and specialisations, available statistics are not sensitive enough to allow disaggregation by detailed NACE, ISCO, and International Standard Classification of Education (ISCED) levels. Further disaggregation of data on regional or local levels often leads to unreliable results. Also, inter- and intra-sectoral transitions of the labour force are difficult to spot when using available statistics.

To compensate data limitations, in depth qualitative research (for example, interviews and focus groups) is instrumental in getting more accurate views on skills demand in the priority sectors. Relevant insights and information require good access to stakeholders, receptive public administrative institutions and companies, and resources to cover the territory and sub-sectors properly.

The research revealed that companies/businesses involved in priority domains for smart specialisation are key drivers for innovation and often find local/specific solutions to address skills shortages (either through the organisation of in-company trainings or through attracting trainers from abroad, if the technology employed is quite specific). Therefore, support to business training is crucial, especially for SMEs.

From the ongoing research in the two countries, it has emerged that both Moldova and Montenegro face various forms of skills mismatches reflected in shortages, gaps, and an inefficient utilisation of available human capital.

The specific skills requirements of the selected priority areas call for both skills generated through formal education programmes at secondary, post-secondary, and tertiary levels, continuous trainings, various training formats, (re-)training, upskilling, and reskilling in a lifelong learning context.

The inclusion of the skills dimension within the smart specialisation strategies is crucial and should ideally accompany the process of identifying the economic potential and selection of priority areas. This can allow right and timely provision of relevant training, targeting both current students, workforce, and businesses.

References

Cedefop (European Centre for the Development of Vocation Training) (2002): Declaration of the European Ministers of Vocational Education and Training, and the European Commission, convened in Copenhagen on 29 and 30 November 2002, on Enhanced European Cooperation in Vocational Education and Training – "Copenhagen Declaration". URL: https://www.cedefop.europa.eu/files/copenahagen_declaration_en.pdf [07 July 2020].

European Commission (2017): Strengthening Innovation in Europe's Regions - Strategies for Resilient, Inclusive and Sustainable Growth. URL: https://ec.europa.eu/regional_policy/en/information/publications/communications/2017/strengthening-innovation-in-europe-s-regions-strategies-for-resilient-inclusive-and-sustainable-growth [07 July 2020].

European Training Foundation (ETF) (2019a): Policies for Human Capital Development: South Eastern Europe and Turkey - An ETF Torino Process Assessment. URL: https://www.etf.europa.eu/en/publications-and-resources/publications/policies-human-capital-development-south-eastern-europe-and [07 July 2020].

European Training Foundation (ETF) (2019b): Skills Mismatch Measurement in ETF Partner Countries. URL: https://www.etf.europa.eu/en/publications-and-resources/publications/skills-mismatch-measurement-etf-partner-countries [07 July 2020].

European Training Foundation (ETF) (forthcoming): ETF Country Reports on Skills for Smart Specialisation.

OCED, ETF, EU and EBRD (2019): SME Policy Index: Western Balkans and Turkey 2019 – Assessing the Implementation of the Small Business Act for Europe. URL: https://www.oecd-ilibrary.org/docserver/g2g9fa9a-en.pdf?expires=1594115206&id=id&accname=guest&checksum=5A7AC760E4F1FD2B1B82A02FF928B864 [07 July 2020].

European Commission, Latvian Presidency of the Council of the European Union, and Ministry of Education and Science/Republic of Latvia (2015): Riga Conclusions 2015 on a New Set of Medium-Term Deliverables in the Field of VET for the Period 2015-2020, as a Result of the Review of Short-Term Deliverables Defined in the 2020 Bruges Communique. URL: https://www.eqavet.eu/Eqavet2017/media/Policy-Documents/Riga-Conclusions-2015.pdf?ext=.pdf [07 July 2020].

Websites

European Commission – Centres of Vocational Excellence: https://eacea.ec.europa.eu/erasmus-plus/actions/centres-of-vocational-excellence_en

European Commission – EU Policy in the Field of Vocational Education and Training (VET): https://ec.europa.eu/education/policies/eu-policy-in-the-field-of-vocational-education-and-training-vet_en

European Commision, Joint Research Center – Smart Specialisation: https://ec.europa.eu/jrc/en/research-topic/smart-specialisation

Ministry of Science of Montenegro: http://www.mna.gov.me/en/ministry.

Online Platform for Inderscience Publishers journal content: https://www.inderscience-online.com/doi/pdf/10.1504/IJTTC.2002.001781

SMEs and the Retrospective Acquirement of Vocational Qualification by Semi-Skilled and Unskilled Workers in the Federal State of Hesse

Oliver Lauxen and Christian Müller

Background: The Vocational Retraining of Semi-Skilled and Unskilled Workers

Compared to other countries, the labour market in Germany is strongly structured according to occupations. The vocational training system is highly established and formal qualifications are universally recognised (Kirpal 2006). The German occupational concept forms the predominant organisational principle of vocational training and was already developed in the Middle Ages, when craftsmen first completed an apprenticeship before being allowed to do their professional work. During industrialisation, the model of craft training was adopted for other areas of activity and transformed into a dual training system at the beginning of the 20th century (Greinert 2006, Kupfer 2011). The trainee is prepared for the job in a vocational school and in a company and has adapt to qualification standards, professional ethics, and codes of conduct (Kirpal 2006). A landmark is the Vocational Training Act (*Berufsbildungsgesetz/BBiG*), which came into force in 1969; it regulates training in the majority of professions and is still valid today (Greinert 2006).

Vocational education and training in Germany have always been directed mainly professionally and less driven by educational policy. Therefore, the German vocational training system (vocation and education training/VET system) and universities are relatively uncoupled. According to Educational Sociology, there is a hierarchy behind this: a university course is open to the upper socio-economic groups, whereas vocational training is intended for the broad lower and middle socio-economic groups (Kupfer 2011).

The significance of the occupational concept becomes evident when looking at the qualifications of employees in Germany. The official employment statistics of the Federal Employment Agency (*Bundesagentur für Arbeit*) distinguish between employees with a university degree, employees with formal vocational qualification, and employees without formal vocational qualification or a university degree. In the Federal State of Hesse, a total of 63.8 per cent of the 2,912,841 employees had completed formal vocational qualification by 30 June 2017, and 19.5 per cent had completed a university degree; only 16.7 per cent (486,454 people) worked without formal vocational qualification (Demireva and Larsen 2019).

In Germany, persons without formal vocational qualifications are particularly affected by unemployment, even more so during a economic crisis such as caused by the current COVID-19 pandemic. More than half of all unemployed people in 2018 had no formal vocational qualification (Röttger et al. 2019). Accordingly, professional qualification processes in Germany are geared towards achieving recognised formal qualifications. Vocational qualification is based on the occupational principle of professionalism and specialisation (Greinert 2008). Since the mid-1980s, the Federal Ministry of Education and Research (*Bundesministerium für Bildung und Forschung/BMBF*) has strongly supported the opportunity to access further qualification for semi-skilled and unskilled workers. For years, research and development programmes have been financed by the Ministry, most recently as regional structural development projects (Baethge and Severing 2015). In the meantime, however, the Federal Government's major funding system has come to an end. It is assumed that regional network structures have been implemented successfully and that the programme will run independently as intended by the last major funding initiative (BIBB 2016). Looking at the wide variety of vocational training programmes in Germany, only 7.4 per cent relate to training focused on the retrospective acquisition of vocational qualification (BIBB 2016). In comparison, 21 per cent of the programmes deal with vocational orientation and 28 per cent with vocational preparation (BIBB 2016).

Against the background of an increasing shortage of skilled workers (Demireva et al. 2019, Lauxen et al. 2020), the topic of training leading to the retrospective acquirement of vocational qualification in a recognised occupation becomes more important. The companies' traditional strategy of simply training more new skilled workers is limited by the declining number of young people and the trend towards academic degrees. Whereas vocational retraining was originally an education policy strategy for the social integration of disadvantaged target groups, the opportunity is increasingly regarded as an instrument to cover the demand for skilled workers by providing further training for semi-skilled and unskilled workers already working in the company (Heisler 2015).

An alternative to gain the qualification for a recognised occupation other than the regular vocational education and training is the so-called external examination (*Externenprüfung*). In the Federal State of Hesse, a specific funding programme for the application and support of this qualification path exists. Nevertheless, there are hurdles in the application process giving rise to several questions, which we will answer in the empirical part of the article.

The External Examination as a Possibility for the Retrospective Acquirement of Vocational Qualification

The external examination aims at facilitating the possibility of professional qualification for people who do not have acquired one yet, but who have gained a lot of work experience instead. It offers the opportunity to acquire a qualification without completing the regular two or three-year training programme (Fink et al. 2019a). The admission of a person to the external examination is decided by the Chambers of Industry and Commerce (*Industrie- und Handelskammer/IHK*) and the Chamber of Crafts (*Handwerkskammer/HWK*) as representatives of the companies (Bläsche et al. 2017). In the Federal State of Hesse, there are ten Chambers of Industry and Commerce and three Chambers of Crafts, each of which is responsible for certain parts of the state as well as for certain professions (Fink et al. 2019a).

In order to be allowed to take the external examination, one has to prove that they have worked in the profession for at least 1.5 times of the usual training period required. As the regular vocational training period lasts three years, this means that an applicant for the examination must be able to prove working in the profession for at least 4.5 years. However, justified exceptions to this rule are possible (Schreiber et al. 2012); for example, professional experience and educational qualifications acquired overseas can be taken into account for the admission.

After the admission by the chamber, the person has the choice to prepare for the examination independently or to take a preparatory course with a trainer. Most participants opt for the preparatory course with a trainer, and just under a third prepare independently, mostly those with a higher school qualification (Schreiber et al. 2012). The preparatory courses primarily teach the necessary theoretical knowledge for the examination (Lauxen et al. 2018).

Promotion of the Retrospective Acquirement of Vocational Qualification in the Federal State of Hesse

While the programmes targeted at the retrospective acquirement of vocational qualification at national level have largely expired, the promotion of it is still in the focus of political activities in Hesse. With the ProAbschluss initiative, the Hessian Ministry of Economics, Energy, Transport and Housing (*Hessisches Ministerium für Wirtschaft, Energie, Verkehr und Wohnen/HMWEVW*) is supporting semi-skilled and unskilled workers in obtaining a vocational qualification through the external examination. The ministry promotes an advisory and support structure for companies and employees including competent advice centres in all 26 local districts.[110] On top of that, the state of Hesse covers half of the costs for preparatory courses for the external examination and half of the examination fees with an instrument called *Qualifizierungsscheck*. In addition to state funds, resources from the European Social Fund (ESF) are also used.

The ProAbschluss initiative focuses on people without a vocational qualification who are in employment. In addition to this, there are other support programmes in Germany, above all by the Federal Employment Agency (*Bundesagentur für Arbeit*), which are aimed primarily at unemployed people. In the following, however, the focus will be on employees without a vocational qualification.

Use of the External Examination and Obstacles for the Retrospective Acquirement of Vocational Qualification

Despite all the support options, only very few people in Hesse (like in other parts of Germany) take an external examination. In 2017, 1,854 external examinations were taken, which corresponds to 5.7 per cent of all 32,607 final examinations in that calendar year. In the period from 2012 to 2017, there was even a steady

---

[110] For further information, see the website of the ProAbschluss initiative: www.pro-abschluss.de.

decline (Figure 1). While 2,055 people passed an external examination in 2012, the number of participants was only 1,854 in 2017. This is a decrease of almost 10 per cent over the entire period. However, the number of participations rose slightly in 2018, which is the last reporting year available.

Figure 1: Participation in external examinations in Hesse from 2012 to 2018

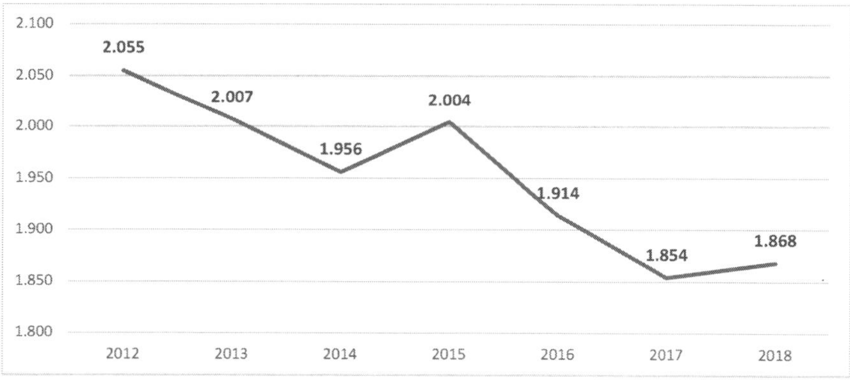

Year	Participants
2012	2,055
2013	2,007
2014	1,956
2015	2,004
2016	1,914
2017	1,854
2018	1,868

Source: Fink et al. (2019a: 7).

The target occupations of the participants in 2017 were diverse. They included commercial occupations, occupations in logistics, industrial occupations, occupations in trade, and occupations in catering. About 61 per cent of the participants in external examinations in 2017 were male (Fink et al. 2019a).

The obstacles to the retrospective acquirement of vocational qualification are complex. They lie partly in the employees themselves, who are insufficiently informed about the possibility of external examination or afraid of failure due to poor learning experience.[111] Other obstacles can be found in the regional economic structure and in the companies (Lauxen and Werle 2018), but also on the part of the training providers, most of whom do not offer any preparatory courses for external auditing (Lauxen et al. 2018). In addition, the attitude of the individual chambers as responsible bodies for post-qualification differs in how they promote it. All these factors play a significant role in why both the absolute number of external examinations and their share in all final examinations vary greatly between regions (Fink et al. 2019b).

---

[111] For a comprehensive presentation, see Fink et al. 2019b.

Questions for the Empirical Part

In the empirical part of the article, we investigate the stance of SMEs in Hesse on the retrospective acquirement of vocational qualification: Are they familiar with the possibilities? What practices do they follow? Do they enable employees without a professional qualification to take an external examination?

These questions can be answered using a typology of companies developed by the Institute for Economics, Labour and Culture (*Institut für Wirtschaft, Arbeit und Kultur/IWAK*), Centre of Goethe-University Frankfurt am Main, as part of the scientific monitoring of the ProAbschluss initiative (Werle et al. 2018). The data basis for this consists of 33 expert discussions with multipliers and 42 qualitative interviews with executives and human resources (HR) managers from Hessian companies. The typology allows for a deeper understanding of the role of the HR policy in SMEs and can also lead to novel ideas on how to improve educational counselling and further promote the retrospective acquirement of vocational qualification.

Methodological Approach: Use of Qualitative Interviews to Capture the Perspective of Companies

A literature review revealed hardly any studies on the company perspective on the retrospective acquirement of vocational qualification by semi-skilled and un-skilled workers. Therefore, a qualitative and explorative research design was chosen (Helfferich 2014). Before the actual company survey, 33 expert discussions were held with multipliers from business associations, chambers, and business development agencies among others. Some of the discussions were very short. The main purpose was to find ways to address companies for the company survey. However, they also gave first insights into how the retrospective acquirement of vocational qualification is looked at in the respective branch.[112]

The interviews with executives and HR managers from Hessian companies started in December 2017. The acquisition of participants took place partly with the help of the multipliers, partly with the support of the consultants of the Pro-Abschluss initiative, via internal IWAK contacts, and via regular acquisition

---

[112] For a detailed description of the methodology, see Werle et al. 2018.

(*Kaltakquise*). By March 2018, we had contacted 179 companies by phone. Of these, 137 did not take part in the survey. A few were excluded because they did not meet the criteria, such as the size of an SME or industry inclusion criteria. By researching the companies' websites, we were able to rule out the possibility that such companies were contacted at all. 38 companies were excluded because there were no skilled or unskilled workers due to legal requirements or the complexity of the work. The other companies simply had no interest in participating.

Between December 2017 and March 2018, 42 guide-based interviews were conducted. This was usually done on-site at the company. The companies surveyed belong to industries in which external audits are carried out in Hesse, namely, construction, the chemical and pharmaceutical industry, the electronic industry, retail trade, gastronomy, craft, the metal industry, the logistics industry, the manufacturing industry, and the cleaning industry. Most of them were medium-sized companies (50 to 250 employees) from all parts of Hesse. It was difficult to approach small businesses (one to 49 employees).

The interviews were analysed in terms of content (Mayring 2007). Companies with similar operational combinations of characteristics were grouped into types (Kluge 2000). The company typology was secured through a communicative validation with three companies randomly selected from the sample (Ziegaus 2006). In two cases, there was an on-site appointment; in another case, the validation was carried out by telephone.

Results: A Typology of SMEs

With the help of a company typology (Werle et al. 2018, Lauxen and Werle 2018), we bundled different perspectives of SMEs on the topic of the retrospective acquirement of vocational qualification by semi-skilled and unskilled workers. The companies were initially roughly distinguished according to whether they

- only teach and instruct semi-skilled and unskilled workers and after that, those employees remain in auxiliary activities,
- further qualify semi-skilled and unskilled workers so that they assume qualified functions,
- and qualify semi-skilled and unskilled workers so that they can obtain the targeted professional qualification retrospectively.

For further typification, we examined the extent to which other operational characteristics occurred in combination. The following characteristics proved to be relevant for the typification:

- the perceived need for skilled workers (How does the company perceive the labour market situation?),
- the quality of information about the retrospective acquirement of vocational qualification (Does the company have information regarding the retrospective acquirement of vocational qualification?),
- the breadth of orientation of the personnel policy (Is the need for skilled workers only covered by traditional measures such as training?),
- and the existing qualification formats for semi-skilled and unskilled workers (Which format does the company utilise?).

The characteristics above could be used to further subdivide companies that only train and induct employees without vocational qualifications. The same is true for the companies who promote professional qualifications. This resulted in a typology with five company types (Figure 2). In companies of the Types I, II, and III, semi-skilled and unskilled workers do not have the opportunity to obtain a professional qualification. This is only possible in companies of the Types IV and V.

These types are ideal types, which means that the associated companies in the sample are not necessarily similar in every respect. Occasionally, there may be a company that can be assigned to more than one type, because the training strategy of departments for semi-skilled and unskilled workers differs.

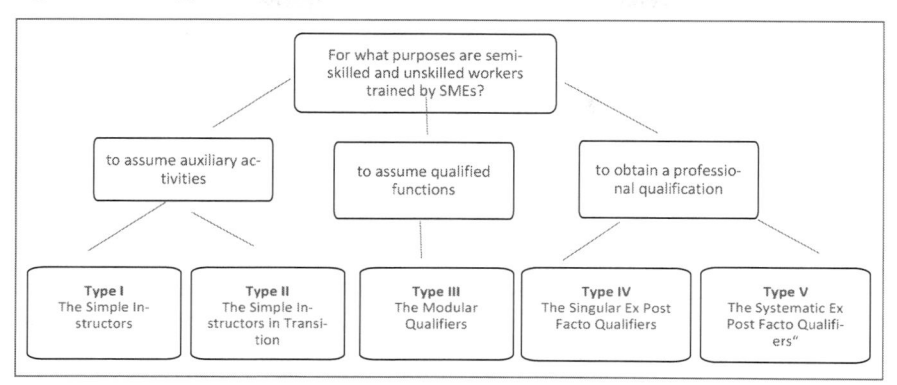

Figure 2: Five types of SMEs

```
                    For what purposes are semi-
                    skilled and unskilled workers
                       trained by SMEs?
         /                    |                    \
to assume auxiliary ac-   to assume qualified    to obtain a professio-
      tivities                functions           nal qualification
      /        \                  |                  /         \
  Type I      Type II          Type III          Type IV       Type V
The Simple In-  The Simple In-  The Modular    The Singular Ex Post  The Systematic Ex
  structors   structors in Transi-  Qualifiers    Facto Qualifiers    Post Facto Qualifi-
                  tion                                                       ers"
```

Source: Lauxen et al. (2018: 21).

Type I and Type II: The Simple Instructors and the Simple Instructors in Transition

The "simple instructors" (Type I) do not experience a shortage of skilled workers and therefore see little need for formal qualification of semi-skilled and unskilled workers that goes beyond learning and induction training. Many of these companies primarily perform auxiliary activities that do not require a formal degree. Companies with a higher share of skilled workers are attempting to quickly bring semi-skilled and unskilled workers into regular vocational training. The "simple instructors" cover their personnel needs through traditional personnel policy measures such as training, recruitment on the labour market, or the use of temporary workers. They do not consider the possibility of retrospective acquirement of vocational qualification by semi-skilled and unskilled workers. Their personnel policy is rather narrowly focused.

This also applies to the "simple instructors in transition" (Type II). In these companies, however, the technical requirements are somewhat higher than for Type I companies. A shortage of skilled workers is noticeable and traditional personnel policy measures appear to be no longer sufficient. The "simple instructors in transition" simply lack knowledge and information about the possibilities of the retrospective acquirement of vocational qualification. However, during the interviews they showed a strong interest in it.

Type III: The Modular Qualifiers

The "modular qualifiers" (Type III) enable employees without a vocational qualification to perform the same tasks as skilled workers with a professional qualification. They have great difficulties recruiting skilled workers and have therefore made HR policy broader than Type I and Type II companies. The "modular qualifiers" employ non-specialist people without qualifications and then qualify them to take on activities usually performed by skilled workers. The qualification is mostly done in-house; only larger SMEs tend to use further external training offers. It takes place in modules that are comparable to individual modules of the respective training framework. The participants thus complete individual parts of the regular vocational training. The "modular qualifiers" sometimes have considerable information deficits regarding the retrospective acquirement of vocational qualification. In many companies, however, the formal vocational qualification is simply of little added value. Enabling the takeover on skilled worker functions in the company appears to be entirely self-sufficient.

Type IV and Type V: The Singular Ex Post Facto Qualifiers and the Systematic Ex Post Facto Qualifiers

The "singular ex post facto qualifiers" (Type IV) rarely offer the opportunity to gain professional qualification, whereas the "systematic ex post facto qualifiers" (Type V) do this on a regular basis. Companies of both types suffer from a pronounced shortage of skilled workers and are well-informed about the possibilities of the retrospective acquisition of vocational qualification. However, the "singular ex post facto qualifiers" use the retrospective acquirement of vocational qualification less as a strategic instrument; their personnel policy is more traditional and narrowly focused. The retrospective acquirement of vocational qualification becomes more focused either when there are peaks in orders, or when employees without a vocational qualification themselves request corresponding qualification wishes to the company management. In these cases, external training is used, as the companies have very few internal structures for this. The "systematic ex post facto qualifiers" have a broad personnel policy; employees without a professional qualification are systematically in the focus. These companies tend to be the larger ones among the SMEs.

Examination of the Results

As the company typology shows, it is not the affiliation to a specific industry or a specific company size that determines whether companies support the retrospective acquirement of vocational qualification by employees without vocational qualification. Rather, it is conducive that companies

- feel pressure to act due to a shortage of skilled workers,
- are informed about the possibility of obtaining vocational qualification via the external examination,
- include people without professional qualifications in their HR policy,
- and use existing qualification structures within the company or contacts to external training providers for employees without vocational qualifications, too.

Counselling can influence these factors (Lauxen and Werle 2018): The "simple instructors" (Type I), who see no need for qualification because their employees mainly perform simple tasks, are not very receptive to information about the retrospective acquirement of vocational qualification. The "simple instructors in transition" (Type II) are quite different: They are looking for alternatives to cover their skilled labour needs and are grateful for information on implementation and funding opportunities. They may very quickly become Type IV or Type V companies. The "modular qualifiers" (Type III) are a heterogeneous group: Some companies could be interested in the certification of internal qualification modules, as such a certification would make it possible to promote these modules via the ProAbschluss initiative, whereas others still lack any information on the retrospective acquirement of vocational qualification.

The IWAK presented ideas for type-specific counselling to the consultants of the ProAbschluss initiative in face-to-face interviews. Together, it was reflected on what the results of the study mean for the work of a consultant in the respective region (Lauxen et al. 2019). In addition, the results were discussed in a workshop together with the consultants, and all consultants received the project report in printed and electronic form.

The profound exchange with the operational actors in the ProAbschluss initiative is an important part of the scientific monitoring by the IWAK. The labour market monitoring is not only aimed at the progress of the initiative for the client, but also to carry out practice-related studies to provide data and impulses for the operational actors' work. For this purpose, both quantitative and qualitative research and evaluation methods are used.

As shown above, the number of external examinations has not increased in the Federal State of Hesse in recent years. The reluctance of many companies becomes more understandable when having a closer look at the results of the study: Across all types of companies, the interviewees expressed anxiety that employees might change the company after gaining a professional qualification. From a human capital theory point of view, this makes sense: investing in further training of employees is risky for a company (Bellmann et al. 2015, Käpplinger 2016). If the employee's retention rate fluctuates, the investment in human capital for the company would be lost. Specific training seems less risky than general training, because the skills acquired would not easily transfer to other companies. Even though the human capital theory approach may not go far enough and other motives play a role, too, as do social negotiation processes, there is a fundamental divergence of interests between employees and employers (Käpplinger 2016). Interviews with employees in the process of acquiring vocational qualification retrospectively also illustrate this (Fink et al. 2019b).

The retrospective acquirement of vocational qualification is not an attractive business for training providers. Most of the training providers do not offer that type of training (Koschek and Samray 2018, Lauxen et al. 2018), which contributes to the lack of awareness of the external examination. In any case, the retrospective acquirement of vocational qualification does not have a good reputation in Germany; it is seen as a competition for regular vocational training (Dauser et al. 2012). Modular training offers targeted at the retrospective acquirement of vocational qualification are part of a controversial political debate (Gutschow 2015, Heisler 2015). All in all, this makes it difficult for consultants to submit suitable offers to companies.

A limitation of the study is the size of the sample. For a qualitative study, 42 interviews are certainly a lot, but of course the data is not representative in a quantitative sense. Nevertheless, the typology seems to reflect the attitudes and operational practices of the companies in the area of the retrospective acquirement of vocational qualification quite well. According to the ProAbschluss consultants, the typology is comprehensible, realistic, and practical (Lauxen et al. 2019). It facilitates orientation for less experienced consultants and helps them to understand the perspective of the companies.

Conclusion and Outlook

According to forecasts, the shortage of skilled workers in Hesse will become an increasingly pressing issue in the coming years. A shortage of 135,070 employees with vocational training is predicted by 2024 (Demireva et al. 2019). This shortage corresponds to 7 per cent of the skilled workforce in 2017. It is less due to economic reasons, but rather due to an immense age-related need for replacement due to the retirement of the so-called baby-boomers.

Against this background, the importance of the retrospective acquirement of vocational qualification by employees is likely to increase in the coming years. There is potential in it to secure skilled labour beyond traditional strategies such as training, employment of temporary work, or recruitment abroad. The target group is already working in the company, knows structures and processes, and has important implicit knowledge. Investment in training can also strengthen the organisational commitment of employees (Meyer and Herscovitch 2001).

In order to make the retrospective acquirement of vocational qualification by employees possible, companies need information and advice on the subject on the one hand and support in expanding their traditional HR policy on the other hand. The ProAbschluss consultants provide information and advice. However, the advisory structure of the ProAbschluss initiative is not a permanent structure, but a project structure linked to the approval of funding and political will. The Federal Employment Agency (*Bundesagentur für Arbeit*) is currently establishing new structures in educational counselling or expanding existing structures: With the Qualification Opportunities Act (*Qualifizierungschancengesetz*), which came into force in January 2019, all employees in Germany now have a legal right to educational counselling. Currently, it is still unclear to which extent the advice structures and advice practice will change because of this. However, it does not seem to make much sense to completely reorganise the structures and networks that have been developed over the years as part of the ProAbschluss initiative.

Virtual regional planning workshops, which the IWAK will carry out together with HR managers in various regions of Hesse in 2020, serve to support the expansion of personnel policy in SMEs. As part of the planning workshops, HR managers in SMEs are to be supported in securing their quantitative and qualitative personnel requirements against the background of demographic and technical developments. The aim is to check to what extent existing support options from external organisations are already taking effect and how they can be more closely aligned to the needs of SMEs, if necessary. Even though the planning workshops address the qualification of employees at all qualification levels, the subject of the retrospective acquirement of vocational qualification has a particular importance, as the demand for qualified personnel is growing due to the increasing digitalisation of companies.

References

Baethge, Martin/Severing, Eckart (2015): Sicherung des Fachkräftepotenzials durch Nachqualifizierung. In: Baethge, Martin/Severing, Eckart (Eds.): Sicherung des Fachkräftepotenzials durch Nachqualifizierung: Befunde - Konzepte - Forschungsbedarf. Bielefeld: W. Bertelsmann Verlag, pp. 7-16.

Bellmann, Lutz/Dummert, Sandra/Ebbinghaus, Margit/Krekel, Elisabeth M./Leber, Ute (2015): Qualifizierung von Beschäftigten in einfachen Tätigkeiten und Fachkräftebedarf. In: Zeitschrift für Weiterbildungsforschung 38 (2), pp. 287–301.

BIBB (Bundesinstitut für Berufsbildung) (2016): Datenreport zum Berufsbildungsbericht 2016. Informationen und Analysen zur Entwicklung der beruflichen Bildung. URL: https://www.bibb.de/dokumente/pdf/bibb_datenreport_2016.pdf [03 March 2020].

Bläsche, Alexandra/Brandherm, Ruth/Eckhardt, Christoph/Käpplinger, Bernd/Knuth, Matthias/Kruppe, Thomas/Kuhnhenne, Michaela/Schütt, Petra (2017): Qualitätsoffensive strukturierte Weiterbildung in Deutschland. Working Paper Forschungsförderung Nr.5 der Hans-Böckler-Stiftung. URL: https://www.boeckler.de/pdf/p_fofoe_WP_025_2017.pdf [03 March 2020].

Dauser, Dominique/Krings, Ursula/Schröer, Wolfgang (2012): Nachqualifizierung (junger) Erwachsener in Forschung und Praxis. In: Loebe, Herbert/Severing, Eckart (Eds.): An- und Ungelernte werden zu Fachkräften. Abschlussorientierte modulare Nachqualifizierung regional verankern. Bielefeld: W. Bertelsmann Verlag, pp. 15–30.

Demireva, Lora/Rand, Sigrid/Larsen, Christa (2019): Zukünftige Entwicklungen auf dem Arbeitsmarkt in Hessen und seinen Regionen bis 2024: Prognoseergebnisse und Strategieansätze. Abschlussbericht von regio pro. URL: http://regio-pro.eu/download/2019/Endbericht_regio_pro.pdf [03 March 2020].

Demireva, Lora/Larsen, Christa (2019): Ausführliche Dokumentation der Prognoseergebnisse bis 2024. Tabellenband. URL: http://www.regio-pro.eu/download/2019/Tabellenband_Ausfuehrliche_Dokumentation_der_Prognoseergebnisse.pdf [03 March 2020].

Fink, Miriam Sophie/Lauxen, Oliver/Müller, Christian (2019a): Nachqualifizierung in Zahlen: Berufs- und regionalspezifische Datenanalysen 2019. Mapping zum Stand der Nachqualifizierung in Hessen. URL: https://www.proabschluss.de/fileadmin/downloads/IWAK/Dossier_Berufs-_und_regionalspezifische_Datenanalysen_2019.pdf [03 March 2020].

Fink, Miriam Sophie/Lauxen, Oliver/Müller, Christian (2019b): Die Perspektive hessischer Beschäftigter: Mapping zum Stand der Nachqualifizierung in Hessen. URL: https://www.proabschluss.de/fileadmin/downloads/IWAK/Dossier_Beschaeftigte_2019.pdf [03 March 2020].

Greinert, Wolf-Dietrich (2008): Beschäftigungsfähigkeit und Beruflichkeit - zwei konkurrierende Modelle der Erwerbsqualifizierung? In: bwp Berufsbildung in Wissenschaft und Praxis 37 (4), pp. 9-12.

Greinert, Wolf-Dietrich (2006): Geschichte der Berufsausbildung in Deutschland. In: Arnold, Rolf/Lipsmaier, Antonius (Eds.): Handbuch der Berufsbildung. 2., überarbeitete und aktualisierte Auflage. Wiesbaden: Springer Verlag für Sozialwissenschaften (VS), pp. 499-508.

Gutschow, Katrin (2015): Potenziale nutzen durch berufliche Nachqualifizierung. In: Baethge, Martin/Severing, Eckart (Eds.): Sicherung des Fachkräftepotenzials durch Nachqualifizierung. Befunde - Konzepte - Forschungsbedarf. Bielefeld: W. Bertelsmann Verlag, pp. 17-34.

Heisler, Dietmar (2015): "Berufswechsler" in der beruflichen Nachqualifizierung. In: Baethge, Martin/Severing, Eckart (Eds.): Sicherung des Fachkräftepotenzials durch Nachqualifizierung. Befunde - Konzepte - Forschungsbedarf. Bielefeld: W. Bertelsmann Verlag, pp. 53-69.

Helfferich, Cornelia (2014): Leitfaden- und Experteninterviews. In: Baur, Nina/Blasius, Jörg (Eds.): Handbuch Methoden der empirischen Sozialforschung. Wiesbaden: Springer Verlag für Sozialwissenschaften (VS), pp. 559-574.

Käpplinger, Bernd (2016): Abschlussbezogenes Lernen: Orientierungen für Beraten und Planen zwischen betrieblichen Interessenkonfigurationen. In: Hessische Blätter für Volksbildung 3, pp. 259–267.

Kirpal, Simone (2006): Arbeitsidentitäten in vergleichenden Perspektiven: Die Rolle der nationalen und sektoralen Kontextvariablen. In: Europäische Zeitschrift für Berufsbildung 39 (3), pp. 25-54.

Kluge, Susann (2000): Empirisch begründete Typenbildung in der qualitativen Sozialforschung. In: Forum: Qualitative Social Research 1 (1). URL: www.qualitative-research.net/index.php/fqs/article/view/1124/2497 [03 March 2020].

Koschek, Stefan/Samray, David (2018): Strategien zur Qualifizierung Bildungsferner aus Anbietersicht. In: bwp Berufsbildung in Wissenschaft und Praxis 47 (1), pp. 25–29.

Kupfer, Antonia (2011): Bildungssoziologie. Theorien - Institutionen - Debatten. Wiesbaden: Springer Verlag für Sozialwissenschaften (VS).

Lauxen, Oliver/Pichler, Tristan/Schmid, Alfons (2020): Arbeitskräfterückgang und betriebliche Ausbildung in der Region Rhein-Main: IWAK-Betriebsbefragung im Herbst 2019. URL:

http://www.iwak-frankfurt.de/wp-content/uploads/2020/02/RM_Bericht.pdf [03 March 2020].

Lauxen, Oliver/Müller, Christian/Fink, Miriam Sophie (2019): Kurzbericht zu den Reflexionsgesprächen mit den ProAbschluss-Beratungskräften 2018. Unveröffentlichter Projektbericht.

Lauxen, Oliver/Werle, Jasmin/Fink, Miriam Sophie (2018): Die Perspektive hessischer Bildungsanbieter 2018: Mapping zum Stand der Nachqualifizierung in Hessen. URL: https://www.proabschluss.de/fileadmin/downloads/IWAK/Dossier_Bildungsanbieter_2018.pdf [03 March 2020].

Lauxen, Oliver/Werle, Jasmin (2018): Nachqualifizierung von Beschäftigten in Unternehmen: Wie Betriebe besser unterstützt werden können. In: bwp Berufsbildung in Wissenschaft und Praxis 47 (5), pp. 38-42.

Mayring, Philipp (2007): Qualitative Inhaltsanalyse: Grundlagen und Techniken. 9. Auflage. Weinheim/Basel: Beltz.

Meyer, John P./Herscovitch, Lynne (2001): Commitment in the Workplace: Toward a General Model. In: Human Resource Management Review 11 (3), pp. 299-326.

Röttger, Christof/Weber, Brigitte/Weber, Enzo (2019): Qualifikationsspezifische Arbeitslosenquoten. URL: http://doku.iab.de/arbeitsmarktdaten/qualo_2019.pdf [03 March 2020].

Werle, Jasmin/Lauxen, Oliver (2018): Die Perspektive hessischer Unternehmen 2018: Mapping zum Stand der Nachqualifizierung in Hessen. URL: https://www.proabschluss.de/fileadmin/downloads/IWAK/Dossier__Die_Perspektive_hessischer_Unternehmen_2018.pdf [03 March 2020].

Schreiber, Daniel/Gutschow, Katrin/Weber-Höller, Robin/Gei, Julia (2012): Anerkennung beruflicher Kompetenzen am Beispiel der Zulassung zur Abschlussprüfung im Rahmen der Externenregelung: Abschlussbericht. Bonn: Bundesinstitut für Berufsbildung.

Unger, Tim (2010): Berufliche Identität im Lebenslauf. In: Büchter, Karin (Ed.): Enzyklopädie Erziehungswissenschaft. Weinheim/München: Juventa, pp. 1-32.

Ziegaus, Sebastian (2006): Die Kommunikative Sozialforschung in der Forschungsliteratur seit 1973. Zeitschrift für qualitative Bildungs-, Beratungs- und Sozialforschung 7 (2), pp. 293-312.

Websites

Initiative ProAbschluss: www.proabschluss.de

Regionale Beschäftigungs- und Berufsprognosen (regio pro): www.regio-pro.eu

3.2. Human Resource Development and Retention Management

How Do SMEs Contribute to Sustainable Employability in Times of Crisis? An Explorative Study in Northern Italy

Mattia Martini and Dario Cavenago

Introduction

The attention to the issue of employability has grown in recent years as a consequence of transformations that are affecting the national and local labour market (Green et al. 2013). In particular, the traditional job security is lost with the shift from the "linear career model" to the "boundary-less career".[113] As a consequence, it becomes important for workers to continually strengthen their employability in order to cope with the increasingly frequent changes in their career paths. Furthermore, it is expected that due to the digital transformation on the labour market, some occupations will disappear, and others will substantially be modified. Workers will have to be ready to adapt to new requirements of skills and abilities and to be employable both at their current as well as at prospective employers. Finally, employability represents a critical resource for individuals to face times of economic crisis when re-engineering, downsizing, and layoff are commonplaces and when the individual's ability to "relocate" in the labour market and reinvent themselves plays a key role.

Individual employability partly depends on personal resources, in particular on human ("know-how"), social ("know-who"), and psychological capital ("know-why"); they affect a person's chances of success in the labour market. However, employability is both an individual and institutional/organisational responsibility (Zhang et al. 2015). Individuals are expected to acquire knowledge, skills and abilities that are appreciated by the employers (both actual and prospective) and

---

[113] „Linear" (or traditional) career models are grounded in a long-term relationship between the individual and one or two companies over the individual's working life. The emerging „protean" or „boundaryless" career, on the other hand, involves different changes of jobs, roles, and employers in the working career path (Eby et al. 2003).

make themselves more "employable" over time. Additionally, different actors such as the government, schools, universities, public and private services for employment and training, and employers have the responsibility to provide opportunities for people to enhance their human, social, and psychological capital in a life-long learning perspective.

As many studies have suggested, a worker's employability largely develops through their working experience (Martini et al. 2019; Martini and Cavenago 2017; Van Harten et al. 2016; De Vos et al. 2011; Van der Heijden et al. 2009; De Grip and Sanders 2004; De Vries et al. 2001; Groot and Maassen 2000). Accordingly, the employers play a key role in strengthening (or hindering) the employability of their employees. An employer can support the employability of their workers by providing programmes and initiatives that promote their development and growth within the organisation and/or by helping the employees in dealing with job changes and career transitions in the labour market.

The literature on the subject discusses the benefits and risks of investing in employability from the perspective of organisations (Van Harten et al. 2020). On the one hand, researchers believe that investing in employability may allow a company to have better performing, more flexible and more committed workers. On the other hand, researchers also point out the risk for the employers of not being able to recover from the investment made, as strengthening employability increases the marketability and possibly turnover of employees. Besides the benefits and risks, some of the research literature points out that enhancing the employability of employees means adopting a sustainable way of human resource management (HRM) strategy and designing practices aimed to help workers dealing with job insecurity and work-related changes (Ehnert et al. 2014).

Northern Italy, like many other countries in the world, is now facing the health emergency due to the so-called Corona virus (SARS-CoV-2). The pandemic and the resulting lockdown of about half of all global business activities will lead to an unprecedented economic crisis. In a recent report, the International Labour Organisation (ILO) points out that the number of hours worked will drop by 6.7 per cent in the entire world in the second quarter of 2020 and the crisis will cancel the equivalent of 195 million full-time workers (ILO 2020). Consequently, solutions must be found that limit the loss of jobs and the dispersion of human capital. Therefore, it is critical to understand if and how small and medium-sized enterprises (SMEs) deal with employability and sustainable employment to face the current economic recession and expected crisis.

The present chapter reports the results of an explorative study conducted with the owners and human resources (HR) managers of six SMEs in Northern Italy. The study aims to examine whether and to what extent the SMEs integrate the concept of employability within their HR strategies, and how they explicitly or implicitly contribute to develop their workers' employability.

The present study draws back to 2011, when the Italian economy was in the midst of an economic crisis that had started in 2009. Thus, although dated, the results of the study could be useful to predict and steer the behaviours of SMEs towards their employees when facing an economic crisis, such as the one that is expected as a result of the COVID-19 crisis.

The chapter begins by presenting the reference literature and then the rational for examining employability within SMEs in Monza and Brianza. It proceeds to describe the research conducted and to discuss the results of the explorative analysis. At the end, conclusions and implications are presented.

Literature Review

HRM and economic literature offer a wide range of definitions of employability. Nevertheless, all definitions of employability are about work and people's ability to be employed. In essence, employability is the "capability to move self-sufficiently within the labour market to realize potential through sustainable employment" (Hillage and Pollard 1998; Fugate and Kincki 2008; Rothwell and Arnold 2007; Van der Heijde and Van der Heiijden 2006; Fugate et al. 2004; De Grip and Sanders 2004; Forrier and Sels 2003; Groot and Maassen 2000).

The employability literature also distinguishes between "internal" and "external employability". "Internal employability" concerns the ability of the employee to keep their actual job, while "external employability" relates to their ability to find a new job in the external labour market. The likelihood of being externally employable is largely connected to the possession of a valuable general and transversal human capital, whereas that of being internal employability largely (if not exclusively) depends on specific human capital, and then professional skills which are necessary to effectively carry out the work within a specific organization (De Cuyper and De Witte, 2011). In what follows, we refer to external or general employability, though most of the arguments and results are also valid in the context of internal employability.

Individual employability largely depends on knowledge and skills. Accordingly, those who have a higher formal education as well as a range of generic skills and labour market experience are supposed to have better chances of getting new employment (Van der Heijde and Van der Heijden 2006; Hillage and Pollard 1998). Furthermore, McQuaid and Lindsay (2005) consider transferable skills to have the most impact on one's employability. They distinguish between basic, key and high-level transferable skills. Basic transferable skills refer to skills such as literacy and numeracy; key transferable skills refer, for example, to problem-solving and communication; and high-level transferable skills include self-management and commercial awareness. However, Fugate and Kincki (2008) describe employability as a psychosocial construct that embodies individual characteristics that foster adaptive cognition, behaviour, and affect, and enhance the individual-work interface. The authors furthermore stress the importance of considering five personal traits that can foster individual employability; these traits are "openness to changes at work", "work and career resilience", "work and career proactivity", "career motivation", and "work identity".

At the organisational level, employability means increased investments in all forms of employee development with an emphasis on providing general or marketable skills that are in demand at other firms (Craig et al. 2002; Baruch 2001). Within the firm, such skills can be acquired through formal and informal learning (Van Der Hejden et al. 2009). Accordingly, organisations may adopt a wide range of personnel development practices to enhance the individual's suitability for work. It starts with formal training, which is targeted at long-term rather than short-term development issues and contributes to develop transferable skills rather than solely firm-specific human capital (Baruch 2001). Informal learning opportunities mainly depend on the extent to which firms design rich, autonomous, and challenging jobs, and organise work through working groups, task rotation, and multitasking (De Grip and Senders, 2004; De Grip et al. 2004; Groot and Maassen 2000). Meanwhile, firms that promote employability are also expanding internal mobility and the above measures can then further be encouraged by stimulating horizontal and vertical flows, such as shifts to other functions at the same level of the hierarchy (horizontal) or to a higher level (vertical) (De Vries et al. 2001). Furthermore, employers can adopt performance evaluation systems to identify the causes of the discrepancies between workers' performances and organisational expectations, and provide follow-up and improvement plans accordingly. Finally, employability may occur as result of career support initiatives (Van Dam 2004), including personal relationships, such as coaching, mentoring, and tutoring.

Although employee development is vital in maintaining and developing the overall capabilities of the organisation, there is a debate about the benefits and risks for companies that invest on employability development (Van Harten et al. 2020). In this vein, a pessimistic and an optimistic vision can be distinguished.

The supporters of the pessimistic vision suggest the existence of an "employability paradox" (De Cuyper and De Witte 2011), emphasising the risks associated with any investments for the development of employability. The assumption behind the employability paradox is that companies risk to lose their investments in employability, as they possibly also stimulate greater turnover of their most valuable employees. According to the human capital theory assumptions (Becker 1983), employers should prefer to focus their investments on firm-specific human capital that is not easily appropriable for competitors. Following these arguments, enhancing employees' employability would not be a convenient strategy for employers.

On the contrary and from a more optimistic perspective, sustaining employability is considered to be a source of sustainable competitive advantage for organisations (Goshal and Moran 1997). From this perspective, investing in employees' employability is considered an effective strategy for attracting, motivating, and retaining talents (Ellstrom and Nillson 2012), as it leads to greater employee commitment (Benson 2006). The underlying assumption here is that when employment-security cannot be longer guaranteed by the employers, employability becomes the basis for an alternative employment relationship (Craig et al. 2002; Galunic and Anderson 2000; Estienne 1997; Iles et al. 1996 among others). Accordingly, developing employability means to guarantee that the employees' skills are up-to-date and marketable when they unexpectedly become unemployed. Building on the social exchange theory, it is assumed that when employees perceive a greater support from their employers for their employability, they will reciprocate the organisation through greater commitment, loyalty, and work-performance (Galunic and Anderson 2000).

Recent empirical study questions the assumptions of the "employability paradox" and provides support for the optimistic view on employability development (Rodrigues et al. 2019; Nelissen et al. 2017). Despite this, there are still many doubts regarding the employer's orientation and commitment of adopting an employability development strategy (Marzec et al. 2009; Baruch 2001; De Vries et al. 2001). According to this, many employers are reluctant to offer generic skill development and prefer job-specific training that brings immediate results to the organisation (Carbery and Garavan 2005). In addition, an employability strategy may fail in sustaining organisational commitment, as its effectiveness also depends on the willingness and capability of employees in taking advantage of the learning opportunities provided by the employers (Thijssen et al. 2008). As a consequence (and according to some empirical evidence), the adoption of an employability approach is more frequent in knowledge-intensive organisations and sectors (Marzec et al. 2009), where the presence of high-skilled workers is greater (De Vries et al. 2001).

Beyond the fact that companies may or may not adopt an employability strategy when managing their employees, the former can be distinguished according to the extent that they offer workplace development opportunities for workers. For example, some authors suggest that investments in formal training are usually higher in larger enterprises (Waddoups 2011) due to their high financial resources. In addition, the largest industrial firms frequently adopt high-performance work systems (HPWS's) which are used to increase employees' competence, flexibility, and performances (Appelbaum et al. 2000). Evidence also suggests that the most varied employability practices were usually applied in SMEs (Marzek et al. 2009), as their flat structures, decentralisation and job rotation guarantee broad informal learning opportunities for their employees (Patton et al. 2000).

Empirical Context

The province of Monza and Brianza in Northern Italy is one of the fastest growing areas in Italy in terms of economic activity. The local area is characterised by a strong industrial tradition and the presence of many SMEs employing about 40 per cent of the total workforce. Some trends of the labour market at the local level make the issue of employability particularly relevant for SMEs. During the economic crisis that started in 2009, the increase of labour market flexibility occurred alongside downsizing, restructuring, delay rings, plant closures, and delocation, with direct consequences for employees such as layoffs and involuntary job terminations. All these trends resulted in a substantial reduction of long-term job security for workers and an increase of employment mobility and job turnover rates in the labour market of Monza and Brianza (Mezzanzanica 2011). One of the consequences of the immensely increased job insecurity was the undermining of the credibility of a model of employment organised around the stability of a long-term employment relationship, which seems to be especially the case in SMEs. In this context, the development of employability may represent an effective strategy for SMEs. In addition, due to increased international competition, human capital became a particularly critical resource for the manufacturing SMEs in Monza and Brianza. Many SMEs increasingly look for high-skilled workers (mainly technicians and specialized workmen) and were more aware of the importance of formal and innovative HRM (Martini 2012).

Method

Data for this study was collected through a research conducted in 2011 together with SMEs in the province of Monza and Brianza. In the first phase of the research conducted, a survey was administered with a representative sample of small, medium, and large organisations to shed light on the adoption of high-performance work practices (HPWPs). The study subsequently proceeded by collecting qualitative data from six case SMEs.[114] The aim of the qualitative phase was to examine to what extent SMEs embrace an employability policy to manage their employees and how they contribute to developing the employability of their employees.

---

[114] This chapter was born in the context of a broader research started in 2011 (still ongoing), conducted by the authors and a team of professors and researchers from the University of Milan-Bicocca. The research on employability aims at exploring the conditions of development of employability in companies and testing the impact of the support of employability on the organisational performance. In 2019, the research led to the development of different tools designed to calculate the Company Employability Index (CEI) and launch an observatory on employability (https://maunimib.unimib.it/osservatori/employability-lab/).

The choice of a multiple-case study was due to the research objective, which was not to identify different approaches and characteristics, but rather to trace out a common trend in the action of SMEs. Furthermore, this choice mitigates the limitations of qualitative research that provides little basis for scientific generalisation (Stake 2006). Although the research results cannot be considered statistically relevant, they give a clear vision of the phenomenon and enrich its exploration. Furthermore, in order to neutralize the effects of the firm's dimensions, both small and medium-sized companies were included. The participating enterprises have chosen not to reveal their identity due to the sensitivity of the subject under study, so specific names will not be mentioned. The main characteristics of the six SMEs are shown in Table 1.

Table 1: Characteristics of SMEs involved

	SME_A	SME_B	SME_C	SME_D	SME_E	SME_F
Core function	Production of plant and equipment for storage and logistics	Production of screw jacks, bevels, and phasers	Production of photovoltaic modules and turnkey plants	Production of screws and special fasteners	Production/distribution of components and systems for plumbing installation	Production of alimentation systems for cars and motorcycles
Number of employees	38	55	120	186	233	245
Foundation (year)	1956	1981	2000	1926	2010	1933
Respondent (role)	Owner	Owner	HR Manager	HR Manager	HR Manager	HR Manager

Source: the authors.

The principal source of investigation were twelve semi-structured interviews (two for each firm) carried out with HR managers, or, where this role was not present, with the enterprise's owner. Each interview was conducted by two researchers, recorded and transcribed for the most important parts; the same researchers also led two focus groups, once with the smaller-sized enterprises (SME_A, SME_B, and SME_C) and once with the larger (SME_D, SME_E, and SME_F). The interview protocol was constructed on the basis of previous empirical research (Groot and Maassen 2000; Baruch 2001; De Vries et al. 2001; De

Grip and Senders 2004; De Grip et al. 2004; Van Dam 2004; Van Der Heiden et al. 2009; Marzec et al. 2009) and the data analysis was carried out through the construction of matrices describing the variables analysed in the various cases, thereby making comparisons easier (Stake 2006).

Results

The Employability Orientation of SMEs

The first aim of the interviews was to examine HR managers' or owners' awareness of the idea of employability. Respondents were asked whether they embrace and/or would embrace an employability strategy to manage employees and then to discuss the barriers and the enhancing factors.

One finding from the interviews is that employers naturally do not focus their strategic personnel management on the development of long-term employability of their employees to maintain them fit for the labour market in general and possibly for the work at other companies. Indeed, the main priority of the SMEs surveyed is to create and develop firm-specific skills that are directly applicable in their current working context. For example, the HR manager of SME_D states that *"developing employability is a problem that we never face, while it is a priority for us that our employees are able to develop skills which would be useful and applicable in our business environment"* (Interview No. 4, 12 June 2011)[115]. Furthermore, the wish to benefit from the human capital developed in their company themselves seems to prevail among the respondents. The risk to lose their employees and the according investments to the competition makes the adoption of an employability strategy less attractive for the SMEs. For example, the owner of SME_B asserts that *"the firm cannot worry about what will happen to their employees. Our employees can develop employability through a working experience in a small business. Then, I don't care to create it and the fact that others can benefit bothers me"* (Interview No. 2, 5 June 2011).

---

[115] All quotes from the interviews have not been corrected (concerning typos, grammar, and other mistakes), so as not to change their meaning.

However, it seems that some external and internal conditions to the SMEs limit their willingness to invest in their employees' employability. Participants highlight that the economic crisis, combined with a higher competition from developing and newly industrialised countries (China, in particular) forced the SMEs to focus on short-term objectives and containing labour costs. Accordingly, a proper implementation of an employability strategy at the organisational level came with high costs and its outcomes will only be visible in the long-run. As the HR manager of SME_E states, *"the employability of our employees is not a priority (...). In this period, we have to reduce costs and the response must be quick and easy (...). Our overriding goal is to improve efficiency in order to survive, to justify the investment and give a semblance of stability for the future"* (Interview No. 5, 20 June 2011). Caring about the employees' employability is not considered to be an effective short-term strategy, as respondents believe that its potential benefits would be visible only over a longer period of time. For example, the manager of SME_F states that *"an attitude of this type constrains the development of employability as the impact of the most advanced human resource management practices is greater in the long run, as these need to be integrated in the work environment in order to lead to concrete benefit"* (Interview No. 6, 28 June 2011).

The respondents also emphasise that a strategy aimed at enhancing employability would not be appropriate if the expectations of employees are still focused on job-security. As stated by the owner of SME_B, *"the choice of the employee to enter and remain in the company always depends on employment security that the organisation can guarantee (...). The goal of the most workers is still on the lifetime job rather than of professional development"* (Interview No. 2, 5 June 2011). As a consequence, it seems to be more effective for the SMEs to guarantee job-security, offer high levels of remunerations and provide internal career opportunities to attract and retain employees. In this regard, respondents emphasise the importance of government interventions, which aim at reducing the rigidity still characterising the Italian labour market (in particular, high costs for the dismissal of employees) and may contribute to create a new culture of work among people that is more focused on taking advantage of life-long learning and the development of opportunities. As the owner of SME_A claims, *"as long as the mentality of people does not change, the introduction of innovative policies* and practices of personnel management, such as those related to the development of employability, are not feasible within our organisations" (Interview No. 1, 3 June 2011).

The respondents also suggest that workers' expectations and preferences vary according to their age and educational level. More specifically, young workers (between 25 and 40 years) and those employed in skilled occupations (such as technicians and professionals) may be more interested in a professional development opportunity than others. For example, the manager of SME_E indicates that *"in my organisation, workmen and the lowest skilled workers only look for permanent jobs and salary increases (...). On the contrary, young office workers and technicians are quite sensible to the development opportunities that we can offer to them"* (Interview No. 5, 20 June 2011). Therefore, diversifying the HRM strategy according to different targets groups was considered to be the better option for SMEs.

Finally, some SMEs must deal with labour unions, which, according to the interviewees, are particularly concerned about ensuring job protection, wage increase, and internal career progressions to the overall labour force. In this regard, the HR manager of SME_F describes that *"where we try to innovate our HRM, we always find a unionized counterparty which is completely detached from the business logic and still anchored to old ideologies"* (Interview No. 6, 28 June 2011).

The Employability Support from SMEs

Apart from a deliberate commitment to supporting employability, our interest was also to understand what chances employees of SMEs might have or might not have to develop their knowledge, skills, and abilities for employability. In this regard, the preliminary quantitative analysis suggested that, due to the way work is organised and managed, employees in SMEs have many learning opportunities, sometimes more than those employed in larger organisations. Thus, the second aim of the interviews was to examine how SMEs effectively contribute, explicitly or implicitly, to develop the employability of their employees. The results show that firms enhance their employees' employability by offering training programmes focused on working experience, personal relations, and evaluations systems.

Firstly, formal training through courses organised internally and/or externally is used by all the SMEs analysed in this study, though the larger companies provide these programmes to a greater extent. In line with the findings reported above, the primary purpose for SMEs is to build or strengthen skills which are directly applicable to their working environment. Moreover, as training is considered to be an expansive activity, it is specifically used in order to target key personnel and aimed at responding to specific organisational needs. For example, all the SMEs provide training to facilitate the new placement process; SME_C, SME_D, SME_E, and SME_F offer training even for supporting internal career transitions, and SME_F provides training also in response to organisational restructuring. Finally, the SMEs never adopt development plans centred around long-term professional needs of their employees. Indeed, although all the examined SMEs had to lay off workers due to the economic crisis, no one provides outplacement services to the involved employees. Respondents stress the importance of investing in general and behavioural skills which they consider to be required to effectively fill most of the occupations and roles within their organisation. More specifically, most of the respondents claim to offer training programmes aimed at developing transferable skills such as leadership, teamwork, problem solving, negotiation, flexibility, and stress management. The SMEs help their employees to develop skills that may contribute to increase their marketability in the external labour market through formal training programmes.

However, employability enhancement within the examined SMEs largely takes place through the working experience and informal learning mechanisms. Decentralisation, multi-tasking, and working groups are widespread within all the six organisations. As claimed by the managers of SME_D, "*it is mainly through the autonomous or semi-autonomous working groups that our employees have the opportunity to acquire generic skills. Indeed, in working groups, employees choose their own leaders, have considerable autonomy, must solve operational problems and are directly responsible for the quality of the products and the achievement of agreed objectives*" (Interview No. 4, 12 June 2011).

Moreover, SMEs with less than 100 employees, such as SME_A and SME_B, organise work through job-rotation, multi-tasking, and shared responsibilities. The larger companies perceived the importance of introducing flexible working practices, too; for example, SME_F had recently introduced a system of total quality management (TQM), which was aimed at increasing the degree of responsibility and strengthening the employees' multitasking. Finally, internal mobility flows are not the norm in the smaller SMEs, but the opportunities for growing vertically and horizontally increased with the size of the firm. In SME_D, SME_E, and SME_F, for example, more than 70 per cent of the new vacancies were intended for internal employees, and promotions required employees to face greater responsibilities and challenging tasks.

Respondents also agreed that young employees within their organisation have high chances to develop their skills and knowledge, especially by interacting with senior colleagues. Indeed, mentoring, tutoring, and coaching are frequently used by the SMEs. In case SMEs provide mentoring for new hires, they also make extensive use of the apprenticeship contract when hiring very young persons without any previous working experience. Such an apprenticeship contract lasts between three and four years and requires young workers to be continuously supported and trained by an experienced colleague. SME_C also used coaching external services for its technical and managerial employees.

Finally, the performance evaluation is a process by which the contribution of the employee is measured and the information it yields are used for employee development. However, such a practice is not widespread within examined SMEs. More specifically, the formal performance evaluation is considered by the respondents as an activity too complex that requires many resources to be effectively implemented. Despite this, the HR manager of SME_C points out that *"in small enterprises, employees and supervisors often work very closely, the performance evaluation and the provision of feedbacks on performances and behaviours is a daily process, even if mainly informal"* (Interview No. 3, 10 June 2011).

Conclusion and Implications

Building on a qualitative study with six manufacturing SMEs in Northern-Italy, this chapter examines the employability orientation of SMEs and their effective contribution to enhancing their employees' chances in the labour market.

Firstly, the negative outlook towards employability seems to prevail among SMEs. In a period characterised by an economic crisis, SMEs have shown some resistances to deliberately investing in employee employability. On the contrary, they preferred to make targeted investments on skills that are easily and immediately applicable to the workers' jobs and tasks and can hardly be appropriated by competitors. Moreover, it seems that the employment relationship within SMEs is still based on the long-term job security and workers do not fully perceive the value of the investments realised by their employers for employability development. Therefore, SMEs prefer to invest in job stability, wage growth and career opportunities rather than in sustainable employability.

Although employability is not a valuable strategy for SMEs to manage their personnel, they implicitly contribute to the employee's employability. Indeed, the employment relationship within SMEs seemed to be direct, informal, and often personal. This feature favours the development of an employability within SMEs that is largely based on formal training, working experiences, personal relations, and evaluation practices. Furthermore, there also seem to exist some differences between SMEs. For example, while larger organisations (between 120 and 249 employees) provide formal training, enhancement of transferable skills, and career opportunities, the smallest organisations mainly contribute to employability development by ensuring rich and varied working experiences and providing support from experienced mentors and tutors.

Although the economic crisis from 2007 to 2012 is not fully comparable to the effects on the economy that will result from the COVID-19 pandemic, the results from the present study may provide some insights for decision-makers on how to face the next economic downturn.

On the one hand, the insight from the study is that in times of economic crisis, opportunistic behaviours towards human capital may prevail among SMEs. In these challenging times they tend to prefer short-term investments and the reduction of labour costs. In order to avoid or at least limit the dispersion of human capital and promote behaviours aimed at preserving labour and ensuring human capital regeneration in an organisational citizenship perspective, it could be necessary to provide adequate incentives and financial support. In Italy, such economic incentives have already been planned by the national government and included in a presidential decree[116]. However, it is also important that these incentives support payrolls and financial liquidity and allow SMEs to plan in the

---

[116] Decree of the President of the Italian Republic No. 18 of 17 March 2020, Enhancement Measures of the National Health Service and Economic Support for Families, Workers and Businesses Related to the Epidemiological Emergency from COVID-19.

medium to long-run. With the help of such instruments, the government could lead SMEs to contemplate the retention of their employees and save jobs in view of an economic recovery over time.

On the other hand, most of SMEs workers could gain knowledge, skills, and abilities that render them competent, flexible, and easily relocatable. The ways in which work and tasks are organised in SMEs help them to be particularly resilient and ready to face organisational and job changes. Accordingly, it could be more feasible for SMEs to convert or modify their production and business models to meet the emerging market needs. In the recent months, examples of this kind have multiplied in Italy during the COVID-19 crisis. For example, the Carillo Home, a SME in the Province of Monza and Brianza, took just three weeks to convert its first production line from sheets to polypropylene surgical masks. Similarly, the textile company Montrasio has adapted its employees and machinery to the production of one million surgical masks per day.

In doing so, SMEs are helping the society to better manage the health emergency and to preserve or even create jobs. In fact, as the owner of Montrasio states: "We are considering hiring other staff because we cannot neglect our traditional production which remains our core business"[117]. To date, these kind of initiatives from SMEs seem to be adequate and concrete responses to the economic crisis and capable of guaranteeing the lasting life of SMEs and the continuity of their work.

References

Appelbaum, E./Bailey, T./Berg, P./Kalleberg, A. (2000): Manufacturing Advantage: Why High-Performance Work Systems Pay Off. New York: Cornell University Press.

Baruch, Y. (2001): Employability: A Substitute for Loyalty? In: Human Resource Development International 4 (4), pp. 543-566.

Becker, G. S. (1983): Human Capital: A Theoretical and Empirical Analysis with Special Reference to Education. Chicago: University of Chicago Press.

---

[117] cf. https://milano.corriere.it/notizie/cronaca/20_febbraio_27/coronavirus-mascherine-vendita-monza-montrasio-azienda-aicurzio-brianza-riconvertita-013b6a8a-598e-11ea-af71-899699a3d6d8.shtml.

Benson, G. (2006): Employee Development, Commitment and Intention to Turnover: A Test of Employability Policies in Action. In: Human Resource Management Journal 16 (2), pp. 173-192.

Carbery, R./Garavan, T. (2005): Organisational Restructuring and Downsizing: Issues Related to Learning, Training and Employability of Survivors. In: Journal of European Industrial Training 29 (6), pp. 488-508.

Craig, E./Kimberly, J./Bouchikhi, H. (2002): Can Loyalty be Leased? In: Harvard Business Review 80 (3), pp. n/a.

De Cuyper, N./De Witte, H. (2011): The Management Paradox. In: Personnel Review, 40 (2), pp. 152-172.

De Grip, A./Sanders, J. (2004): Training, Task Flexibility and the Employability of Low-Skilled Workers. In: International Journal of Manpower 25 (1), pp. 73-89.

De Grip, A./Van Loo, J./Sanders, J. (2004): The Industry Employability Index: Taking Account of Supply and Demand Characteristics. In: International Labor Review 143 (3), pp. 211-233.

De Vos, A./De Hauw, S./Van der Heijden, B. I. J. M. (2011): Competency Development and Career Success: The Mediating Role of Employability. In: Journal of Vocational Behaviour 79 (2), pp. 438-447.

De Vries, S./Gründemann, R./Van Vuuren, T. (2001); Employability Policy in Dutch Organisations. In: International Journal of Human Resource Management 12 (7), pp. 1193-1202.

Eby, L. T./Butts, M./Lockwood, A. (2003): Predictors of Success in the Era of the Boundaryless Career. In: Journal of Organizational Behavior 24, pp. 689-708.

Ellstrom, P. E./Nillson, S. (2012): Employability and Talent Management: Challenges for HRD Practices. In: European Journal of Training and Development 36 (1), pp. 26-45.

Ehnert, I./Harry, W./Zink, K. (2014): Sustainability and HRM: An Introduction to the Field. In: I. Ehnert, I./Harry, W./Zink, K. (Eds.): Sustainability and Human Resource Management. New York: Springer, pp. 4-30.

Estienne, M. (1997): An Organisational Culture Compatible with Employability. In: Commercial and Industrial Training 29 (6), pp. 194-199.

Fagiano, D. (1993): Training is the New Job Security. In: Management Review 82 (8), p.4.

Forrier, A./Sels, L. (2003): The Concept Employability: A Complex Mosaic. In: International Journal of Human Resources Development and Management 3 (2), pp. 102–214.

Fugate, M./Kinicki, A. J. (2008): A Dispositional Approach to Employability: Development of a Measure and Test of Implications for Employee Reactions to Organisational Change. In: Journal of Occupational and Organisational Psychology 81 (3), pp. 503–527.

Fugate, M./Kinicki, A. J./Ashforth, B. E. (2004): Employability: A Psycho-Social Construct, its Dimensions, and Applications. In: Journal of Vocational Behavior 65 (1), pp. 14-38.

Galunic, D./Anderson, E. (2000): From Security to Mobility: Generalized Investments in Human Capital and Agent Commitment. In: Organisational Science 11 (1), pp. 1–20.

Goshal, S./Moran, P./Bartlett, C. A. (1997): Employment Security, Employability and Sustainable Competitive Advantage. URL: https://flora.insead.edu/fichiersti_wp/inseadwp1997/97-20.pdf [01 June 2020].

Green, A. E./De Hoyos, M./Barnes, S.-A./Owen, D./Baldauf, B./Behle, H. (2013): Literature Review on Employability, Inclusion and ICT. Report 1: The Concept of Employability with a Specific Focus on Young People, Older Workers and Migrants. URL: http://ipts.jrc.ec.europa.eu/publications/pub.cfm?id56059 [01 June 2020].

Groot, W./Maassen, H. (2000): Education, Training and Employability. In: Applied Economics 32 (5), pp. 573-581.

Hillage, J./Pollard, E. (1998): Employability: Developing a Framework for Policy Analysis. London: Department for Education and Employment.

Iles, P./Forster, A./Tinline, G. (1996): The Changing Relationships Between Work Commitment, Personal Flexibility, and Employability: An Evaluation of a Field Experiment in Executive Development. In: Journal of Managerial Psychology 11 (8), pp. 18-34.

International Labour Organization (ILO) (2020): ILO Monitor: COVID-19 and the World of Work. Second Edition. Updated Estimates and Analysis. URL: https://www.ilo.org/wcmsp5/groups/public/---dgreports/---dcomm/documents/briefingnote/wcms_740877.pdf [01 June 2020].

Martini, M./Cavenago, D./Marafioti, E. (2019): Enhancing the Employability of Temporary Agency Workers: The Interplay Between Agency Support and Client Company Investments. In: International Journal of Human Resource Management, pp. n/a (DOI: 10.1080/09585192.2019.1579750).

Martini, M./Cavenago, D. (2017): The Role of Perceived Workplace Development Opportunities in Enhancing Individual Employability. In: International Journal of Training and Development 21 (1), pp. 18-34.

Martini, M. (2012): Le condizioni di sviluppo delle human capabilities nelle imprese della Brianza. In: Cavenago, C./Martini, M. (Eds.): Human capabilities e sviluppo aziendale. Rome: Aracne.

Marzec, I./Van der Heijden, B. I. J. M./Scholarios, D./Van der Schoot, E./ Jdrzejowicz, P./Bozionelos, N./Epitropaki, O./Knauth, P./Mikkelsen, A./Van der Heijde, C. (2009): Employability Management Practices in the Polish ICT Sector. In: Human Resource Development International 12 (4), pp. 471-492.

McQuaid, R. W./Lindsay, C. (2005): The Concept of Employability. In: Urban Studies 42 (2), pp. 197-219.

Mezzanzanica, M. (2011): Il mercato del lavoro in provincia di Monza e della Brianza: Contesto e quadro di sintesi. In: Mezzanzanica, M. (Ed.): La ripresa possibile. Milano: Guerini e Associati.

Nelissen, J./Forrier, A./Verbruggen, M. (2017): Employee Development and Voluntary Turnover: Testing the Employability Paradox. In: Human Resource Management Journal 27 (1), pp. 152-168.

Patton, D./Marlow, S./Hannon, P. (2000): The Relationship Between Training and Small Firm Performance: Research Frameworks and Lost Quests. In: International Small Business Journal 19 (11), pp. 535-557.

Rodrigues, R./Butler, C. L. /Guest, D. (2019): Evaluating the Employability Paradox: When Does Organisational Investment in Human Capital Pay off? In: International Journal of Human Resource Management 31 (9), pp. 1134-1156.

Rothwell, A./Arnold, J. (2007): Self-Perceived Employability: Development and Validation of a Scale. In: Personnel Review 36 (1), pp. 23-41.

Stake, R. E. (2006): Multiple Case Study Analysis. New York: Guilford Press.

Thijssen, J. G. L./Van der Heijden, B. I. J. M./Rocco, T. S. (2008): Toward the Employability-Link Model: Current Employment Transition to Future Employment Perspectives. In: Human Resource Development Review 7 (2), pp. 165-183.

Van Dam, K. (2004): Antecedents and Consequences of Employability Orientation. In: European Journal of Work and Organisational Psychology 13 (1), pp. 29-51.

Van der Heijden, B. I. J. M./Boon, J./Van der Klink, M./ Meijs, E. (2009): Employability Enhancement Through Formal and Informal Learning: An Empirical Study among Dutch Non-Academic University Staff Members. In: International Journal of Training and Development 13 (1), pp.19-37.

Van der Heijde, C. M./Van der Heijden, B. I. J. M. (2006): A Competence-Based and Multidimensional Operationalization and Measurement of Employability. In: Human Resource Management 45 (3), pp. 449-476.

Van Harten, J./De Cuyper, N./Guest, D./ Fugate, M./Knies, E. (2020): Introduction to Special Issue on HRM and Employability: Mutual Gains or Conflicting Outcomes? In: International Journal of Human Resource Management 31 (9), pp. 1095-1105.

Van Harten, J./ Knies, E./Leisink, P. (2016): Employer's Investments in Hospital Workers' Employability and Employment Opportunities. In: Personnel Review 45 (1), pp. 84–102.

Zhang, M. M./Bartram, T./McNeil, N./Dowling, P. J. (2015): Towards a Research Agenda on the Sustainable and Socially Responsible Management of Agency Workers Through a Flexicurity Model of HRM. In: Journal of Business Ethics 127 (3), pp. 513–523.

Waddoups, C. J. (2011): Firm Size and Work-Related Training: New Evidence on Incidence, Intensity, and Training Type from Australia. In: Journal of Labor Research 32 (4), pp. 390–413.

Innovation and Sustainable Inclusive Employment: Evidence from the „Regio Insubria" During the COVID-19 Outbreak

Moreno Baruffini

Introduction

In a globalised and ever-changing world, the concept of competitiveness of a territory changes and evolves with it. The estimate of the competitive level of a region, therefore, has multiple facets and lends itself to various interpretations. Uncertainties on a political level, the strong impact in international economic cycles of international powers, the presence (or the threat) of restrictive policies for the trade constitute structural difficulties. Moreover, the recent crisis caused by the COVID-19 pandemic is just an additional example that could trigger a succession of events that would lead to sector shocks or to more or less marked economic crises.

The Great Recession that started in 2008 has indeed shown that financial crises can have long-term effects on productivity. The long-term growth trajectory can be reduced by a protracted period of reduction of investments, caused by a financial collapse, directing the economic system towards a less prosperous path. At the same time, the advent of the fourth industrial revolution is producing, among other effects, an acceleration of innovative cycle. It is causing the obsolescence of business models at a faster pace (Larsen et al. 2016).

These renewal processes create opportunities for new entrants and reduce the barriers for the transfer of technologies and innovation. Still, they imply the presence of difficulties or crises in sector growth. In order to meet these challenges, different mechanisms are needed to reduce the risk of new financial crises and the ability to manage the socio-economic effects of innovation. For these reasons, economies who want to succeed in the present era must (WEF 2018):

- be resilient, building mechanisms to prevent financial crises, and to respond to external shocks;

- be agile, embracing change rather than opposing it. Workers, companies, and leaders should be able to change how they operate and take advantage of new opportunities to produce goods or provide services with new approaches;
- build an innovative ecosystem, in which innovation is stimulated at all levels, and all economic actors contribute to creating the best conditions to bring out new ideas, new products, and services;
- and a dopt an anthropocentric approach to economic development. That is, to recognize centrality to human capital for economic prosperity, adopting policies that do not inhibit the potential of the human factor, necessary determinant for long-term economic growth.

The general concept that the World Economic Forum (WEF) wants to reiterate is that in a world of continuous and unpredictable evolution, the intent of policymakers should be to ensure that the speed of changing scenarios and the introduction of new technologies will ultimately translate into better living conditions and prosperity for the population.

In this context, small and medium-sized enterprises (SMEs) are the central innovators, because they are agile, embracing the change rather than resisting. They constitute an innovative ecosystem, in which innovation is encouraged at all levels, and all economic actors contribute to creating the best conditions to bring out new ideas. Finally, they usually adopt an anthropocentric approach to economic development, that is, to recognize the centrality of human capital for economic prosperity and to adopt policies that do not inhibit the potential of the human factor.

Therefore, the main objective of this article is to investigate how SMEs are innovators of sustainable and inclusive employment and to what extent SMEs contribute to changing value chains in current transformations of production systems and human resources management (HRM).

In order to achieve this objective, a case study of different trans-border enterprises is developed. It aims at discovering the peculiarities emerging from the trans-border economic environment between Canton Ticino (Switzerland) and the neighbouring Italian provinces. The information gathered will allow recognising how sustainable and inclusive employment has an impact on the routines and tasks performed by SMEs.

This result could subsequently become the basis for further academic research, analysing how they develop new forms of work. It could analyse, for example, the transformation of production systems induced by the digitalisation and robotisation after the lockdown imposed due to the COVID-19 outbreak.

The article is organised as follows: The next section describes some theoretical foundations of the subsequent case study. The third section focuses on the methodology used. In the fourth section, the information gathered is presented and described. In the last section, the main conclusions and implications are presented. Some limitations of the article and future lines of research are also defined.

Theoretical Framework

Enterprises, particularly SMEs, play a crucial role in creating sizeable jobs around the globe. According to the study "World Employment and Social Outlook 2017: Sustainable Enterprises and Jobs" (conducted between 2003 and 2016), "the number of full-time employees within SMEs nearly doubled, with the share of total employment attributable to SMEs rising from 31 per cent to 35 per cent" (ILO 2017: 17).

Innovation is an essential source of competitiveness and job creation for enterprises. "Innovative firms, overall, tend to be more productive, create more jobs, employ more educated workers and offer more training. They also hire more female workers" (ILO 2017: 120). Moreover, the report also finds that

> "[i]n some cases, however, innovation has led to more intensive use of temporary workers (particularly, in firms with product and process innovation) and a higher concentration of women in temporary employment. For example, firms implementing product and process innovation tend to employ more temporary workers than non-innovators by over 75 per cent" (ILO 2017: 134).

> "Providing formal training for permanent employees is associated with higher wages, higher productivity and lower unit labour costs, while increasing the use of temporary employment is associated with lower wages and lower productivity, without any implications for unit labour costs" (ILO 2017: 142).

> "Evidence indicates that, on average, enterprises that provide formal training to their full-time permanent employees pay 14 per cent higher wages, are 19.6 per cent more productive and have 5.3 per cent lower unit labour costs, compared with those that do not offer training. Alternatively, on average, having a higher share of temporary employment by ten

percentage point is associated with lower average wages by 2.6 per cent and lower productivity by 1.9 per cent, which, thus, does not give a competitive advantage in terms of their unit labour costs" (ILO 2017: 51).

Globalisation and competitiveness are critical issues when addressing HRM. Since many emerging markets are promoting their growth through young human resources (HR), often drawing on resources from other countries, SMEs must face up these threats to obtain and maintain a sustainable competitive advantage. As a consequence, sometimes, companies have difficulties finding and retaining the best human capital.

Generally, according to the literature, the most valuable HR are those who have computer skills and who demonstrate high flexibility (Deery and Jago 2015). Such characteristics are defined by changes in economic models, which in turn, however, must undergo social changes.

For many years, several HR experts have been worried about the approaching terms of the professional careers of the so-called "baby boomers", who have long formed a vast reservoir of labour and consumption (Pânzaru 2005). Furthermore, the so-called "millennials" currently make up the segment of HR, which is growing in most countries. Millennials sharply differ from previous generations: They must feel they are an active part of a structure or business, and in any case, they give more importance to the family than to work. Consequently, leisure time and the possibility of playing sports, improving one's training, or dedicating oneself to improving social well-being are important factors for them.

Finally, there is also a theme linked to the "attrition" of HR (Ployhart et al. 2006), which, subject to many stimuli or deadlines, can go into crisis. Therefore, it is also necessary to foresee rotation times or change of work times.

Methodology and Field of Research

The case study methodology (Yin 2013) has been used in this article in order to understand procedures applied in the professional world and to obtain some practical examples. Through this methodology, this article provides information about the trans-border economic environment between Canton Ticino (Switzerland) and the neighbouring Italian provinces. The study was carried out at some SMEs that operate in the area of interest, selected according to their dimension (micro, small and medium-sized enterprises) and their economic branche (secondary and tertiary economic sector).

Semi-structured interviews were initially planned to be conducted with HR managers (or equivalent) during the spring of 2020, but because of the lockdown imposed due to the COVID-19 pandemic, it was decided to send and collect questions and answers by email. Replies were collected from three respondents.

First was the CEO of a newly established company promoting carpooling (according to the EU, it is a micro-enterprise, employing less than ten employees; European Commission: 2012). The founders of this start-up identified an "untouched" market. They started from a concept of "attackable market", given that throughout the world, "carpooling" and "shared mobility" was very fashionable in all its forms, including apps like BlablaCar and Uber, at the time. However, there was still a "virgin market", namely, that of those who go back and forth to work every day by their car - a driver and four empty seats - and nothing had yet been done to optimise this type of movement. They consequently proposed a solution including a "click on a smartphone", an applied technology in step with the times, and a focus on "sharing". The company was founded in 2015.

The second interviewee was the HR manager of the Swiss branch of a pharmaceutical industry network (according to the EU definition, it is a medium-sized enterprise, employing less than 250 employees). The enterprise was founded in Ticino in the first half of the 1960s. The first production centre, located near Lugano, was sized in considering an activity limited to Switzerland. Still, within a few years, its pharmaceutical specialities aroused a lot of interest and gained the trust of Swiss doctors, which contributed to extending the activities to other European countries. The Swiss enterprise holds a significant strategic as well as commercial and scientific-clinical role within the company group: It acts as the centre for the production of the main specialities intended for the group's operating companies as well as for third-party customers in Europe, the USA, and Asia; exports make up 90 per cent of the total production.

Last was an HR consultant of a company that conducts research, selection, and evaluation of commercial, administrative, accounting, technical, middle, and top management profiles (according to the EU definition, it is a small-sized enterprise, employing less than 50 employees). The company also performs ad hoc training courses, structured on specific company needs, and professional and individual coaching courses. It also implements services for companies aimed at increasing their business through business development strategies.

The diversity in the economic sector of the companies and in the roles of those who answered (both in terms of position in the organisational structure and the formal one) led to different pieces of evidence, characterised by different looks and different sensitivities.

The questions submitted to respondents came from previous research and from the European Network on Labour Market Monitoring (EN RLMM)[118] and have been analysed together with the informants in the case studies:

- To what extent does your SME contribute to changing value chains in current transformations of productive systems and workforce management?
- To what extent are SMEs (or start-ups) involved in the spread of new employment and new forms of work linked, for example, to the transformation of production systems induced by the digitalisation and robotisation (such as smart working and teleworking among others) as well as by regional, national, and global competition? Will these processes create better jobs in SMEs or create disparities?
- How are SMEs embedded within local actors' networks in order to proceed with training and labour market supply policies?
- What type of innovative HR practices and work organisations, if any, do SME develop when they participate in sustainable development strategies?

Case Studies Findings

The objective of this paper is to investigate how SMEs are innovators of sustainable, inclusive employment and to what extent SMEs contribute to changing value chains in current transformations of productive systems and HRM. Information obtained by the respondents, often summarized, are described below:

The Contribution of SMEs to Changing Value Chains

Continuous modernisation is one of the most valuable aspects for the innovation in SMEs and therefore, research and development is one of the central issues

---

[118] http://regionallabourmarketmonitoring.net.

signalled by companies. This can consist of applying new solutions to well-know problems (for example, traffic jams) or to invest in human capital training in order to maintain a creative environment in the firm (as done in the pharmaceutical sector). This can help workers to respond to challenges of the greater flexibility that the market imposes.

The carpooling enterprise CEO described the central idea of its firm as follows:

> "We studied the 'carpooling' phenomenon, and we came to hypothesise an additional incentive for commuters, which was economical for them, but also useful for the environment and society: by sharing the car, traffic is reduced, as well as accidents and pollution. Instead of having four cars for four people, you have one car for four people. We then went to find a method that constituted a flywheel. We developed a specific solution for commuters that would guarantee them not only the saving of fuel by sharing - in Switzerland, on average, employees who do this practice, per person, save from 1,200 to the 2,000 Swiss francs a year - but also an additional profit, which was an incentive" (Interview A, 11 March 2020: 1).

> "The incentives we imagined and implemented are connected to the two types of customers that we have identified: companies with particular sensitivity and more attentive to corporate social responsibility (CSR), who, in turn, can incentivise employees who, sharing the car through company welfare, implicitly help the environment; and the Municipalities, which can incentivise citizens who perform good practices in other ways. Therefore, we have developed a solution aimed at these two types of customers" (Interview A, 11 March 2020: 1).

> "The innovative current platform which, with a proprietary algorithm, manages the matching between supply and demand of commuter transport with completely cashless payment systems, will soon be integrated with new features that will emphasize driving style and active and passive safety of the vehicle used" (Interview A, 11 March 2020: 1).

The Pharmaceutical HR manager highlighted the pursuit of continuous innovation:

> "As a pharmaceutical company, we are constantly looking for innovative and technological solutions to automate our processes, freeing up resources for the execution of increasingly specialised and highly qualitative tasks. Our driver is the pursuit of continuous improvement and, in this regard, in project management, we use design techniques to share the skills and knowledge of all of us. From an human resources point of view, we play a business partner role to the extent that we encourage the training and development of human capital present in the company to be able to respond to the challenges of the greater flexibility that the market imposes" (Interview B , 1 April 2020: 1).

Finally, the HR consultant of the recruitment company highlighted the importance of flexibility in terms of tasks:

"Our company operates supporting companies that come from different sectors in many ways, providing support not only in terms of recruitment and training but also by advising and helping companies to reorient themselves on the market. Nowadays, who advises and recruits manpower gives an important contribution to the world of work, to help companies identify their needs and provide non-standardised answers" (Interview C, 6 April 2020: 1).

All three respondents highlighted the importance of continuous innovation; those from smaller firms put more emphasis on process innovation, while the HR manager highlighted the importance of the links between business partners.

The Spread of New Employment and New Forms of Work

Internships, mainly devoted to students of the local university, are strong incentives for innovation and human capital empowering. Regarding this topic, the carpooling enterprise CEO argued:

"Over the years, my firm has activated internships with students enrolled at the University of Lugano in Switzerland, focusing on highly qualified profiles, and who have carried out an internship related to their study programme. In particular:

a) Internship A1, a student enrolled at the Faculty of Economic Sciences, collaborates in taking care of relationships with local partners in the Canton of Ticino (Municipalities, Companies), prepares project reports, collaborates with the firm to achieve the shared objectives, collaborates in the management of information stands, collaborates in customer support, collaborates in the creation of information material, performs administrative tasks;

b) Stage A2, a student enrolled at the Faculty of Economic Sciences, collaborates in taking care of relations with local partners in the Canton of Ticino (Municipalities, Companies), prepares project reports, collaborates with the company in the realisation of shared objectives, collaborates in the management of information stands, collaborates in customer support, collaborates in the creation of information material, performs administrative tasks;

c) Stage B, a student enrolled at the Faculty of Informatics, designs solar power systems for displays and e-paper for electric poles for parking reservation with plate, deals with making small hardware changes to the devices, small administrative functions (relations with the hardware and software vendors) and customer support." (Interview A, 11 March 2020: 2).

"My firm also took advantage of the personal research service of the Unemployment Service (reporting of a vacancy to the IT system - COLSTA data bank -), and hired a collaborator who took care of managing relationships with local partners in the Canton of Ticino (the Municipalities, companies, event organisers), collaborating with the company to achieve shared objectives; collaborating in the acquisition and management of events in the Swiss and European Territory; collaborating in the management of information stands; managing contacts with the company partners and suppliers of internal and external services; actively managing the marketing and communication sector for the development of effective communication tools; managing social media; collaborating in customer support; collaborating in the creation of information material; performing administrative duties. The same was then called to be taken over by the public office of the city of Lugano" (Interview A, 11 March 2020: 2).

One of the most useful points for HR is talent preservation and smart working. However, few companies manage to offer these peculiarities. Nevertheless, during the COVID-19 crisis, the teleworking has been used spreadly. In this regard, the pharmaceutical HR manager explained:

"The Pharma Valley in which we operate becomes a starting point for solid synergies with companies related to us for an avant-garde Ticino and the sharing of good practices. As the HR Department, we work closely with line managers to ensure a selection process that allows us to select the best resource and the candidate to start his/her company experience in the best way" (Interview B, 1 April 2020: 1).

"The exceptional situation we are experiencing has naturally led our company to activate solutions for teleworking. Thanks to our IT Department, we were able to put people in a position to be able to work remotely" (Interview B, 1 April 2020: 1).

The HR consultant of the recruitment company emphasised the opportunity given by smart working:

"We are slightly involved in the processes of digitisation or reorientation of the workforce towards smart working concepts. However, we are adapting ourselves to this new system of work, also by taking advantage of an emergency period that will create many opportunities for companies that will be able to seize them. I believe that smart working can increase the productivity of employees and collaborators, thus increasing the productivity of the company" (Interview C, 6 April 2020: 1).

Respondents recognised internships as strong incentives for human capital empowering and they highlighted the capital importance of teleworking as an opportunity to tackle the difficulties due to the outbreak.

Training and Labour Market Supply Policies

Many companies are developing training modules to find employees, or to operate in support of other enterprises. On the one hand, this can allow the firm to gain visibility, and concurring in design labour supply policies can boost the general labour market on the other hand. Moreover, CSR pushes firms to search for talents in the local area.

In this respect, the carpooling enterprise CEO said:

"We provide local actors - companies and public bodies - with a tool to observe employees mobility needs, plan and monitor corporate carpooling incentive campaigns and evaluate their results. The service market strategy follows the B2B2C business model: My firm involves the company to launch carpooling among its commuting workers, who become users and travellers. In Italy, the mobility manager is a figure provided by law; each company of a certain size should have a person responsible for developing the company's mobility policies; the important thing is to provide it with the appropriate tools and training, and our mission is precisely this: to explain to mobility managers the tools they have available, some traditional, others more innovative. They range from encouraging season tickets to public transport, to activating company shuttles, or to carpooling as we see it" (Interview, 11 March 2020: 2).

"In Ticino, my firm has collaborated with SUPSI and USI on research projects, having been recognised as one of the most innovative companies in the sector; for example, it offered support to the European SocialCar project and the three experimentation phases foreseen by the project" (Interview, 11 March 2020: 2).

"The SocialCar project[119] financed under the Horizon 2020 framework programme of the European Community, had the ambition to demonstrate that there are concrete possibilities to exploit the synergies between private transport and the public one thanks to the carpooling systems. To this end, SocialCar has developed an app for smartphones and has tested its effectiveness through a three-phase trial, carried out in parallel in twelve European countries" (Interview, 11 March 2020: 2).

"My firm also wants to give priority to young people who have studied here, and the precondition is the growth of society, so the company asks for collaboration from institutions and society" (Interview, 11 March 2020: 2).

Regarding the importance of attracting talent, the pharmaceutical HR manager said:

"In our case, the partnerships with the trade associations that are promoters for us and the related companies of our instances are solid. At the same time, with a view to our Corporate Social Responsibility policy, we return to the territory as much we can by training a nursery of young professionals, working closely with the professional training division and the other actors connected to it. As for the supply of labour, we are working on the digitalisation of our processes, maybe we will soon be able to benefit more and more even in this phase of artificial intelligence and algorithms to make everything as scientific as possible" (Interview B, 1 April 2020:1).

The HR consultant of the recruitment company highlighted the importance of links between firms:

---

[119] http://www.socialcar-project.eu.

"We are a young reality, but already well integrated. The link with our partners helps us to generate a growing number of relationships; we support staff recruitment and training, but, as I said before, with excellent advice and not only as executors, as well as giving real added value" (Interview C, 6 April 2020: 1).

All in all, access to public funds and a broad network between different firms were recognised as crucial factors.

Innovative HR Practices and Work Organisations

Innovative HR practices can affect the development of the business and let a firm become more and more valuable in the local and global environment. However, it is not easy to develop these competences. Regarding these options, the car-pooling enterprise CEO stated:

"My company is still a small Startup that has not fully become a mature company, and we have not yet adopted innovative HR practices. We learn a lot from the continuous relationship with those who are our corporate customers" (Interview A, 11 March 2020: 3).

Also, the consultant of the recruitment company stated that they are not actors in this type of business choice (Interview C, 6 April 2020: 1). On the contrary, the pharmaceutical HR manager stated:

"Our company has a solid propensity for the sustainability of corporate processes and policies. As an HR function, we reiterate the centrality of the person, be it a collaborator or a patient; in fact, we believe that people make a difference in a company. We take care to make the life of our collaborators and end consumers better; in this regard, we have conceived a series of specific products and services" (Interview B, 1 April 2020: 1).

From this, it can be concluded that only medium-sized enterprises are currently developing innovative HR practices.

Discussion and Conclusions

Uncertainties on a political level or a crisis such as the COVID-19 pandemic are critical issues that can affect the economic environment. Moreover, social changes such as the ageing of the population or the change in general tastes can also affect the social environment.

SMEs are the central innovators in this environment because they are agile and they constitute an innovative ecosystem in which innovation is encouraged at all levels; also, they usually adopt an anthropocentric approach to economic development.

The main objective of this article was to investigate how SMEs are innovators of sustainable and inclusive employment and to what extent SMEs contribute to changing value chains in current transformations of productive systems and HRM. Hence, the research aims to understand to what extent SMEs are involved in the spread of new employment and new forms of work linked, for example, to the transformation of production systems induced by the digitalisation and robotisation. Two objectives have been accomplished, aiming at responding to the research question. Firstly, we analysed some SMEs in the area of research as case studies. Secondly, we described what type of innovative HR practices and work organisations SMEs develop when they participate in sustainable development strategies.

- From this work, the following general conclusions can be derived:
- Continuous modernisation is one of the most valuable aspects for innovation of SMEs and therefore, research and development is one of the central issues signalled by companies. This can help workers to respond to the challenges of the greater flexibility that the market imposes.
- Internships, mainly devoted to students of the local university, are strong incentives for innovation and human capital empowering.
- Many companies are developing training modules to find employees or to operate in support of other enterprises. CSR pushes firms to search for talents in the local area and is a growing trend in the area.
- Finally, innovative HR practices can affect the developing of the business and let a firm become more and more effective in the local and global environment.

A further prosecution of this research considering different external factors such as region, country, or industrial sector as well as different internal factors such as organisational composition, culture, or leadership style, seems promising. It could shed light on how these factors influence the innovation of SMEs and their thrust to sustainable employment.

References

Deery, Margareth/Jago, Leo (2015): Revisiting Talent Management, Work-Life Balance and Retention Strategies. In: Int. J. Contemp. Hosp. Manag. 2015 27, 453–472.

European Commission (2012): What is an SME? URL: https://ec.europa.eu/growth/smes/business-friendly-environment/sme-definition [09 July 2020].

International Labour Office (ILO) (2017): World Employment and Social Outlook 2017: Sustainable Enterprises and Jobs: Formal Enterprises and Decent Work. Geneva: ILO.

Larsen, Christa/Rand, Sigrid/Schmid, Alfons/Holopainen, Päivi/Jokikaarre, Pirita/Kuusela, Katri/Alapuranen, Niina (Eds.) (2016): Digital (R)evolution and Its Effects on Labour: Opportunities and Challenges for Regional and Local Labour Market Monitoring. München, Mering.

Pânzaru, Ciprian (2005): Some Considerations of Population Dynamics and the Sustainability of Social Security System. In: Procedia - Social and Behavioral Sciences 2015 183, pp.68-76.

Ployhart, Robert E./Weekley, Jeff. A./Baughman, Kathryn (2006): The Structure and Function of Human Capital Emergence: A Multilevel Examination of the Attraction-Selection-Attrition Model. In: Academy of Management Journal 49 (4).

Rodríguez-Sánchez, Josè-Luis/González-Torres, Tais/Montero-Navarro, Antonio/Gallego-Losada, Rocio (2020): Investing Time and Resources for Work-Life Balance: The Effect on Talent Retention. In: Int. J. Environ. Res. Public Health 2020 17.

World Economic Forum (WEF) (2018): Global Competitiveness Report 2018. Cologny/Geneva: WEF.

Yin, Robert K. (2013): Case Study Research: Design and Methods (5th ed.). Thousand Oaks, CA: SAGE Publications.

Websites

European Network on Labour Market Monitoring (EN RLMM): http://regionallabourmarketmonitoring.net

SocialCar project: http://www.socialcar-project.eu

Recruiting and Retention in SMEs in Hesse – Qualitative Insights

Jenny Kipper

Introduction and Theoretical Framework

Small and medium-sized enterprises (SMEs) are important factors for growth and stability of the German economy and, furthermore, they are quite often incubators to generate innovative ways of employment strategies, new ways of human resource management, and sustainable inclusive employment. Therefore, it is important to monitor this type of organisations[120] not only from an economic point of view but also from a pedagogical perspective.

As specified by the European Commisssion the most common definition for SMEs also in Germany is along their number of employees and turnover or their total balance sheet:

Table 1: Definition of SMEs

Company category	Staff headcount	Turnover	or	Balance sheet total
Medium-sized	< 250	≤ € 50 m		≤ € 43 m
Small	< 50	≤ € 10 m		≤ € 10 m
Micro	< 10	≤ € 2 m		≤ € 2 m

Source: European Commission (2012).

Over 99 per cent of companies in Hesse are SMEs.[121] They play a key role for the regional and local labour markets and economic structures. At the same time, they seem to suffer a lot in crises such as the current COVID-19 pandemic since

---

[120] The terms "company", "enterprise", and "organisation" will be used as synonyms.

[121] cf. https://wirtschaft.hessen.de/wirtschaft/das-rueckgrat-der-wirtschaft.

they need to be very flexible concerning employee handling and products/services. They are often depending on one person (the owner) and their limited financial resources. Therefore, SMEs are only as flexible as their managers are and as their budget allow.

The monitoring of the Hessian SMEs seems to be typical for the monitoring structure on SMEs throughout Europe: there exists only basic data that is not systematically analysed, collected at one place, or completed with additional data for a accurately fitting analysis and thereof developed measures (cf. HMWEVW 2018: 5). The Hessian Ministry of Economics, Energy, Transport and Housing tries to bundle the relevant data every two years and provide a first insight into the SME situation in Hesse.[122] As mentioned above, over 99 per cent of the companies in Hesse are SMEs. In 2018, over 64 per cent of the employees in Hesse are engaged with SMEs and most of them are not located in urban areas. 81,7 per cent of the apprentices in SMEs are acquiring knowledge and competences they need for their future jobs.[123] In 2015, 90,1 per cent of the SMEs have been micro enterprises (with one to nine employees).

Not only the German and Hessian figures are impressive. The SMEs are playing worldwide a key role when looking at employment structures. The International Labour Organization (ILO) stated in 2017 that in the 13 years before the number of people employed by SMEs has increased significantly and is now nearly twice as much as in 2003 (cf. ILO 2017: 11ff.).

These few figures above demonstrate that many employees and the economy are depending on the economic stability of SMEs and, therefore, it is quite relevant to gain more insights into these enterprises to understand their uniqueness, their organisational structure, how they manage employment, secure innovative ways of employment as sustainable inclusive employment, find forms for retention management, and in how far they are supported by regional and local structures, especially in times of crises. Also, the analysis of the entrepreneur itself is very interesting in this context.

Therefore, a qualitative perspective on SMEs could complement the quantitative statistics to show details for a deeper understanding of the ways SMEs act, the

---

[122] cf. https://wirtschaft.hessen.de/wirtschaft/das-rueckgrat-der-wirtschaft.

[123] cf. https://www.ifm-bonn.org/statistiken/mittelstand-im-ueberblick/#accordion=0&tab=0.

situations they are confronted with, and the solutions they generate for most of their challenges as these seem to differ from big enterprises they compete with in the war for talent concerning recruiting and retention (cf. Ernst & Young 2011). Thus, this is the main objective of this paper. As Sames/Schäfer show in their analysis, there are different types of characteristics of SMEs depending on the focus of the research. They developed a typology to explain how the organisations are dealing with industry 4.0 and show, that not every organisation is quickly adapting to new situations (cf. Sames and Schäfer 2017) even if exactly this seems to be the reputation of SMEs. This, again, refers to the fact, that we need to gain more insights into the individual culture, their structures, and hierarchies.

To answer the questions above the article applies the results of six interviews in urban and rural areas in the state of Hesse. In combination with the quantitative data mentioned above this could serve as a starting point for further academic discussion, related research, and to develop factors for a systemic approach to monitor the landscape of Hessian SMEs. The paper is structured simply into four main chapters. The following one describes the research process. The third chapter presents and illustrates insights and results in relation to the areas of interest described hereinafter. The last section closes this analysis with a conclusion and some implications for further monitoring and research on SMEs also from a pedagogical point of view[124].

Research Process

The predominant data and research on SMEs are based on quantitative data. This type of data is not suitable to gain insights into the behaviour of the SMEs as a specific type of organisations. Therefore, a qualitative approach has been chosen.

For the field of research, SMEs as organisations in urban and rural areas are focused to evaluate differences in:
- employment strategy and practise,
- support structure, local/regional cooperations/networks, and

---

[124] This means focusing on learning processes in personal but also in organisational development, in this case especially related to the biography of the entrepreneurs.

- forms of employment in times of crises as for example the current COVID-19 pandemic.

Five interviews with owners of SMEs and one interview with a Human Ressource Manager of an SME have been planned and executed. The following branches have been chosen:

- IT and services/consulting[125] – a branch which profits from the pandemic,
- Leisure and tourism – a branch that is strongly affected by the pandemic, and
- Retail – a branch that is partially affected.

The data gathering has been executed with semi-structured interviews (cf. Meuser and Nagel 1994)[126]. The field of research have been six organisations[127] that are presented in the table below to give a first impression on the field of research and to make the following analysis more comprehensible.

All six interviews have been transcribed[128] and anonymised for the analysis as far as necessary and so that data examples could be used to explain and complete the description of the results[129].

---

[125] In this case it is consulting on data security. It is known that not all consulting companies profit from the current crisis.

[126] All interview partners have been contacted directly through a written approach and to ensure a most differentiated perspective on the organisations there has only been management asked for an interview. The topic of the interview needed to be explained in a few sentences upfront to the interview to gain the acceptance for the interview process. The questions of the interview have not been shared beforehand to ensure that there are still answers spontaneously. The semi-structured interviews allow to reconstruct knowledge, experiences, and action strategies of the organisations leaders and in the meantime give insights into the daily business with examples for the topics mentioned above. The interview guide has been used as a flexible thematic guide through the interview topics. Most important was, that the narration part of the interview partners was as high as possible. The following topics have been covered: characteristics of the human resource work (recruiting, retention management, qualification, role-models, and innovation), inclusive employment of relevant target groups, regional and local support, networks and cooperations, and challenges of the situation during the COVID-19 pandemic.

[127] The definition of SME is based on the EU Classification (European Commission 2012).

[128] A simple way of transcription has been chosen to guarantee a good reading experience. All interviews have been done in German and have been translated into English afterwards. The transcription has been done according to Kuckartz and Rädiker (2019).

[129] Due to reasons of data security and anonymisation, all information that could lead to the organisations or interviewed persons are deleted or anonymised.

The analysis of the interviews has been done on the basis of the qualitative content analysis (cf. Mayring 2004) to focus on the above-mentioned topics.

Table 1: Overview on analysed organisations

Organisation A	Organisation D
Number of employees[130]: 35 Interviewpartner: Human Resource Manager, male Branch: IT/software industry Region: rural area Duration of interview: 46.24 minutes Interview technology: phone interview Comment: interview time was late in the evening beyond regular working hours during the lockdown.	Number of employees: 5 Interviewpartner: company owner, male Branch: tourism/leisure industry (campsite) Region: rural area Duration of interview: 54 minutes Interview technology: personal interview Comment: interview took place in the evening; place of the interview was the garden of the company owner a few weeks after lockdown
Organisation B	**Organisation E**
Number of employees: 19 Interviewpartner: company owner, male Branch: leisure industry (dance company) Region: urban area Duration of interview: 31.30 minutes Interview technology: personal interview Comment: interview took place in the organisation during lockdown; conversation after the official interview went on for another 30 minutes.	Number of employees: 18 Interviewpartner: company owner, male Branch: services/consulting industry (consulting on data-security) Region: urban area Duration of interview: 54.55 minutes Interview technology: personal interview Comment: interview took place in the office rooms of the organisation during late lockdown time.
Organisation C	**Organisation F**
Number of employees: 5 Interviewpartner: company owner, female Branch: retail industry (small retail shop and café in a village) Region: rural area Duration of interview: 23.12 minutes Interview technology: personal interview Comment: interview took place around lunchtime, when the organisation was closed; place of the interview was the living room of the company owner; interview was a few weeks after lockdown.	Number of employees: 79 Interviewpartner: company owner, male Branch: tourism industry (hotel and restaurant business) Region: urban area Duration of interview: 33.57 minutes Interview technology: personal interview Comment: interview took place in the rooms of the organisation after reopening during late lockdown time.

Source: the author.

---

[130] Number of employees, not full-time equivalent (FTE).

Qualitative Insights and Results

The following chapter provides insights into the six interviews. The results are structured along the main categories and are shown in a descriptive way. This allows to gain a picture inside the organisations.

Characteristics of Employment Strategy and Practise

Most common for all six companies is the fact, that the human resource management is not at all standardised. It is always oriented towards the specific employees and the business needs, no matter how big the SME is. The managing director of the organisation F gets to the point in just a few words: "It is enormously extensive what we do there for the people [...] it is individual every time." (Interview F, minute 00:16:17ff.). This is one of the main differences compared to big enterprises. Even when these organisations have a human resource manager to serve the relations between employees and the management of the company, it is not said, that this brings in more standardisation, for example in the way of recruiting as the following chapters show.

Recruiting

When looking at differences concerning SMEs and big enterprises, it is obvious, that SMEs are less attractive to employees. Therefore, the SMEs need to use very flexible and different ways to fill vacancies and be competitive in the war for talent (cf. Peters, Goesmann and Hellert 2013, Ernst & Young 2011, Jasper and Horn 2009).

In most ways, recruiting is a task of the managing director and all six interviewed persons had their own ways to fill vacancies. The most common approach to find new employees is, to use the own network. The following examples have been highlighted in the interviews and show the variety of recruitment activities:

- "post and pray", as recruiters would say[131] (what normally does not work but is still tried in a first step),
- cooperations with universities,
- offer an intern, change it into a trainee and then finally into a fulltime position,
- instruct a recruitment agency in a foreign country,

---

[131] That means to post a job advertisement, for example, on a carreer platform.

- ask the own network if they know a fitting person or somebody who is looking for a job, or even
- recruit a known person from a client company that is looking for new challenges.

Employees, who are most looked for, are heterogeneous. There are two major groups coming from Germany or foreign countries that have been mentioned in the interviews: young professionals, just graduated, and/or dropouts from universities.[132]

All respondents stated, that recruiting the right employees is challenging and time consuming. To make their companies more interesting and the people willing to sign a contract, they offer a lot of support for example for a relocation (Interview B) or the manager from the company F, who offers own apartments, so that the candidates do not have to search on their own in urban areas, even if it is not easy for himself:

> "So we take care of everything, beginning by the apartment, that we, yes, we do just use our contracts, let me put it that way, because the housing market ist just not the easiest especially to get it affordable, and now real estate scout, you can forget that. This is only possible through connections. So, we use this here in our costumers, it goes into the newsletter and so on and so forth. We'll tell you where to apply for a bit of support and so on." (Interview B, minute 00:28:08)

They also spoke about examples, where they had been searching for a job for the partners, if the candidate was not willing to relocate alone or was not able to commute between home and work.

Finally, it could be summarised that the whole recruitment process is challenging and time consuming for the entrepreneurs as they are searching in a wider field, they are looking for less attractive target groups and need to spend more time and effort to find the right candidates. They need not only to offer a job, but additionally other incentives to gain attractivity.

Role Models for Human Resource Management

As the before mentioned procedures show, the entrepreneurs need inspiration and creativity in order to come up with measures. It is very surprising, that nearly

---

[132] It must be stated, that the sample had just six interviews and in these special cases no one mentioned other potential candidates such as employed people with vocational training or just finished trainees.

all of the interviewed persons said, that they have no role model or an organisation that is inspiring them, as the managing director from company E said:

> "It may sound a bit extremely arrogant, it is not meant to be, but to be honest, I don't look at others. I actually do my thing very, very mindlessly." (Interview E, minute 00:50:06ff.)

The other interviews show the same phenomenon related to the action strategy. The entrepreneurs focus on their business idea, observe the market, and try to look at the situation from a holistic perespective to secure the economic survival of their company. Therefore, they need no role model. Just one of the interviewed persons remembered that he gets his ideas still out of his past time at university and the companies he served in the past. This is even more worth mentioning when it comes to the point of employee retention.

Retention Management

Retention management is one of the key points in SMEs. Their efforts to find the right person is much higher than in big enterprises, related to wages and organisational structures or even the branding, so that they need to compensate this with a longterm relationship between employee and company. Furthermore, the fact that the single employee counts more regarding to organisational knowledge and client relationship, forces the company managers to find creative ways of supporting their employees in all relevant issues as the manager of company F stated:

> "And then you just have to show continued creativity to realise that it's not about walking around the area, saying I finance the driver's license for the people or walking around, saying I get apartments for all the people. This is the wrong way, but you have to listen to the person and you have to understand what the person, where the shoe pinches for the person." (Interview F, minute 00:23:50ff.)

This leads to several ideas that could be found in all interviews, such as:

- culture-related ideas
    - create and live a family culture,
    - create a culture of courage and appreciation
    - trusting new employees with full responsibility from their first day onwards at the company
- structure-related ideas
    - flexible work (concerning time, processes and content) oriented on the needs of the employee,

- short ways concerning decision-making (not persisting on hierarchies),
- employee-related ideas
    - take care of every employee as a single person,
    - taking over the financial part of special further training (language, driver license),
    - giving everybody a chance, space, and enough time for the own personal (individualised) development,
    - support with public authorities related topics,
    - taking over mediation and conflict management for private topics,
    - car pool, company car, or
    - giving and searching jobs also for the partners of the employees

These examples show the variations the company owners can choose to support their employees. It could be seen, that retention management is proceeded along two big categories: culture, organisational structure, and offering incentives, such as further education, social support, and benefits.

One part mentioned above is also to further training and education. That will be described separately below as it seems an existential point for SMEs.

Further Training and Education

An employee, that can do his/her job, is a match-winning point for SMEs that compete, in most areas, with big enterprises or many other SMES. None of the interviewed managers would tolerate an employee, that cannot handle his/her job due to missing competences.

The statements concerning this topic have been very different but mostly the same in one point: they are doing the training of their employees in informal ways. The company manager of the organisation E explains, why it is not an option for him to send his employees to an external provider:

"[Since] the X[133] training as a data protection officer has a different weighting, as I want to put it like that carefully. You get a certain material communicated, you become very afraid of liability, the speakers there are all highly respected experts in their field. No question about it, but in that case it was like that, the employee is now no longer with us, he came back and was suddenly afraid to send any comments to the clients. Yes, because now he has heard from X[134] how problematic everything is. And we have an approach here: nothing

---

[133] Anonymised provider.

[134] Anonymised provider.

is problematic at first, but rather there is a problem and we will solve it." (Interview E, minute 00:20:10)

The managing director of the organisation C has the same opinion:

"So, how I deal with a customer, for example, yes, or how I, how I conduct a critical discussion then. So a customer is dissatisfied with the performance, yes, then I do a short soft skills training, so to speak, because I am also very well trained there, luckily, in this area as a trainer, moderator, and consultant, yes, that does belong to my work, and it may be that I just do a soft skills training then. But this very strongly on the job, so it is not off the job, that we somehow crouch together somehow and or that we get someone externally, but this is then directly on the job." (Interview C, minute 00:42:47)

That is what they call „hand raising" (Interview E, minute 00:18:54f.). But they are doing this just for one purpose: the quality of their services. And, therefore, the employee must bring passion and the initiative to learn new things:

"They must keep up, quite simple. If I don't know how a crème brûlée is made, [...] then I have to let it be shown to me, and if I can't do it myself the next time, then you are of no use, then you won't have any fun either. So, either you are really willing to learn and then you have to accept it. And a spark is always a part of it [...]. It's not about doing it just somehow, but to do it well. You can clean up a seminar room or you can clean up a seminar room." (Interview F, minute 00:31:50ff.)

The manager of the organisation A quotes that it takes an employee around one year to be able to perform in his organisation the way they they should as it needs so many times to understand the services, the products, and the structures also when they are an SME. But he is also one of the two, that mandates an external provider. The managing director from organisation B also takes the option to send his employees to external courses, when he cannot offer the content by himself, especially the soft skill topics.

The four other interviewed persons are doing all qualifications by themselves or do not need them as their hired candidates are qualified enough. They also expect their employees to bring in self-initiative and dedication to learn by themselves.

What could be stated for further education and training is, that the manager offers several ways for the development of their employees, most of them inhouse but always oriented on the specific needs and situation and only if the employee shows intrinsic motivation.

Inclusive Employment

„How can you be so stupid to hire a woman?" (Interview E, minute 00:34:19ff.) This question has been asked to one of the interview partners and it shows, that also in SMEs it is not self-evident to hire and support special target groups such as for example women or international employees.

Therefore, it is much more remarkable that in all six organisations it has not been stated that these candidates are often the better ones as the following example shows:

> "A [female] friend of the driver, she was riding along, they are from East Romania, and he said, well, can't the girl work anything for you? Then I hired her for the scullery. And she couldn't speak the least bit German but worked her way up to the cold dishes' manager. It's enormous what she manages in the kitchen, without any training and all. She speaks German impeccably. And at some point, she came from the scullery, it was tight that afternoon, and ice-cream cups had to be rolled and that was indeed a funny task. Anyone, who has ever been to a sundae post in any shop knows that it will be a lot of gossiping and handling, and this is the fastest sundae maker I have ever seen. And then she worked her way into the kitchen and is now basically the core competence of the cold dishes." (Interview F, minute 00:17:09ff.)

The company owner explains that he has supported an employee, he has not even searched for, and she took the chance for her personal development and is now a solid part of the team and furthermore in a key position for the kitchen services.

What becomes visible in all interviews is, that the entrepreneurs are searching for good employees, no matter from which country, which gender, what age, or for example physical constitution. The owner of organisation D even works with only elder persons.

Flexible Ways of Working

To ensure also sustainable and inclusive employment they need to offer flexible ways of working such as working more in high season and reducing work in the rest of the year, working from everywhere and whenever its guaranteed that the job is done in time, changing shifts regularly and also at short notice. If they did not agree on the above-mentioned options, it would be impossible for them to retain their employees for a longer time.

Support Structure, Local/Regional Cooperations/Networks

Even if there is a lot of discussions about policy frameworks to support SMEs, none of the interviewed persons described the use of local or regional support or cooperation.

Some of the companies are important for the regional economy but do not get any support from the region as the person from organisation B explains:

> "I have not received any political support, although I have tried to use networks. That was really difficult, even if the city's economic promoter always says, talk to us, but then nothing happens." (Interview B, minute 00:30:41ff.)

One from organisation E elaborates:

> "It's more the private networks. Sure, if now, let's say, you have a difficult personnel situation, you would have to find someone quickly, the agency for employment also has a website, I can place ads anywhere, but this is also a service, it's not a structure, which I, that is there, yes, but it many cases it does not help me." (Interview E, minute 00:39:06ff.)

That is what all company owners said. They need private networks to secure hiring and retention, but they are not integrated in regional or local structures that help facing challenging situations on a long and short-term basis. Some of them have tried to establish a relationship within local policy support structures and relevant persons as the managing director of company B explained. However, this way has not been successful for them concerning daily challenges as recruiting, retention management, or support in times of crises.

Knowing this, the fact, that in times of crises networks and supporting structures are essential, it is quite interesting to look at the next category.

Employment in Times of the COVID-19 Pandemic

It could not be said for all analysed SMEs, that they really do have a challenging time due to the COVID-19 pandemic. There can be found different ways of handling the challenge and it is important, what the owner of company B says: "It all depends on me somehow, it depends on how my mood is." (Interview B, minute 00:29:09ff.).

The results are not surprising. There can be found companies such as organisation A that has to go into short-time work even though they are in the IT-sector and were ready to make their work processes more flexible. And there can also be found companies such as organisation F, that had to shut down completely due to the pandemic. There has been no chance to flexibilize work although the employees wanted to work, as the owner describes:

> "I can't pay you, but you can take a box of water from the basement or whatever, then they said that the boss had already paid enough. In good times we stick together, in bad times, too." (Interview F, minute 00:27:05ff.)

This phenomenon could also be seen in organisation C, that also had to close completely for clients, but some work still must be done due to maintenance reasons. The employees had still been working and the management agreed to pay the gap between short-time allowance and the normal wage. There has only been the smallest organisation, that had to dismiss one employee due to the pandemic. The restrictions after could not been handled in another way and the company was to small to cover the financial losings.

What really seems interesting is, what could be seen in organisations E and F and it is the same as described in the beginning: it depends on the management and their mindset/attitude:

> "I went into a little bell of my own and looked, what is really going on? What is happening here right now? And I said, I'm not going to do anything at first, on the contrary indeed. I didn't say I just don't do anything at all, but I said, now I'm really getting weaving with the people we have." (Interview E, minute 00:44:58ff.)

The owner knows, that the employees need guidelines and a role model in such times. Therefore, they focus on company culture and spirit to support their employees. Both had the same mindset, even if one company has short-time work and all consequences of the complete lockdown and the other one had no changes or financial losses. This could be an interesting way to handle times of crises and needs to be in the focus of further research.

Conclusion and Implications

The insights above show, that there is still room for professionalisation, when we think of supporting the biggest group of companies in the Hessian labour market. Some of the branches, that the companies come from, are suffering greatly during the COVID-19 pandemic and did not find any support. Even before, they had no systematic support, while building up their company or running their business.

The results show in many cases that human resource management is highly individualised along the employees' needs and the business processes.

What has been surprising is, that there seems to be no relevant difference between rural and urban areas or a causality when talking about company size (in this group of micro and small enterprises) and industry, when we are focusing on the following points:

- employment strategy and practise,
- support structure, local/regional cooperations/networks, and
- ways of employment in times of crises.[135]

Retention management is a key topic in SMEs and the analysis before show, that the entrepreneurs are aware of competing with the big enterprises in the war for talent (cf. Broich 2015).

All the ways, the organisations find to handle the crisis, to deal with recruiting issues, to develop employment strategies, or to build up a relevant network, all depends on the company owner and/or manager. The way, that this personality influences the company culture, find ways of developing new ideas, and is role model for all employees, counts more than any structure, network, or recruiting plan.

The following points can be taken as a conclusion from the short analysis above.

From a pedagogical point of view, there need to be much more research that focuses on the biographical points of entrepreneurs (cf. Sievert 2016). To learn about their biographies enables to develop fitting support concepts, to understand which further education and/or training could support them during different development steps of their organisations, and to consult new entrepreneurs.

For a systematic monitoring it can be stated, that it is not enough to simply collect data on company size (employees and revenue) from different perspectives. To understand SMEs in a deeper way and to support them in times of a crisis, there should also, for example, factors be considered such as:

- high- or low season times,
- age of persons that can be recruited as potential candidates,
- origin of persons that can be recruited as potential candidates,

---

[135] As we know, that labour markets differ from urban to rural areas. There should follow further qualitative research.

- ways of recruiting,
- (personal) networks used on a regular basis,
- special target groups that can be included as employees,
- ways for retention management depending on company size, branch, and area,
- possible ways of flexibilisation in work structure and processes.

The developing of qualitative insights to complement the current quantitative monitoring would be helpful to understand and support SMEs and the entrepreneurs. As the analysis above can only give some small insights into "the live of SMEs" there is still – from both perspectives: monitoring and pedagogics – the need for further research to build up basic knowledge and a systematic monitoring approach. Also, the ideas for the monitoring of further factors, as suggested above as a first collection, should be discussed further.

At the end, I want to thank all persons who took time for an interview during the lockdown in spring 2020. It has been a hard time to reorganise their businesses during this crisis and therefore it is so much more worth mentioning, that above all they blocked their time to help with reporting about and explaining their experience and knowledge for supporting labour market research.

References

Broich, Dennis Julius (2015): Mitarbeiterbindung in KMU: Analyse von Instrumenten und Maßnahmen. Hamburg: Igel Verlag.

Bundesministerium für Wirtschaft und Energie (BMWi) (2018): Wirtschaftsmotor Mittelstand 2018: https://www.bmwi.de/Redaktion/DE/Publikationen/Mittelstand/wirtschaftsmotor-mittelstand-zahlen-und-fakten-zu-den-deutschen-kmu.pdf?__blob=publicationFile&v=36 [12 June 2020].

Ernst & Young (2011): Agenda Mittelstand: Talent Management im Mittelstand: Mit innovativen Strategien gegen den Fachkräftemangel. Ernst & Young.

European Commission (2012): What is an SME? URL: https://ec.europa.eu/growth/smes/business-friendly-environment/sme-definition [18 June 2020].

Hessisches Ministerium für Wirtschaft, Energie, Verkehr und Landesentwicklung (HMWEVW) (2018): Hessischer Mittelstandsbericht 2018. URL: https://wirtschaft.hessen.de/sites/default/files/media/hmwvl/hessischer_mittelstandsbericht_2018_hmwevl.pdf [12 June 2020].

Holz, Michael/Schlepphorst, Susanne/Schlömer-Laufen, Nadine: Unternehmertum im Fokus: Worauf der Erfolg der Hidden Champions baut. URL: https://www.ifm-bonn.org//uploads/tx_ifmstudies/policybrief_01_2020.pdf [12 June 2020].

International Labour Office (ILO) (2017): World Employment and Social Outlook 2017: Sustainable Enterprises and Jobs: Formal Enterprises and Decent Work. Geneva: ILO.

Jasper, Gerda/Horn, Judith (2009): Untersuchung zum Rekrutierungsverhalten von Unternehmen. In: Bundesministerium für Bildung und Forschung (2009): Reihe Berufsbildungsforschung 5.

Kuckartz, Udo/Rädiker, Stefan (2019): Datenaufbereitung und Datenbereinigung in der qualitativen Sozialforschung. In: Baur, Nina/Blasius, Jörg (Eds.): Handbuch Methoden der empirischen Sozialforschung. Wiesbaden: Springer Fachmedien, pp. 441-456.

Mayring, Philipp (2004): Qualitative Inhaltsanalyse. In: Flick, Uwe/von Kardorff, Ernst/Steinke, Ines (Eds.) (2004): Qualitative Sozialforschung: Ein Handbuch. Reinbek: Rowohlt Taschenbuch-Verlag, pp.468-475.

Meuser, Michael/Nagel, Ulrike (1994): Expertenwissen und Experteninterview. In: Hitzler, Ronald/Honer, Anne/Maeder, Christoph: Expertenwissen: Die institutionalisierte Kompetenz zur Konstruktion von Wirklichkeit. Opladen: Westdeutscher Verlag, pp. 180-192.

Peters, Ute/Goesmann, Christina/Hellert, Ulrike (2013): Rekrutierung in kleinen und mittelständischen Unternehmen: Eine Bestandsaufnahme. In: Institut für Arbeit und Personal (Iap) Schriftenreihe 4.

Sames, Gerrit/Schäfer, Maria (2017): Industrie 4.0: Typologie der Unternehmen im Mittelstand. URL: http://digdok.bib.thm.de/volltexte/2018/5206 [19 June 2020].

Sievert, Andrea (2016): Existenzgründung als biographische Chance: Berufliche Selbständigkeit im Kontext lebensgeschichtlichen Lernens. Wiesbaden: Springer Fachmedien.

Kranzusch, Peter/Icks, Annette/Levering, Britta (2019): Herausforderungen für den Mittelstand: Update der Unternehmersicht 2019. URL: https://www.ifm-bonn.org//uploads/tx_ifmstudies/IfM-Materialien-279_2019.pdf [12 June 2020].

Websites

Hessian Ministry of Economics, Energy, Transport and Housing (Hessisches Ministerium für Wirtschaft, Energie, Verkehr und Landesentwicklung/HMWEVW) – regular reports on the situation of SMEs in Hessen: https://wirtschaft.hessen.de/wirtschaft/das-rueckgrat-der-wirtschaft

Institut für Mittelstandsforschung (IfM) Bonn – data on the status-quo, development, and problems of SMEs: https://www.ifm-bonn.org/statistiken/mittelstand-im-ueberblick/#accordion=0&tab=0

4. OUTLOOK – SMES ACROSS EUROPE

SMEs – Labour and the Challenge of Competitive Sustainability

Marco Ricceri

Premise

The challenge of sustainable development in its many economic, environmental, and social aspects, which involves deeply the system of small and medium-sized enterprises (SMEs) cannot fail to take into account the radical change of scenario caused by the sudden and unexpected sanitary and economic crisis that has invested the world in the first months of 2020. As an introduction to the better understanding of this passage and to get an idea of the sudden and unexpected character with which this crisis occurred as well as of its profound implications, it is useful to recall, by way of example, some authoritative positions expressed in the period between the end of 2019 and the beginning of 2020.

COVID-19: A "Major Strategic Surprise" and Its Impact

At the end of 2019, precisely on 17 December 2019, the European Commission officially presented the document on the "Annual Sustainable Growth Strategy 2020" (COM 2019, 650 final), with these opening sentences:

> "The European economy is now in its seventh consecutive year of growth. The economy is expected to continue expanding in 2020 and 2021, even though growth prospects have weakened. Labour markets remain strong and unemployment continues to fall, though at a slower pace. Public finances continue to improve, our banking system is more robust and the foundations of our Economic and Monetary Union are stronger." (COM 2019, 650 final)

Just over a month later, on 29 January 2020, in the Commission's presentation of the "Commission Work Programme for 2020" (COM 2020, 37 final), no reference is made in this basic-document on the SARS-CoV-2, already widespread in Europe; the presentation confirms an optimistic vision of the future: "There is plenty of room for optimism and pride. After years of crisis management, Europe can now look forward again. This work programme frames the way ahead and allows us to find solutions to issues that have divided us in the past". These documents prove, in practise, the absence of any suspicion of the crisis that was exploding in Europe and the world just in the same period. The main concerns expressed for 2020 are, in fact, concentrated on the uncertainties caused by the geopolitical situation and by international trade tensions, due to their negative impact on investment decisions.

In the same month January 2020, the Economist Intelligence Unit (EIU), the Economist Group's research and analysis division, published a forecast report on the "Five Main Risks to the World Economy in 2020" (EIU 2020). The list of risks includes: the possible negative consequences of US-Iranian tensions on the world oil price, the effects of a possible breakdown in commercial relations between the United States (US) and the European Union (EU), the possibility of recession in emerging markets due to the burdens of accumulated debts, and the abandonment of Asia by major financial bodies due to protracted popular protests in Hong Kong. But among the main risks, the EIU also includes the emergence of the coronavirus epidemic and its "lasting impact on the global economy", with a 20 per cent probability (EIU 2020)."The global economic impact of the coronavirus outbreak - this is the EIU forecast- is set to be more profound than that of severe acute respiratory syndrome (SARS), a similar virus that spread from China in 2003, owing to the much larger role that China plays in the global economy today" (EIU 2020: 5).

However, much depends on the length of the period in which China, like the rest of the world, will know how to stop the spread of the virus and normalise economic activities. In any case, in the course of 2020, numerous international exporters are destined to experience significant financial difficulties, due to the negative repercussions of this situation on trade flows and economic systems destined to record a heavy drop in gross domestic product (GDP) growth rates.

On 1 May 2020, the United Nations Department of Economic and Social Affairs (UNDESA) published the Monthly Briefing on the World Economic Situation an Prospetcs, entitled "Severe Downturns in Labour-Intensive Sectors Spell Trouble for Global Inequality" (UNDESA 2020), in which a clear assessment of the new situation is presented: "The global economic downturn caused by the COVID-19 pandemic - the UN document states - is shaping up to be the worst since the tragically consequential Great Depression". To this historical appeal, the UN adds a comparison with the financial and economic crisis of 2008 and highlights the following element: "Although similar in terms of their impact, especially on employment and income, key differences make the current crisis particularly dangerous" (UNDESA News 4 May 2020). In fact, in 2008 the crisis was primarily financial and banking, with the fall of the stock markets and the freezing of credit, which led to heavy negative consequences for the real economy and employment levels. Instead, the United Nations (UN) report explains,

> "[...] this time, soaring unemployment came first as many businesses were forced to shutter because of nationwide lockdowns in most developed economies. Rising unemployment and shrinking revenues are choking the demand for products and services, which will inevitably lead to sharp increases in bankruptcies and even more lay-offs. Millions of low-skilled workers employed in retail trade, restaurants, sports and recreation became the first casualties, as the pandemic containment measures largely shut down economic activities in these sectors. The pandemic is disproportionately hurting those who are least able to withstand an economic shock: low-skilled, low-wage workers both in formal and informal sectors...The negative distributional consequences of the pandemic are likely to be more pronounced than the global financial crisis in terms of scope and magnitude, as low-income households will be hit simultaneously both on the economic and health fronts." (UNDESA News 4 May 2020)

To this general assessment, the UN document adds particularly alarming forecasts for two specific sectors: travel and tourism and manufacturing production, sectors in which the largest number of small and medium-sized enterprises (SMEs) operate. In the first mentioned sector, that of travel and tourism, the International Air Transport Association (IATA) estimates a 38 per cent drop in passenger traffic in 2020, compared to 2019 levels, which translates into USD 252 billion revenue loss from passenger. Moreover, the document adds, if global tourism were to collapse, - a sector that employs more than 300 million people - the consequences would be catastrophic in many realities, where the loss of income combined with limited opportunities to find jobs in other sectors of the economy would lead to high and widespread levels of poverty.

Heavy negative consequences due to the COVID-19 pandemic are also expected in the manufacturing sector, which employs over 460 million people worldwide. "As the pandemic continues to spread – the document states – manufacturing activities have stalled or are slowing down around the world" (UNDESA 2020: 3).

The fall of manufacturing activities could spill over across national borders through the global trade networks: "such a spillover effect would be potentially disastrous for global manufacturing, as nearly half of the world's exported goods and services [...] involve inputs from more than one country" (UNDESA News 4 May 2020). And more: "A prolonged economic crisis - reducing global demand for manufacturing, especially for durable goods - could destroy millions of manufacturing jobs worldwide, particularly in manufacturing-dependent economies" (UNDESA 2020: 3).

The fall in global demand which was already under pressure due to growing trade tensions, will inevitably have serious consequences on the income levels of businesses and individuals.

This long introductory call to three emblematic positions is useful, in our opinion, to understand better how in a short period of just over four months, the sudden appearance of the COVID-19 pandemic around the world, together with the tragic loss of many lives, has radically changed the scenario of world economic development to which the vast and articulated system of SMEs also refers. We are faced with what numerous analysts, undoubtedly weak in forecasts but with a fervent creative imagination, hastened to define with an effective term as a "major strategic surprise". A surprise that in a very short time registers a passage from the commitment for new development plans marked by a substantial optimism, such as that mentioned in the EU document of December 2019, to the recognition by the UN in early May 2020 of the "disastrous" character of the situation arisen in the world, the "worst situation after the tragic Great Depression of the thirties in the last century".

Obviously the possibilities of reaction and correction of this unexpected situation are linked to a multiplicity of factors such as, for example, the promotion of new forms of solidarity, cooperation, competitive rules between the main regional areas of the world, the concrete implementation of the commitments on balanced growth so many times proclaimed by the main international coordinations, and the reaction capacity of the main development actors: states, businesses, workers, civil society organisations, local communities, and families.

The New UN Commitments for the Sustainability of Development

One thing is sure: the crisis of these months has highlighted even more than has happened so far the limits of the current development model and the value of the UN commitment to pursue a different path than in the past by promoting a new world order based on the sustainability of growth, in its multiple economic, environmental, and social aspects. The fundamental reference is to the general goals and specific targets approved with the UN Agenda 2030 in September 2015, objectives certainly not legally binding, but of great recognised and shared political value, with respect to which in recent years a general mobilisation of international institutions and agencies, states and main public and private operators have been activated.

The breakdown of the current development processes caused by the COVID-19 pandemic shows that the efforts made so far by the international community in this decidedly innovative direction have clearly been insufficient, as was also openly recognised in the "Global Sustainable Development Report (GSDR) 2019" presented by the United Nations (UN 2019) and discussed in the High Level Political Forum organised on 11 September 2019 precisely with the aim to assess the progress made by the initiatives promoted by the states in the fulfilment of the commitments foreseen by the 2030 Agenda on sustainable development. This open and internationally shared complaint and the pandemic crisis impose a decisive change in the policies for sustainable development and objectively give greater strength to the commitments and guidelines contained in the strategic documents approved by international institutions and states on the matter. This set of commitments and guidelines are well delineated, for example, in the documents approved by the European Union and expressly also concern the complex system of SMEs.

In this regard, it should be recalled that the United Nations 2030 Agenda for Sustainable Development "Transforming Our World" (UN 2015), within the framework of the 17 general goals and the 169 specific targets, has also included an objective that refers specifically to SMEs. The reference is to strategic goal no.8: "Promote sustained, inclusive and sustainable economic growth, full and productive employment and decent work for all"; and, inside it, to the specific target no.8.3 which states precisely: "Promote development oriented policies that support productive activities, decent job creation, entrepreneurship, creativity and innovation, and encourage the formalization and growth of micro, small and medium sized enterprises, including through access to financial services".

The achievement of this specific target, for which the UN also provides states with precise guidelines, takes on more precise meanings in light of the additional policies that are illustrated in the subsequent "GSRD 2019" Report of 11 September 2019 (UN 2019), already mentioned above. For example, where the fundamental role of private sector companies in sustainable development is recognised, the states are urged to promote incentive policies to encourage private investment in common public goods, to support private companies in directing their production of goods and services towards quality rather than quantity of development. These are all decidedly innovative and important recommendations to guide in particular the activity of the world of SMEs, which we find also at the basis of the promotional strategies of other international institutions, such as the European Union, and many states (UN 2019).

The New EU Strategy for "Competitive Sustainability" and the Role of SMEs

On 11 December 2019, the EU Commission communicates to the Council and to the major Community institutions the political project of "The European Green Deal" presented as "an integral part of the Commission's strategy to implement the United Nations' 2030 Agenda and the sustainable development goals" and subsequently, on 17 December 2019, the "Annual Sustainable Growth Strategy 2020". The two documents, among other things, present indications of further steps, projects, and measures approved in the following months.

The main ones include: the "European Green Deal Investment Plan – EGDIP", (COM 2010, 21 final), reinforced by the definition of the operational tools, the Just Transition Mechanism and the Just Transition Fund (COM 2020, 22 final); the proposal for a "European Climate Law" (COM 2020, 80 final); "A New Industrial Strategy for Europe" (COM 2020, 102); "A SME Strategy for a Sustainable and Digital Europe" (COM 2020, 103 final); the "Circular Economy Action Plan" (COM 2020, 98 final); "A Roadmap for Recovery. Towards a More Resilient, Sustainable, Fair Europe" (European Council 2020a). Note that most measures are presented, as an organic whole, in March 2020, that is precisely in the period of maximum explosion of the sanitary and economic crisis caused by COVID-19 pandemic.

The relevant fact is that this set of documents constitutes, in practice, the European translation of the UN commitments for sustainability; and that a particular area of intervention concerns the world of SMEs. The principles and guidelines defined in these documents present a decidedly innovative approach compared to the past, expressing a clear awareness both of the leading role that the European Union can and intends to play worldwide, and of the profound changes to be made in sector policies. We are, in essence, facing to a new reference framework that applies to public policies as well as to private operators; and the concrete steps taken so far by the European authorities to give a new impetus to the path of truly sustainable development indicate the unprecedented opportunities that they intend to offer in particular to the business world, especially small and medium-sized ones.

The European Green Deal sets a specific strategic goal: that of climate neutrality by 2050, enshrined in law; and also establishes that all EU policies must be oriented and contribute to its achievement. As an intermediate objective, the Commission aims to reduce greenhouse gas emissions by at least 50 to 55 per cent by 2030 compared to 1990 levels. The promotion of the circular economy in the European system is functional to these objectives. In this regard, the commitment to involve the production world is very clear. Thus, states the Commission document:

> "Achieving a climate neutral and circular economy requires the full mobilisation of industry. It takes 25 years – a generation – to transform an industrial sector and all the value chains. To be ready in 2050, decisions and actions need to be taken in the next five years [...]. The transition is an opportunity to expand sustainable and job-intensive economic activity. There is significant potential in global markets for low-emission technologies, sustainable products and services. Likewise, the circular economy offers great potential for new activities and jobs [...]. The European Green Deal – the document continues – will support and accelerate the EU's industry transition to a sustainable model of inclusive growth [...].The circular economy action plan will include a 'sustainable products' policy to support the circular design of all products based on a common methodology and principles. It will prioritise reducing and reusing materials before recycling them. It will foster new business models and set minimum requirements to prevent environmentally harmful products from being placed on the EU market. Extended producer responsibility will also be strengthened." (COM 2020, 640)

In line with the UN commitments, the European Union therefore sets out to promote a new development model, a decision that entails profound structural transformations in the productive world. The fact that the plan is established by law, on the one hand, undoubtedly adds strength to the related provisions, and, on the other hand, requires entrepreneurs to equip themselves and to follow carefully the evolution of this complex of provisions to acquire the ability to understand all implications and to grasp positively the opportunities for expansion and growth.

In this regard, it is interesting to note that the European Union declines the UN strategic goals and the three dimensions - economic, environmental, and social - in which such goals are articulated by adding the adjective "competitive" to the more general term of sustainability, as to mark particular attention to the world of business and work. Consequently, the EU identifies four strategic axes on which to operate - environment, productivity, stability, and fairness - and focuses on the dissemination of digital and clean technologies to promote the transition of the European production system to a sustainable economic model and achieve a global leadership in this area.

In the strategy for competitive sustainability for 2020, the European Commission selects two particular areas of intervention: a) productivity growth, to give an impulse to recover the delays accumulated at an international level compared to the main regional areas; b) finance for development, to promote greater support for innovation and investment in the economy, guaranteeing companies easier access to the financing they need to grow, innovate, and expand. In particular, the document specifies, SMEs must be able to "take full advantage of the integration in cross-border value chains and the seamless merger between industry and services that characterizes the digital era" (COM 2020, 650).

In the subsequent communication of 10 March 2020 on "A New Industrial Strategy for Europe" (COM 2020, 102 final), the Commission confirms its commitment to operate in all its policies on "twin ecological and digital transitions" with investments in new technologies and widespread innovations of products and production processes intended to create new markets and business models. Functional to this new strategy are the building up of a solid digital single market, based on valid and adequate systems of technical regulation of standards and certifications, as well as the definition and application of a specific approach in European and national policies reserved for SMEs, an "SME-to-SME approach", for the contribution that this type of business can make to large companies. "The growing number of young, techsavvy SMEs can help more established industrial firms to adapt their business models and develop new forms of work for the digital age. This has already created new opportunities and start-ups should be supported to help build the platform economy" (COM 2020, 102).

The development of the circular economy "will ensure a cleaner and more competitive industry by reducing environmental impact, alleviating competition for scarce resources and production costs". According to the Commission, the commitment to support companies in this conversion effort has value "as much as the environmental and moral imperative"; furthermore, his predictions are that "applying circular economy principles in all sectors and industries has the potential to create 700,000 new jobs across the EU by 2030, many of which in SMEs" (COM 2020, 102).

Together with this new industrial strategy policy and the provisions to reduce obstacles to the construction of the single market (COM 2020, 93 final and COM 2020, 94 final), on the same day, 10 March 2020, the European Commission presented the strategy document, which was specifically dedicated to the system of SMEs: "A SME Strategy for a Sustainable and Digital Europe" (COM 2020, 103 final). A strategy defined as "fundamental" for the implementation, inter alia, of the European Green Deal, the Action Plan for the Circular Economy, the European Data Strategy, the European pillar of social rights, and which is linked to the previous support plans and programs, in particular: the Small Business Act of 2008, the Start-up and scale-up initiative of 2016, the Competitiveness Program for Small and Medium-Sized Enterprises (COSME) and the SME Support Actions funded under the Horizon 2020 programme and European structural investment funds.

Due to their value, the European Commission document first refers, in the introduction, to the commonly known situations and data:

> "Europe's 25 million small and medium enterprises (SMEs) are the backbone of the EU economy", so the opening of the document. These businesses "employ around 100 million people, account for more than half of Europe's GDP and play a key role in adding value in every sector of the economy. SMEs bring innovative solutions to challenges like climate change, resource efficiency and social cohesion and help spread this innovation throughout Europe's regions. They are therefore central to the EU's twin transitions to a sustainable and digital economy. They are essential to Europe's competitiveness and prosperity, economic and technological sovereignty, and resilience to external shocks. As such, they are a core part of the achievement of the EU's industrial strategy." (COM 2020, 103)

> "SMEs are deeply woven into Europe's economic and social fabric. They provide two out of three jobs, bring training opportunities across regions and sectors, including for low-skilled workers, and support society's welfare, including in remote and rural areas. Every European citizen knows someone who is an entrepreneur or works for one. The daily challenges of

European SMEs to comply with rules and access information, markets and finance are thus challenges for the whole of Europe." (COM 2020, 103)

"SMEs are very diverse in terms of business models, size, age, and entrepreneurs' profiles, and draw on a diverse talent pool of women and men. They range from liberal professions and microenterprises in the services sector to middle-range industrial companies, from traditional crafts to high-tech start-ups. This strategy recognises their different needs, helping companies not just to grow and scale up, but also to be competitive, resilient, and sustainable. It therefore sets out an ambitious, comprehensive and cross-cutting approach, based on horizontal measures helping all kinds of SMEs as well as actions targeting specific needs." (COM 2020, 103)

The SMEs strategy defined by the European Commission envisages actions based on the following three pillars, partly already announced in the January 2020 European Green Deal: a) capacity building and support for the transition to sustainability and digitalisation; b) reducing regulatory burdens and improving market access; c) improving access to finance.

"The objective - the document specifies - is to unleash the power of Europe's SMEs of all kinds to lead the twin transitions. It aims to considerably increase the number of SMEs engaging in sustainable business practices as well as the number of SMEs employing digital technologies. Ultimately, the goal is that Europe becomes the most attractive place to start a small business, make it grow and scale up in the single market." (COM 2020, 103)

Such a goal, according to the Commission, can only be achieved through a strong operational partnership between the EU, the member states and their regional and local authorities. In fact, in Europe, many SMEs are well equipped, since they are flexible, highly technological, innovative, and committed to the values that guide sustainability and the circular economy. Almost a quarter of SMEs in Europe already make the transition possible and offer ecological products or services on the market; many SMEs (including social economy enterprises) are already doing a lot for the communities in which they are based.

But many other enterprises, on the other hand, find it difficult to switch to more sustainable business models. According to the Commission's communication on new SME strategy, one third of SMEs confirm having to deal with too complex administrative and legal procedures when trying to make their businesses more efficient in terms of the resources employed (COM 2020, 103: 2).

Even on the adequate use of data made possible by the digital economy, the Commission's reports reveal significant difficulties for businesses. Only 17 per cent of SMEs have successfully integrated digital technologies into their businesses, compared to 54 per cent of large companies. Traditional SMEs are often uncertain in their choice of digital business strategy, have problems tapping large repositories of data available to larger companies and shy away from advanced artificial intelligence (AI)-based tools and applications. At the same time, they are very vulnerable to cyber threats. Finally, there is the fact that often in both the digital and sustainability transition processes, start-ups and established SMEs are challenged by a lack of skilled employees or experienced managers; for a quarter of European SMEs this deficiency is the most important problem (COM 2020, 103: 4f.).

Over 70 per cent of firms report that difficulties accessing talent is an obstacle to new investment across the EU. The shortage of staff with adequate skills is particularly acute for digitalisation and new technologies, as 35 per cent of the workforce currently have poor or absent digital skills. It should be added that SMEs often do not have the same resources as large companies to invest in training their employees.

In order to intervene effectively in this situation and strengthen the operational capacity of businesses, the Commission provides numerous targeted service structures, funds and plans, such as: i) the advice provided by the "Europe Enterprise Network (EEN)", the "European Resource Efficiency Knowledge Center" (EREK), and the "European Institute of Innovation and Technology" (EIT) whose action will be geared in particular by providing to local authorities useful tools such as "regional schemes for innovation"; ii) the funds approved with the "European Green Deal investment Plan"; iii) the organisation of a network composed by 240 "Digital Innovation Hubs" (DIH) spread in every region of Europe and supported by investments in the digital Europe programme and structural funds; iv) the set up of common European data spaces for reliable and secure data sharing, with guaranteed access to all companies, in particular SMEs, and the organisation of a market dedicated to cloud services to promote the spread of cloud computing by SMEs while ensuring fair contractual conditions; v) the protection of intellectual property for SMEs by launching a specific action plan on intellectual property (only 9 per cent of SMEs are currently able to protect their intellectual property); vi) digital training courses for SME employees financed under the "Digital Europe Program" and with the collaboration of universities and local training bodies, to promote the acquisition of skills in areas such as artificial intelligence, cyber security, or the blockchain. The Commission also announces the revision of the "European Skills Agenda" and the launch of a pact for professional skills to meet the needs of SMEs.

> "European SMEs experience legislation as complex and burdensome, especially due to the different procedures in Member States. [...] Complying with regulations, standards, labels and administrative formalities affects SMEs more than bigger companies due to their limited financial and human resources. [...] Despite progress since the adoption of the Small Business Act, the cumulative impact of regulation remains a major problem for SMEs." (COM 103, 2020)

It is on the basis of these considerations relating to the obstacles that the complexity of the regulatory systems poses for the SMEs development that the European Commission envisages a great effort of simplification to be promoted in collaboration with the member states according to the three principles already agreed at Community level for some time : "Think Small First" (assume the SMEs interests in public policies), "once only" (supply at once of the documentation required by public administrations), "digital by default" (digital pre-definition of the documents required and to be sent to public administrations) (COM 2020, 103: 7).

For its part the Commission is committed strengthening the specific "Regulatory Fitness and Performance Programme (REFIT)", and the new "Fit for Future Platform", which systematically monitors existing EU legislation in order to reduce burdens and simplify it, based on the new principle. "one-in, one-out" (OI-OO) aimed at reducing in a single act the incoming and outgoing transmission of the documents requested to companies. Among the various initiatives announced by the Commission in this area, the following are worth mentioning: a) a new political initiative, "EU Start-up Nations Standard" for the identification of best practices to be disseminated among member states in order to simplify rules and procedures for SMEs, in particular start-ups, with reference to the transfer of people, goods, and services abroad. The aim is to facilitate their exports, cross-border cooperation, collaboration between companies and between them and research centers and universities; b) a new, particular area of intervention selected by the Commission concerns collaboration with the member states to simplify public procurement procedures in order to promoting greater participation by SMEs.

The European strategy also addresses another SMEs key problem related to difficulties in accessing public and private financing with a set of provisions aimed at organising "a conducive regulatory environment, sufficient and aligned EU and national funding, as well as access to networks of companies and investors" (COM 2020,103: 13).

The measures announced include: a) support for the spread of the use of crypto assets and the adoption of digital tokens by SMEs, investors and intermediaries, in alignment with the EU's upcoming "Digital Finance Strategy" and through a more adequate use of the "European Blockchain Services Infrastructure (EBSI)", and b) the further enhancement of financial and guarantee interventions in favour of SMEs through the instrument of a specific "SME IPO Fund" within the "InvestEU programme".

A final aspect concerns the governance system of all the measures intended to promote the SMEs development in Europe; governance that the Commission intends to build on a strong EU-Member States partnership; and, the Commission explains:

> "[...] as many SMEs are deeply rooted in regional and local ecosystems where they provide jobs, training, tax revenues and social welfare, this commitment must extend to regional authorities. The strategy's implementation will be underpinned by a strong partnership of all actors who share responsibility for delivery - EU, national, regional and local authorities, SMEs and investors. It will involve regular political stocktaking of progress, measurement and monitoring." (COM 2020, 103)

The complex of the main measures presented by the European Commission in March 2020, linked to the launch of the European Green Deal and aimed at promoting the digital and sustainable twin transition of the Community production system, is complemented by a "Circular Economy Action Plan. For a cleaner and more competitive Europe" (COM 2020, 980 final) aimed at making a major contribution to achieve climate neutrality by 2050 and to decoupling economic growth from the use of resources, while ensuring at the same time the long-term EU competitiveness.

Starting from the consideration that "half of total greenhouse gas emissions and more than 90 per cent of biodiversity loss and water stress come from resource extraction and processing", the European plan aims to involve the traditional economic operators in an accelerated transition process towards a regenerative growth model that gives back to the planet more than it takes, advance towards keeping its resource consumption within planetary boundaries. This model, therefore, must contribute "to reduce its consumption footprint and double its circular material use rate in the coming decade" (COM 2020, 98).

According to the Commission, the set up of this new development model offers important opportunities and advantages to the business world, including small and medium-sized ones. In any case, the Commission considers that "this progressive yet irreversible transition to a sustainable economic system is an indispensable part of the new EU industrial strategy (COM 2020, 98).

The action plan presents the main areas of intervention as follows:

> "Building on the single market and the potential of digital technologies, the circular economy can strengthen the EU's industrial base and foster business creation and entrepreneurship among SMEs. Innovative models based on a closer relationship with customers, mass customisation, the sharing and collaborative economy, and powered by digital technologies, such as the internet of things, big data, blockchain and artificial intelligence, will not only accelerate circularity but also the dematerialisation of our economy and make Europe less dependent on primary materials." (COM 2020, 98)

The plan also presents a first set of indications relating to "sustainable products" on which the European Commission intends to concentrate its support actions, incentives, and funding, in order to provide companies with precise guidelines on the new opportunities it intends to offer. The first list of products indicated includes: electronics and ICT, batteries and vehicles, packaging, plastics, textiles, construction and building, food, water, and nutrients.

With respect to these first indications, the Commission announced that in 2021, in collaboration with the Member States, they will proceed to the definition of a wider "sustainable product policy framework" as a fundamental reference of all the promotional provisions connected to the start and dissemination of the new circular economy model (a legislative proposal is envisaged for 2021). This framework will not be limited only to the indication of the products but will be integrated into an organic way also with the indication of services and sustainable business models that "will constitute the norm" as well as of the ways to transforming consumption patterns so as avoiding first of all the waste production. "This product policy framework will be progressively rolled out, while key product value chains will be addressed as a matter of priority. Further measures will be put in place to reduce waste and ensure that the EU has a well-functioning internal market for high quality secondary raw materials" (COM 2020, 98).

The definition of the strategic product framework is integrated by the Commission with an additional plan for action to support the necessary investments at territorial level, in regions and cities, so as to ensure that all regions benefit from the transition. Cohesion policy funds will be directed towards this end, which will help territorial entities to implement circular economy strategies by strengthening the industrial fabric and value chains. Particularly important will be the initiatives aiming to assist cities which are linked to the proposal of the European urban initiative, to the "Intelligent Cities Challenge" and "Circular cities and regions" programmes. The circular economy will be among the priority sectors of the Green City Accord.

The Commission document also prefigures the expected benefits, citing the Cambridge Econometrics, Trinomics, and ICF study (2018), on the impact of circular economy policies on the labour market: in fact it is calculated that European GDP could increase 0.5 per cent by 2030, accompanied by the creation of 700,000 new jobs. In the year 2018, the number of jobs linked to the circular economy in the EU is estimated at around 4 million units. In addition, the Commission states that "there is a clear business case for individual companies too: since manufacturing firms in the EU spend on average about 40 per cent on materials, closed loop models can increase their profitability, while sheltering them from resource price fluctuations" (COM 2020, 98).

> "For citizens – the Commission points out - the circular economy will provide high-quality, functional and safe products, which are efficient and affordable, last longer and are designed for reuse, repair, and high-quality recycling. A whole new range of sustainable services, product-as-service models and digital solutions will bring about a better quality of life, innovative jobs and upgraded knowledge and skills." (COM 2020, 98)

The fact is that up to 80 per cent of products environmental impacts are determined in the design phase, but the "take-make-use-dispose" linear pattern does not provide producers with sufficient incentives to make their products more circular. Hence the new strategic intervention, based on a mix of mandatory and voluntary actions, which gives a new impetus to the EU initiative in pursuing the goal of sustainability.

For its part, the European Commission is fully aware that

> "the transition to the circular economy will be systemic, deep and transformative, in the EU and beyond. It will be disruptive at times, so it must be fair. It will require an alignment and cooperation of all stakeholders at all levels - EU, national, regional and local, and international. Therefore, the Commission invites EU institutions and bodies to endorse this Action Plan and actively contribute to its implementation, and encourages Member States to adopt or update their national circular economy strategies, plans and measures in the light of its ambition." (COM 2020, 98)

For businesses, in particular for small and medium-sized innovative ones, it will be very important to understand the implications and equip themselves to seize the opportunities of this transition from a linear economy to a circular economy now decidedly launched at European level.

The need for a profound adaptation to the new strategy is also envisaged for the world of work. For example, the Commission is well aware of this, as demonstrated by what it says in relation to the strategic plan:

> "Circularity can be expected to have a positive net effect on job creation provided that workers acquire the skills required by the green transition. The potential of the social economy, which is a pioneer in job creation linked to the circular economy, will be further leveraged by the mutual benefits of supporting the green transition and strengthening social inclusion, notably under the Action Plan to implement the European Pillar of Social Rights." (COM 2020, 98: 15)

To this end, the Commission announces an update of the Skills Agenda, the launch of a Pact for Skills, to be implemented with large-scale-multi-stakeholder partnerships as well as with the Action Plan for the Social Economy, the promotion of further investments in education and training systems, in lifelong learning and social innovation, within the framework of the European Social Fund Plus.

The descriptive framework of the main EU plans for sustainable development in the industrial sector and related services, also with particular reference to the activities of small and medium-sized companies, is completed with the reference to the commitments contained in the "Road Map for Recovery" approved on 23 April 2020 by the European Council, in the midst of the sanitary and economic crisis. Also, in this document, the green transition, and digital transformations, both functional to the launch of a competitive sustainability model, are at the center of political decisions together with the construction of a fully functioning European single market. It is a further confirmation of the innovative direction in which the European Union and the member states have decided to act soon:

> "[...] the Green transition and the Digital transformation - clearly states the Council's final statement - will play a central and priority role in relaunching and modernising our economy. Investing in clean and digital technologies and capacities, together with a circular economy, will help create jobs and growth and allow Europe to make the most of the first-mover advantage in the global race to recovery." (European Commission 2020)

As for the single market, it must be considered that the "value and supply chains that have been disrupted must be re-established" and to this aim "it is vital to restore and to further deepen the Single Market as a key component of our prosperity and resilience" (European Commission 2020).

Comments

The organic strategy of ecological and digital twin transition developed by the Commission undoubtedly presents a fundamental contribution from Europe to sustainable development. In a first step it is appropriate to reflect on the fact that this strategy was elaborated and presented precisely in the period of the great world shock of the sanitary and economic crisis caused by the spread of the so-called Coronavirus (SARS-CoV-2), a crisis that even evokes the Great Depression of the last century, as recalled in the aforementioned United Nations monthly report of 1 May 2020 (UNDESA 2020).

It is therefore a strategy triggered in a situation of great uncertainty, widespread and profound difficulties in identifying the general conditions for a possible, valid recovery of development; in any case in a situation that will be marked by profound changes in the ways of people's life and their communities, in the organisation of economic systems and production processes. How can we promote the recovery of these economic systems, on what basis? Will we continue in the globalisation process, albeit in different ways, or will we witness the beginning of what has been defined as an unprecedented de-globalisation process? What alternatives are we facing?

An example of this reflection spread in all circles, governmental and not, on the possible future can be found in the type of questions posed by Philippe Pochet, the director of the European Trade Union Institute (ETUI) who has tried to prefigure four scenarios related to the inevitable direct and indirect intervention of the state in the economy. Will it be a weak or a strong intervention? Will it rely on the recovery of strong neoliberalism (first scenario) or will it be characterised by invasive forms of intervention, linked in an extreme case to new forms of authoritarianism (second scenario)?Will the choices go in favour of recovering economic growth at any price to minimise business bankruptcies and unemployment by operating mainly in the short and medium term (third scenario)? Or, in alternative, will the ecological transition be accelerated to that model of sustainable development already envisaged in international agreements, by operating mainly on common goods and also in a long-term perspective (fourth scenario)?

Obviously, different contact and intersection situations may arise between different scenarios. But it is certain that the recovery process, to be valid and not ephemeral, will entail an inevitable, albeit partial, change in production preferences, with the reorganisation of the value production chains, and the related trading systems, precisely in order to overcome the limits that emerged with the COVID-19 pandemic and the crisis it caused.

The Need to Act with a New Integrated and Intersectoral Approach in Development Policies

The choice of the European Union, based on the decisions and acts we have examined, confirms the will to move in the direction characterized by the fourth scenario, to support a green and digital transition towards a growth model based more on quality than on the quantity of development . But, this is the point to be underlined, the measures taken so far seem to be quite far from the need to promote the structural changes envisaged with that integrated and intersectoral approach that would be necessary for such a policy, in order to be able to deal organically, effectively, all-encompassing, systemic, the set of problems, tensions, ruptures that the adoption of the new growth model inevitably entails. We cannot see, for example, in the important EU documents the overcoming of the intervention logic that continues to operate for sectoral silos, for separate compartments and areas of action, an overcoming that has long been strongly recommended by international institutions such as the UN or the OECD. It deals with the fundamental problem still open related to the governance of the structural change processes that the EU intends to promote, to which the problems of an intersectoral planning of these processes are also closely linked.

The goal of systemic transformations cannot be separated from an overall assessment of the costs and benefits that this order of interventions in the real economy inevitably entail. For example, as the aforementioned UN "GSDR 2019" report claims:

> "Transitions towards sustainability can have significant impacts on employment, workers' families and communities, reducing or eliminating jobs in polluting industries and creating jobs using modern cleaner production. The deployment of new technologies and automated production that are part of such transitions can also reduce total labour demand even for skilled workers. That trade-off may be beneficial for the environment and for society at large, but it comes with human costs for affected workers, their families and immediate communities. To make those transitions socially acceptable, it is essential to take

into account the millions currently employed in resource intensive sectors and others who will lose their jobs." (UN 2019)

This position, shared by member states inside UN, requires for example the organisation of systemic interventions involving businesses, territories, and the world of work. Hence, the need that the incentive and support policies for new business activities are accompanied, within the same provisions, by parallel actions aimed at adapting the functions, services, and performances of the labour markets structures as well as of other related bodies. A concrete example: it would be most desirable and useful that the recent Commission decision to organise 240 Digital Innovation Hubs (DIH) in the regions of Europe also provided for an organic integration of these new centers with the regional labour services, as with other service structures, such as those operating in vocational training, since all these structures, although operating in different areas, face decisive problems for the promotion of competitive sustainability. In essence, it should be an opportunity for the organisation of real multipurpose and multifunctional European reference poles to be able to aggregate the numerous activities and services, both public and private, which are currently acting too separately and un-coordinated from each other, on a large common innovation project. Such a systemic combination of measures, and therefore of operating structures, is all the more urgent the more the structural adjustment needs, related to both the pandemic crisis and the green and digital transition, to also impose profound changes in traditional ways of working, in the organisation of its contribution to the levels of corporate productivity, in the relationship between working life and private life; and those who choose or are forced to work in conditions radically different from the past and enter a lasting situation of uncertainty and economic and social precariousness do not always find adequate protection in the trade union organisations that have hitherto represented the world of work.

The problem is well present in the aforementioned UN recommendations:

> "During previous eras of technological change, workers' organizations helped ensure that conditions at work improved, and wages rose so that productivity gains were more widely distributed, and social cohesion strengthened. They could continue to play such roles in the near future; however, a broader coalition including governments and employers could be more effective, especially given the decline of workforce participation in labour unions in many countries and sectors. Disruptive new technologies and globalization indicate that significant numbers of people may work as self-employed workers, or under non-standard labour contracts, for example in platform labour markets ....With those trends in mind, the ILO's Commission on the Future of Work has recommended measures, such as universal

labour guarantees to cover all workers irrespective of contractual status, and governance systems for labour platforms." (UN 2019)

A systemic integration of the multiple sectoral interventions into a single organic project objectively still largely remains to be built, at European level and in many member states. All the more, as it was already mentioned, that the European provisions for the green and digital transition have been taken in a context of great general uncertainty about the common economic future due to the real risk of closure and bankruptcy of hundreds of thousands of businesses of all sizes throughout Europe. The reference to the value of the European Pillar of Social Rights -moreover a document of indicative political value–that we find in several documents, from the Annual sustainable growth strategy of Dec. 2019 to the SME development strategy, in March 2020, is undoubtedly an important fact but it is not sufficient if the corresponding measures are not included in the context of the support and incentives approved for the business world. We are therefore always within the context of that approach for sectoral silos whose overcoming is advocated by the most important international institutions.

The Need for New Tools to Qualify the Business-Territory Relationship

Another fundamental aspect that should be the subject of greater consideration by the European authorities concerns the relationship between the business world and their reference territories. This is all the more important for SMEs - among which we should not forget the important role played by the micro enterprises - which generally acquire their innovative operational capacity precisely from the material and immaterial values of the territories and their communities, in a relationship that is continuous, organic, and functional. The spread, evolution, and often the success of the industrial districts in which these companies are concentrated is a demonstration of the value of this inter-relation system for the quality of business activities.

In Italy, for example, official statistics (ISTAT 2019) have identified the existence of 141 industrial districts which represent about a quarter of the Italian production system in terms of both businesses (24.4 per cent) and employees (24 per cent). Among the main characteristics of the Italian industrial district model we find production specialisation, flexibility, good opportunities to draw on qualified human resources, a widespread orientation among companies to compete but also to collaborate, to network, a socio-economic fabric favourable to the entrepreneurial initiative.

Inside the district, craft and industrial businesses use working side by side, often in the supply chain, with strong complementary connections even outside the district itself; all elements that make easier the circulation of product and market information, technology transfer, the creation of relationships of trust and continuous synergies. Over time, in particular in recent years, the Italian districts have undergone an evolution characterised, in many cases, by what has been defined as a verticalisation process due to the prevailing of the role of a leading company, that is a company that for results, turnover, size and capacity for innovation and competition ended up taking on a strategic role of reference for the other district companies.

One of the most important Italian banks, Banca Intesa San Paolo, in a 2018 study, has highlighted this districts transition from a horizontal to a vertical model and has surveyed 1,600 companies that for their large operational capacity have passed from small to medium-size and have established themselves as growth champions for the whole local system. Another important aspect to recall concerns the fact that at the basis of the functioning of the local district we find not only codified rules but above all unwritten rules that are the result of habits in interpersonal relationships, a widespread desire to do and do well, the values shared by a community and its territory; unwritten rules that directly affect its structure, productivity, and performance.

Hence the acknowledgment, shared by many experts, that the Italian industrial district is an economic and territorial reality, but above all a social reality. A reality, it must be added incidentally, which facilitates the socialisation of community relations, the integration of industry in the territory, and where the cultures of the area certainly do not have a lower influence than the corporate performance allocated therein in determining the success or failure the overall economic activities of the district system. In short, it is a complex reality that can also be difficult to replicate in other contexts, but from which useful suggestions and indications for common challenges can be drawn, especially when structural transition processes towards new development models such as those envisaged by the European Union are promoted. But it is right in front of these widespread industry modelsand territorial realities with economic, social, and cultural values and experiences that are closely intertwined with each other – and such realities are well present in all Europe - that the intersectoral systemic approach becomes an obligatory step in the planning out and implementation of promotional projects and measures, as it should have been for all the measures approved in recent months at community level.

The Need for a Sound Governance for the New Environmental and Social Policies

In particular, the path that has been opened for the set up of the circular economy requires all development actors to show in their public documents a broader sense of purpose to be certified in the legislative provisions, regulations, corporate budgets, the latter to be transformed into "integrated corporate budget" in order to highlight the real contribution by private companies to the social and environmental values of the territories, a particularly difficult challenge for the SMEs' system; in a broader sense, it requires the adoption of a new governance model, commonly defined as "Environmental Social Governance ESG", as well as the widespread application of an adequate system for measuring the values produced by each operator, public and private.

In this time of deep structural crisis, the political choice to place the company at the center of the circular economy requires a resolute step change in the interpretation of the development phenomena together with the use of more coherent and valid approaches and assessment methodologies, less sectoral than has been done so far, able of grasp the movement and contribution of the individual variables, but above all the relationships between them and the overall developed impact. It is the obligatory path for what the EU has defined in terms of "competitive sustainability".

References

BRICS VII Summit (2015): Long Term Strategy, Document, General Principles. URL: http://brics2016.gov.in/upload/files/document/5763c20a72f2d7thDeclarationeng.pdf [10 July 2020].

Cambridge Econometrics and Trinomics and ICF (2018): Impacts of Circular Economy Policies on the Labour Market: Final Report. URL: https://circulareconomy.europa.eu/platform/sites/default/files/ec_2018_-_impacts_of_circular_economy_policies_on_the_labour_market.pdf [10 July 2020].

Castellani D. Rullani, E./ Zanfei, A. (2017): Districts, Multinationals and Global/Digital Networks. In: Rivista Economia e PoliticaIndustriale 44 (4), pp. 429-447.

Economist Intelligence Unit (EIU) (2020): Top Five Risks to the Global Economy in 2020. URL: https://www.eiu.com/n/top-five-risks-to-the-global-economy-in-2020 [10 July 2020].

Eurofound (2019): Energy Scenario: Employment Implications of the Paris Climate Agreement. Luxembourg: Publications Office of the European Union (EU).

Eurofound (2020): Labour Market Change: Trends and Policy Approaches Towards Flexibilisation, Challenges and Prospects. Luxembourg: Publications Office of the European Union (EU).

Eurofund and European Commission Joint Research Centre (2019): European Jobs Monitor 2019: Shifts in the Employment Structure at Regional Level. Luxembourg: European Union (EU).

European Commission and Centre for Strategy and Evaluation Services (CSES) (2002): Benchmarking of Business Incubators. Brussels: CSES.

European Commission (30 September 2008): A Small Business Act for Europe, Communication from the Commission to the European Parliament, the European Economic and Social Committee, the Committee of the Regions, COM (2008) 394, Final/2, Bruxelles.

European Commission (28 November 2018): A Clean Planet for all A European Strategic Long-Term Vision for a Prosperous, Modern, Competitive and Climate Neutral Economy, Communication from the Commission to the European Parliament, the European Council, the Council, the European Economic and Social Committee, the Committee of the Regions, the European Bank of Investments, COM (2018) 773, Bruxelles.

European Commission (11 December 2019): The European Green Deal, Communication from the Commission to the European Parliament, the European Council, the Council, the European Economic and Social Committee, the Committee of the Regions, COM (2019) 640 final, Brussels.

European Commission (11 December 2019): The European Green Deal, Communication from the Commission to the European Parliament, the European Council, the Council, the European Economic and Social Committee, the Committee of the Regions, COM (2019) 640 final, ANNEX, Brussels.

European Commission (17 December 2019): Annual Sustainable Growth Strategy 2020, Communication from the Commission to the European Parliament, the Council, the European Central Bank, the European Economic and Social Committee, the Committee of the Regions, the European Investment Bank, COM (2019) 650 final, Brussels.

European Commission (17 December 2019): Proposal for a Joint Employment Report from the Commission and the Council accompanying the Communication from the Commission on the Annual Sustainable Growth Strategy 2020, COM (2019) 653 final, Brussels.

European Commission/von der Leyen, Ursula (2019): Speech in the European Parliament Plenary Session, President-Elect of the European Commission, European Parliament.

European Commission (2020): SME Regional Policies. URL: https://ec.europa.eu/growth/smes/business-friendly-environment/regional-policies [10 July 2020].

European Commission (14 January 2020): European Green Deal Investment Plan, COM (2020) 21 Final.

European Commission (14 January 2020): Proposal for a Regulation of the European Parliament and of the Council for establishing a Just Transition Fund, COM (2020) 22 final.

European Commission (14 January 2020): Proposal for a Regulation of the European Parliament and of the Council for establishing a Just Transition Fund, COM (2020) 22 final, ANNEX 1-3.

European Commission (29 January 2020): Commission Work Programme 2020. A Union that strives for more, Communication from the Commission to the European Parliament, the Council, the European Economic and Social Committee and the Committee of the Regions, COM (2020) 37 final, Brussels.

European Commission (19 February 2020): European Strategy for Data, COM (2020) 66 final, Brussels.

European Commission (04 March 2020): Proposal for a Regulation of the European Parliament and of the Council establishing the Framework for Achieving Climate Neutrality and Amending Regulation (EU) 2018/1999 (European Climate Law), COM (2020) 80 final, Brussels.

European Commission (10 March 2020): A New Industrial Strategy for Europe, COM (2020) 102 final, Communication from the Commission to the European Parliament, the Council, the European Economic and Social Committee, the Committee of the Regions, Brussels.

European Commission (10 March 2020): A SME Strategy for a Sustainable and Digital Europe, Communication from the Commission to the European Parliament, the Council, the European Economic and Social Committee, the Committee of the Regions, COM (2020) 103 final, Brussels.

European Commission (10 March 2020): Indentyfying and addressing barriers to the Single Market, Communication from the Commission to the European Parliament, the Council, the European Economic and Social Committee, the Committee of the Regions, Brussels, COM (2020) 93 final, Brussels.

European Commission (11 March 2020): Circular Economy Action Plan. For a cleaner and more competitive economy, Communication from the Commission to the European Parliament, the Council, the European Economic and Social Committee, the Committee of the Regions, COM (2020) 98 final, Brussels.

European Commission (11 March 2020): Circular Economy Action Plan. For a cleaner and more competitive economy, Communication from the Commission to the European Parliament, the Council, the European Economic and Social Committee, the Committee of the Regions, COM (2020) 98 final, ANNEX, Brussels.

European Commission (10 March 2020): Long term action plan for better implementation and enforcement of the single market rules, Communication from the Commission to the European Parliament, the Council, the European Economic and Social Committee, the Committee of the Regions, COM (2020) 94 final, Brussels.

European Council (21 June 2019): A New Strategic Agenda2019-2024. Brussels: European Union (EU).

European Council (12 December 2019): Conclusions, European Council meeting, EUCO 29/19. Brussels: European Union (EU).

European Council (2020a): A Roadmap for Recovery. Towards a more resilient, sustainable and fair Europe. URL: https://www.consilium.europa.eu/media/43076/26-vc-euco-statement-en.pdf [10 July 2020].

European Council and European Commission (2020b): Joint European Roadmap Towards Lifting COVID-19 Containment Measures. Brussels: European Union (EU).

Eurostat (2018): Private Investments, Jobs and Gross Value Added Related to Circular Economy Sectors. URL: https://ec.europa.eu/eurostat/tgm/refreshTableAction.do?tab=table&plugin=1&pcode=cei_cie010&language=en [10 July 2020].

Istituto Nazionale Statistica (ISTAT) (2011): Censimento Distretti industriali (Industrial Districs, Census). URL: https://www.istat.it/it/archivio/150320 [10 July 2020].

Organization for Economic Co-Operation and Development (OECD) (2018): Global Material Resources Outlook to 2060. Paris: OECD Publishing.

Organization for Economic Co-Operation and Development (OECD) (2019): OECD SME and Entrepreneurship Outlook 2019. Paris: OECD Publishing.

Piore, M. J./Sabel, C. F. (1984): The Second Industrial Divide: Possibilities for Prosperity. New York: Basic Books.

Pochet, Philippe (2020): Four Scenarios for Europe's Future after the Crisis. URL: https://www.socialeurope.eu/four-scenarios-for-europes-future-after-the-crisis [10 July 2020].

Statista (2019): Number of small and medium-sized enterprises (SMEs) in the European Union in 2018, by size. URL: https://www.statista.com/statistics/878412/number-of-smes-in-europe-by-size [10 July 2020].

United Nations (UN) (2012): The Future We Want: International Conference on Sustainable Development RIO+20, Agenda Item 10, A/Conf.216/L.1, Rio de Janeiro (Brazil), June 13-22, 2012.

United Nations (UN) (2015): Transforming our World: The 2030 Agendafor Sustainable Development, A/RES/70/1, New York, September 2015.

United Nations (UN) (2019): The Future is Now: Science for Achieving Sustainable Development, Global Sustainable Development Report (GSDR) 2019 New York, 11 September 2019.

United Nations (UN), Department of Economic and Social Affairs (UNDESA) (2020): Monthly Briefing on the World Economic Situation and Prospects n.137. URL: https://www.un.org/development/desa/dpad/publication/world-economic-situation-and-prospects-may-2020-briefing-no-137 [10 July 2020].

Valenduc Gérard (2018): Technological Revolutions and Societal Transitions. URL: https://papers.ssrn.com/sol3/papers.cfm?abstract_id=3180000 [10 July 2020].

von der Leyen, Ursula (2019): A Union that Strives for More: My Agenda for Europe, Political Guidelines for the Next European Commission 2019-2024. URL: https://ec.europa.eu/commission/sites/beta-political/files/political-guidelines-next-commission_en.pdf [10 July 2020].

Websites

Organization for Economic Co-Operation and Development (OECD), Centre for Entrepreneurship, SMEs, Regions and Cities: www.oecd.org/cfe/sme

United Nations (UN), Sustainable Development Goals, Goal #12: Ensure Sustainable Consumption and Production Patterns: https://www.un.org/sustainabledevelopment/sustainable-consumption-production/

United Nations (UN), Department of Ecnomic and Social Affairs (UNDESA): News on World Economic Situation and Prospects: https://www.un.org/development/desa/en/news/policy/wesp-monthly-briefing-may.html

Afterword

To say that small and medium-sized enterprises (SMEs) form the backbone of the European economy is an understatement, as they constitute 99 per cent of all companies and employ more than 66 per cent of the European workforce. Their role in regions and communities goes beyond the economic activity, as they provide jobs, services, and opportunities to most of the population, particularly in isolated or rural areas.

Nevertheless, in a rapidly changing world, SMEs find it particularly difficult to adapt to changes, most of them being microenterprises (with three or less employees). They constitute an immensely diverse picture, ranging from tech start-ups and restaurants to family-owned and industrial middle-sized companies. This diversity must be considered when dealing with the different paths ahead for SMEs. The recent SME strategy of the European Union (EU) for a sustainable and digital Europe highlights these facts, and the special issues they face due to their size in terms of access to funding, digitalisation, and working conditions (including health and safety, training and ongoing training), industrial relations, exporting, and public tendering. Less than 25 per cent of European SMEs are ready for the transition necessary to overcome these challenges (European Commission 2020).

At the European Economic and Social Committee (EESC), we welcome the strategy of the European Commission, as enabling SMEs to adapt, scale up, and enjoy the advantages of the single market while creating a levelled playing field and fostering the digital and fair environmental transition is a goal we certainly all share (EESC 2020). We hope that it will give a new impulse to the "think small first" principle, which is still far from being complete. Moreover, in our position paper on it, we highlight the special challenges and actions necessary, so that they can compete on equal footing with larger companies (EESC 2020).

Nevertheless, some aspects included and some aspects missing in the EU strategy paper concern us, for example, the so-called "gold-plating" of EU regulations by Member States. The term, which intuitively might suggest "unnecessary red tape", is often used to attack social and environmental standards that go even beyond EU law demands. Still, we should remember that EU law is there to provide a common ground and a minimum base, never to limit protection of consumers, workers, and the environment. If anything, regulatory adaptation must be a race to the top. While "cutting red tape" and making economic activity easier is certainly a shared objective, it should not be used to lower the standards that define the social market economy.

Another concerning aspect is the fail to mention, beyond incidentally, the role of all social partners in the process of innovation, transition, and digitalisation. Workers and trade unions are a fundamental piece of the puzzle, without which SMEs can neither work nor develop. The average small size of such companies presents extra challenges to workers' rights and participation, consultation, and information. Furthermore, the share of employees in micro and small companies who actually benefit from social dialogue institutions at the workplace displays a broad variability (European Commission 2013). Additionally, the particular character of the relationship between the employer and the employees on the one hand, and the institutional resources generated by the national industrial relations system on the other hand are the main factors affecting the development and practice of social dialogue. For these reasons, at the EESC, we urge the participation of the social partners in the SME Strategy and the European Semester (EESC 2020). The EU has taken numerous steps in ensuring workers' voice in companies (Voss and Pulignano) when it comes to cross-border issues, reinforcing national legislation for mergers and other operations. Furthermore, recent research shows, clearly, that companies which integrate workers in their decision-making process are consistently more successful, long-lasting, and sustainable than the ones which do not (ETUI 2019, Voss and Pulignano).

Enforcement is a third dimension of the regulation debate continuum that is also vacant, and it should not be. Beyond the issues of supposed "gold-plating", the need "to cut red tape", or the need for more stringent social and environmental standards, there is a clear necessity for effective enforcement with sufficient legislative tools and monetary resources.

If SMEs are to adapt, transform, compete, and succeed (as some are already doing), they cannot do so by merely applying top-down programmes to their working methods and workforce. They must take onboard the workers, which in return will surely improve the level of skill capture and retention. In the case of transparent working conditions, for instance, the EESC already recognised "the particular situation of natural persons acting as employers, and micro and small enterprises, which may not have the same resources available to them as medium and larger enterprises when fulfilling their obligations under the proposed directive. The EESC therefore recommends that the European Commission and Member States should provide appropriate support and assistance to such entities, to help them meet these obligations" (EESC 2018).

SMEs, as mentioned above, play a role in their communities beyond the economic one by means of their local and regional integration. And while their size might bring difficulties in terms of fixed costs, it also allows them to be flexible and innovate in a way larger companies, by their sheer size, simply cannot. Clear social and environmental standards and regulation are key elements in this process of innovation; they enable companies to engage in fair competition that is beneficial to themselves, workers, consumers, and the economy. When clear standards or a sufficient enforcement of such are missing, we often observe a race to the bottom, where companies purely aiming at price efficiency outperform innovative and responsible ones and pass on so-called "negative externalities" of precarious employment, exploitation, and environmental damage on to society. It is, therefore, more important than ever to take stock of the already good practices in place by many SMEs in terms of innovation and sustainability, and for the EU to act as an enabler of this transition, ensuring a levelled playing field for fair competition. As this anthology shows, the change is already happening. The EESC and social partners at the European level will continue working to ensure it happens in the best conditions possible for companies, workers, consumers, and the environment.

Oliver Roepke

Chairman, Group II - Workers
European Economic and Social Committee (EESC)
Brussels (Belgium)

References

European Commission (2013): "Fitness Check" on EU Law in the Area of Information and Consultation of Workers (Commission Staff Working Document). Brussels: European Commission.

European Commission (2020): Communication from the Commission to the European Parliament, the Council, the European Economic and Social Committee and the Committee of the Regions: An SME Strategy for a Sustainable and Digital Europe (Working Document). Brussels: European Commission.

European Economic and Social Committee (EESC) (2018): Proposal for a Directive of the European Parliament and of the Council on Transparent and Predictable Working Conditions in the European Union. Brussels: EESC.

European Economic and Social Committee (EESC) (2020): Strengthening SMEs: Way Forward to a Dedicated SME Strategy Position Paper. Brussels: EESC.

ETUI (2019): Benchmarking Working Europe 2019. Brussels: ETUI.

Voss, E./Pulignano, V. (forthcoming): An EU legal framework on Safeguarding and Strengthening Workers' Information, Consultation and Participation. Brussels: EESC.

INFORMATION ON THE AUTHORS

Roman I. Antonenko is an MA in Financial Analysis, National Research University - Higher School of Economics, Moscow.

Roman I. Antonenko
National Research University Higher School of Economics
Myasnitskaya Street, 20
101000 Moscow
Russia
Phone: +7 (495) 771-32-32
E-mail: Antonenkori609@gmail.com
Homepage: www.hse.ru

Dr Michał Barański is a leader of the Labour Law and Social Policy Research Team at the Institute of Legal Sciences at the University of Silesia in Katowice and an attorney-at-law. He participates in an international research project titled "Implementation and Enforcement of EU Labour Law in Visegrad Countries", under which he prepared the study "Adapting the Polish Labour Law to the EU Law in the Subject of Working Time". He is editor-in-chief of the academic journal "Z Problematyki Prawa Pracy i Polityki Socjalnej" ("Problems of Labour Law and Social Politics") and member of the Polish Section of the International Society for Labour and Social Security Law (ISLSSL) as well as of the European Network on Regional Labour Market Monitoring (EN RLMM) at the Goethe University in Frankfurt am Main (Germany).

Dr Michał Barański
Institute of Legal Sciences
Faculty of Law and Administration
University of Silesia in Katowice
Bankowa, 11b
40-007 Katowice
Poland
E-mail: michal.baranski@us.edu.pl
Phone: +48 32 3591547

Dr Moreno Baruffini has been a post-doc researcher at the Institute for Economic Research (IRE) at the Università della Svizzera italiana (USI) since June 2014. Moreno Baruffini graduated with honours from the Politecnico di Milano

(Italy) with a dissertation in regional sciences. He worked at the Metodi E Tecnologie Innovative per la Didattica (METID) Centre at the Politecnico di Milano and at the Institute of Earth Sciences of the University of Applied Sciences of Southern Switzerland (SUPSI). In his PhD dissertation at the Faculty of Economics, Università della Svizzera italiana (USI), he analysed labour market flexibility, security, and complexity in the Swiss context. He is currently the Manager of the Observatory for Economic Dynamics (O-De). Moreno Baruffini's academic work concerns the analysis of the Swiss regional economy, the European cross-border labour markets, and border-regional economics, specifically focusing on trans-border mobility.

Dr Moreno Baruffini
Institute for Economic Research (IRE)
Via Maderno 24
CP 4361
6904 Lugano
Switzerland
Phone: + 41 (0)58 666 41 16
E-mail: moreno.baruffini@usi.ch
Homepage: www.ire.eco.usi.ch

Dr Ernesto Dario Calò is PhD in "Communication, Social Research, and Marketing" at the Department of Communication and Social Research of Sapienza – University of Rome. For five years, he has collaborating with the University Chairs of Complex Organisational Systems, Socio-economic Systems, Strategic Marketing, and International Business. He has research experience in the fields of social and cultural change, electoral sociology, political marketing, and business management, publishing several articles both on a national and international level. Currently, he is doing research on the consequences of the COVID-19 with reference to music cultural industries and on business models for Industry 5.0 and sustainable development.

Dr Ernesto Dario Calò
Department of Communication and Social Research
Sapienza – University of Rome
Via Salaria, 113
00198 Rome
Italy
E-mail: ernesto.calo@uniroma1.it
Homepage: www.coris.uniroma1.it

Dr Milena Cassella is PhD in "Communication, Research, Innovation" and Research Fellow at the Department of Communication and Social Research at the Sapienza University of Rome. She deals with cultural industries as organisational systems, collaboration networks and social capital. She has research experience and publications on national and international level on crowdfunding for cultural projects, organisational culture, effects of evaluation systems on research, and teaching within the Italian University. Currently, she focuses on platformisation of cultural production and the role of knowledge workers in organisations with a high innovation content.

Dr Milena Cassella
Department of Communication and Social Research
Sapienza – University of Rome
Via Salaria, 113
00198 Rome
Italy
E-mail: milena.cassella@uniroma1.it
Homepage: www.coris.uniroma1.it

Professor Dario Cavenago is Full Professor in Management at the Department of Business and Law, University of Milano-Bicocca. He presides over the two-year Master of Science programme in Management and Service Design (MAGES) and is the Director of the master programme in Management for Human Capital Development (MACU). Among his main research interests are: the role of human capital within the firm with a focus on innovation; knowledge management within strategic change in cities; local governments and network systems; social entrepreneurship and non-profit organisations; and governance and business models.

Professor Dario Cavenago
Department of Business and Law, University of Milano-Bicocca.
Via Bicocca degli Arcimboldi, 8
20126 Milano
Italy
Phone: +39 0264487487
E-mail: dario.cavenago@unimib.it
Homepage: https://www.unimib.it/dario-cavenago

Olesya V. Dmitrieva is a PhD candidate at the Department of Economic and Financial Strategy of the Moscow School of Economics, Lomonosov Moscow State University.

Olesya V. Dmitrieva
Lomonosov Moscow State University
Leninskie Gory, Lomonosov Moscow state University d1, str. 61
119234 Moscow
Russia
Phone: +7 (916) 719-12-19
E-mail: Olesya.dmitrieva@icloud.com
Homepage: mse.msu.ru

Professor Cosmin Enache is a professor at the West University of Timisoara, Finance Department. He has expertise in public economics, holding a PhD degree in Economics/Finance with a thesis on fiscal policy and economic growth. He received a postdoctoral grant financed by European Social Fund (ESF), which was focused on the social and economic effects of social security public expenditures in the context of recent demographic transition process. This research topic was also the subject of his habilitation thesis. He has several publications in the ISI Web of Science journals. Current research interests include the sustainability of public pension systems, labour market as well as computational and Bayesian methods for population projections.

Professor Cosmin Enache
West University of Timisoara
Finance Department
Research Group on Social and Economic Complexity
Blvd. V. Parvan, 4
300223 Timisoara
Romania
Phone: +40 256 592 167
E-mail: cosmin.enache@e-uvt.ro
Homepage: www.feaa.uvt.ro

Professor Renato Fontana is Full Professor of Complex Organisational Systems at the Department of Communication and Social Research at the Sapienza University of Rome. He was President of Teaching Area in Communication for Enterprises and Organisations and was the General Secretary of Italian Association of Sociology – AIS (2004-2007). In the last 20 years, he has collaborated with the EU, ILO, and UN. He has authored several articles and books both on the national and international level. He has research experience in the fields of technological innovation, social and cultural inequalities, labour markets, and gender issues. Currently, he is doing research on new occupational profiles in the knowledge economy in Italy and in Europe.

Professor Renato Fontana
Sapienza – University of Rome
Department of Communication and Social Research
Via Salaria 113
00198 Rome
Italy
Phone: +39 06 499 18 456
E-mail: renato.fontana@uniroma1.it
Homepage: www.coris.uniroma1.it

Dr Martine Gadille (PhD in Economics, Aix Marseille University), is a researcher in Business Administration at the Institute of Labor Economics and Industrial Sociology (LEST-CNRS 7317, French National Centre for Scientific Research/ CNRS). Her research areas are regional governance of innovation, knowledge management, and micro and meso learning dynamics.

Dr Martine Gadille
L.E.S.T
35 avenue Jules Ferry
13626 Aix-en-Provence, Cedex 01
France
E-mail: martine.gadille@univ-amu.fr

Dr Karine Guiderdoni-Jourdain (PhD in Management Sciences, Aix Marseille University) is an assistant professor in Management Science at Aix-Marseille University and affiliated to the Institute of Labour Economics and Industrial Sociology (LEST-CNRS 7317). She is currently leading research on international support services for SMEs and on the internationalisation of family-managed SMEs.

Dr Karine Guiderdoni-Jourdain
L.E.S.T
35 avenue Jules Ferry
13626 Aix-en-Provence, Cedex 01
France
E-mail: karine.guiderdoni-jourdain@univ-amu.fr

Dr Jenny Kipper is a pedagogue with a focus on organisational development and consulting. She worked in different types of organisations such as big enterprises, research institutes, small consultancies, or start-ups. Currently, she is a lecturer at Goethe-University and Frankfurt University of Applied Sciences for topics related to organisational theories, consulting, change management, qualitative methods, and personal development. In parallel, she does smaller consulting projects on organisational development and coaching so that lecturing and consulting benefit from each other.

Dr Jenny Kipper
An den Banggärten, 24a
61118 Bad Vilbel
Germany
Phone: +49 6101 5028708
E-mail: info@drkipper.de

Dr Christa Larsen is a social scientist. She works in the fields of labour markets, regional development, and empirical methods. Christa Larsen studied sociology, political science, and economics at the Universities of Duisburg and Bielefeld (Germany) and at the University of Oregon (United States). In her dissertation at the University of Essen (Germany), she applied multi-level models in the field of socialisation. She has research experience in the fields of methods and statistics with a focus on quantitative network analyses, as well as in education and professional training, labour markets, socialisation, and gender relations. Since 2002, she has been based at the Institute for Economics, Labour and Culture (IWAK) in Frankfurt am Main and has been acting as managing director of the institute since 2008. Her current scientific work concentrates on regional labour market monitoring, regionalised analyses of labour markets for health workers, setting up labour market information systems, and conducting regional forecasts.

Dr Christa Larsen
Institute for Economics, Labour and Culture (IWAK)
Centre of Goethe University Frankfurt am Main
Senckenberganlage 31
60325 Frankfurt am Main
Germany
Phone: +49-(0)69-7982-2152
E-mail: c.larsen@em.uni-frankfurt.de
Homepage: www.iwak-frankfurt.de

Dr Oliver Lauxen is a nursing scientist. He has worked as an elderly care nurse and as a charge nurse in nursing homes and home health care services. He studied Nursing and Health Sciences at the Protestant University of Applied Sciences in Darmstadt (Germany) and graduated with a master's degree. Since 2010, he has been a researcher at the Institute for Economics, Labour and Culture (IWAK) at the Goethe-University, Frankfurt am Main. His current scholarship focuses on regionalised analyses of labour markets for healthcare workers and the experiences of nurses from abroad.

Dr Oliver Lauxen
Institute for Economics, Labour and Culture (IWAK)
Centre of Goethe University Frankfurt am Main
Senckenberganlage 31
60325 Frankfurt am Main
Germany
Phone: +49 (0)69 798 25457
E-mail: lauxen@em.uni-frankfurt.de
Homepage: www.iwak-frankfurt.de

Professor Katalin Lipták is an associate professor, head of department, and vice-dean for education at the Faculty of Economics, University of Miskolc, Hungary. She is an economist and jurist. Her research fields are regional labour market processes, regional economics, and labour law. She is currently researching the evolution and development of the labour market and the changing labour market processes as well as the social and solidarity economies. She is a member of the Hungarian Regional Science Association and of the Editorial Board of Észak-magyarországi Stratégiai Füzetek.

Professor Katalin Lipták
Department of Employment Policy and Labour Market
Institute of World and Regional Economics
Faculty of Economics
University of Miskolc
3515 Miskolc
Hungary
E-mail: liptak.katalin@uni-miskolc.hu
Phone: +36 46 565-111/2023

Professor Mattia Martini is Assistant Professor in Management at the Department of Business and Law, University of Milano-Bicocca. He has participated in different national and European-founded projects relat-ed to the governance of labour market services, the human capital develop-ment systems and the management of sustainable innovation. His main research interests relate to organization and management, with particular reference to social and personal services in the fields of employment and healthcare, and a focus on human capital and employability development.

Professor Mattia Martini
Department of Business and Law, University of Milano-Bicocca.
Via Bicocca degli Arcimboldi, 8
20126 Milano
Italy
Phone: +39 0264487544
E-mail: mattia.martini1@unimib.it
Homepage: https://www.unimib.it/mattia-martini

Professor Ronald McQuaid is Professor of Work and Employment at the University of Stirling's Management School. He has published many books and scientific and policy papers on employment, employability, entrepreneurship, and SMEs.

Professor Ronald McQuaid
Stirling Management School
University of Stirling
FK94LA Stirling
Scotland, UK
E-mail: ronald.mcquaid@stir.ac.uk

Professor Gábor Mélypataki is an assistant professor at the Faculty of Law, University of Miskolc, Hungary. His research fields are civil service law, social innovation and labour law, and labour law digitalisation. He is currently researching the connection between labour law and new trends and technologies as reflected in social innovation. Also, he is co-president of the Subcomittee of Labour Relations at the Hungarian Academy of Sciences. Furthermore, he works as a mediator at the Labour Advisory and Dispute Resolution Service and at the Chamber of Commerce and Industry of Borsod-Abaúj-Zemplén County and is a member of the editorial staff of the European Review for Alternative Conflict Solution and Dispute-Resolution (ERADR).

Professor Gábor Mélypataki
Department of Agriculture and Labour Law
Institute of Civil Law
Faculty of Law
University of Miskolc
3515 Miskolc
Hungary
E-mail: melypataki.gabor@uni-miskolc.hu; jogmega@uni-miskolc.hu
Phone: +36 46 565-111/2384

Cristina Mereuta is a Labour Market Specialist at the European Training Foundation (ETF). Her responsibilities include research and capacity development related to skills needs identification, skills anticipation and matching, and transition from school to work and skills mismatches. Before joining the ETF, Cristina worked for the Ministry of Labour and Social Protection of Romania, where her responsibilities included serving as Head of the Employment Policy Unit and expert in international relations. Her work also covered expert contributions to international and European projects or initiatives focused on activation, skills development, and social integration. Cristina holds a master's degree in political sciences from the National School of Political Sciences and Public Administration in Bucharest (Romania) and attended training and experience exchange programmes in the area of employment, social affairs, and European affairs.

Cristina Mereuta
European Training Foundation
Villa Gualino
Viale Settimio Severo, 65
10133 Torino
Italy
Phone: +39 0116302451
E-mail: cristina.mereuta@etf.europa.eu
Homepage: www.etf.europa.eu

Christian Müller studied Vocational Education and Political Science at the Justus-Liebig University in Gießen (Germany), with academic stays at the University of Granada (Spain) and the University of Antioquia in Medellin (Colombia). He worked as a teacher at an international German school in Santiago de Cali (Colombia). Since 2018, he has been a researcher at the Institute for Economics, Labour and Culture (IWAK) at the Goethe-University, Frankfurt am Main, and works in the ProAbschluss initiative. His research focuses on vocational training, further education, and professional socialisation.

Christian Müller
Institute for Economics, Labour and Culture (IWAK)
Centre of Goethe University Frankfurt am Main
Senckenberganlage 31
60325 Frankfurt am Main
Germany
Phone: +49 (0)69 798 28923
E-mail: chr.mueller@em.uni-frankfurt.de
Homepage: www.iwak-frankfurt.de

Professor Zoltán Musinszki is an associate professor and vice-dean for Scientific and Accreditation Affairs at the Faculty of Economics, University of Miskolc, Hungary. His fields of research are management control, management, and cost accounting. He is currently researching the evolution and development of controlling and cost systems for SMEs and their social innovation aspects. He is a member of the Quality Assurance Committee of the Hungarian Accreditation Committee and of the Management and Controlling Association as well as of the Editorial Board of Controller Info. He is furthermore editor-in-chief of Hantos Periodika and chairman of the Editorial Board.

Professor Zoltán Musinszki
Institute of Finance and Accounting
Faculty of Economics
University of Miskolc
3515 Miskolc
Hungary
Phone: +36 46 565-111/2213
E-mail: musinszki.zoltan@uni-miskolc.hu

Professor Irina V. Novikova is a Dr Sc (Econ), Professor at the Department of Economic and Financial Strategy of the Moscow School of Economics, Lomonosov Moscow State University, and Leading Researcher Fellow of the Strategic Studies Center at the Institute of Complex Systems Mathematical Research, Lomonosov Moscow State University.

Professor Irina V. Novikova
Lomonosov Moscow State University
Leninskie Gory, Lomonosov Moscow state University d1, str. 61
119234 Moscow
Russia
Phone: +7 (962) 2931309
E-mail: NovikovaIV5@gmail.com
Homepage: mse.msu.ru

Dr Nina Oding is a senior researcher and the head of the research department at the Leontief International Centre for Social and Economic Research in St. Petersburg, Russia. As an expert and project coordinator, she has acquired vast experience in developing and managing research programmes and policy consulting projects as well as in researching urban economics and regional development. She conducts studies focused on issues related to the transformation economy, budgetary federalism, public sector reform, and spatial planning. Nina Oding is a team leader and deputy director of international projects commissioned by the WB, TACIS, EU, USAID, and DFID. Her current scientific work focuses on regional development issues and regional labour markets.

Dr Nina Oding
International Centre for Social and Economic Research "Leontief Centre"
Krasnoarmeyskaya, 7
190005 St. Petersburg
Russia
Phone: +7-981-2746-88-30
E-mail: oding@leontief.ru
Homepage: www.leontief.ru

Professor Ciprian Panzaru is a professor at the West University of Timisoara, Sociology Department. He coordinates disciplines such as Sociology of Migration, Labour Economics, Social Mobility, and Economic Sociology. His areas of interest include agent-based modelling, computational sociology, international migration, labour market issues, and population forecasting. He attended the postdoctoral programme in Economics, financed by the European Social Fund (ESF), studying the effect of demographic changes on social security systems. He was a visiting researcher at the Department of Applied Economics of the Free University of Brussels (DULBEA) and a visiting professor at the Artois University

(France). Currently, he leads the Research Group on Social and Economic Complexity at the West University of Timisoara.

Professor Ciprian Panzaru
West University of Timisoara
Sociology Department
Research Group on Social and Economic Complexity
Blvd. V. Parvan 4
300223 Timisoara
Romania
Phone: +40 256 592 167
E-mail: ciprian.panzaru@e-uvt.ro
Homepage: www.cpanzaru.socio.uvt.ro

Daniel Porep is a social scientist. He studied sociology, economics and modern history at the University of Potsdam and focused on methodology, statistics, and social structure analysis. He has worked since 2008 in the field of labour market monitoring for the Federal State of Brandenburg and currently works in the Divison WFBB Labour at the Brandenburg Economic Development Board (WFBB – Wirtschaftsförderung Land Brandenburg GmbH).

Daniel Porep
Brandenburg Economic Development Board (Wirtschaftsförderung Land Brandenburg GmbH)
Friedrich-Engels-Straße, 103
14473 Potsdam
Germany
Phone: +49 331 704457-2912 / Fax: 49 331 704457-11
E-mail: daniel.porep@wfbb.de
Homepage: arbeit.wfbb.de
Homepage: www.fis-brandenburg.de

Borja Pulido Orbegozo studied Business Administration and Management at the University of the Basque Country (UPV-EHU). Since 2016, he has been working at the Technical Bureau at Lanbide, the Basque Employment Service, in the field of Labour Market Observatory (LMO) and in the production of labour market indicators (LMI). He has furthermore been advising the Management of the Public Employment Service as well as various departments of the Basque Government. Previously, he has worked in private entities, carrying out tasks similar to the current ones.

Borja Pulido Orbegozo
Lanbide-Basque Employment Service
Jose Atxotegi, 1
01009, Vitoria-Gasteiz
Spain
Phone: +34 945 06 24 16
E-mail: b-pulido@lanbide.eus
Homepage: www.lanbide.eus

Professor Marco Ricceri, expert on European social and labour policies, is acting as secretary general of the EURISPES, a primary Italian research institute in the economic, social, and territorial development. Marco Ricceri is also a coordinator of the Ethic Committee of the European Agency of Investments (AEI), Geie, (Florence-London); a member of the Steering Committee of the International Association for Social Quality-IASQ (Amsterdam-The Hague); enrolled in the list of "Pool of Reviewers" of the European Science Foundation-ESF (Strasbourg) for "European Social Policy" and "Industrial Relations"; and a chairman, Scientific Committee, European Network on Labour Market Monitoring (EN RLMM), IWAK Institute, Goethe University (Frankfurt am Main). Furthermore, he is a university docent on "Global Government-Global Governance", GESAM Master course, University of Venice Ca'Foscari. In 2012, Ricceri was awarded as "Honorary Doctor" by the Institute of Europe IE-RAS, Russian Academy of Sciences.

Professor Dr Marco Ricceri
EURISPES - The Secretary General
Via Cagliari, 14
00198 Roma
Italy
Phone: +39 06 44202211 / Mobile: +39 338 9766007
E-mail: eurispes.intl-dept@libero.it, riccerimarco@hotmail.com
Homepage: www.eurispes.eu

Professor Alfons Schmid is a professor of economics at the Johann Wolfgang Goethe University in Frankfurt am Main. His main areas of research are regional developments in the employment and labour market, new information technology and its impacts on employment situation, regional competitiveness, and attitudes in the context of the welfare state.

Professor Alfons Schmid
Society for Economics, Labour and Culture (GEWAK)
Centre of Goethe University Frankfurt am Main
Senckenberganlage 31
60325 Frankfurt am Main
Germany
Phone: +49 (0)69 798 28229
E-mail: alfons.schmid@em.uni-frankfurt.de
Homepage: www.iwak-frankfurt.de

Dr Robert Tchobanian (PhD in Economics, Aix Marseille University), was a researcher in social-economics at the Institute of Labour Economics and Industrial Sociology (LEST-CNRS 7317, French National Centre for Scientific Research/CNRS) during this study. His research areas are industrial relations and information and communication technologies (ICT) usage in organisations.

Dr Robert Tchobanian
Résidence Beausoleil, Bat K
avenue H. Mauriat
13100 Aix-en-Provence
France
E-mail: robert.tchobanian@gmail.com

Dr Aline Valette-Wursthen is a socio-economist. She works in the field of continuing vocational training system, early school leavers' tracer studies on local labour markets, regional training governance, and territorial social dialogue. She has research experience in the field of public policies and evaluation, recently including issues of lifelong guidance. She studied at the University of Aix-Marseille (France) and holds a PhD in Labour Economic titled "Changing Patterns of Labour Market Segmentation in France and the United Kingdom? A Wage and Job Stability Approach". Since 2008, she is based at the French Centre for Research on Education, Training and Employment (Céreq), and since September 2018, she works as a senior researcher at the Work, Employment and Professionalisation Department. Her current scientific work concentrates on branches employment observatories, French training, and employment public policies and reforms.

Dr Aline Valette-Wursthen
Céreq
10 place de la Joliette
BP21321
13567 MARSEILLE cedex 02
France
Phone: +33 4 91 13 28 52
E-mail: aline.valette@cereq.fr
Homepage: www.cereq.fr

Pirita Vuorinen holds a Master of Science in Economics from the Plekhanov Russian University of Economics in Moscow (Russia), DEA Sciences de Gestion from IAE Caen, University School of Management in Caen (France), and a Master of Arts in Economics from the College of Europe in Bruges (Belgium). Pirita has been working with the European Training Foundation (ETF) in Turin since 2012 on VET governance, SBA assessment, Torino Process, and the local dimension of skills, with a focus on innovation and competitiveness. Before joining the ETF, Pirita worked for the United National Development Programme (UNDP) for ten years, where her most recent responsibilities included serving as Head of the sub-offices of the UNDP in Iraq and Russia and working in the private sector development programme for Iraq. Prior to that, Pirita worked in the private sector for various multinational corporations.

Pirita Vuorinen
European Training Foundation
Villa Gualino
Viale Settimio Severo 65
10133 Torino
Italy
Phone: +39 0116302278
E-mail: pirita.vuorinen@etf.europa.eu
Homepage: www.etf.europa.eu

Dr Aleksandra Webb is a lecturer in the Management Work and Organization Division of the University of Stirling's Management School and has been a co-researcher on several European research projects related to skills, labour markets, and the impact of digitalisation on higher education.

Dr Aleksandra Webb
Stirling Management School
University of Stirling
FK94LA Stirling
Scotland, UK
E-mail: a.k.webb@stir.ac.uk